BORDERLINE PERSONALITY DISORDERS

The Concept, the Syndrome, the Patient

BORDERLINE
PERSONALITY DISORDERS

The Concept, the Syndrome, the Patient

Edited by
PETER HARTOCOLLIS, M.D., Ph.D.

INTERNATIONAL UNIVERSITIES PRESS, INC.
New York

Library of Congress Cataloging in Publication Data

International Conference on Borderline Disorders,
    Topeka, Kan., 1976.
    Borderline personality disorders.

    Sponsored by the Menninger Foundation and the National
Institute of Mental Health.
    Bibliography: p.
    Includes index.
    1. Pseudoneurotic schizophrenia — Congresses.
I. Hartocollis, Peter. II. Menninger Foundation,
Topeka, Kan. III. United States. National Institute of
Mental Health. IV. Title [DNLM: 1. Personality
disorders — Congresses. WM100 1615b 1972]
RC514.I525 1976   616.8'9   77-6152
ISBN 0-8236-0575-2

                    Fourth Printing, 1979

            Manufactured in the United States of America

CONTENTS

Preface

The term borderline has existed for a long time in psychiatry. It used to indicate serious pathology of doubtful diagnostic affiliation. Because it meant both too many things and too little, new, less ambiguous terms began to appear — pseudoneurotic schizophrenia, psychotic character, as-if personality — terms signifying a special affinity to one or another traditional diagnostic category. Then, during the last decade, a new notion was advanced, which is now gaining momentum — that all these hybrid terms actually refer to a broad but unique category of mental patients. The term borderline was readopted.

And yet there is still no consensus about its legitimacy as a unique psychiatric category; no agreement as to what patients, what cluster of symptoms, what dynamics, what degree or range of pathology, what incidence, what prognosis, and what treatment one should keep in mind when reading and talking about the so-called borderline. Although one faces similar problems in dealing with schizophrenia, especially in trying to explain its origins, there has been little difficulty in agreeing that schizophrenia exists, at least as a syndrome. Whenever it becomes difficult to recognize it as such, it is precisely because of the existence of borderline cases — when the issue becomes that of borderline as distinct from schizophrenic disorders.

This volume is a product of the International Conference on Borderline Disorders held in Topeka, March 19-21, 1976, which was a sequel of the International Conference on Psychiatric Conditions held in Paris, February 23-26, 1972, itself a sequel of the International Colloquium on Psychosis held in Montreal, November 5-8, 1969. The Topeka conference sought to bring together representative exponents of the "borderline" concept, colleagues impressed enough with its validity to have adopted it in their clinical and research work. The conference was to afford such workers an opportunity to exchange views and argue points in the face of new findings, their own and others'; to appraise similarities and compare differences; to strive for a realistic evaluation of the situation concerning borderline disorders.

Implicit in all these goals was the need to establish a common language, to define the concept "borderline," if possible, to the satisfaction of all concerned — behavioral scientists and mentalists, clinicians and researchers alike. If a large proportion of the contributors represent a psychoanalytic bent, this merely reflects the fact that the initiative and most of the work in the area of borderline disorders have been carried out by psychoanalysts and psychoanalytically oriented colleagues. I am ready to acknowledge that the organizers of this conference and the Menninger Foundation, which hosted it in Topeka, are psychoanalytically oriented; but as some of the most significant work in the field took place at the Menninger Foundation (I refer here to the work of such familiar authors as Rapaport, Schafer, Knight, Ekstein, and Kernberg), I hardly need apologize for the prominent place psychoanalysis was accorded at this conference.

I should emphasize, however, that no particular point of view, psychoanalytic or other, guided our thinking in choosing program participants. What counted was the expertise and relevance of the data each contributor had to offer. We asked not only for good descriptions of behavior, but also for a view of the intrapsychic. We wanted to examine the question of origin, and so we invited researchers concerned with genetics, infant development, and family background. We tried to include those with a global, statistical, epidemiological approach, as well as those familiar with the human condition from the inside, the conceptualizers of the mind. We sought to bring together the hard-core scientists whose projects involve carefully controlled populations in experimental wards or the community, and the soft-core mentalists, the healers and the introspectionists whose observations and insights are based primarily on clinical practice in the private office. We were aware of the risks involved — how the use of metapsychological concepts might render the clinician's observations impotent or meaningless; how the effort to reach the depth of human experience might narrow the perspective of the problem; how elegant statistics might make us lose sight of the individual; how jealous concern for the right methodology might split apart clinicians and behavioral scientists. I point out each of these risks because the very nature of the subject invites them — something that became quite obvious during the conference. And we wanted to make these risks obvious in order that workers in the field — clinicians as well as researchers, psychoanalysts and empirical scientists alike — might become more concerned about them and listen to each other more respectfully in the future.

To what extent we succeeded, this volume may tell. The formal contributions are all here. Yet a great deal of what happened during the conference has been left out — the group discussions, the questions and the information the audience contributed; the spontaneous, unrehearsed contributions of the program participants, the speakers themselves and their discussants, the colleagues who chaired the meetings and monitored the exchange with the audience, the participants at large. Our debt to all those who directly or indirectly helped with the program and the conference as a whole is acknowledged below, but only the particular contributions of those whose papers form the various chapters of the book are identified as such. Ideas of other participants, however, are reflected in my introductions to the various sections of the book. I hope those who contributed these ideas will recognize them and forgive my decision to use them without acknowledging their origin on each occasion.

I wish to express my appreciation to all those who helped me organize and carry out the conference that resulted in this book, beginning with Dr. Roy Menninger, President of the Menninger Foundation, who entrusted me with the task and placed at my disposal all necessary professional and technical resources of this organization.

The program committee stood loyally by my side with advice and encouragement. Its members were Dr. Tobias Brocher, Director of the Center for Applied Behavioral Sciences and Distinguished Professor in the Menninger School of Psychiatry; Mr. D. C. Gerstenberger, Assistant Administrator of the C. F. Menninger Memorial Hospital; Dr. J. Cotter Hirschberg, Distinguished Professor and Dean of Faculty in the Menninger School of Psychiatry; Mrs. Marsha Sheahan, Information Services; Dr. Sydney Smith, Chief Clinical Psychologist, Director of Psychology Training, and Editor of the *Bulletin of the Menninger Clinic;* Dr. William H. Smith, Senior Staff Psychologist and, at the time, Director of Psychology at the C. F. Menninger Memorial Hospital; Dr. Philip Woollcott, Director, Menninger School of Psychiatry and Department of Education; Mrs. Carole J. Dillingham, Secretary of the C. F. Menninger Memorial Hospital, all at the Menninger Foundation.

To the above I should like to add Drs. Colette Chiland, John G. Gunderson, and Otto F. Kernberg, who were there from the very beginning, even before I myself came in eventually to take over the responsibility for organizing the conference in Topeka. All three were instrumental in the selection of the contributors. Dr. Samuel Keith joined us in time, as official representative of NIMH's interests and support.

The following colleagues served as chairpersons, panelists, group discussion leaders, and reporters: Drs. Ann Appelbaum, Ramon C. Ganzaraín, A. Cesar Garza-Guerrero, Michael Harty, Alfredo Namnum, Robert L. Obourn, Ishak Ramzy, Herbert E. Spohn, Normund Wong, and Hugo J. Zee, all at the Menninger Foundation; Dr. John S. Kafka of the Washington Psychoanalytic Institute and George Washington University; Dr. Ernst A. Ticho of the Baltimore-District of Columbia Psychoanalytic Institute and George Washington University; and Dr. Robert Rubinstein of the Mount Zion Hospital and San Francisco Institute of Psychoanalysis. To all of them I offer my sincere thanks.

Peter Hartocollis, M.D., Ph.D.

Foreword

Several convergent lines of investigation have recently focused attention on the borderline disorders. To investigate the possible interface or overlap with schizophrenia, current research has examined clinical, psychological, familial, and genetic descriptions of the syndrome. Hampered by the lack of a widely accepted, reliable, and valid diagnosis, study has progressed on the strength of individual leadership and convictions without the opportunity for interaction and collaboration. While it is important not to close off promising directions for research, it is also necessary and desirable to look for cooperation from those of differing theoretical persuasions. The papers presented at the Menninger-National Institute of Mental Health Conference on borderline disorders demonstrated the dedication and effort of those working in this area. The conference itself provided the opportunity for open communication among investigators which will certainly enhance scientific progress toward achieving a united research effort.

The National Institute of Mental Health, through its Division of Extramural Research Programs, Clinical Research Branch and Center for Studies of Schizophrenia, and its Office of Program Development and Analysis, hopes that its contribution to the support of this conference has brought further clarity to a perplexing condition which has been responsible for much human suffering. All clinicians have had experience with borderline patients and probably have spent much time pondering a wide variety of questions. We feel that through research many of the questions that daily face the clinician can be answered. What defines a borderline disorder? What is its etiology? What are its psychodynamics? Its most effective treatment? Its prognosis? Can its manifestations be prevented? Some answers are available to us now, but much of our current knowledge must be replicated, and probably much must be confirmed through the initiation of carefully designed studies. If progress is to be made, however, the unfortunate estrangement that all too often exists between clinicians and researchers in this area must be ended. Whatever the factors that influence this schism, and I am certain there are many, the effect is counterproductive. Problems like the borderline disorders are clinical problems and require the blending of the best clinical understanding with the most precise and careful research designs if they are to be resolved. The National Institute of Mental Health believes that the conference reported on in these pages represents a major step in this direction.

We look forward to further development of knowledge in this area and anticipate the accumulation of much valuable information in the next few years. We have seen the progress of research on depression and schizophrenia and hope that similar progress will be made toward understanding the borderline disorders. Without the opportunity to share the research results with the clinicians who can most immediately use them, however, much of the scientific impact of these results would be lost. We therefore extend our sincere appreciation to the Menninger Foundation for their massive efforts in organizing and cosponsoring this major opportunity for interested people to share their thoughts and data on borderline disorders. We urge, moreover, that this conference serve not only to summarize what is currently known about borderline disorders, but also to stimulate meaningful and productive work in the future.

Samuel J. Keith, M.D.
Assistant Chief
Center for Studies of Schizophrenia
National Institute of Mental Health
Rockville, Maryland

I

THE CONCEPT

I come to explore the wreck.
The words are purposes.
The words are maps.
—From *Diving into the Wreck:
Poems 1971-72,* by Adrienne Rich

What does the word borderline mean? Is it a historical accident or a conceptual entity? Is it a concept defining a psychic reality, or merely an artifact, another label in the long list of psychiatric nosology? Nearly every article in this book, explicitly or by implication, struggles with this multiple question—the first two in a more general, philosophical way.

Bion's essay raises more questions than it seems to answer. And yet his questions, subtle as they are, have a reassuring effect. He does not like to settle questions. With André Gide, he believes that the answer is the misfortune of the question. A question may appear simple, but the answer to a real question is an impossible one. Bion's concept of the borderline is Freud's "caesura" of birth. Man's life is determined as much by chance as by choice. A multitude of facts and problems are involved in life choices. Choice is the integration of such facts and problems, the integration being determined by the limitation of our inner resources. For Bion, the fundamental human need is to alleviate one's sense of ignorance. Human beings clamor for knowledge, but ignorance is filled with knowledge. There is more irony than mystery in Bion's ideas. Bion addresses himself to the tragedy of man's fate, and the essence of tragedy is irony.

Though a Frenchman, André Green is temperamentally closer to Bion than any Anglo-Saxon contributor in this volume. He is more a philosopher and a logician, more a playwright or tragic actor, than a clinician. His point of view is global, sweeping. His concept of the borderline transcends the pathological to become in essence the question of mind and body, good and evil, true and false, being and nonbeing. He points to "tertiary" processes, consisting of conjunctive and disjunctive processes, acting as intermediaries between primary and secondary logic. He emphasizes the role of symbolization in the conjunctive functions of tertiary processes; symbolization requires the splitting of two elements and their conjunction creates a third element, which is composed of the two split-off elements, each one remaining the same and becoming in their union a different one.

Emotional Turbulence

WILFRED R. BION, M.D.

The entity familiar to members of the medical, psychiatric, and psychoanalytic professions under the usually adequate designation "borderline patient" or "borderline psychotic" is in no way familiar to laymen and workers in other fields. It therefore seems possibly illuminating to approach the conference's topic as the "thing itself" usually presents itself to the medically unsophisticated and to work from this to the more familiar medical definitions. We are all familiar with the term latency. I want to forget the usual usage temporarily, for it is easy to focus on laten*cy* rather than *what* is latent. I find it useful to consider that in latency what is latent is *emotional turbulence.*

When the quiet, cooperative, nicely behaved boy or girl becomes noisy, rebellious, and troublesome, the emotional upheaval rapidly ceases to be limited by the physiological boundaries of what we call John, Jack, Jill, or Jean in his or her corporeal frame. Into this emotional field the psychiatric worker enters. His problem can be seen in its hideous, practical reality when he is called upon — usually too late — to pronounce on the admirable (though to exceptionally intuitive authorities *not* so admired), docile child, and strongly suspects schizophrenia, or when he must judge the depression (or admired liveliness) of a manic-depressive psychosis. In choosing "emotional turbulence" I include its counterpart and opposite.

THE CAESURA OF BIRTH: CHOICE AND CHANCE

Leonardo's *Notebooks* contain many drawings of water swirling in turmoil, of hair in disorder. Milton, in *Paradise Lost*, writes in his Invocation to Light at the start of the Third Book, "Won from the void and formless infinite." We can think of other works by artists,

3

poets, priests, which call up similar pictures or thoughts from our own experience. It is not my intention to interpret, psychoanalytically or otherwise, these instances of human creation. I wish to recall them so that you may invoke similar images from your own scientific, artistic, or religious inheritance, whatever is for you most evocative of a period of mental turbulence similar to that with which psychoanalysts deal. I do not stress adolescence because for most psychoanalysts that conception is too strong; latency is too weak. I would that analysts recall periods of mental turmoil that have evoked the most turbulence in themselves.

To clarify "too strong," I take the term "caesura" from Freud's (1926) "Inhibitions, Symptoms and Anxiety": "There is much more continuity between intra-uterine life and earliest infancy than the impressive caesura of the act of birth would have us believe" (p. 138). Freud's summary can itself be described as one in which the "impressive caesura" is *too* impressive to allow us to suppose that the fetus might have a proto-mind and personality or could develop its proto-mind into a mind after birth.

Repression, said Freud, is *not* an event that takes place once; the caesura of birth, like the caesura of death, is impressive because it apparently takes place only once. It is hard to observe that repression is a kind of death. Breakdown, neurosis, psychosis may, in their turbulence, be difficult to discern; it may be a birth inseparable from the repression and death. In analysis we often have reason to think we may be unable to penetrate the impressive caesura of resistance or its varieties.

Can any growth take place without repression? Is progress inseparable from repression of the previous state? Does any thought occur without resistance to the thoughts *not* selected? Is there any feeling or idea that is not subject to resistance as an inevitable part of choice or change? Is anything separable from anything else in the way one word can be separated from another, or one physical body from another?

The problems of decision are reactivated as emotional turbulence and as a cause of or precipitation from it. On occasions when the turbulence is great enough, it is dramatic — as at birth, death, adolescence, or the onset of senility. Decisions are evolved in the community, family, group, and individual; people with a psychoanalytic vertex have committed themselves to thought and discussion. The decision and the discussion of it entails a considerable preceding process of maturation. A patient, whether a child or not, requires some degree of precedent experience. There are limits, even if we do not know what they are, beyond which the analysand is too young or too senile, too retarded or too precocious. We consider only what lies between these somewhat shadowy precincts — the limits of wavelength that bind the polyspectral "area."

There must be choice; this entails being tolerant enough to view the emotional turmoil. The turmoil observed has to be split — artificially, verbally. Some persons appear unable to make these verbal splits without feeling that they have in fact physically split. The next element in choice depends on chance, that is, on some force other than the conscious human being who chooses. The matters dictated by chance cannot be discussed by us in advance because this is an open-ended problem confronting any group, any individual, any society. In individual analysis it is possible to discuss what is going on between the two people who are participating. The analysand can keep the analyst informed and the analyst can do his best to interpret the information made available to him. The patient, who is usually in a state of turmoil, has first to decide what he will choose to talk about. Patients frequently say, "I can't think of anything to talk about today," or, "I have an awful lot to talk about but don't really want to talk about any of it." These statements have their counterpart in a group where the members seem uncertain what to discuss. Sometimes one particular person is anxious to put forward his view; at other times nobody wants to say what he is thinking about and the group becomes duller and duller, less and less communicative. The person leading the group must then consider what he should do with the situation which is unknown to him but which the chance of that particular session presents to his inspection. Here again there is chance, namely, events discernible in the turbulence. The individual in analysis may not be communicative, but he is nevertheless upset. It is wise for the analyst to assume that people do not spend time and money on analysis unless they are disturbed — no matter how smooth, straightforward, and apparently simple the view they present for the analyst's inspection. The same applies to the group; the individual members certainly have problems. But a group inspection provides a chance to see what interaction there is between the emotional situation that is apparently restricted to the individual and the way it spills over and affects other group members.

One disadvantage of the group situation is that seeing, say, six or ten people at the same time leads one to suppose that there are six or ten discrete personalities present. In other words, the distinct physiology of the participants is so dominant that one is liable to assume that the personality is similarly bounded by physical appearance. The "dramatic" effect of having the personalities present makes one suppose that the important thing is what any individual participant is saying or doing—another caesura in short. A similar situation exists with the individual who, it is assumed, has no problem dating from before birth—this dramatic event appears to present a caesura which cannot be penetrated.

In the Greek city-state where the numbers were small, democracy could operate; every individual was able to know sensibly what was going on. The people could collect in a forum and each individual could exercise his senses on material presented for his inspection. In small groups it is possible to be available to the forces that are operative; the reactions of the group can be seen. In addition to paying attention to what is actually said, we can be open to whatever else is going on—tones of voice, smiles, gestures, silences, and overt signals from one person to another. A wide spectrum of events is thus open to our inspection; there is a turmoil of communications. But however chaotic the situation, however psychotic or neurotic the phenomena seem to be, the analyst must be sufficiently tolerant of them to be able to observe what is going on. He is then faced with the problem of what, if anything, he proposes to say; saying something involves choice and the events therefore have to be ordered. What takes place is a splitting of the total situation artificially into various elements, an ordering of these elements, and a reintegration to bring these perceptions together again.

The expectation of the group can be so intense that it can hardly wait to hear what is going to be said. This expectation stimulates a great many feelings which can be so intense that the group becomes resistant to *any* emotion and falls silent. Expectation has been overaroused (including expectation of disappointment or disillusionment). A barrier (resistance, prohibition, caesura) is erected to protect the solution of the previous problem, to separate the present from the past, the future from the present; this barrier can become impenetrable to further development. On the other hand, the group *can* develop if the caesura is an illuminating idea.

This situation is inadequately described by terms like caesura, resistance, or cure. A polyvalent word is needed to bring together the actual elements, or a representative number of them, involved in one caesura. What I am describing signals cessation of an epoch; the patient feels "cured" by an interpretation (or misinterpretation), or sees some point which hitherto has been obscure. The tendency is for the patient to want to say, if he can verbalize it at all, "That settles it now, I don't want it to be unsettled." Having achieved illumination, he does not want any more. This is more observable in a group, when it is presented with an idea it has not had before. If the members see the point, this stimulates closure, converting the open-ended problem into a closed solution, settled once and for all. But there is no solution once and for all; each solution opens another universe. The situation, except for that point where a breakthrough in analysis has occurred, is wide open again—a vast, open-ended problem. The individual is now free to learn more, but unless he wishes to do so it cannot from his point of view be regarded as a satisfactory "cure."

IGNORANCE: SOURCE OF KNOWLEDGE

To turn to a few questions. Without any suspicion of Socratic irony, I would make it clear that the questions are serious ones. Although I know they are simple questions, I am aware that the answers may be unexpectedly difficult.

As an example of the simple answer to a question, I offer a joke illustrated in *Punch* magazine. A small boy draws an adult's attention to a lark singing in the sky. He states, "Hi, mister, there's a sparrer up there and 'e can't get up and 'e can't get down and 'e ain't 'alf 'ollering." This discovery made by a small boy gives information which might otherwise escape attention.

Another anecdote taken from the same source. A small boy speaking to his father says, "What's that, Daddy?" The answer: "A cow." "Why is it a cow, Daddy?" Answer: "Because his Mummy and Daddy were cows." "Why were they cows, Daddy?" These three simple questions asked one after another take one directly into realms of complexity which include problems still unsolved. This is true not only of the questions, but also of the answers, because like all really good answers, they stimulate still more questions. Any good solution to a problem causes the subject illuminated to reveal further questions and further problems.

A simple question: When is a human being born? Individuals may give me an answer in the particular instance of their own birth. I would then ask: When was your personality born? When did you first see light? When did your optic pits become capable of seeing light? Were your optic pits susceptible to pressure, giving the impression of light, adequate in the sense of stimulating the sensation of sight, inadequate in the sense that what you "saw" is not what is called adult or mature sight? I could ask a similar question about the auditory pits.

Some more questions and answers: What are you doing? Thinking. How do you know that you are thinking? My *phrenes* are going up and down. That answer is plausible; anybody can see that when a person begins to breathe heavily, in and out, it is reasonable to suppose that that state is caused by the diaphragm, as we call it, or *phrenes*, as the Homeric Greeks called it. Like the lark, it has an obtrusive characteristic; the answer is comprehensible, it would seem to be correct. How does somebody think? Their *phrenes* go up and down. It is a good answer in this respect: it stimulates still further questions. In the time of Democritus of Abdera people began to suspect that the inert and somewhat useless mass of stuff they carried about in their skulls—the brain—was connected with thinking; thinking might be a function of that material which seemed to terminate the parasympathetic, sympathetic, and central nervous systems.

During the Second World War, I encountered the Matrix test, imposed on members of the British army. Men were expected to choose one pattern out of several to complete a page of incomplete patterns. The number of correct answers was matched against the number of failed answers and it was thereby supposed that you had a rough-and-ready intelligence test. There were complications. One man, for example, was certain that the tests could not be so ludicrously simple and proceeded to measure the patterns offered and the vacant spaces. Consequently, his score was zero. Theoretically this would mean that he had a very low intelligence. If this man's personality is assessed psychiatrically, the problem becomes more complex. He may not be stupid, but why is he so suspicious? Why can he not believe that a simple answer is the correct one?

Ignorance is filled with knowledge; there are numerous answers to the questions that arise if it is supposed that the human animal has a mind. Why is it a cow, Daddy? And why is Daddy or Mummy not a cow? As a psychoanalyst I could fall back on the works of Freud; I could fall back on articles by Melanie Klein, Abraham, and others too numerous to mention. But I will first fall back on a simple answer: People do not often deliberately and consciously withhold information when they are expected to provide it. That would be a conscious example of presenting the inquirer with a blank space. There are, however, certain failures to answer which Freud (1926) considers to be unconsciously withheld—that is, they are not deliberate attempts at falsification, deception, and evasion. There are other occasions when a person exhibits doubt, or presents an answer that seems to be unsatisfactory. Freud calls this false memory, intended to fill the space left empty by the amnesia. This suggestion is fruitful; it leads to more questions and inquiries which I would extend still further. If it is true that the human being, like nature, abhors a vacuum, cannot tolerate empty space, then he will try to fill it by finding something to go into that space presented by his ignorance. The intolerance of frustration, the dislike of being ignorant, the dislike of having a space which is not filled can stimulate a precocious and premature desire to fill the space. One should therefore always consider that our theories, including the whole of psychoanalysis, psychiatry, medicine, are a kind of space-filling elaboration not in essence dissimilar to the belief that the lark in the sky is "a sparrer that can't get up and can't get down and ain't 'alf 'ollering." In other words, the practicing analyst has to decide whether he is promulgating a theory or a space-filler indistinguishable from a paramnesia.

Anybody who reminds the human animal that it knows very little is likely to be unpopular. Human beings clamor for some kind of authoritative statement to take the place of both ignorance and the exercise of curiosity; they hope, in that way, to put a stop to disagreeable feelings of ignorance and the repetition of the questions. The repeated questions may even be what is known as repetition compulsion. But repetition compulsion may in fact be a spark of human curiosity which has hitherto failed to be extinguished by any authoritative statements from whatever source.

We are familiar with being expected to provide the answers to questions. In examinations, as candidates, we are invited to provide answers to the questions asked, and our examiners are usually and plausibly thought to be entitled to fail us if we do not know those answers. But here again, one wonders whether this is a kind of disguise — anger at being frustrated, at being unable to be presented with a plausible answer to the question we ask and are asked by other people. We identify both with those who ask questions and with those who are supposed to know the answers. I mentioned that I did not wish to be suspected of Socratic irony, not the least because Socrates came to an unfortunate end — a result of asking questions. It is possible that the same danger will arise if our answers make what appears to be closed, open-ended.

In view of the advances made by the human monkey, who has become powerful enough to blow himself off the face of the earth, the situation is urgent. It is a race between his capacity for inhibiting knowledge, his own or other people's, and his capacity for advancing his ability to make "tricks." Walt Whitman wrote: "I am the teacher of athletes. He who spreads a wider chest than my own proves but the width of my own. He best honors my style who learns under it to destroy the teacher." Students may learn today not only through what they are taught by their universities, but also through themselves.

INHIBITION AND INITIATIVE: THE ETERNAL DILEMMA

I should be sorry to give the impression that because I am not filled with panic I therefore tell a harmless bedtime story. I would, without alarm, draw attention to a situation which is now one of urgency. It is a question of whether the paramnesias, the answers that are immediately comprehensible, that can be used to fill up the space of our ignorance, mislead us into extreme danger; whether the powers of the human mind match its destructiveness. So far the human being has survived and preserved a capacity for growth.

The gifted person may be able to draw and thus communicate visual images to others, people with less capacity to intuit. Leonardo's drawings of hair and water give a good idea of what turbulence "looks like." Mental turbulence, whether one's own or that of the community in which one lives, is much more difficult to depict; its existence and significance cannot be understood if the turbulence is not observed. Today almost any newspaper displays signs of turbulence; it exists in areas which have hitherto been regarded as civilized. If turbulence is demonstrated, the reply is likely to be, "What about it? We all know this." That is an example of the caesura; it is hard to penetrate what we "all know" and to suggest that there may be something that has *not* yet emerged from the turbulence, just as there may be something — we do not know what — that led to the turbulence. Are we then to inhibit the turbulence? Or are we to investigate it? From a certain point of view it would seem simple to answer that question. Universities and "learned societies" consider it wise to investigate, to exercise curiosity on the observed turbulence (the problem) *and* the theory believed to be a satisfactory explanation of the problem. Curiosity has itself to be under scrutiny while being exercised; we must not be directed toward understanding other problems by inhibiting observation of our own curiosity.

In a group with a diversity of opinions and views available, a diversity of characters we can observe and be observed by, what procedure should we adopt? All the members of the group represent different states of mind; each state of mind may be seen as an integer, an integrated whole, as something we might describe as human nature, human mentality, or human character. We could investigate it more easily by "splitting" these different "vertices" into states of mind corresponding to the anatomical structures of the individual human beings. But is personality bound by the physiology of the person, or is there an integration corresponding with the statement, *"Vox populi, vox Dei"*? If there is a cultural characteristic, it might express itself by favoring certain thoughts and disfavoring others. A caesura, difficult to penetrate is created. (It is curious that this term "caesura" was misprinted in the original paper by Freud as "censure," so that it was even then, accidentally of course, unconsciously described as a censor, an inhibition.)

Recently the primitive artist appears to have penetrated the caesura between cultivated and primitive; the cultivated artist seems prepared to learn, or allow himself to be aware of, the elements the primitive artist wishes to convey. Rimbaud was one of the early articulate people who listened to the inarticulate; Baudelaire, Shakespeare, and Homer formulated the states of mind of the people among whom they lived and were able to penetrate states of mind which did not then exist — ours. Such persons find some method by which what they have to say is made available to the people to whom they wish to say it. In the process of making it acceptable, what they have to say may be softened, made so tolerable and so bearable that its substance is lost to sight. Only the beauty of the work of art is seen; the *Odyssey, Iliad,* or *Aeneid* are mere poems. What lies behind the beautiful formulation, drawing, painting, music is lost; only the beauty remains. It appears almost accidental if something escapes from the prevalent force of the inhibitory authority. Instead of listening to music, someone listens to the radio interferences; there is a vast breakthrough of listening with more powerful instruments focusing on the interference; radio astronomy is born. Whether anybody wants to hear what they might hear thanks to increased powers of understanding is an open question. The approach usually made by the combined wisdom of culture, the godlike omnipotence of the people, is to dismiss the newly discovered formulation as a construction — and then to erect a monument which it is hoped will be sufficiently weighty to keep the underlying corpse buried. The other procedure is equally efficacious — the deification or glorification of the person or thing disturbing the placid surface by saying, "Yes, you are a god just like us" and inviting the individual to join the Establishment. There are thus two means available to deal with the newborn idea or discovery, namely, to bury it or to idealize it; to say the person is a genius — and therefore beyond us — or to say the person is crazy — and therefore beyond us. (The latter are safer locked in a mental hospital from which the "sanity" of the people cannot be penetrated.) Both mechanisms are discernible—but only at a distance. "These things happen—but not here. My colleagues and I don't behave like that." It is difficult to see that "My colleagues and I" behave *just* like that. I can scrutinize myself as I am always available, whether awake or asleep; it is both difficult and unpleasant.

The escape from self-knowledge is easy and can be extremely violent (by self-murder). The group or society can, similarly, solve all its problems by killing another group or society or culture. These murderous impulses have so far not been adequate because the murderer is penetrated by the thing he murders, or the society is penetrated by the culture it is trying to destroy; the religion becomes impregnated with the religion whose place it is attempting to take.

Chance is out of man's control.
Choice involves inhibition and initiative.
That is at present the basic dilemma.

REFERENCE

Freud, S. (1926), Inhibitions, symptoms and anxiety. *Standard Edition*, 20:87-172. London: Hogarth Press, 1962.

The Borderline Concept
A Conceptual Framework
for the Understanding of Borderline Patients:
Suggested Hypotheses

ANDRÉ GREEN, M.D.

"However, there are some things the Other cannot see."
—Charlotte, in A. Morgenstern's
"Experiences within a Borderline Syndrome"

Just as the hysteric was the typical patient of Freud's time, the borderline is the problem patient of our time, remarked Knight (1953) more than twenty years ago. We may question Knight's opinion regarding Freud's own patients, for they can no longer be understood simply within the limits of their hysterical neurosis (Deutsch, 1957). But there is little question when it comes to borderline patients and our time. In fact, Freud's (1918) own case of the Wolf Man may well serve as the paradigm for many of our current concerns in psychoanalytic treatment and theory. The mythical prototype of the patient of our time is no longer Oedipus but Hamlet.

Since the first clinical descriptions of the borderline patient almost half a century ago (Stern, 1938), an enormous amount of work—clinical data, technical variations, theoretical constructs— has accumulated in the psychoanalytic literature. We now say we are ready for a decisive confrontation of our established ideas with a new insight. If we limit ourselves to the clinical data, we can safely assume that we will find large areas of common experience. If we

Faculty Member, Paris Psychoanalytic Institute; Vice President, International Psychoanalytic Association, Paris, France.

15

discuss techniques, however, it is more probable that we will disagree. If we speak of theory, it is almost certain that we shall part ways. In short, we can share our perceptions but not our conceptions — perhaps because we nurture different preconceptions.

In what follows, I shall examine the borderline as a concept, for I believe that behind the descriptive rubric there in fact lies a unique concept. I shall then restate some of the models used by the major contributors to our present knowledge of borderline pathology. And finally, I shall propose my own conceptualization and trace it to the clinical findings and conceptual models of others. I do not promise to settle the problem, for that might lead me to oversimplification and schematization. I offer my personal view, trying to obey the command of intelligibility without sacrificing the complexity of the concept.

THE TERM DEFINED

The word borderline, used to define a certain category of patients, belongs neither to the vocabulary of traditional psychiatry, nor to the terminology developed by psychoanalysis. Freud identified some new clinical entities, which have since been accepted by nonanalytic psychiatrists, but he did not define a category of borderline patients as such. Seeking help from the *Oxford English Dictionary* (Burchfield, 1972) engenders disillusionment: "borderline is a line of demarcation." But we find added: "borderline case (esp. Psych.): one verging on insanity" (p. 329). So the contradiction emerges. Our clinical experience tells us that the border of insanity is not a *line*; it is rather a vast territory with no sharp division: *a no-man's-land* between sanity and insanity.

Freud does not propose a category of borderline patients, but he stresses the opposition between the obligations of abstract conceptualization and clinical reality. In "Analysis Terminable and Interminable" (1937), he writes: "We know that the first step towards attaining intellectual mastery of our environment is to discover generalizations, rules and laws which bring order into chaos. In doing this we simplify the world of phenomena; but we cannot avoid falsifying it, especially if we are dealing with processes of development and change. What we are concerned with is discerning a *qualitative* alteration, and as a rule in doing so we neglect, at any rate to begin with, a *quantitative* factor. In the real world, transitions and intermediate stages are far more common than sharply differentiated opposite states" (p. 228). Here is our challenge. In dealing with transitions or intermediate descriptive steps, should we not attempt to go beyond them, to cross the border from the phenomenological to the theoretical? Should a theoretical generalization necessarily be linked to the two broad areas of psychopathology, neurosis and psychosis, as something between them? Or should the borderline case be accorded an identity of its own?

If we now turn to our professional dictionaries, we are confronted with a variety of approaches. Laplanche and Pontalis (1967) give the following definition of borderline: "Term most often used to designate psychopathological troubles lying on the frontier between neurosis and psychosis, particularly latent schizophrenias presenting an apparently neurotic set of symptoms" (p. 54). They stress the vagueness of the field covered by such a definition, which includes psychotic, perverted, and delinquent personalities; they seem to prefer that the term be more closely linked to "pseudoneurotic schizophrenia." Implied here are two concepts: the borderline as a neurotic set of symptoms is a fallacy, and the borderline as a psychotic set of symptoms is schizophrenia.

Moore and Fine (1967) give the following definition in their glossary: "A descriptive term referring to a group of conditions which manifest both neurotic and psychotic phenomena without fitting unequivocally into either diagnostic category" (p. 19). Apparently no different from the French definition. But in fact the American glossary implies a difference. Even though its authors' further comments stress the defensive nature of the borderline's neurotic symptoms, what I find important for my investigation is that, according to their definition of the borderline, neither kind of symptom, neurotic or psychotic, fits the traditional conception of neurosis or psychosis.

Rycroft (1968) is less equivocal. He observes that the borderline case defies any attempt at classification. Yet he considers the problem from the point of view of psychosis alone and observes that in the borderline personality structure the defense is of a psychotic type, though the person's behavior is not. Parenthetically, Rycroft rejects the idea that neurosis and psychosis are mutually exclusive.

As consulting dictionaries has proved of little help, let me pause for a moment and ask: Who or what is borderline? The important thing about such a question is the distinction between to *have* something borderline and to *be* borderline. I can *be* a citizen or a *heimatlos,* but to be borderline — that is difficult for me to conceive.

The professional dictionaries tell me this much: borders are located at different places by different experts. So let me turn to my own personal experience. What are my borders? The skin envelope or container comes immediately to mind. But as definite and important as it may appear to me, my skin container is discontinuous. The tissue of flesh is interrupted by other tissues, or it presents holes, which act as gates. We can call them custom houses or inspectors: eyes, ears, nose, mouth, anus, urethra, vagina. Mouth, anus, sex organs — the so-called erotogenic zones — are important because they function in two ways: in and out. I am thus presented with two problems. The first is the nature or structure of the border; the second is the circulation in and out of its gates. But what are the borders or frontiers of my psyche? What are the laws governing the circulation through the gates of my psychic borders? What is the relation of the psyche and its borders to these gates? Two types of laws come to mind, two laws working in tandem — the pleasure-unpleasure principle and the reality principle. The reality principle is of particular importance for my investigation as it pertains to the existence or nonexistence of the object, hence of the self.

Several types of borders are encountered in nature: lines or surfaces, with or without circulation through the frontier, or an osmotic membrane, which affords communication with an adequate selection of what has to be taken in or kept out, or, if there is trouble, what has to be rejected, what is unwelcome inside; and finally, a blurred division in some state of intersection, a border resembling the meeting of two clouds. In case of danger, an osmotic border can open up to unburden the inside from the troublesome stimuli. But other measures are possible: for instance, the stultification of the line, a kind of mortification, or the blurring of the border, creating instead a fragile border, a no-man's-land. To be a borderline implies that a border protects one's self from crossing over or from being crossed over, from being invaded, and thus becoming a *moving border* (not *having*, but *being* such a border). This in turn implies a loss of distinction between space *and* time.

It is rather obvious that even apparently ordinary definitions of the borderline contain nuances betraying different points of view. In my view, one should not try to understand the symptoms of the borderline patient in terms of psychosis. Neither should one try to identify the borderline's psychotic condition with schizophrenia. Finally, I would question the generally accepted notion that neurotic symptoms have a definite function. Before elaborating on my point of view, however, I propose that we examine some other models.

CONCEPTUAL FRAMEWORKS AND MODELS OF BORDERLINE STATES

My intention is not to review the extensive literature on the subject. I shall therefore restrict myself to the work and views of those who have dealt with borderline cases in the psychoanalytic situation. I propose to classify such contributions in terms of three lines of thought: Freudian, Kleinian, and Winnicottian.

There are very few indications in Freud's own work that help in understanding borderline cases. In "Neurosis and Psychosis" Freud (1924a) states:

> . . . it will be possible for the ego to avoid a rupture in any direction by deforming itself, by submitting to encroachments on its own unity and even perhaps by effecting a cleavage or division of itself. In this way the inconsistencies, eccentricities and follies of men would appear in a similar light to their sexual perversions, through the acceptance of which they spare themselves repressions.
>
> In conclusion, there remains to be considered the question of what the mechanism, analogous to repression, can be by means of which the ego detaches itself from the external world. This cannot, I think, be answered without fresh investigations; but such a mechanism, it would seem, must, like repression, comprise a withdrawal of the cathexis sent out by the ego [pp. 152-153].

Several points are relevant to our discussion: the ego's avoidance of rupture, presumably of its borders, "in any direction"; the ego's submission to "encroachments" (today we would probably use the term impingements); the defense mechanism of ego "cleavage or division of itself" (which today we would call splitting); the assumption that we need to create a clinical model for the ego deformation analogous to the sexual perversions; and finally, the hypothesis that ego cleavage (splitting) must involve a withdrawal of cathexis, which would make it a psychotic mechanism.

Freud (1924b) follows up his reflections on the nature of psychosis. He states: "neurosis does not disavow the reality, it only ignores it; psychosis disavows it and tries to replace it" (p. 185). It is obvious that the concept of disavowal is different from repression in that disavowal is a psychotic mechanism dealing with external reality, whereas neurosis and repression deal with internal reality. Freud elaborates on this point: "In a psychosis, the transforming of reality is carried out upon the psychical precipitates of former relations to it — *that is, upon the memory-traces, ideas and judgements which have been previously derived from reality and by which reality was represented in the mind*" (1924b, p. 185; italics mine). Freud indicates the crucial role that cognition and the ability to deal not only with drives but also with ideas and judgments play in psychosis. Freud's statement underscores the importance of Bion's (1962) concept of the K (knowledge) and his emphasis on thought processes in psychosis. The creation of a neo-reality in psychosis is analogous to the neurotic *world of fantasy*, "a domain which became separated from the real external world at the time of the introduction of the reality principle" (Freud, 1924b, p. 187). The final lines of Freud's article stress the difference between psychosis and neurosis in the use of fantasy — anticipating Winnicott's work on "playing," and that of Klein, Segal, Khan, and myself, among others, on "symbolism" and borderline states:

> But whereas the new, imaginary external world of a psychosis attempts to put itself in the place of external reality, that of a neurosis, on the contrary, is apt, *like the play of children* [italics mine], to attach itself to a piece of reality — a different piece from the one against which it has to defend itself — and to lend that piece a special importance and a secret meaning which we

(not always quite appropriately) call a *symbolic* one. Thus we see that both in neurosis and psychosis there comes into consideration the question not only of a *loss of reality* but also of a *substitute for reality* [Freud, 1924b, p. 187].

Freud's search for an answer to the problem of psychosis led him to the dynamics of borderline thinking, described in his article on "Negation" (1925). In my view, Freud's pair of opposites — Yes or No — coexist with a neither-Yes-nor-No mental structure, which, with regard to reality, finds expression in the feeling that the object is and is not real, or the object is neither real nor unreal (fantasied).

We may schematize Freud's ideas in the following manner:

	(IR)	(ER)
Pr_2	P — UP Yes-No	Pr_2 Yes-No
Pr_1	UP — P Yes	?

At first a vertical border separates "good" psychic reality (IR) from "bad" external reality (ER). This division coincides with the separation of "Yes" (inside) from "No" (outside), according to the pleasure-unpleasure principle. A second development is represented by the horizontal border, which separates the pleasurable and unpleasurable inside. But because of repression, what corresponds to the unpleasurable in the conscious-preconscious corresponds to the pleasurable in the repressed. The vertical and horizontal lines thus indicate the separation between psychic reality (IR) on the left and external reality on the right (ER). In psychic reality, we have the secondary process (Pr_2) on the conscious level, with pleasurable (P) and unpleasurable affects (UP) linked with a Yes-or-No system (Yes-No), corresponding to the secondary process (Pr_2) of the external world. Hence a similarity between the conscious and the real. On the other hand, in psychic reality we also have the repressed, i.e., the system of a reversed opposition of the pleasurable-unpleasurable affect (antagonistic to the corresponding conscious affects) and a system of judgment where "No" is unthinkable. Hence a conflict between the conscious and the unconscious and, in turn, between the unconscious and the external world. But we can assume that the unconscious is in some sort of correspondence with the unknown (?) of the external world.

This set of propositions is echoed in "Analysis Terminable and Interminable" (1937), an inexhaustible source of ideas for psychoanalysts with regard to theory and practice. Here once again Freud reiterates his belief in the importance of early traumas or early ego distortions with fixations to primitive defense mechanisms. He embellishes this with formulations about constitutional factors and peculiarities of the libido (inertia, viscosity, extreme fluidity and mobility of the cathexes), factors he seems to take for granted, but which require in fact a thorough investigation of their meaning and origin. On the other hand, even if not all of us agree with Freud's conception of the death instincts, few would deny the crucial importance of aggression — even if variously understood and conceptualized — in the etiology of psychosis and borderline states.

I would place the work of Bergeret (1974a) along this theoretical developmental line. His extensive knowledge of the literature allows him to make a good synthesis. He describes two kinds of disorganizing traumas. An early infantile trauma, with severe frustrations and the threat of object loss, leads to a precocious pseudo latency. This kind of disorganizing trauma accounts for a common body of borderline states (*tronc commun des états-limités*) and a provisional ego organization. A second kind of disorganizing trauma may occur in late adolescence — adolescence itself becoming prolonged beyond its normal end. Such trauma, accompanied by disruptive anxiety states, results in the reorganization of the provisional ego toward three alternative pathological outcomes: neurosis, psychosis, or psychosomatic regression. Two other ways of negotiation are found by the beleaguered ego: perversion and character disorder.

Another developmental theory basically along Freudian lines is that of Kernberg (1975). His formulations are supported not only by his own clinical experience, but by his vast knowledge of the literature, which he is able to reinterpret and integrate in an original and imaginative way.

As Kernberg's writings on the borderline personality organization are well known, I shall limit myself to his general frame of reference. Kernberg uses a double-sided model: structural and genetic-dynamic. This structural point of view has reference to (a) a topographical model as developed by Freud, (b) Hartmann's ego psychology, and (c) the structural derivatives of object relations. Borderline states, according to Kernberg, are characterized by: (a) nonspecific manifestations of ego weakness, (b) a shift toward primary-process thinking, and (c) specific defensive operations, which he views from the vantage point of internalized object relations.

Kernberg stresses the importance of splitting between "good" and "bad" internal objects and self-images. He believes that the major defect in the development of borderline pathology lies in the individual's incapacity to synthesize the positive and negative introjections and identifications. Note that Kernberg considers the borderline personality organization not as fluctuating or labile, but as a stable type of structure.

From the genetic-dynamic point of view, Kernberg stresses the importance of oral fixations. His conceptualization in this respect is distinct from the Kleinian view, which he criticizes. But along with Klein, he believes that pregenital aggression induces premature development of oedipal striving.

In conclusion, I shall define Kernberg's theory as a *borderline* one — bordering between ego psychology and the Kleinian point of view.

We may now turn to the work of Melanie Klein and her followers. I refer to only one of Klein's papers, "Notes on Some Schizoid Mechanisms" (1946), which I find particularly relevant to the subject of borderline disorders. Most important is her assumption that object relations exist from the beginning of life. She also emphasizes the destructive potential of the infant mind and its primitive defenses of splitting, idealization, and projective identification. Moreover, she recognizes the importance of the narcissistic nature of schizoid object relations and describes the connection between schizoid and manic-depressive phenomena. Segal and Rosenfeld, among other followers, have elaborated and developed Klein's views with reference to adult borderline patients.

Special mention should be made of Bion's work. Even though nearly all his contributions are focused on the problems of psychosis, his 1957 paper "Differentiations of the Psychotic from the Nonpsychotic Personalities" is an important contribution to the literature of borderline disorders. The richness and originality of Bion's ideas defy summarization. His contributions are most significant in that they confront Freud's ideas about the psychic apparatus, especially as it concerns thought processes, and Klein's conceptualization of object relations, especially her view of projective identification as a basic defense mechanism. Bion points to the precocious mental development or "precipitation" of psychotic individuals and argues that defense should be conceived not in terms of regression, but as rapid "anticipation"—something that impairs the development of the psychic apparatus for secondary-process thinking. His recognition of depressive functions in language processes is also an original and relevant contribution. Instead of a maturational use of language resources, there is, according to Bion, a fixation to "ideograms," which hinders the evolution of thought processes toward a mind structure dependent on verbal thought.

In his later work (1962), Bion assumes the existence of three factors: L (love) and H (hate), with K (knowledge) as a primary concept of equal importance to love and hate. He also postulates the relations $O \rightarrow K$, where O stands for the unknowable object and the state of the unknowable (godness, absolute truth, the infinite), leading to a state of knowledge that deals with what is acknowledgeable. Finally, his analysis of the relation between "container" and "content" offers valuable clues to the study of the psychic structures.

But it is Winnicott (1958, 1965, 1971a, 1971b) who is specifically, in my opinion, *the analyst of the borderline.* His inimitable style and original conceptualization do not lend themselves to easy summarization. Winnicott's apparent clarity is misleading, and frequently one reads authors inspired by his contributions who do not do justice to the subtle and rich complexity of his ideas. His emphasis on the "facilitating environment," "primary maternal concern," and "holding" has led to a shift of attention from the over-all internal object to the role of the external object. In fact, however, Winnicott is much more interested in the *interplay* of the external and the internal. What he directs our attention to is precisely the *area of the intermediate,* and the failure to create it. He gives us a joint model of clinical setting and psychic functioning. He describes the fate of symbolization and the impairment of the functional value of the transitional field, as well as transitional phenomena in borderline cases, by insisting on the fact that for these patients the setting and the analyst do not represent the mother—they *are* the mother. His conceptualization of the "false self" refers to the effects of an overdemanding adaptation to the need-supplying object.

Much less attention has been given to Winnicott's late concepts of "noncommunication," "void," and "emptiness." His theory of the "gap" and the impossibility to create out of it another form of reunion with the object in the building of the "potential space" opens new horizons of understanding, inducing the analyst to new ways of observing his own reaction as a tool for comprehending the paradoxes of borderline systems of thought. In what he calls "the negative side of relationships," Winnicott (1971b) gives useful clues for the understanding of clinical features of the borderline individual, in whom a sense of lack and a feeling of nothingness predominate. Countertransference thus becomes the analyst's privileged instrument for work with such patients. The analyst must pay attention not only to what is present, but also to the missing links, which are not hidden but experienced as gaps, the only things that are real for the borderline patient. The essence of Winnicott's thought is contained in the last lines of *Playing and Reality* (1971b), which he names his "tail piece." Here he defines conceptualization (the psychic functioning that creates the subjective object) and perception (the objectively perceived object), pointing out an inherent paradox, "one that we must accept and that is not for resolution."

Winnicott's work has influenced Khan's (1974) and Milner's (1968) theoretical development. Khan has given us the concept of the "cumulative trauma," describing infantile neurosis as a "false self organization" and pointing out the role of the interplay of the analyst's senses in the appraisal of transferential manifestations. The necessity to establish a contractual distance prevents the analyst from indulging in merging regressions or intruding into the secrecy of the patient's "potential space." Like Winnicott, Khan is aware of the importance of the aliveness of the analytic situation.

Milner has outstandingly illustrated the modifications required for analytic work with borderline patients. Her major contribution lies in the recognition of the need for tolerance of unorganized states in the analyst's mind, from which growth and creativity stem. Her contributions to the dynamics of symbolism and her criticism of the conceptualization of primary process as a lower form of psychic activity constitute the basis of a better understanding of primary-process thinking in borderline disorders. I would like to add here that in borderline thinking we have the result of a destructive perversion of primary-process thinking, rather than a genuine expression of what primary process is supposed to be in infancy.

I have made only one reference to the French literature, but as I have been strongly influenced by it, I feel that I should not close this section without mentioning some important, even though indirect, contributions to the borderline psychopathology by my fellow countrymen. Bouvet's (1967) description of pregenital structures and especially of depersonalization neurosis, as well as the work of his followers from the Paris school of psychosomatics (Marty, Fain, M'Uzan, and David), have enriched our understanding of the borderline. Bouvet's concept of *rapprocher* and of psychic distance has been carefully applied to the handling of difficult cases. Lacan's (1966) ideas on psychosis, especially his attempt to clarify Freud's concept of "deferred action," of "foreclosure" (*Verwerfung*) and its role in his theory of the Name of the Father are stimulating, even if other aspects of Lacan's writings may be highly questionable.

To conclude this partial review of the literature, I shall list the issues relevant to our topic: (1) the role of the *ego, the self*, and *narcissism*, with the early defense mechanisms of dissociation and splitting, and their consequences: decathexis and projective identification; (2) the function of *object relations*, with special attention to pregenital aggression and its influence on thought processes; (3) the presence of *psychotic anxiety* and its impact on the binding function of psychic processes, with consequences for verbal thought; (4) the failures in the creation of a *transitional space*, with the dual, coexisting function of the pleasure principle and the reality principle, and a double-bind pattern of relations; (5) the *condensation of pregenital and genital aims*, giving a double meaning to each of them, which automatically refers one to the other; (6) the role of a *complementary relation* in the analytic setting, the countertransference becoming a conveyor for the patient's communication more than an obstacle to his understanding; and (7) the notion of *psychic dis-*

tance, necessary to avoid both lack of communication and intrusion.

THE CONCEPT OF THE BORDERLINE

Most, if not all, of the preceding contributors base their theoretical assumptions mainly on the genetic point of view. Even those who take into account the topographic model and the concomitant structural point of view subsume it under an over-all genetic rubric. In his "Outline of Psycho-Analysis" Freud (1940a) wrote:

> A child's first erotic object is the mother's breast that nourishes it; love has its origin in attachment to the satisfied need for nourishment. There is no doubt that, to begin with, the child does not distinguish between the breast and its own body; when the breast has to be separated from the body and shifted to the *'outside'* because the child so often finds it absent, it carries with it as an *'object'* a part of the original narcissistic libidinal cathexis. The first object is later completed into the person of the child's mother, who not only nourishes it but also looks after it and thus arouses in it a number of other physical sensations, pleasurable and unpleasurable [p. 188].

In this instance Freud conceived the birth of the object as separate from the child's own body as a gradual process. But on other, earlier occasions, he spoke about a clear-cut separation from the outset (1925). His concept of the original reality ego indicates that he saw the child as able to distinguish between internal and external sources of excitation from the beginning. Such ideas seem contradictory unless we assume that there is a distinction between inside and outside that antedates the distinction between the child's body and the mother's breast. Indeed, in his paper on "Negation," Freud (1925) made a clear-cut distinction between the pleasure principle and the reality principle, which arises with the development of reality testing. As he put it, ". . . it is evident that a precondition for the setting up of reality-testing is that objects shall have been lost which once brought real satisfaction" (p. 238). In Freud's view, at least as I understand it, this development is not a progressive, slow change, since it requires the function of judgment to decide whether

the object exists or not. The function of judgment is related to primary instinctual impulses and "is not made possible until the
creation of the symbol of negation has endowed thinking with a first
measure of freedom from the consequences of repression and, with
it, from the compulsion of the pleasure principle" (p. 239).

Because of the sovereignty of the reality principle, the realm of
fantasy is created as a private domain. This development allows for
an important observation: each time a separation occurs between a
couple of mental opposites—two terms, two functions, two processes—at least one of the two split-off elements tends to reinclude
some part of the opposite, excluded element.

On the other hand, if the psychic apparatus has the *illusion of a
mutative transformation*, a retrospective view of its former functioning allows us to assume that, in fact, the transformation was
gradual, involving the overlapping of different models of functioning, of two areas, and of the dual relation between the self and the
object.

Let us now shift our attention to some other relevant metapsychological concepts formulated by Freud. Let us consider the
nature of the topographic model. Freud (1933) states:

> In thinking of this division of the personality into an ego, a
> super-ego and an id, you will not, of course, have pictured sharp
> frontiers like the artificial ones drawn in political geography.
> We cannot do justice to the characteristics of the mind by linear
> outlines like those in a drawing or in primitive painting, but
> rather by areas of colour melting into one another as they are
> presented by modern artists. After making the separation we
> must allow what we have separated to merge together once
> more. You must not judge too harshly a first attempt at giving a
> pictorial representation of something so intangible as psychical
> processes. It is highly probable that the development of these
> divisions is subject to great variations in different individuals; it
> is possible that in the course of actual functioning they may
> change and go through a temporary phase of involution [p. 79].

The function of judgment is established gradually. Conversely,
the reconstruction in the psychic apparatus of the past experience of

this gradual process as a mutation is important for the establishment of the judging process in reality testing. The major difficulty therefore lies in the coexistence of different ego states: tolerance of "shadows, doubts and mysteries" and/or capacity to decide between the Yes and the No, the existent and the nonexistent. Imagination and rationality are so necessary to each other that any imbalance in the one would be detrimental to the other, leading to a global impairment of mental functioning.

In "Civilization and Its Discontents," Freud (1930) discusses the blurring of mental frontiers that occurs even in normal persons and relates it to the return of an undifferentiated infantile state of mind, characterized by an "oceanic feeling." He concludes: "The fact remains that only in the mind is such a preservation of all the earlier stages alongside of the final form possible, and that we are not in a position to represent this phenomenon in pictorial terms" (p. 71).

Here again we find Freud wishing to use pictorial metaphors, even though he is aware of their inadequacy. The pictorial way of communicating, in theory or in mental functioning, has a transitional function between the two other main modes of human communication: affects, which in essence are not representatible in pictorial form, and thought, which consists of relations independent of the terms it brings into relation. Splitting is therefore a normal process enabling one to achieve communication out of the verbally uncommunicable affects and thought processes. As such, splitting never disappears but undergoes transformations with the help of a holding, containing, *optimally distant, and time-delaying object.* Even though splitting can separate, it never succeeds in a complete way. This is also true in a clinical sense with the "Splitting of the Ego in the Process of Defence," as Freud (1940b) pointed out in his posthumously published paper, where the concept of disavowal is once more implicated.

In a companion paper Freud (1940a) brings forward the importance of splitting in the psychoses. Even in the severely disturbed patient suffering from hallucinatory confusion, the normal ego is not totally absorbed by the regressive condition—*a fortiori* in less severe cases. As Freud puts it: "Two psychical attitudes have been formed instead of a single one—one, the normal one, which takes account of reality, and another which under the influence of the instincts detaches the ego from reality. The two exist alongside of each other. The issue depends on their relative strength" (p. 202).

I would like to close this section by showing that not only are the frontiers between the ego and reality variable, but even the instinct, as Freud conceived it, undergoes analogous variations in its intrinsic functioning. According to Freud (1915), "an 'instinct' appears to us as a *concept on the frontier* between the mental and the somatic, as the psychical representative of the stimuli originating from within the organism and reaching the mind, as a measure of the demand made upon the mind for work in consequence of its connection with the body" (pp. 121-122; italics mine).

This so frequently quoted, deceptively simple statement of Freud's can be a source of endless reflection. My understanding of it is as follows:

1. The instinct (*trieb*) is a concept.

2. The concept is on the *frontier* between two domains.

3. Freud opposes one single word, the "mind" (*seele*), as the function of the "mental" (*psychische*), to two words expressing the same idea: the "somatic" (*somastisch*), or the "organism," and the "body" (*körper*). One may raise the question: Are these different synonyms used to avoid fastidious repetition, or do the words in fact refer to semantic distinctions?

4. The instinct is a *psychical representative* of stimuli. This psychical representative must not be confused with the *ideational representative*, which, along with a quota of affect, forms the instinctual representatives in the psyche.

5. The instinct is defined as a *process*, a progression involving pressure or energy, which can only be felt and understood as a measure of a demand upon the mind for work. In my opinion, it is clear that the measure of such a demand for work is of variable strength, and the frontiers between the organism and its mind are not sharply delineated. So within this concept of the frontier (*grenzbegrief*) one can also think of borderline states between the somatic and the mental or psychic, between the body and the mind, on which a process of transformation is at work.

In conclusion, we can say that *nowhere* does there exist clear-cut splitting: within the instincts; between body and mind; within the ego and its interrelations to the id, the superego, and reality. Therefore we have to consider the borderline as a *moving and fluctuating* frontier, both in normality and in severe illness, and as the most basic concept in psychoanalysis, which cannot be understood in pictorial terms (representations) but has to be conceived in terms of processes of transformations of *energy* and *symbolization* (force and meaning).

On the other hand, one basic function of the psyche is to strive for *separation* in order to foster adaptation, individuation, and autonomy. But these aims will not be attained unless the *disjunctive* process is accompanied by a *conjunctive* one, where the aim is to reestablish communication with the split-off elements to the extent possible. This is the work of *symbolization*, which requires the splitting of two elements and their conjunction in order to create a third element, which is composed of the two split-off elements, each of them remaining the same and becoming in reunion a different one.

A HYPOTHESIS OR CONCEPTUAL FRAMEWORK CONCERNING BORDERLINE PATIENTS

As I indicated earlier, the borderline case is less of a frontier than a no-man's-land, an entire field whose borders are vague. Its population has to be sorted out. Grinker's (1977) attempt is in this respect a classificatory one. Yet we are in need of not only catalogues of symptoms or of classificatory tables, but also of ordinal concepts. To this end, I shall propose a conceptual framework, announced on a previous occasion (Green, 1975), and extracted from the analytic situation. I would like to stress that the borderline cases closer to neurosis often afford us the greatest opportunity to grasp the nature of the problem, because they are amenable to the deep scrutiny of psychoanalytic investigation. Illustrative case material may give the reader the impression that the patient is neurotic, but the analyst knows that he is dealing with a borderline case. This knowledge is based on the affective quality of the patient's communication and the analyst's own inner response to it, which are difficult to convey in writing — unless one writes poetry.

In this connection, I should mention the function of countertransference, which can serve as a very precise tool in the understanding
of borderline patients.

To begin with, one must trace the hypothetical limits of the
psychic field. There are two, of a different nature: *soma* and *acting*.
In my analysis of Freud's definition of an instinct (*trieb*), I pointed
to the multiplicity of terms attributed to the somatic sphere and
raised the question of synonymity or semantic difference. Here I
shall draw a distinction between the somatic, which I relate to the
organism (a biological entity), and the body, which I relate to libidinal cathexis. We assume that the aim of an instinct is achieved by
what Freud calls "specific action," which can transform a helpless
situation into a satisfactory experience after the failure of
hallucinatory wish-fulfillment. We know that "acting out" is the
opposite of a specific action (in Freud's sense). The main function of
acting out — or reactive behavior — is to pare or to parade. I have in
mind the French word *parer,* meaning to cope with, to counteract,
to protect oneself, to avoid, to ward off. The aim here is to precipitate the organism into action in order to bypass psychical reality.
Thus, one might say that the psychical field is delineated by both aspects of the instinct: its source (somatic) and its aim (acting). It is
difficult to assign one basic function to the psychic field, as it seems
to have more than one. But in order to clarify my idea, and at the
risk of oversimplifying things, I shall advance a hypothesis.

Freud assumed that the basic function of the psychic field was
the *lowering of unpleasurable tension.* Hartmann's ego psychology
assumes that the basic function is *adaptation*, an assertion not
contradictory to Freud's, though implying a shift in emphasis. The
British School considers that *growth* is this basic function. I suggest
that this basic function is *representation*. This should be understood
in a very broad sense, as including representation of both the
external and the internal world. It also includes a pluralistic mode
of representation, not only through an ideational content but also
through acts, affects, bodily states, language, ideas, and thoughts.
As Castoriadis-Aulagnier (1975) suggests, it is as if any activity of
the psychic apparatus had the function of building the representation of whatever is to be represented, and also the representation of
the functioning of the psychic apparatus itself. The psychical field is

under a double influence: the *pressure* of the instinct pushing toward the realization of the specific action, and the impact of the need-satisfying object through representation.

Freud has endlessly stressed the importance of reality testing in distinguishing between representation, which obeys the pleasure principle, and perception, which is under the power of the reality principle. The aim of the instinct requires, especially at the beginning, a devoted person to act as a need-satisfying object, and at the same time as substitute for the child's embryonic ego. Both functions are fused and embodied in the mother's breast — i.e., the mother's care. The child's ego acts individually when separation between breast and child finally takes place. This gradual process is evidently accompanied by periodic phases of reunion with the object, when the former phase is re-established in fact; and of periodic phases when the child tries to re-establish, alone, the lost paradise of fusion with the maternal object or breast. But the inevitable frustrations and disappointments of the growing process compel him to tolerate, alongside the feeling of well-being, the discontent and anger which are fixated in archaic forms of representation, for which Bion (1957) has proposed the concept of the "ideogram." The attempt to separate the "good" from the "bad," the pleasurable from the unpleasurable, and the obligation to achieve separation instead of giving birth to the distinction between self and object (inside and outside, somatic and psychic, fantasy and reality, "good" and "bad") engender splitting in borderlines. In a set of complementary, opposite terms, each separated term admits the symmetrical complement; for example, the shadow of its light, its phantom more than its fantasy. But inevitably, it will be again reunited in some other area of the psychic space. In severely disturbed cases the result is a radical exclusion: splitting.

To some extent, splitting is necessary to the work of the psychic apparatus, which must not be overburdened and overwhelmed by tension and has, in order to survive, to refind the *quality* of well-being. On the other hand, radical splitting puts aside and away factors indispensable for the work of representation. Therefore splitting, instead of functioning as a useful limitation, causes amputation in the ego. For, with regard to the kind of splitting I am talking about here, not only destructive instinctual representations are split off, but also, in the same process, important parts of the ego itself (Bion, 1962, 1963).

The cause of splitting is understood differently, depending on one's conceptual framework. For Freud the splitting I am discussing is an expression of the death instinct, as opposed to the unifying action of Eros. For Melanie Klein it is also the result of the death-instinct operations, but as related to the fear of annihilation and directed toward the object. Freud's death instinct is a separating force, which operates primarily internally, even at the cellular level, without necessarily being felt as destructive; rather it is seen as disjunctive. In Klein's theory, it is the *affect* and not the idea of destruction that comes into play. For Winnicott splitting or dissociation is also related to destruction but with major differences. First, Winnicott assumes that early destructive experiences, because of the ego's immaturity, cannot be felt as such; lacking integration, they are more like unthinkable "agonies." Second, the attitude of the external environment is of utmost importance in containing these disintegrated states.

In my view, splitting is hardly conceivable without its complementary term: confusion. The child's splitting is a very basic reaction to the object's attitude, which can be twofold: (1) a lack of fusion on the part of the mother, to the effect that even in the actual experiences of encounter the child meets a *blank breast*; (2) an excess of fusion, the mother being unable to renounce for the sake of her child's growth the paradisiac bliss regained through the experience of pregnancy.

The child-breast separation is bound to a double consent, a two-party contract relating mother and child with reference to a potential third party—the father—who is present from the beginning in the mother's mind. The paradoxical result of splitting in this instance is that (a) something will be excluded, warded off, disavowed, and in fact become unworkable or unthinkable; and (b) the split-off terms will come back in a manner analogous to the return of the repressed, with the difference that they will have an intrusive, persecutory quality by way of projective identification. In other words, splitting in this instance results in the polarity "loss-intrusion."

It would be quite erroneous to think that splitting occurs only or mainly during the separation of the external from the internal. In fact, splitting also occurs, and perhaps even predominantly, between psyche and soma, and consequently between bodily sensations and affects. This dissociation may take subtle forms, as in the isolation process disjoining affect representation and thought. Needless to say, motor action itself may also be split off from the psychic world. What I want to stress here is that the two frontiers established by splitting are between the somatic and the libidinal body on the one side, and between psychical reality and external reality, involving the libidinal body and action, on the other.

As a consequence, we may assume that the split-off soma will intrude into the psychic sphere in the form of psychosomatic symptoms, hysteria, or hypochondriasis. The difference between psychosomatic symptoms and conversion hysteria is that whereas conversion symptoms are built in a symbolic fashion and are related to the libidinal body, psychosomatic symptoms are not of a symbolic nature. They are somatic manifestations loaded with refined, "pure" aggression. Hypochondriacal symptoms, on the other hand, are painful representations of somatic organs filled with narcissistic, delibidinized and destructive libido.

Considering the second frontier, one may assume that there is the same lack of symbolization in "acting out." Insofar as it is a symptom, acting out may have a symbolic meaning for the analyst, but none from the patient's point of view. It is a mere discharge, the patient being blind to its possible meaning. It is not linked to anything other than its manifest, rationalized content. Here lies the difference between acting out and parapraxis, which is something devoid of meaning but which rapidly acquires a meaning by means of the associations that follow its narrative. In short, we may say that somatic (or psychosomatic) reactions and acting out have the same function: discharge to ward off psychic reality.

One can now understand the difference between splitting and repression. In repression, the psychic energy is bound. Links are intact and recombined with other representations or affects—id derivatives. The original terms in the associative link are replaced by others, but the linking function is only transformed, not altered. In splitting, the links are destroyed or so impaired that only by intensive effort can the analyst guess what they could have been. I therefore strongly object to the notion that borderline patients engage in primary-process thinking.

The implications of this differentiation between repression and splitting are of momentous importance. The return of the repressed gives rise to signal anxiety. The return of the split-off elements is accompanied by feelings of severe threat, of "helplessness" (Freud's *hilflosigkeit*), "annihilation" (Klein, 1946), "nameless dread" (Bion, 1970), "disintegration" or "agonies" (Winnicott, 1958). When the narcissistic cathexes are mainly threatened, the experience is characterized by "blankness" (Green, 1969).

Let us now consider the concepts that define the psychic sphere, for so far I have only examined those elements rejected from the psychic sphere. They are the same: *splitting* and *repression*. Just as repression is a mechanism directed inward, splitting here is active on its inner side. Let me clarify what I mean.

The idea of splitting in the psychic sphere poses problems. It is clear that splitting in borderline disorders is not the same as repression in neurosis or splitting in the psychoses. I have pointed out that repression in neurosis is accompanied by internal symbolization, which can be witnessed in the return of the repressed. With respect to psychosis, we may say that splitting acts as minute splitting, as Klein and her followers have observed. Nor is splitting in the borderline simply reduced to the kind of cleavage that takes place in depression, though depression and mental breakdown are constant threats in borderline disorders. In my opinion, the specificity of the borderline lies in the fact that splitting develops on two levels: splitting *between* the psychic and the nonpsychic (soma and outside world) and splitting *within* the psychic sphere. The splitting between the inside and the outside is determined by the constitution of an ego container, and ego holder or ego envelope, whose limits are well delineated but do not function as a protective shield. In fact, ego boundaries are largely elastic. Nevertheless this flexibility is not conducive to adaptive behavior; rather, it acts like a fluctuation of expansion, retraction, or both, in coping with *separation (loss) anxiety, intrusion (implosion) anxiety*, or both. This variability of ego boundaries is not felt as an enrichment of experience but as a loss of control, as the last defensive measure against implosion, disintegration, or loss. This ego envelope, this inefficient shield, protects the vulnerable ego, which is both rigid and lacking cohesiveness. The inner splitting reveals that the ego is composed of different, noncommunicating nuclei. These ego nuclei can aptly be designated as *archipelagos*.

By means of this metaphor I shall try to describe some unique characteristics of these psychic structures. Instead of a myriad of islands surrounded by an ocean, one might think of isolated pieces of land delineated by void space. These islands remain without the possibility of connection with each other. There is a lack of cohesiveness, a lack of unity, and above all a lack of coherence and an impression of contradictory sets of relations — roughly speaking, the coexistence of contradictory thoughts, affects, fantasies, but moreover contradictory byproducts of the pleasure principle, the reality principle, or both. This failure in integration gives the observer a feeling of aloofness, an absence of vitality, as these separated islands of egos (self-object relations) do not succeed in forming one individual being. In my view, these islands of ego nuclei are less important than their surrounding space, which I have described as void. Futility, lack of awareness of presence, limited contact are all expressions of the same basic emptiness that characterizes the experience of the borderline person. Again, like Bion, I stress the importance of the linking function or, to remain in Freud's conceptual framework, of the binding function of Eros. The discourse of the borderline is not a chain of words, representations, or affects, but rather — like a pearl necklace without a string — words, representations, affects contiguous in space and time but not in meaning. It is up to the observer to establish the missing links with his own psychic apparatus.

I have suggested that the mechanism of splitting operates alongside a mechanism best identified as primary depression. In my view, all other mechanisms of psychic defense (projective and introjective identification, denial, omnipotence, etc.) are consequences of the basic mechanism of splitting, which is one of the two polar mechanisms of the psychic apparatus. The other polarity is depression. By depression I do not mean what is usually described by this term, but rather a *radical decathexis*, which engenders blank states of mind without any affective components, pain, or suffering. The clinical features associated with this mechanism are a series of phenomena about which borderline patients complain: difficulty of mental representations, impairment of concentration, impossibility of thinking — all of which have been described before as *blank psychosis* (Donnet and Green, 1973). It is the psychotic kernel. This primary depression may lead either to a random recathexis by instinctual energy (predominantly aggression) and a reinforcement of splitting, or to feelings of nonexistence and unreality of self- and object images. When there is a chance for further maturation, the normal depressive position becomes a regressive pool for this primary depression. To ward off the threat of primary depression, precipitate and premature object relations occur, and adolescence is inordinately prolonged. Impossibility of mourning and of tolerating guilt feelings are striking features responsible for acting out, psychopathic or as-if personality behavior, polymorphous perversions, drug addiction, and alcoholism. These two basic mechanisms, splitting and primary depression, take place within the inner reality of the self. I have already commented on the elasticity of ego boundaries as a mode of reaction to loss, separation or intrusion anxiety, or both.

In my view, one needs to consider *two borderline areas* in the psychic apparatus. First, an intermediary area between the unconscious and the conscious-preconscious; its manifestation is the dream. Second, the area of play or illusion — Winnicott's "potential space." Borderline patients are characterized by a failure to create functional byproducts of the potential space; instead of manifesting transitional phenomena, they create symptoms to fulfill the function of transitional phenomena. By this I do not mean to say that borderline patients are unable to create transitional objects or phenomena. To say such a thing would be to ignore the fact that many artists are borderline personalities. In fact it can only be said that, from the point of view of the psychic apparatus of such individuals, transitional objects or phenomena have no functional value, as they do for others.

As many workers in the field have realized, dream analysis in the treatment of the borderline is, as a rule, unproductive. The reason seems to be that borderline patients' dreams do not express wish-fulfillment but rather serve a function of evacuation. As Bion (1962) has pointed out, the "dream barrier" is an important function of the psychic apparatus. It seems that in borderline cases, even though the dream barrier is effective, the dream's purpose is not the working through of instinct derivatives, but rather the unburdening of the psychic apparatus from painful stimuli or, in Bion's terms, from "accretion." The dreams of borderline patients are not characterized by condensation but by concretization. One can also observe dream failures in these patients: wakening in order to prevent dreaming or to find themselves surrounded by a strange, disquieting atmosphere, which constitutes a transitional dream state akin to a nightmare. In more successful instances, dreams are actualizations of the self in the dream space, attempts to reformulate traumatic experiences (Khan, 1974). In such instances, the most significant thing in analyzing a dream is not the dream's latent content but *the dreamer's experience.*

Let us now turn to another aspect of the problem. The content of the unconscious is made up of object relations, involving either part objects or whole objects (persons). The history of object relations is made up of pregenital fixations and regressions in a more or less predictable sequence of preoedipal and oedipal phases of development. In describing "blank psychosis," Donnet and I (1973) have proposed the concept of *bi-triangulation* or *tri-dyadic relationships.* In this type of Oedipus-like complex, there is a triangular relationship in which the two parental figures are experienced as affective polar opposites.

A normal person nurtures ambivalent feelings, both positive and negative, for each parent. In borderline persons, however, there is a split between the two parents along the notions of the "bad" and the "good," the "persecutory" and the "idealized"; one parent is felt as "all bad" and the other as "all good." In this relationship the "good" parental object is perceived as weak and ineffective and the overvaluation of the "good" idealization is of no help against the omnipotent "badness" of the other parent. The fear that abandonment by the "bad" intruding parental object will lead nowhere but to a desert, and that the idealized "good" object is unavailable, too distant and unreliable, brings the borderline patient to an insoluble dilemma. Shapiro and his co-workers (1975) have described how the borderline may be the receptacle of complementary disturbed parents, each projecting onto the child the denied part of his or her sick personality. However, the division of good and bad between two objects uncovers that of one two-sided object.

When Winnicott postulated the concept of the "false self," he gave us a way of understanding the function of narcissistic features in borderline patients. As the "false self" is built not on the patient's real experiences, but on the compliance to the mother's image of her child, the "false self" organization serves the object's narcissism rather than that of the self—hence one paradox of the existence of narcissistic features and the feeling that they are of a different nature from the usual features of so-called narcissistic personalities. The answer to this contradictory assessment is that the "false self" is supplied by a borrowed narcissism—the object's narcissism. Consequently, the mental functioning of the bewildered analyst appears as the double of the patient's mental functioning and object relations: symmetrical, complementary, or opposite.

It is quite remarkable that the dead-end issues facing the borderline patient are experienced by him not only in his mental functioning and object relations as reactivated in the transference, but also in his real life. They force him to move constantly from one place to another, to travel far away in order to escape the "bad" object and reach the "good" one in some ideal holy land, only to be recaptured by some substitute figure of the "bad" object, some silly agent of the "bad" object sent to torment him and bring him back to his detested nest.

Concerning the borderline's mental functioning, one may observe a paradoxical mode of elaboration. I have already commented on the role of splitting. I can add that the different components of the psychic apparatus are all confused. There is no clear distinction between thoughts, representations, and affects. Rational thinking is difficult because the thought processes are loaded with massive quantities of affects, and they cannot be detached from the instincts except by way of an intensive splitting, sometimes accompanied by magical beliefs and narcissistically invested omnipotence. Also, in considering the borderline's mental representations, one can see that there is such a conglomeration of affects and representations that affects act in fact as representations and representations act as affects. Moreover, one can say that acting (as opposed to specific action) is the true model of the mind here, whether directed inward, producing psychosomatic symptoms, or outward, by way of acting out. Acting is not limited to actions; fantasies, dreams, words take the function of action. Acting fills space and does not tolerate the suspension of experience. The reason for such intolerance for the suspension of experience is the belief that no creation, no knowledge can emerge from it. Suspension is equated with inertia or, as Khan (1974) has described it, resource-less dependence. Basic trust is fundamental for the acceptance of passivity. Passivity is always felt as the supreme threat, open to all kinds of dangers in the hands of the omnipotent "bad" object.

I shall now propose a final hypothesis with respect to the border-line's judgment and reality testing. According to the reality principle, the psychic apparatus has to decide whether the object is or is not there: *"Yes" or "No."* According to the pleasure principle, and as negation does not exist in the primary process of the unconscious, there is only "Yes." Winnicott has described the status of the transitional object, which combines the "Yes" and the "No," as the transitional is- and is-not-the-breast. One can find precursors of Winnicott's observations in Freud's description of the cotton-reel game (1920) and in his description of the fetish (1927). But I think that there is one more way of dealing with this crucial issue of deciding whether the object is or is not, and that is illustrated by the judgment of the borderline patient. There is a fourth possible answer: *neither "Yes" nor "No."* This *is* an alternate choice to the refusal of choice. The transitional object is a *positive refusal*; it is either a "Yes" or a "No." The symptoms of the borderline, standing for transitional objects, offer a *negative refusal of choice:* neither "Yes" nor "No." One could express the same relation in experiential terms by asking the question: "Is the object dead (lost) or alive (found)?" or "Am I dead or alive?"—to which he may answer: *"Neither Yes nor No."*

A related concept that may prove useful to our discussion is Lacan's (1966) "absence." As I understand it, the concept refers to neither loss nor death. Lacan's "absence" has an intermediate status, being halfway between intrusion and loss. Excess of presence is intrusion; excess of absence is loss. The presence-absence pair cannot be dissociated. The two terms are interrelated, as are perception and representation. But a tremendous effort is necessary in order to be able to tolerate absence, to differentiate it from loss, and to give to the representational world its full role in one's imagination and thought. Only the absence of the object can be the stimulus for imagination and thinking, in other words, for psychic creativeness and aliveness. Winnicott's (1965) concept of the capacity to be alone *in the mother's presence* and Bion's (1970) *negative capability* come to mind.

To conclude, I would like to offer one more hypothesis. This concerns the notion of *tertiary process*, not materialized but made of conjunctive and disjunctive mechanisms in order to act as go-between of primary and secondary process. It is the most efficient mode of establishing a flexible mental equilibrium and the richest tool for creativity, safeguarding against the nuisance of splitting, whose excess leads to psychic death. Yet splitting is essential in providing a way out of confusion. Such is the fate of human bondage, that it has to serve two contrary masters — separation and reunion — one or the other, or both.

REFERENCES

Bergeret, J. (1974a), *La personnalité normale et pathologique*. Paris: Dunod.
_____ (1974b), La dépression et les états-limites. Paris: Payot.
Bion, W. R. (1957), Differentiation of the psychotic from the non-psychotic personalities. In: *Second Thoughts*. London: Heinemann, 1967, pp. 43-64.
_____ (1962), *Learning from Experience*. New York: Basic Books.
_____ (1963), *Elements of Psycho-Analysis*. New York: Basic Books.
_____ (1970), *Attention and Interpretation*. London: Tavistock Indications.
Bouvet, M. (1967), *Oeuvres Psychoanalytiques,* Vol. I. Paris: Payot.
Burchfield, R. W., ed. (1972), *A Supplement to Oxford English Dictionary*. Oxford: Clarendon Press.
Castoriadis-Aulagnier, P. (1975), *La Violence de l'Interpretation*. Paris: Presses Universitaires de France.
Deutsch, F. (1957), A footnote to Freud's "Fragment of an analysis of a case of hysteria." *Psychoanal. Quart.*, 26:159-167.
Donnet, J. L., & Green, A. (1973), *L'Enfant de ca. Psychanalyse d'un entretien. La Psychose blanche*. Paris: Editions Minuit.
Freud, S. (1915), Instincts and their vicissitudes. *Standard Edition*, 14:117-140. London: Hogarth Press, 1957.
_____ (1918), From the history of an infantile neurosis. *Standard Edition*, 17:7-122. London: Hogarth Press, 1955.
_____ (1920), Beyond the pleasure principle. *Standard Edition*, 18:7-64. London: Hogarth Press, 1955.

_____ (1924a), Neurosis and psychosis. *Standard Edition*, 19:149-153. London: Hogarth Press, 1963.

_____ (1924b), The loss of reality in neurosis and psychosis. *Standard Edition*, 19: 183-187. London: Hogarth Press, 1961.

_____ (1925), Negation. *Standard Edition*, 19:235-239. London: Hogarth Press, 1961.

_____ (1927), Fetishism. *Standard Edition*, 21:152-157. London: Hogarth Press, 1961.

_____ (1930), Civilization and its discontents. *Standard Edition*, 21:64-145. London: Hogarth Press, 1961.

_____ (1933), New introductory lectures on psycho-analysis. *Standard Edition*, 22:5-182. London: Hogarth Press, 1964.

_____ (1937), Analysis terminable and interminable. *Standard Edition*, 23:216-269. London: Hogarth Press, 1964.

_____ (1940a), An outline of psycho-analysis. *Standard Edition*, 23:144-207. London: Hogarth Press, 1964.

_____ (1940b), Splitting of the ego in the process of defence. *Standard Edition*, 23:275-278. London: Hogarth Press, 1964.

Green, A. (1969), La nosographie psychoanalytique des psychoses. In: *Problems of Psychosis*, Vol. I, ed. P. Doucet & C. Laurin. Amsterdam: Excerpta Medica.

_____ (1973), *Le Discours Vivant: La Conception Psychoanalytique de l'Affect.* Paris: Presses Universitaires de France.

_____ (1975), The analyst, symbolization and absence in the analytic setting (on changes in analytic practice and analytic experience). *Internat. J. Psycho-Anal.,* 56:1-22.

Grinker, R. R., Sr. (1977), The borderline syndrome: A phenomenological view. *This Volume,* pp. 159-172.

Kernberg, O. F. (1975), *Borderline Conditions and Pathological Narcissism.* New York: Jason Aronson.

Khan, M. (1974), *The Privacy of the Self.* New York: International Universities Press.

Klein, M. (1946), Notes on some schizoid mechanisms. *Internat. J. Psycho-Anal.,* 27:99-110.

Knight, R. P. (1953), Borderline states. *Bull. Menninger Clinic,* 17:1-12.

Lacan, J. (1966), *Écrits,* Paris: Editions Seuil.

Laplanche, J., & Pontalis, J.-B. (1967), *The Language of Psychoanalysis,* trans. D. Nicholson-Smith. New York: Norton, 1973.

Milner, M. (1968), *The Hands of the Living God.* New York: International Universities Press, 1969.

Moore, B. E., & Fine, B. D. (1967), *A Glossary of Psychoanalytic Terms and Concepts.* New York: Amer. Psychoanal. Assn.

Rycroft, C. (1968), *A Critical Dictionary of Psychoanalysis.* New York: Basic Books.

Shapiro, E. R., Zinner, J., Shapiro, R. L., & Berkovitz, D. (1975), The influence of family experience on borderline personality development. *Internat. Rev. Psycho-Anal.,* 2:399-412.

Stern, A. (1938), Psychoanalytic investigation of and therapy in the borderline group of neuroses. *Psychoanal. Quart.,* 7:467-489.

Winnicott, D. W. (1958), *Collected Papers: Through Pediatrics to Psychoanalysis.* New York: Basic Books.

_____ (1965), *The Maturational Processes and the Facilitating Environment.* New York: International Universities Press.

_____ (1971a), *Therapeutic Consultations in Child Psychiatry.* New York: Basic Books.

_____ (1971b), *Playing and Reality.* New York: Basic Books.

II

EXPLANATORY FORMULATIONS

> To say that some parts of Plato
> and Sir Thos More are as wild
> as the ravings of Bedlam.
> — From *Cantos LXVII,*
> by Ezra Pound

The papers in this section deal with the concept of borderline in a more circumscribed fashion. Rinsley's approach is from a psychoanalytic object-relations point of view, which in essence is that of most of the other contributors, in particular Mahler and Kernberg. In fact, Rinsley openly acknowledges his reliance on Mahler's and Kernberg's ideas about borderline patients. Rinsley's article is placed first because of the comprehensive nature of his historical introduction.

Mahler's developmental point of view weighs heavily on contemporary thinking, if not yet in clinical practice, concerning borderline patients. Her contribution, worked out in collaboration with Louise Kaplan, is built around the cases of two children, whom some readers may recognize from Mahler's previous writings. But there is more detail, and the emphasis is different. The article's main thesis is that borderline as well as narcissistic patients do not proceed through the ordinary developmental sequence that culminates in a viable Oedipus complex and in neurosis. Mahler and Kaplan offer a precise and detailed understanding not only of subphase vulnerability, but also of subphase adequacy. They examine the interlocking strands of narcissism, psychosexual development, and object relations throughout the separation-individuation process; point out the relevance of the subphase hypothesis for the

45

understanding of borderline and narcissistic phenomena; and illustrate how psychoanalytic research based on child observation complements and refines later reconstructions in the diagnostic and treatment work.

Kernberg's structural point of view is well known from his earlier writings. Green and Rinsley, in their respective articles, have reviewed and analyzed Kernberg's main theoretical points concerning the borderline personality organization. According to Kernberg, borderline personality disorders have in common a specific, stable form of pathological intrapsychic structure. They are not merely disorders somewhere in transition between psychosis and neurosis or vice versa, rather, they are disorders related to a fixed, highly structured personality organization. As regards the impression that there are indeed quantitative and qualitative differences between borderline disorders and the neuroses or psychoses, Kernberg makes a concerted effort to establish a method, in terms of a "structural interview," that would allow for a reliable differential diagnosis. This is the central theme of his article. As Kernberg points out, in this diagnostic effort he is more concerned with what goes on structurally than with the origins of the condition.

Grinberg's article deals with the problem of diagnosis, but not in terms of the usual concern about the borders with schizophrenia or neurosis. Building on Melanie Klein's concept of schizoid and depressive positions, he distinguishes between two types of borderline patients, the "schizoid" and the "melancholoid." Such a distinction allows him to account for the diverse dynamics and different prognoses that characterize borderline patients.

In the final article of this section, Chiland and Lebovici describe their experience with borderline children in France. These children's manifest pathology seems to transcend national borders.

An Object-Relations View
of Borderline Personality

DONALD B. RINSLEY, M.D., F.A.P.A., F.R.S.H.

The concept of the borderline personality, which is increasingly prominent in the current literature (Wolberg, 1973), may be set forth in a variety of ways, each of which illustrates the current state of evolution of psychiatric and psychodynamic theory, diagnosis, and clinical practice. For some, the diagnosis borderline personality implies a clinical syndrome intermediate between two other differentiable categories of psychopathology, namely, psychosis and psychoneurosis (Kernberg, 1972; Masterson, 1973, 1974; Masterson and Rinsley, 1975). Or borderline patients may be viewed basically as neurotics who periodically or episodically display the signs and symptoms of illness of a degree which may be labeled as psychotic (Fenichel, 1945). Or, in accordance with the work of Hoch and Polatin on "pseudoneurotic schizophrenia" (1949), the borderline patient may be considered the victim of a basically schizophrenic disorder, the symptoms of which to a greater or lesser degree masquerade as neurotic. This view reflects the opinion of many clinicians, such as Kolb (1973), who classifies patients suffering from "borderline syndrome" under the rubric of schizophrenia; Ekstein (1966), who considers psychotic and borderline children in terms of a similar proneness to regression; and Pine (1974), who concludes that there is no significant difference between borderline and psychotic childhood disorders.

The concept of the borderline may also be used to encompass a wide variety of persons otherwise diagnosable as suffering from one

Associate Chief of Psychiatry for Education, Topeka Veterans Administration Hospital; Fellow in Advanced Studies, Department of Education, The Menninger Foundation, Topeka, Kansas; Clinical Professor of Psychiatry, University of Kansas School of Medicine, Kansas City, Kansas.

or another form of "character" pathology (Boyer and Giovacchini, 1967). One may thus subsume under the rubric borderline the spectrum of schizoid, infantile, narcissistic, hysterical, paranoid, inadequate, impulse-ridden, polymorphous-perverse, and alloplastic personalities whose symptomatology falls short of more florid psychosis. Of notable historical significance in this regard is Helene Deutsch's (1942) formulation of the as-if (*als ob*) personality. As-if personalities, who are basically schizoid, correspond to Grinker, Werble, and Drye's (1968) third subgroup of borderline patients: those devoid of the capacity for warmth and affection and deficient in self-identity.

The distinction between the neuroses and borderline conditions emphasized by some (Kohut, 1971), is disputed by others (Ritvo, 1974). Whereas the former conceptualizes neurotic conditions in terms of the classical transference neurosis and borderline conditions in terms of pathologically persistent narcissism, the latter consider such a distinction overdrawn (Loewald, 1974). If the distinction between borderline and neurotic disorders appears unclear to some, that between borderline disorders and psychosis, especially in childhood, appears similarly unclear. The borderline child is characterized as unable successfully to separate self- and object representations, with an associated failure of introjection (Rosenfeld and Sprince, 1963). Impairment or failure of self-object differentiation is likewise cited as the basis for child psychosis (Mahler, 1968). Similarly, Kernberg (1968) cites a "quantitative predominance of negative introjections" as the prime contributing factor in the etiology of borderline psychopathology, while Mahler (1968) cites a predominance of negative introjections as etiologic for infantile psychosis.

Even so cursory a review as that presented here readily confirms the unsettled nature of the nosology and psychodynamic significance of the concept of borderline disorders. The wide range and pleomorphic nature of borderline symptomatology certainly add to it. In contrast, the view of borderline disorders I shall develop here is based on the following considerations:

1. The diagnosis "borderline syndrome" constitutes a theoretically, clinically, etiologically, and heuristically valid and specific nosologic category.

2. The clinical symptomatology, level of developmental fixation, and therapeutic response of borderline patients allow their placement, as it were, along a spectrum of psychopathology between the psychoneurotic and the psychotic.

3. The etiology of the borderline syndrome, and the developmental arrest basic to it, are known.

4. The particular deficiency in object relations common to borderlines, which differentiates them from psychoneurotics and psychotics, is likewise known.

5. Based upon these considerations, a rationale for the treatment of borderline patients may be developed.

Historical Antecedents to an Object-Relations Theory of Borderline Personality

The historical basis for the development of an object-relations theory of borderline personality organization may be said to have been laid down in the early, classic psychoanalytic studies of depression (melancholia). Abraham (1912) describes the depressed person's feelings of inner impoverishment, emptiness and "badness," and inability to love, coupled with the need to project aggression (hate) onto others to create, as it were, a congeries of what Melanie Klein (1932) later terms external persecutors. Abraham (1916) postulates the melancholic's regression to the stage of oral cannibalism, such that the "lost" object is devoured. Later (1924) he postulates the anal expulsion and subsequent annihilation of the lost object and advances the important distinction between the melancholic who expels it and the obsessional who retains it. Abraham theorizes that the melancholic at first expels, then later reintrojects the lost object and narcissistically identifies with it, a sequence based in turn on Freud's (1917) earlier formulation concerning the melancholic's regression from object love to narcissistic identification as a consequence of the persistence of narcissistic object choice. Freud clearly perceived in the melancholic the persistence of that form of object relations that proceeds from failure to achieve the differentiation of self from object, so that the latter variously and significantly reflects ("mirrors") the former (Kohut, 1971; Mahler, 1968, 1974).

Rado (1928) develops a concept of depression, sometimes termed his "double-introjection" theory, which despite certain theoretical shortcomings, nonetheless contains important inferences concerning the metapsychology of depression. According to Rado, the melancholic introjects the lost object as a split, dyadic "good object" and "bad object" — the former, symbolic of the beloved but potentially punitive parent surrogates, is incorporated into the superego, and the latter into the ego. Rado's concept of the split good-bad introject had important echoes in the later contributions of such theorists as Melanie Klein and Fairbairn.

Melanie Klein's (1932, 1935, 1940, 1946) contributions to the metapsychology of depression and to object-relations theory are too well known and extensive to permit a comprehensive restatement here. Of particular importance for this discussion, however, is her concept of the depressive position of infancy, during which the infant experiences a transition from reliance upon part-object relations to reliance upon whole-object relations. In accordance with her view, while in the depressive position, and due to his inability to perceive a preponderance of good internal objects, the infant denies the terror associated with the potential loss of his good object by denying the object's complexity. The object thus becomes either "all good" or "all bad" — in effect, a split object. Klein concludes that the infant is able to mourn only if the good lost object is a whole object. The persistence of splitting thus precludes adequate mourning, and hence adequate working through of object loss. Her view of the infant as, in effect, "unsure" of his good objects recalls Abraham's earlier description of the melancholic's feeling of inner impoverishment, which is accompanied by a perceived inability to love.[1]

Fairbairn's (1941) further elaboration of these and related considerations must now be looked at. He differentiates three sequential stages in the development of object relations:

1. *Infantile dependence* includes: (a) an *early oral stage,* during which the infant seeks only a part object, i.e., the maternal breast;

---

[1] I have elsewhere (1968a) commented on the important relation between deficiency or impoverishment of ego libido and a dearth of internalized good objects, as noted in schizoid states.

and (b) a *late oral stage,* termed "mother-with-the-breast," during which the whole object (mother) is dealt with as a part object (breast).

2. *Quasi-independence,* which he considers a stage of transition between infantile and later adult dependence, is characterized by progressive relinquishment of relations based on primary identification in favor of relations with differentiated objects, and by "desperate endeavours ... to separate from the object and ... to achieve reunion with the object." During this stage, developmental progress occurs in terms of "dichotomy and exteriorization" (externalization) of the object, thereby differentiating self from object, and endowing the externalized object with the characteristics of reality.

3. *Mature dependence,* during which both accepted and rejected objects become externalized, involves the achievement of the ability to perceive and interact with the "external" object as a whole object, that is, as an object that combines within itself both "good" or libidinal and "bad" or aggressive characteristics.

Fairbairn places particular emphasis on the vicissitudes of the splitting of "good" and "bad" objects during the transitional or quasi-independent stage, and he cites his now famous transitional techniques, by means of which the person attempts to regulate the process of differentiation of self from object. Schematized in somewhat revised form, these techniques are:

1. *Paranoid technique*: "good" (accepted, libidinal) object is internalized; "bad" (rejected, aggressive) object is externalized.

2. *Hysterical technique*: "good" object is externalized; "bad" object is internalized.

3. *Obsessional technique*: both "good" and "bad" objects are internalized.

4. *Phobic technique*: both "good" and "bad" objects are externalized.

Fairbairn (1951) goes on to postulate the infant's need to split the internalized bad object into two parts which he terms, respectively, an exciting object (*E. O.*) and a rejecting object (*R. O.*). The endopsychic consequences of this are of pervasive importance in the genesis of borderline and schizoid conditions, to which reference will be made later.

Jacobson's (1954, 1964) contributions to an understanding of the metapsychology of borderline and psychotic states may be said to center upon two basic conceptions. The first of these involves the developmental vicissitudes of self- and object representations, while the second concerns the degree to which these representations retain the characteristics of, and in psychotic states regress to, early infantile self- and object images. With respect to the former, progressive development entails and signifies the progressive differentiation of self-representations from object representations such that "self" and "other" become demarcated from each other. In regard to the latter, progressive development signifies the ongoing depersonification ("metabolization") of primitive self- and object representations (Kernberg, 1966) and their transformation or assimilation into otherwise smoothly functioning defensive and representational structures (Rinsley, 1968a). By the same token, reanimation of primitive, infantile self- and object images signals the onset of preoedipal regression with entrance into prepsychotic or frankly psychotic states of function and experience; it represents a destructuralization symbolic of an effacement of internal structural boundaries and of the boundary between "self" and "outside."

Influenced strongly by Jacobson's work, Kernberg, who defines object-relations theory as the psychoanalytic approach to the internalization of interpersonal relations (1971), postulates four sequential stages in their normal development (1972):

Stage 1. Roughly coterminous with the first postnatal month, this earliest stage of development antedates the establishment of the primary, undifferentiated self-object constellation built up in the infant as a consequence of pleasurable, gratifying mother-infant interactions (Jacobson, 1964). Mahler (1968) applies the phrase "normal autism" to this period; the term "presymbiotic" (Rinsley, 1972, 1974a, 1974b) is similarly applicable to it.

Stage 2. Roughly spanning the second and third postnatal months, this second stage of development witnesses the establishment and consolidation of an undifferentiated self-object image or representation of a libidinally gratifying or rewarding ("good") type under the organizing influence of pleasurable or gratifying mother-infant interactions. Concomitantly, a separate "bad" self-object image or representation evolves under the influence of painful or frustrating (i.e., traumatogenic) psychophysiological states. Two self-object affect complexes are thus built up and fixed by memory traces as polar-opposite endopsychic structures. In accordance with Mahler's (1968) formulations, the chronology of this developmental stage includes the inception of the mother-infant symbiosis, which she dates from the second postnatal month and which reaches its peak some two to three months later.

Stage 3. The third developmental stage is reached when the self-image and object image have become differentiated within the core "good" self-object representation. Similarly, a start is made toward differentiation of self-image and object image within the core "bad" self-object representation. According to Kernberg, this stage spans the latter three quarters of the first postnatal year, a period of time which is noted to overlap Mahler's symbiotic phase and her subsequent differentiation and practicing subphases (6-16 months).[2]

Stage 4. Kernberg's fourth developmental stage witnesses the coalescence of "good" and "bad" self-images into the beginnings of an integrated self-concept. Self-images establish coherence and continuity, affects become integrated and undergo further differentiation, and the child's self-concept and social behavior become progressively congruent. At the same time, "good" and "bad" object images also coalesce and the "good" (libidinal) and "bad" (aggressive) images of the mother become integrated into a whole-object maternal concept which progressively faithfully reflects the mother's actuality. Kernberg dates the inception of this stage at some point between the end of the first postnatal year and the second half of the second year, and considers that it continues to evolve throughout the remainder of childhood. In accordance with this chronology, Stage 4 is seen to overlap Mahler's practicing, rapprochement, and object-constancy subphases of separation-individuation.[2]

[2] Kernberg's timing of the Stage 3 and Stage 4 developmental-representational events appears, on both theoretical and clinical grounds, to be premature. Stage 3 events, including the inception of differentiation of self- and object images, hence awareness of one's separateness from the maternal object, typify Mahler's rap-

Kernberg's formulation of the developmental events specific to Stage 4 resembles Fairbairn's conception of how the individual achieves mature dependence, in particular through the mechanism of externalization ("exteriorization") of *both* "accepted" (good, libidinal) and "rejected" (bad, aggressive) objects with ensuing replacement of splitting, as exemplified in his transitional mechanisms, with repression and the assumption of whole-object relations.

In accordance with the phenomenology of Kernberg's developmental schema, psychotic syndromes may be said to result from developmental fixation or arrest at Stages 1 or 2. In those cases that suffer arrest at Stage 1, basically autistic (autistic-presymbiotic) syndromes may be expected to ensue, while arrest at Stage 2 may be expected to result in predominantly symbiotic syndromes. Common to both is failure of differentiation of self from object, and to both the diagnostic term schizophrenia may be said to apply (Rinsley, 1972).

By contrast, developmental arrest at Stage 3, during which self and object begin to differentiate from each other, but only within the core "good" or "bad" self-object representations, yields borderline personality organization. In such cases, self and object remain partially differentiated, whole objects are in effect dealt with as part objects, introjective-projective defenses remain prominent, alternating efforts toward separation from and reunion with the (primal) object are characteristic, and paranoid-hysterical mechanisms typify object relations.

Attainment of Stage 4 signifies arrival at, at worst, a psychoneurotic *modus vivendi*, and at best an essentially healthy one. Borderline personalities, fixated at Stage 3, at their best approach, and often appear to achieve, this degree of integration, while at their worst they regress toward the undifferentiated representational state characteristic of fixation at Stage 2. Persistent reliance upon splitting as a defense mechanism is typical for both psychotic (Stages 1 and 2) and borderline (Stage 3) personalities and accounts for the various manifestations of their respective "weak" egos (Rinsley, 1968b).

---

prochement subphase of separation-individuation (16-25 months), while Stage 4 events typify her subphase of object constancy (24-36 months).

Mahler's numerous and fundamental contributions to an understanding of the development of personality (1968, 1971, 1972, 1974; Mahler, Pine, and Bergman, 1975) emphasize and explicate the complex process of mother-infant symbiosis and the ensuing processes of desymbiotization and separation-individuation. Her now famous subphases of separation-individuation (*differentiation:* 6-10 months; *practicing:* 10-16 months; *rapprochement:* 16-25 months; *object constancy:* 25-36 + months) comprise a chronology of mother-child interactions which center upon the growing child's drive toward progressive self-differentiation as an object separate from the mother and the latter's complementary facilitating responses in relation to it.

It is during the rapprochement subphase that the child begins to perceive the possibility of his own separateness and uniqueness apart from the person of the mother. The child will tolerate the ensuing separation anxiety and utilize it in the service of his ongoing psychological development provided that the antecedent "maternal beacon" has served him well. This means that his prior interactions with the mother have caused him introjectively to distill a preponderance of "good" (libidinal) object representations, which in turn have strengthened the *anlagen* of his corresponding self-representations. At about this time, the child also begins to develop the capacity for object permanency (Piaget, 1937), precursory for the later development of true object constancy, as exemplified in the capacity for evocative recall (Fraiberg, 1969). It may be said that evocative recall represents the achievement of a stable endopsychic state of representational configurations, having superseded the infant's reliance upon magical hallucination and, later, simple recognition memory. The achievement of evocative recall may likewise be taken to signify the inception of replacement of the earlier splitting defense by repression. The healthily developing child's repository of "good" (libidinal) self- and object representations serves, in turn, as an impetus for his increasing use of evocative recall, as what is recalled is positive. In those cases that reflect a preponderance of "bad" (aggressively valent) introjects, the child persists in his reliance upon riddance mechanisms of a projective nature (Rinsley, 1968a), with the ever-present possibility of return of the "projects" (i.e., as persecutors).

In accordance with these considerations, a predominance of "bad" introjects fosters the persistence of splitting defenses, precludes the adequate development of evocative recall, inhibits the inception of whole-object relations and hence, following Klein, effectively thwarts the working through of the depressive position, thereby preventing completion of the developmental tasks associated with the separation-individuation phase. In such cases, whether juvenile or adult, the persistence of paranoid and hysterical transitional mechanisms, as set forth by Fairbairn, is readily discerned clinically, Either one's self or others are "all good" or "all bad," the one remaining, in effect, split from the other. Under such circumstances, where some degree of differentiation of self-representations from object representations has occurred, one legitimately speaks of a borderline disorder; where such differentiation has essentially failed to occur, one legitimately speaks of psychosis. Common to all such cases is the persistence of pre-eruptive or actually disruptive degrees of separation anxiety. In psychosis, such anxiety is of the instinctual variety, with its gross threat to what yet remains of intact ego functions; in borderline disorders, such anxiety assumes a partially structuralized form (Masterson and Rinsley, 1975) with both instinctual and superego (guilt) components, which Masterson (1972, 1973) has termed "abandonment depression."

The Split Object-Relations Unit: Its Origin and Characteristics

Extensive and in-depth clinical experience with borderline adolescents and adults led Masterson and me (1975) to identify a particular endopsychic structure common to borderline personalities, which we could further trace to a particular mother-infant interaction throughout the period of separation-individuation.

> ... *the borderline child has a mother with whom there is a unique and uninterrupted interaction with a specific relational focus, i.e., reward for regression, withdrawal for separation-individuation* ... the unique 'push-pull' quality of this sort of mother-infant interaction becomes powerfully introjected and forms the basis for the progressive development of the borderline syndrome....

The mother's withdrawal of her libidinal availability in the face of her child's efforts toward separation-individuation creates the leitmotif of the borderline child, with the result that the child becomes the unique child of the borderline mother. The borderline mother, herself suffering from a borderline syndrome, experiences significant gratification during the child's symbiotic phase. The crisis supervenes at the time of separation-individuation, specifically during the rapprochement subphase, when she finds herself unable to tolerate her toddler's ambivalence, curiosity and assertiveness; the mutual cueing and communicative matching to these essential characteristics of individuation fail to develop. The mother is available if the child clings and behaves regressively, but withdraws if he attempts to separate and individuate. The child needs the mother's supplies in order to grow; if he grows, however, they are withdrawn from him . . . The images of these two mothers are as it were powerfully introjected by the child as part-object representations together with their associated affects and self representations. Thus is generated the *split object relations* unit . . . which forms so important a part of the intrapsychic structure of the borderline [p. 167].

In accordance with Kernberg's formulations (1966), the fundamental object-relations unit, derived from the infant's internalization of his interactions with the mother, comprises a self-representation, an object representation, and an affective (libidinal; aggressive) component linking them together. This triadic unit has also been called an ego state (Rinsley, 1968a). The object-relations unit of the borderline turns out to be split into *two part units*, each comprising a *part-self representation* and a *part-object representation* together with an associated affect. These two part units represent, respectively, derivatives of the two principal themes of interaction with the borderline mother, that is, the mother's maintenance of her libidinal availability in response to her infant's clinging, regressive behavior, and her withdrawal of her libidinal availability in the face of the infant's efforts toward separation-individuation.

Masterson and I have accordingly termed the two component part units the *withdrawing part unit* and the *rewarding part unit —*

the former invested ("cathected") with aggressive energy, the latter with libidinal energy, and each split off from the other. This splitting of "good" (libidinal, positively valent) from "bad" (aggressive, negatively valent) self- and object representations effectively precludes their integration into whole (positive and negative) self- and object representations, and thus may be seen to represent fixation at Kernberg's Stage 3.

The split object-relations unit of the borderline personality may accordingly be schematized as follows:

1. *Withdrawing* (*Rejecting, Aggressive*) *Part Unit*
    a. *Part-object representation*: A maternal part object which is attacking, critical, hostile, angry, withdrawing or withholding supplies and approval in the face of assertiveness or other efforts toward separation-individuation.
    b. *Affect*: Chronic anger, frustration, feeling thwarted, which cover profound underlying abandonment depression.
    c. *Part-self representation*: A part-self representation of being inadequate, bad, helpless, guilty, ugly, evil, empty, etc.
2. *Rewarding* (*Libidinal*) *Part Unit*
    a. *Part-object representation*: A maternal part object which offers approval, support, supplies, and comfort for regressive and clinging behavior.
    b. *Affect*: Feeling good, being fed, gratification of the wish for reunion.
    c. *Part-self representation*: A part-self representation of being the good, passive, compliant child.

The infant's powerful introjection of the split object-relations unit both results from and further contributes to the persistence of the splitting defense. As a consequence, self-representations and object representations remain only partially differentiated. As long as this endopsychic situation persists, as it does indefinitely in the case of borderline personalities, developmental progress toward the attainment of whole-object relations is effectively thwarted.

As already noted, the borderline mother's libidinal availability in the face of her infant's clinging behavior, which is normal and essential during the symbiotic phase, becomes pathogenic when the infant enters the separation-individuation phase. In the case of the future borderline personality, it becomes represented at that time in the form of the rewarding part unit which, when activated, causes the individual to "feel good." This "feeling good" comes, with time, to be increasingly ego syntonic, as it functions to ward off the enormous anxiety associated in such cases with the prospect of separation-individuation, now represented in the attacking, rejecting maternal part image (withdrawing part unit). As a consequence of countless repetitions of the borderline mother's "push-pull" relation to her infant, the latter's primitive pleasure ego becomes allied with the rewarding part unit; the result of their combined operation in turn fosters the preservation of the fantasy of reunion and the associated ongoing denial of the reality of separateness. The persistent denial of separateness is, in turn, paradigmatic for the impairment of the sense of reality and capacity for reality testing, which finds such protean symptomatic expression in the daily lives of borderline personalities.

A fateful consequence of the persistence of the split object-relations unit is, of course, the persistence of its split-off, archaic self- and object images. Indeed, these could be considered as quasi-pictorialized endopsychic hallucinations which resemble the magical hallucinations by means of which the infant attempts restoration of the "lost" object. These archaic images correspond to Kernberg's (1966) "unmetabolized" or "underpersonified" introjects, linked concretistically to the "real" objects they represent, and comprise the ego and superego forerunners upon which borderline patients often regressively rely. They in turn determine the degree to which borderline patients, not unlike psychotics, continue to utilize various degrees of archaic, pictorial forms of ideation when abstract, categorical thinking would otherwise be required and expected. Further, the readiness with which the borderline projects and introjects them (projective and introjective identification) imparts the peculiarly labile, protean quality so typical of his interpersonal relations, particularly in the therapeutic transference.

It may therefore be concluded that the endopsychic structure of the borderline personality comprises a split object-relations unit, with its powerful residue of unneutralized aggression and its affiliation with the infantile pleasure ego, and a lesser residue, comprising a core of healthy self- and object images affiliated with an "embattled" reality ego (Masterson and Rinsley, 1975). The striking similarity between the split object-relations unit and Fairbairn's split internalized bad object is evident: his affiliated *exciting object* (*E.O.*) and *libidinal ego* (*L.E.*) correspond to the *rewarding part unit*, while his affiliated *rejecting object* (*R.O.*) and *anti-libidinal ego* (*Anti-L.E.*) correspond to the *withdrawing part unit*. Finally, Fairbairn's affiliated *central ego* (*C.E.*) and *ideal object* (*I.O.*) correspond to the "healthy" self- and object images affiliated with the (*embattled*) *reality ego*.

In accordance with this view, the term borderline may be applied to those cases that demonstrate the interrelated problems of pathologically persistent narcissism and incomplete self-object differentiation, regardless of specific or predominant autoplastic or alloplastic symptomatology. In such cases, clinical experience reveals the seemingly endless alternation of feelings of infantile megalomania, and of impotence and worthlessness, which reflect the persistence of the "all-good"/"all-bad" split. The term borderline may be seen to apply to a wide spectrum of personality disorders, including the schizoid-inadequate, the hysterical, and the more purely narcissistic, central to which is the continued operation of the split object-relations unit.

THERAPEUTIC CONSIDERATIONS

Although a detailed consideration of psychotherapeutic technique with borderline personalities, based upon the foregoing discussion, would be beyond the scope of this presentation, several general principles may now be developed.

As Masterson and I (1975) have shown, the borderline patient begins therapy with the feeling that the behavior engendered by the alliance between his rewarding part unit and his pleasure ego is "ego syntonic," that is, it makes him "feel good." He is likewise unaware of the ultimate psychological and psychosocial cost to him incurred by virtue of his denial of the self-injurious and self-defeating nature of the behavior.

From the outset, the therapist begins a process of confrontation and clarification of the self-destructive behavior engendered by the alliance in order to render the latter progressively ego alien. As the symptomatic behavior comes under increasing control, the withdrawing part unit becomes activated, followed by activation of the rewarding part unit and the appearance of further resistance. There now ensues a sequential process, involving resistance, reality clarification, working through of the feelings of abandonment (withdrawing part unit), further resistance (rewarding part unit) and further reality clarification, which leads in turn to further working through.

In those cases in which the circular working-through process proves successful, an alliance is next seen to develop between the therapist's healthy ego and the patient's embattled reality ego; this therapeutic alliance, formed through the patient's having internalized the therapist as a positive external object, proceeds to function counter to the alliance between the patient's rewarding part-unit and his pathologic (pleasure) ego. . . .

The structural realignments which ensue in the wake of the working-through process may now be described. The repetitive projection of his rewarding and withdrawing part-units (with their component maternal part-object representations) on to the therapist, together with the latter's interpretive confrontation thereof, gradually draws to the patient's conscious awareness the presence of these part-units within himself. Concomitantly, the developing alliance between the therapist's healthy ego and the patient's reality ego brings into existence, through introjection, a new object relations unit: the therapist as a positive (libidinal) object representation who approves of separation-individuation + a self representation as a capable, developing person + a 'good' feeling (affect) which ensues from the exercise of constructive coping and mastery. . . .

The working through of the encapsulated rage and depression associated with the withdrawing part-unit in turn frees its component part-self and part-object representations from their intensely negative, aggressively valent affects. As a result, the new object relations unit (constructive self + 'good' therapist + 'good' affect) linked with the reality ego becomes integrated into an overall 'good' self representation, while the split object relations unit linked with the pathological (pleasure) ego becomes integrated into an overall 'bad' self representation; both are now accessible to the patient's conscious awareness as are their counterparts within the person of the therapist. At this point, the patient has begun in earnest the work of differentiating good and bad self representations from good and bad object representations as prefatory to the next step, in which good and bad self representations coalesce, as do good and bad object representations. The stage is now set for the inception of whole-object relations, which marks the patient's entrance into Stage 4. . . .

The de-linking, as it were, of 'raw' instinctual energies from the rewarding and withdrawing part-units renders these energies increasingly available to the synthetic function associated with the patient's expanding reality ego, hence available for progressive neutralization. With this, and concomitant with the progressive coalescence of good-bad self and object representations, splitting becomes replaced by normal repression, with progressive effacement, as it were, of the personified or 'unmetabolized' images associated with the disappearing split object relations unit . . . The patient is now able to complete the work of mourning for these 'lost' images, which characterizes his final work of separation from the mother [Masterson and Rinsley, 1975, pp. 171-172].

Therapeutic confrontation of the borderline patient's symptomatic behavior temporarily evokes the patient's efforts to control it, as a result of early, if transient, efforts toward identification with the therapist. Such efforts are, however, relatively short-lived, as they quickly activate the withdrawing part unit, replete with its hostile, rejective, persecutory, maternal part image; feelings of "badness" and worthlessness; and repository of unneutralized aggression. Thus, the patient's earliest attempts to exert control over his self-defeating and self-injurious behavior activate his long-harbored persecutory representations, which are then willy-nilly projected onto the therapist who in turn becomes, for the patient, an evil predator. The borderline mother of a hospitalized adolescent girl stated this clearly to her family therapist: "You made me very mad last time . . . after I listened to you Tuesday I felt rotten . . . I tried to stop stuffing myself before I went to bed and the more I

thought about what you said about overeating the madder I got . . .
I think you just want me to get mad and that's how you'll get your
kicks!"

Among other things, this communication conveys the patient's
projection of her "bad" and aggressive representation onto the therapist, as well as her counterphobically defended anxiety that the
therapist wants her to be "bad" in order to find a basis for rejecting
her. Quickly, however, she communicates her subjective experience
of activation of the rewarding part unit: ". . . so then you know what
I did . . . I went to the 'fridge' and ate myself blue in the face . . . I
got so stuffed I couldn't breathe and I fell asleep."

Now the patient, to "spite" (i.e., demonstrate and exert control
over) the therapist, regresses to an infantile, oral-narcissistic state
symbolic of the fed, satiated infant who subsequently falls asleep.
She feels "good" and full and has flaunted her self-injurious
symptom (overeating) in the face of the now-fantasied impotent
therapist. The split between the projected, withdrawing part unit
(therapist), who now embodies the patient's partially differentiated
"bad" part-self image and rejecting maternal part image, and the
retained rewarding part unit, with its hedonic part-self image and
its soothing, consoling maternal part image (i.e., food), is evident.

The therapist is now in a position to confront and clarify these
split representations and to begin to link them, with the help of the
patient's memories, dreams, and waking fantasies, to earlier actual
or fantasied historical events which reinforced and overdetermined
the splits as derivatives of the push-pull quality of the mother-child
relation. Many therapeutic hours later the patient notes, "Yes, I
remember mother used to tell me I was crap . . . no good . . . that
I'd never amount to anything . . . No matter what I did it wasn't
good enough for her." She continues, "You know, that's what I
thought about *you* [therapist] . . . that you'd find fault with
everything I did or said . . . you'd put me down."

The patient now refers to the therapist in terms of transference
expectations, utilizing the subjunctive ("would") rather than the
immediate present or future tenses. The therapist is becoming differentiated from the parental representations, in part as a result of
vigorous, ongoing interpretation of the patient's transference projections, especially the negative ones (Kernberg, 1975). Of particu-

lar importance is the sensitive manner in which the therapist must handle the confrontation and interpretation of the rewarding part unit, with its powerful secondary gain associated with the "good" feeling connected to essentially passive, regressive-compliant, and ultimately self-defeating behavior. Within the transference, and by displacement outside it, the patient's repeated efforts to provoke the therapist's approval in the wake of such behavior repeatedly fail; the withdrawing part unit is, in consequence, reactivated and its representations, together with its encapsulated aggression (anger, rage), are in turn reprojected onto the therapist: "You really want me to be nothing . . . I do what you want and all I get is your 'interpretations' . . . Abuse, that's what it is . . . You abuse me . . . Sometimes you make me feel like I'm your slave!"

As the therapeutic work proceeds, the patient becomes aware of her redoubtable tendency to project the split object-relations unit onto the therapist, and, in consequence, she perceives increasingly clearly the presence and operation of the split object-relations unit within herself. She further comes to realize that both part units are deleterious to her (cf. the split internalized "bad" object) and that another part of herself coexists with this "bad" object. A sixteen-year-old adolescent girl stated it: "You know, there's a part of me that wants to grow . . . to grow up and accomplish things . . . I want to prove I can make it . . . I guess you [therapist] want me to make it too . . . Boy, it took me a long time to believe that!"

The "part that wants to grow" comprises the emergent, long-inhibited, healthy object-relations unit comprising *a part-self image* of a maturing, increasingly successfully coping individual, *a maternal part image* of a person (therapist) who accepts, encourages, and rewards (i.e., provides libidinal supplies for) success, and *a linked affect* comprised of mixed aggressive and libidinal valences (libidinalized aggression in the service of successful coping and mastery). The last is seen to represent essentially neutralized energy available for sublimations, the inverse of the *Entmischung*, with the emergence of "raw" instinct, which typifies regression.

As previously noted, the progressive emergence into the patient's conscious awareness of *both* the split ("bad") object-relations unit and the healthy object-relations unit, the latter as a consequence of

the therapist's judicious interpretation of the therapeutic transference, signals the patient's entrance into Stage 4. It conveys the
patient's beginning assumption of mature dependency (Fairbairn),
his awareness of his separateness, and of the coalescence within
himself of *both* "good" (libidinal) and "bad" (aggressive) valences
and representations. It thus represents the inception of whole-object
relations. In terms of the therapeutic transference, the healthy
object-relations unit may be schematized as follows:

1. *Object representation*: A (maternal) image of the therapist,
who approves, encourages, and rewards effective and realistic
planning and coping behavior (i.e., efforts toward mastery).
2. *Affect*: A feeling of gratification (i.e., "good" feeling) in the
wake of achievement (libidinal and aggressive).
3. *Self-representation:* A self-image of a successfully coping,
achieving person.

The integration of both "good" and "bad" representational
structures within one's self, and the recognition that such integration exists also within the therapist, lead to strikingly gratifying
responses from the patient. The aforementioned adolescent girl
stated, "Wow . . . I guess I'm really one person after all . . . I've got
good and bad in me and what I do with them is pretty much up to
me . . . just like you [therapist] . . . you can do it too."

A poignant sequence shortly before termination of therapy of a
seventeen-year-old girl of superior intelligence is illustrative:

Patient: I was reading *You Can't Go Home Again* . . . you know,
the book by Thomas Wolfe. He said it . . . and I thought to
myself that I couldn't go home either . . . and I cried a lot when
I thought that . . . I guess Thomas Wolfe cried a lot too . . .
maybe he cried through his work, his writing.
Therapist: You're crying now and grieving, aren't you?
Patient: Yeah . . . I remember what you said about mourning
and grieving . . . that I couldn't do that when my mother took
off . . . Boy, have I been doing it now.

The final signal that resolution of the split object-relations unit
has begun in earnest is conveyed in the inception and completion of

working through of the departure of the "lost" object, the final mourning of which can only occur in relation to a whole object, which leads ultimately to acceptance of the fact of one's separateness. With this depart the last vestiges of the long-harbored, pre-eruptive abandonment depression with its guilt-laden separation anxiety and the persistent and profound vulnerability to real and fantasied "losses" which characterize all essentially unindividuated personalities.

SUMMARY AND CONCLUSIONS

In accordance with the foregoing, the following inferences and conclusions concerning borderline personality organization and its clinical expression may be developed:

1. Viewed from a developmental standpoint, borderline disorders comprise a protean symptomatic group which is indeed intermediate or transitional between psychotic disorders and psychoneurotic disorders.

2. Subsumable under the borderline rubric is a wide spectrum of personality disorders otherwise classified as schizoid, inadequate, infantile, narcissistic, hysterical, cyclothymic, sociopathic, and so on.

3. The developmental arrest or fixation etiologic for the borderline syndrome occurs during the separation-individuation phase of infantile development, more specifically, during its rapprochement subphase (16-25 months).

4. The basis for the developmental arrest common to borderline personalities is to be found in the relatively stereotypical "push-pull" nature of the mother-infant interaction during that period, specific to which is the borderline mother's libidinal availability (reward, approval, reinforcement) in response to her infant's dependent, regressive, and clinging behavior, and her withdrawal of her libidinal availability (rejection, disapproval, abandonment, negative reinforcement) in response to her infant's efforts toward separation-individuation.

5. The infant's powerful introjection of the essentially doubly binding, "push-pull" relation with the borderline mother in turn

establishes and fixates the *split object-relations unit* with its incompletely differentiated self- and object representations, ongoing reliance upon splitting defenses, reservoir of unneutralized aggression, persistent reunion-refusion fantasies, and, in alliance with the infantile pleasure ego, denial of separateness with associated impairment of reality testing.

6. As a consequence, the borderline personality continues to deal with whole objects *as if* they were part objects and struggles persistently, and not rarely desperately, with them after the fashion of "transitional" objects (Fairbairn, 1941). The persistence of part-object relations, based in turn upon untrammeled reliance upon splitting defenses, precludes the infant's negotiation of the depressive position, with ensuing failure to mourn and persistence of that particular form of partially structuralized separation anxiety which Masterson has termed "abandonment depression," with resultant ongoing vulnerability to real and fantasied separations and "losses."

7. The "all-good"/"all-bad" nature of borderline endopsychic and derivative "external" interpersonal relations, and the various "mirroring" phenomena (Kohut, 1971) and infantile grandiose and persecutory projections common to borderline personalities are considered to result from failure of differentiation of self- and object representations characteristic of fixation at Kernberg's Stage 3 in the development of object relations.

8. Psychoanalytic therapy of borderline personalities requires confrontative and interpretive exposure of the split object-relations unit within the therapeutic transference which, if successful, catalyzes the development of the therapeutic alliance with ensuing restructuring of the patient's endopsychic representations ("healthy object-relations unit"). The resultant depressive working through enables the patient to achieve developmental Stage 4, typified by a sense of personal separateness and wholeness.

REFERENCES

Abraham, K. (1912), Notes on the psychoanalytical investigation and treatment of manic-depressive insanity and allied conditions. In: *Selected Papers of Karl Abraham*. London: Hogarth Press, 1927, pp. 137-156.

_____ (1916), The first pregenital stage of the libido. In: *Selected Papers of Karl Abraham*. London: Hogarth Press, 1927, pp. 248-279.

_____ (1924), A short study of the development of the libido, viewed in the light of mental disorders. In: *Selected Papers of Karl Abraham*. London: Hogarth Press, 1927, pp. 418-501.

Boyer, L. B., & Giovacchini, P. L. (1967), *Psychoanalytic Treatment of Characterological and Schizophrenic Disorders*. New York: Science House.

Deutsch, H. (1942), Some forms of emotional disturbance and their relationship to schizophrenia. In: *Neuroses and Character Types*. New York: International Universities Press, 1965, pp. 262-281.

Ekstein, R. (1966), *Children of Time and Space, Of Action and Impulse*. New York: Appleton-Century-Crofts.

Fairbairn, W. R. D. (1941), A revised psychopathology of the psychoses and psychoneuroses. In: *An Object-Relations Theory of the Personality*. New York: Basic Books, 1954, pp. 28-58.

_____ (1951), A synopsis of the development of the author's views regarding the structure of the personality. In: *An Object-Relations Theory of the Personality*. New York: Basic Books, 1954, pp. 162-179.

Fenichel, O. (1945), *The Psychoanalytic Theory of Neurosis*. New York: Norton.

Fraiberg, S. (1969), Libidinal object constancy and mental representation. *The Psychoanalytic Study of the Child*, 24:9-47. New York: International Universities Press.

Freud, S. (1917), Mourning and melancholia. *Standard Edition*, 14:243-258. London: Hogarth Press, 1957.

Grinker, R. R., Sr., Werble, B., & Drye, R. C. (1968), *The Borderline Syndrome*. New York: Basic Books.

Hoch, P. H., & Polatin, P. (1949), Pseudoneurotic forms of schizophrenia. *Psychiat. Quart.*, 23:248-276.

Jacobson, E. (1954), Contribution to the metapsychology of psychotic identifications. *J. Amer. Psychoanal. Assn.*, 2:239-262.

_____ (1964), *The Self and the Object World*. New York: International Universities Press.

Kernberg, O. F. (1966), Structural derivatives of object relationships. *Internat. J. Psycho-Anal.*, 47:236-253.

_____ (1968), The treatment of patients with borderline personality organization. *Internat. J. Psycho-Anal.*, 49:600-619.

_____ (1971), New developments in psychoanalytic object relations theory. Presented at the 58th Annual Meeting of the American Psychoanalytic Association, Washington, D.C. (Unpublished.)

_____ (1972), Early ego integration and object relations. *Ann. N. Y. Acad. Sci.*, 193:233-247.

_____ (1975), *Borderline Conditions and Pathological Narcissism*. New York: Jason Aronson.

Klein, M. (1932), *The Psycho-Analysis of Children*. New York: Delacorte, 1975.

_____ (1935), A contribution to the psychogenesis of manic-depressive states. In: *Love, Guilt, and Reparation and Other Works*. New York: Delacorte, 1975, pp. 262-289.

_____ (1940), Mourning and its relation to manic-depressive states. In: *Love, Guilt, and Reparation and Other Works*. New York: Delacorte, 1975, pp. 344-369.

_____ (1946), Notes on some schizoid mechanisms. In: *Envy and Gratitude: And Other Works by Melanie Klein.* New York: Delacorte, 1975, pp. 1-24.

Kohut, H. (1971), *The Analysis of the Self.* New York: International Universities Press.

Kolb, L. C. (1973), *Modern Clinical Psychiatry,* 8th ed. Philadelphia: Saunders.

Loewald, H. W. (1974), Current status of the concept of infantile neurosis: Discussion. *The Psychoanalytic Study of the Child,* 29:183-188. New Haven: Yale University Press.

Mahler, M. S. (1968), *On Human Symbiosis and the Vicissitudes of Individuation.* Vol. I: *Infantile Psychosis.* New York: International Universities Press.

_____ (1971), A study of the separation-individuation process: And its possible application to borderline phenomena in the psychoanalytic situation. *The Psychoanalytic Study of the Child,* 26:403-424. New York: Quadrangle.

_____ (1972), On the first three subphases of the separation-individuation process. *Internat. J. Psycho-Anal.,* 53:333-338.

_____ (1974), Symbiosis and individuation: The psychological birth of the human infant. *The Psychoanalytic Study of the Child,* 29:89-106. New Haven: Yale University Press.

_____, Pine, F., & Bergman, A. (1975), *The Psychological Birth of the Human Infant.* New York: Basic Books.

Masterson, J. F. (1972), *Treatment of the Borderline Adolescent: A Developmental Approach.* New York: Wiley-Interscience.

_____ (1973), The borderline adolescent. In: *Adolescent Psychiatry,* Vol. 2: *Developmental and Clinical Studies,* ed. S. C. Feinstein & P. L. Giovacchini. New York: Basic Books, pp. 240-268.

_____ (1974), Intensive psychotherapy of the adolescent with a borderline syndrome. In: *American Handbook of Psychiatry,* Rev. Ed., Vol. II, ed. S. Arieti et al. New York: Basic Books, pp. 250-263.

_____ & Rinsley, D. B. (1975), The borderline syndrome: The role of the mother in the genesis and psychic structure of the borderline personality. *Internat. J. Psycho-Anal.,* 56:163-177.

Piaget, J. (1937), *The Construction of Reality in the Child.* New York: Basic Books, 1954.

Pine, F. (1974), On the concept "borderline" in children: A clinical essay. *The Psychoanalytic Study of the Child,* 29:341-368. New Haven: Yale University Press.

Rado, S. (1928), The problem of melancholia. *Internat. J. Psycho-Anal.,* 9:420-438.

Rinsley, D. B. (1968a), Economic aspects of object relations. *Internat. J. Psycho-Anal.,* 49:38-48.

_____ (1968b), Theory and practice of intensive residential treatment of adolescents. In: *Adolescent Psychiatry,* Vol. 1: *Developmental and Clinical Studies,* ed. S. C. Feinstein, P. L. Giovacchini, & A. A. Miller. New York: Basic Books, 1971, pp. 479-509.

_____ (1972), A contribution to the nosology and dynamics of adolescent schizophrenia. *Psychiat. Quart.,* 46:159-186.

_____ (1974a), Special education for adolescents in residential psychiatric treatment. In: *Adolescent Psychiatry,* Vol. 3: *Developmental and Clinical Studies,* ed. S. C. Feinstein & P. L. Giovacchini. New York: Basic Books, pp. 394-418.

_____ (1974b), Residential treatment of adolescents. In: *American Handbook of*

Psychiatry, Rev. Ed., Vol. II, ed. S. Arieti et al. New York: Basic Books, pp. 353-366.

Ritvo, S. (1974), Current status of the concept of infantile neurosis: Implications for diagnosis and technique. *The Psychoanalytic Study of the Child,* 29:159-181. New Haven: Yale University Press.

Rosenfeld, S. K., & Sprince, M. P. (1963), An attempt to formulate the meaning of the concept "borderline." *The Psychoanalytic Study of the Child,* 18:603-635. New York: International Universities Press.

Wolberg, A. R. (1973), *The Borderline Patient.* New York: Intercontinental Medical Book Corp.

Developmental Aspects in the Assessment of Narcissistic and So-Called Borderline Personalities

MARGARET S. MAHLER, M.D., SC.D.(MED.)
and LOUISE KAPLAN, PH.D.

We believe the outstanding feature of narcissistic as well as borderline personalities is that they do not proceed in the ordinary way through the developmental process that culminates in a well-defined Oedipus complex and in neurosis. We agree with Rangell (1972) that the Oedipus complex—the core of neurosis—may be regarded as the fourth psychological organizer. Its shape, resolution, and mode of dissolution can restructure earlier developmental events. The Oedipus complex represents the acme not only of infantile psychosexual development but also of object relations. It transforms the previous mainly external regulation of narcissism into internal self-esteem regulation by the superego.

Many of our colleagues have found the symbiosis and separation-individuation frame of reference useful in their work with child and adult patients in general, and narcissistic and borderline patients in particular. Nevertheless, although we have delineated the subphases of separation-individuation and come to some general hypotheses about subphase vulnerabilities, we are increasingly aware of the need to be more precise and detailed in our evaluation of what we call subphase adequacy. Such an extension can only be achieved by consideration of the interlocking strands of narcissism

Dr. Mahler is Clinical Professor of Psychiatry Emeritus A.E.C.O.M.; Visiting Professor of Child Psychoanalysis, Medical College of Pennsylvania; Faculty Member, New York and Philadelphia Psychoanalytic Institutes.

Dr. Kaplan is Associate Professor, New York University Clinical Psychology Program; Director, New York Mother-Infant Research Nursery.

and psychosexual development (Spruiell, 1975), in addition to that of object relations of the separation-individuation process. We hope that this broader perspective of the subphase theory will facilitate the assessment of narcissistic and borderline personality organizations.

Eventually it should be possible to determine the progressive subphase adequacy in all three areas of development and in the second half of the third year perhaps gauge whether the preconditions for normal oedipal development and the infantile neurosis prevail. These preconditions entail that self-constancy, that is, individual entity and identity, should be achieved at the end of the rapprochement subphase, in addition to a level of object constancy that facilitates triangular whole-object relations cathected with neutralized libido and aggression. In the psychosexual sphere an emerging and flexible narcissistic genital orientation should be evident. Repression is the main defense mechanism in these important developments.

As we emphasized in the book *The Psychological Birth of the Human Infant* (Mahler, Pine, and Bergman, 1975), a predominantly observational study of the preverbal and primary-process phases of development, the subphase-related progress in object relations could be fairly reliably studied through its *referents*. These referents were furnished by observation of interactive behaviors of the mother-child unit over the course of time, polarized by the two partners of the dual unit. In contrast to progress in object relations, the building of a cohesive, separate, and whole self-representation is elusive. What the infant feels subjectively eludes the observing eye; that is, behavioral referents are barely existent. We may assume, however, that the earliest perceptions are those of bodily sensations. Freud (1923) described the ego as "first and foremost a body-ego" (p. 27).

What we have in mind then is to consider the subphase adequacy or subphase inadequacy of all three strands of preoedipal development. Consideration of the traditional hierarchic psychosexual stages is implicit in the separation-individuation-subphase theory; here we will stress this issue somewhat more than previously.

As for narcissism, in our observational study and later in our film analyses we noted episodes in which the differentiating five- to eight-month-old, surrounded by approving and libidinally mirroring friendly adults, seemed electrified and stimulated by this reflecting admiration. We recognized that an important source of narcissistic libido, the quantity and quality of libidinization of the body ego or body self, is dependent upon early narcissistic supplies. These supplies are contributed in the symbiotic phase as well as in the differentiation and early practicing subphases by fueling by the environment. Imbalances in fueling by the environment will be described in our two sample cases.

Each subphase makes its particular contribution to healthy or pathological narcissism; narcissistic reserves are still being built up, to a great extent, by subphase-adequate mothering in the later subphases. *The autonomous achievements* of the practicing subphase are the main source of narcissistic enhancement from *within*. Most infant-toddlers of the practicing stage show three contributories to narcissism at their peak. These are (in an exaggerated way and in individually different proportions): self-love, primitive valuation of their accomplishments, and omnipotence. During the rapprochement subphase, prior to and dependent on the resolution of the rapprochement crisis, narcissism (particularly omnipotence shaken by the coming of age of representational intelligence) is subphase-specifically vulnerable.

We shall describe below the diametrically opposite vicissitudes of infantile omnipotence, body self-love, self-esteem regulation, and self- and gender formation in two children. These two case studies illustrate what we mean when we speak of the broad spectrum of borderline phenomena. Furthermore, these examples point out the relevance of the subphase hypothesis for the understanding of both borderline and narcissistic phenomena in future investigations.

The sketches of Sy's and Cathy's development have been drawn from *carefully processed,* voluminous observational data of their first three years of life, occasional follow-up material of their nursery and kindergarten and school years, and finally a more systematic follow-up study undertaken at latency age and early adolescence, respectively. We shall not of course regard our project as satisfactorily terminated until we have had the opportunity to analyze two to three children and at least one mother.

SY

We begin with the subphase developmental history of one of our study children in whom, by the middle of the third year, we already found such severe disorders in all three aspects of the separation-individuation process that we predicted borderline personality development (see Mahler, Pine, and Bergman, 1975, p. 200).

Sy's innate ego endowment was better than average, as our controlled observational data and the developmental tests unequivocally indicated. From his sixth or seventh month until the last quarter of his second year, Sy's life was a saga of daytime attempts to extricate himself from his mother's suffocating envelopment and intrusiveness. During the night, on the other hand, he behaved or was seduced into behaving as the "child-lover at the breast." At seven to nine months, when normally the specific bond with mother is at its peak and stranger anxiety appears, Sy strained *away* from his mother's body when she held him.

Sy's slow locomotor maturation complicated matters. Moreover, the mother discouraged every attempt at locomotion as well as other autonomous functions. Phase-specific stranger anxiety was replaced by *stranger preference.* By twelve months of age Sy used his newly emerged ego function of crawling to crawl rapidly away from mother. And if a stranger and mother were to beckon simultaneously, he would unhesitatingly go to the "non-mother." As soon as Sy mastered rapid crawling, Sy's mother redirected his course incessantly—intruding and forcing him to interact with her continually.

Sy had no opportunity to experience the obligatory forms of separation reactions that the other children showed at subphase-adequate times. His differentiation, practicing, and rapprochement subphases were rudimentary and distorted and the subphase characteristics highly confused.

Sy's symbiotic phase pervaded the differentiation process; it interfered with and crowded out the ego-building contributions that the practicing and rapprochement subphases furnish to psychic structuralization. *It was the all-important, almost purely maturational, species-specific emergence of free upright locomotion, as late as at seventeen months, that made Sy suddenly aware that he might suffer object loss.*

The sudden onset of the rapprochement conflict, which Sy experienced without his ego having been prepared for functioning separately (in a clearly delineated practicing subphase), was one of the roots of his deviational development. The absence of a definitive practicing subphase deprived his ego of the capacity to mitigate gradually the impact of his pregenital instinctual drives and deprived him as well of *both* the internal source of narcissism derived from the autonomous ego sphere and the narcissistic enhancement afforded by the normal active, aggressive spurt of practicing.

The period from his seventeenth to twentieth month was a particularly unstable and stormy one. At the beginning of his rudimentary rapprochement subphase, Sy would go to his mother somewhat more often with requests and demands. More often than not his mother completely ignored these requests. At seventeen to eighteen months Sy refused the breast, and promptly developed a sleep disturbance, which allowed his mother to rationalize the reintroduction of her dried breast — a "giant pacifier." At the same time the need for mother increased. Sy clung to her after each nap, cried in the morning, and continued to have difficulty in falling asleep.

By his twentieth month, whatever relation Sy had developed to the object world at large became actively split off as all "bad." He became aggressive to the other children and suspicious toward those at the Center who were previously his friends. Up to then he had been fairly exuberant and trusting. Now he became somber, depressed, and moody.

From the moment he weaned himself, Sy's separation-individuation process was corroded in all three areas previously cited by his excessive castration anxiety, which later amounted to mutilation anxiety. This anxiety was so overwhelming because his ego did not experience the obligatory and normal subphase-adequate fears of object loss, stranger anxiety, separation anxiety, and fear of loss of the object's love at subphase-adequate times. In the psychosexual sphere anal concerns and severe castration anxiety overlapped. Such overlapping was augmented by massive, visual exposure to the sexual organs of nude men, his father's included, in the locker room. At the same time, Sy was permitted to perceive in equally traumatic proportion sights that brought home to him, out of phase, the danger of castration. He would go to urinate in the bathroom but instead would masturbate. He was unable to sit down for fear that his feces, and possibly his penis, would be flushed away. His predilection to expose his penis and frequent utterances, such as "nice penis," "you nice people," indicated, among other signs, the precocious onset and prolonged adherence to the narcissistic-phallic phase of libido development.

The father's dictum was: a baby belongs to the mother as long as he wants her breast. As soon as the son rejects the breast he belongs to the father. Sy's castration anxiety increased significantly in his third year when Sy's father took him over, body and soul. The father duplicated the mother's overstimulation of the first two years. The father's behavior was described thus: "He at once threatens and cajoles, manhandles and caresses, slams about and seduces Sy. When the father's rage reaches a peak, he switches to seductive kissing and tickling. The whole thing is sadistic, sexualized, and hysterical." At the birth of his brother in Sy's thirty-fourth month his mother was in the hospital for a prolonged stay and his father was his only caretaker. Sy was in a frenzied, panicky state. He talked incessantly in gibberish, expressing primary-process ideation.

By age four, Sy had turned violently against his mother and emulated his father's degrading of her. He totally rejected her in his attempt to become big and manly like his father. Sy began to vomit food his mother wanted him to eat and developed an eating problem. During Sy's struggle with identification with father, he turned all his crude aggression against his mother—kicking and biting and shouting at her. In the midst of this turnabout in Sy's fifth year, another fateful traumatization occurred. Sy's father exchanged him for his younger brother, who was at the very age at which the father had taken Sy over from the mother. Whereas Sy had been aggressive, elated, and rather manic in nursery school, now at kindergarten age everybody noted that the sparkle in his eye was gone. Sy turned once again to his mother and became her quasi satellite, in an anxious but subdued alliance against the younger brother and father.

Sy's subphase developmental history was characterized by pro-longation up to his twentieth month of the nocturnal "child-lover-at-the-breast" symbiosis. This, without more than a nominal experiencing of the practicing and rapprochement subphases of separation-individuation, was overlapped by and continued as a bizarrely frank oedipal relation with his mother and later with his father.

From the time he weaned himself and walked, Sy was treated by the mother as her "man," with reciprocal behavior on his part. It is a demonstration in *statu nascendi* and step by step of what Kernberg (1967) describes as the genetic-dynamic analysis of the borderline personality's Oedipus complex. He says: "... what is characteristic of the borderline personality organization ... is a specific condensation between pregenital and genital conflicts, and a *premature* development of oedipal conflicts..." (p. 678).

We could follow, in the second part of Sy's third as well as in his fourth, fifth, and sixth years, the vicissitudes of the failure of the ego's function of normal repression. There were many instances of this failure, but for lack of space we cannot elaborate on them. An example might suffice: Sy remembered minute details about the Center, which the other children had completely repressed. These details were syncretically retained by his ego's pathological memory function.

Sy's behavior at times seemed a caricatured emulation of his mother, at other times he seemed a bizarre diminutive replica of his father. Instead of repression, the extensive splitting operations described by Kernberg resulted in a morbidly combined father-mother image. There was hardly any opportunity for his ego to identify selectively with desexualized and deaggressivized paternal or maternal traits. We observed an unusual confusion between the paternal images and dissociation and lack of neutralization of his erotic and aggressive impulses.

It is very difficult to conceptualize Sy's ego ideal or his identifications and self-representation. The unassimilated introjective identification of part images of mother and father was predominant at the expense of transmuting internalization.

We believe that the positive qualities that saved Sy from psychosis were his excellent endowment, for example the way in which he made up for his slow locomotor development by becoming extremely proficient in gymnastics (his favorite activity was acrobatics). From material gained from him, his mother, and teacher, one can surmise that Sy liked to be away from home. He was the least homesick when the class went to camp. The mother also told of times when Sy did not come home from school but went to his teacher's house instead. He had obviously succeeded in creating an island for himself where his ego developed without constant intrusion and interference by his disorganized, disorganizing, and aggressive environment.

Sy's intrapsychic conflicts can be only guessed at, of course, and we would like to get Sy into analysis, but both parents are opposed to it.

Follow-up home and school interviews of Sy in his eleventh year described him as faring much better than we would have predicted. His academic achievement in an honors class in a local public school is excellent and he is fairly popular with his classmates. The teachers, however, could not suppress their irritation with Sy and his family. They described Sy as a fresh, sexually precocious child who bragged and engaged in disruptive, exhibitionistic clowning and crudely inappropriate sex talk. Moreover, the teachers felt that the parents overestimated Sy's creative and intellectual potential, very often insisting that he be treated specially.

The psychological tests, which were administered without knowledge of the follow-up interviews or the early developmental history, revealed a diagnostic picture of borderline personality organization at the lower level of the borderline spectrum. When tested, Sy's characteristic posture was hunched over and limp, as though his body were totally devoid of muscle tone. He handled the examiner's test materials in a way that suggested that he was appropriating and possessing them — but without active intentionality. In his passivity there was a decided blurring of the boundaries between yours and mine.

Even though Sy's behavior betrayed no signal or social anxiety, he was apparently in a *state of overwhelming anxiety*. The palms of his hands would sweat profusely, leaving moisture on everything he touched. His hands would shake and he looked helpless and vulnerable. Alternately, Sy was often able to pull back and take an active, more rationally bound view of reality. At these times his body was firmly erect and alertly mobilized. His mental functioning also improved and toned up. He concentrated actively and sharpened his previously vague responses. He then smiled happily and even tried to show off.

Such unpredictable alternation in affect states, body posturing, and modes of responding typified Sy's Rorschach responses. Most often, Sy would be pulled into the cards—his loss of distancing was prominent. Repeatedly he would confuse his inner bodily feelings with external perceptions. He yawned, for example, and then said the wolf on the card was tired. Now and then he would project his impulses and then become inundated by the anxiety aroused by his own projections. He experienced the projected impulse simultaneously with the fear of the impulse. Primitive denial and externalization were prominent defenses. Notably absent during the testing were any indicators of shame or guilt and there was very little signal anxiety—only overwhelming primitive anxiety.

When Sy is able to extricate himself, put distance between himself and the stimuli of external reality, he is able to maintain fantasy-reality distinctions. Secondary-process thinking and logic were evident in many of Sy's responses, although it was abundantly clear that his mode of thought organization was subject to easy regression.

In his eleventh year, Sy's good basic endowment has allowed him to extricate himself and create distance, analogous to the way he actively pushed, crawled, and turned away from the engulfing mother-child symbiosis—and thereby escaped outright psychosis. Nevertheless, the prolonged symbiosis has cast its shadow over all future subphases of separation-individuation. It continues as a grossly erotic, overly aggressivized, out-of-phase oedipal constellation which has left an indelible stamp on Sy's body representations.

On the tests, the ego-inundating nature of Sy's castration anxiety was apparent in his body-mutilation fantasies and the fragmented quality of his body representations. Moreover, in Sy's perceptions body parts merged with one another, were interchangeable with one another, and were in fact interchangeable with the inanimate objects of reality.

CATHY

By way of contrast, we will briefly describe the separation-individuation process of Cathy, a child whose development proceeded along more or less neurotic lines, but who at thirteen showed signs of a narcissistic disturbance.

Cathy joined our project at twelve months of age. She immediately conquered our mother-infant room with her spectacular self-assurance and verbal precocity, without the slightest "stranger" and "strangeness" reactions. Her mother—a somewhat colorless, depressive woman—seemed to enjoy Cathy greatly as the narcissistic, glamorous extension of "her self."

Cathy had mastered walking by eleven months. Her exuberance, however, did not include the usual abandon and daring observed in other children in the practicing subphase. Cathy's much praised and encouraged "independence" had been bought at the expense of bodily closeness, i.e., libidinal supplies of her body self. Mrs. C., who stressed that Cathy was not a cuddly baby, never picked her up except for brief comforting followed by distraction tactics.

At around nineteen months Cathy's mood definitely deteriorated. Mrs. C. complained about Cathy's crying, temper tantrums, and often incomprehensible behavior. Her toilet training had been uneventful and she was practically trained by nineteen months without coercion. The mother, however, complained, "She doesn't want me to touch her, to dress her, to put her on the toilet, although she will let others do so." We felt that at this point a "bad" and dangerous maternal part representation was actively split off from the "good object representation." We may also assume that Cathy's moodiness indicated dissociation of aggressive and libidinally invested part-self representations.

We watched our radiant, narcissistic "queen-bee" of the nursery become—intermittently—a petulant, hard-to-understand, and for the moment very aggressive little girl. Not only were we faced with a full-fledged rapprochement crisis, but with a sudden and abrupt collapse of Cathy's omnipotent grandeur. Only many weeks later were we able to piece together the events that culminated in this intense and prolonged rapprochement crisis. Between her sixteenth and eighteenth month Cathy often visited a little boy from the nursery. One day this boy's mother bathed the two children together and Cathy came home declaring that the little boy had *two* belly-buttons.

Six to seven weeks after Cathy's discovery of the anatomical sex difference she became extremely aggressive, pulling the hair of other children in our nursery. The mother recalled that when she took Cathy into the shower to facilitate washing her long, fine hair, Cathy pulled at her mother's pubic hair. *Cathy's desperate search for a penis was quite clear.* Disturbances of both sleep and toileting followed. We felt that Cathy's aggressive provocativeness represented a demand to her mother to make amends for her anatomical shortcoming (even at 27 months of age she asked for a penis for Christmas!).

At two and a half years Cathy briefly wanted mother, father, and herself all to be together. We thought this was to be the beginning of a true phallic-oedipal relation. Cathy, however, soon preferred exclusive dyadic relations, vacillating between selection of *either* father *or* mother. From then on and throughout her second to fifth year, Cathy alternated between weakly energized forays into a triadic relation which included both the mother and the father and frantic claims for exclusive dyadic relations.

Also at two and a half Cathy attempted to give up the bottle, but was unsuccessful. Her mother declared that "the bottle was the only thing that Cathy was really attached to." Her overestimation of her transitional object—the bottle—betrayed a certain pathology in Winnicott's (1953) terms. From her third year on, Cathy required a mirroring, exclusively dyadic relation in order to maintain her ideal state of self. The search for shifting dyadic relations became a major theme in Cathy's life.

When Cathy entered nursery school at three, she turned with her unspecific object hunger to the nursery-school teacher as a mother substitute—entwining her, seeking her exclusive attention. A crisis soon occurred involving child, mother, and teacher. Unable to cope with Cathy's intense need for exclusive attention, the teacher sent her home to her mother. Mrs. C.'s reaction was one of angry depression directed toward the teacher and also toward her own daughter. Cathy, as never before, clung to her mother's body—clutching her thighs. Mother extricated herself by angrily pushing her off. Cathy responded to this dual rebuff by engaging in compulsive talking to an imaginary audience from whom she anticipated mirroring admiration. It was as though Cathy were trying to recapture the ideal state of self she experienced in her twelfth to nineteenth month when she was the omnipotent "queen bee" of the nursery. Even though Cathy's clinging behavior declined, we felt that Cathy had abandoned hope rather than resolved the rapprochement crisis. We believe that the ambivalently loved, needed and hated object, who regarded herself and Cathy as failures, was at this point split off and externalized, in favor of an internally retained, differentiated, negatively cathected self-representation.

Cathy's later school experiences continued to be disappointing. She hated school and at six declared that the children hated her and would not play with her. From her sixth year on Cathy blamed her mother for all the ills of her life, calling her "the worst mother in the world."

In Cathy's seventh year an interview with the father revealed a complex and ever-worsening sadomasochistic relation between his wife and Cathy. He said, "They are more like sisters than a mother and daughter." He also felt that Cathy often daydreamed. He thought it quite natural, however, that Cathy, like daughters in general, should be closer to her mother than to her father.

The outstanding impression conveyed by follow-up interviews, school and home visits when Cathy was thirteen was her sense of her personal inadequacy and low self-esteem. Although her full-scale IQ was 134, her school achievement was in the B minus to C range.

When Cathy was tested her voice was barely audible and she tried to keep her head positioned so that her hair would cover her face. The omnipotent, self-assured, exhibitionistic toddler had become an adolescent who seemed to want to disappear. Whereas the follow-up testing of Sy revealed some of the inner dynamics of borderline personality organization, in the personality picture of Cathy at thirteen we recognized what is typically called obsessive-compulsive personality organization. *Repression* was evident and the additional defenses of reaction formation and isolation were well maintained without evidence of decompensation. Her excessively exalted ego ideal led to easy self-devaluation and to continuing prominence of anxiety and shame. Nevertheless, in contrast to Sy, the affect of guilt was the major regulator of instinct defense activity. Overwhelming panic and diffuse anxiety did not replace *signal anxiety*.

Cathy perceived bodies as hidden, blocked in action, slouched down, and trapped. These images represented her basically *masochistic* orientation. In hindsight we can now hypothesize that these hidden and trapped bodies echoed Cathy's ungratified longings for bodily libidinal supplies during practicing and rapprochement. In turn, the sudden shattering of her omnipotence — her desperate demands for the undoing of her anatomical shortcoming — added to Cathy's growing predisposition to disparage herself and her femininity.

Whereas Sy's body image was distorted, fragmented, and confused with the inanimate, Cathy's body image was intact and well bounded. Nevertheless, Cathy's self-image, her dissatisfaction with herself and with her feminine gender identity was evident. She was disappointed in herself and expected disappointment and defeat in her relations with others.

In Sy we noted perilous regression and the disorganization of secondary-process thinking by condensations and contaminations. Cathy's reality testing was excellent. However, even temporary regressions were forbidden and when things were not "just so" she gave up rather than taking the chance that she might be wrong.

In Cathy's case, we believe that neither the overidealized and overidealizing, all-good, admiring mother-image nor the grandiose, omnipotent ego ideal were gradually adjusted to reality. The infantile self-object image was never cut down to size so that the real mother would be able to match that image. Nor did the ego ideal become reconciled with the realistic potential of Cathy's autonomous actual self-image.

The characteristic and unique feature of Cathy's struggle was her seeking substitutions in the outside world in order to approximate the highly overestimated, exceptional, and exclusive self-object representation unit. She sought these substitutions in dyadic relations that would match the idealized self-object image of her longed-for omnipotent past.

Cathy's mother's inability to provide a balance of libidinally satisfying, intermittent body closeness and to recognize Cathy's hunger for physical contact during practicing led to an intensification of the splitting mechanisms which characterized Cathy's rapprochement period. The narcissistic reserve, which might have enabled Cathy to overcome later narcissistic hurts, was depleted on two fronts during practicing. The excessively exalted ego ideal and the absence of practicing phase-specific libidinal refueling laid the groundwork for inflexible ego ideal and superego structures which would not allow for an adaptive tolerance for ambiguity and ambivalence. Furthermore, during rapprochement itself, Cathy's coercive wooing behavior was once again rebuffed by her mother. But, although Cathy was not prepared to experience a fully developed oedipal constellation, we know that some aspects of an advanced oedipal solution were achieved. This solution was characterized by a repression of the instinctual preoedipal and oedipal strivings. Cathy's narcissistic grandiosity was replaced by masochistic self-disparagement, but whole-object relations remained dominant, even though there seemed to be a potential for homosexual development.

Conclusions

Our aim in this brief presentation was to adumbrate the explanatory power that full utilization of the symbiosis and the separation-individuation-subphase theory contributes to the assessment of later personality organization, provided its complexities are taken into account. Rather than presenting a coordinated system of subphase-related failures in one subphase of the separation-individuation process with a corresponding specific form of narcissistic or borderline personality organization, we have tried to avoid oversimplification and closure.

In our assessments of the personality organization of narcissistic and borderline child and adult patients, the overriding dominance of one subphase distortion or fixation must not obscure the fact that there are always corrective or pathogenic influences from the other subphases to be considered. In Sy's case, for example, the luxuriation of the symbiosis prevented later subphases from making their specific *positive* contributions to personality development. In practicing, Sy was deprived of the internal source of narcissism derived from the autonomous ego sphere as well as the shaping influence of the normal aggression spurt. At the same time the age-appropriate separate self- and body awareness of rapprochement was inundated by castration anxiety and overstimulation of fantasy life. The distorted nature of Sy's oedipal constellation cannot be understood merely from the perspective of the symbiotic phase.

In Cathy's case the rapprochement theme of the search for exclusively dyadic relations to mirror her lost ideal state of self predominated. Yet the specific shape of Cathy's oedipal resolution cannot be adequately understood unless we include the dramatic imbalance in which Cathy's exalted omnipotence was not matched by the necessary body-libidinal supplies to her narcissism during the symbiotic, differentiation, and practicing subphases.

REFERENCES

Freud, S. (1923), The ego and the id. *Standard Edition*, 19:12-66. London: Hogarth Press, 1961.

Kernberg, O. (1967), Borderline personality organization. *J. Amer. Psychoanal. Assn.*, 15:641-685.

Mahler, M. S., Pine, F., & Bergman, A. (1975), *The Psychological Birth of the Human Infant*. New York: Basic Books.

Rangell, L. (1972), Aggression, Oedipus, and historical perspective. *Internat. J. Psycho-Anal.*, 53:3-11.

Spruiell, V. (1975), Three strands of narcissism. *Psychoanal. Quart.*, 44:577-595.

Winnicott, D. W. (1953), Transitional objects and transitional phenomena. *Internat. J. Psycho-Anal.*, 34:89-97.

The Structural Diagnosis of Borderline Personality Organization

OTTO F. KERNBERG, M.D.

I believe that an understanding of the intrapsychic structural characteristics of patients with borderline personality organization can contribute to solving what has heretofore been a difficult problem: the differential diagnosis of borderline disorders from the neuroses and neurotic character pathology, on the one hand, and from the psychoses, particularly schizophrenia and manic-depressive illness, on the other. Structural diagnosis — that is, the diagnosis of the predominant organization of the patient's intrapsychic personality structures — may add significantly to the criteria for differential diagnosis stemming from a purely descriptive or behavioral approach, and to genetic analysis stemming from the study of emotional illness in the patient's biological relatives. I also believe that structural diagnosis requires a special technique of clinical interviewing — a "structural interview" (which I shall describe later) that focuses sharply on the relation between the present interaction of patient and diagnostician, the patient's present interpersonal functioning in general, and the history of his symptomatology.

The descriptive approach focuses on the frequency of the symptoms and on observable, abnormal behavior manifestations. A genetic approach emphasizes the genetic loading of mental disorder in the patient's biological relatives. The combination of descriptive and genetic criteria often enriches the clinical differential diagnosis, particularly in cases related to the manic-depressive or schizophrenic spectrum. A structural diagnosis of borderline personality

Dr. Kernberg is Medical Director, The New York Hospital-Cornell Medical Center, Westchester Division; Professor of Psychiatry, Cornell University Medical College.

organization is more difficult, requires more practice and experience from the clinician, and presents, in terms of research, methodological difficulties which still remain to be resolved. The structural diagnostic approach can, however, be learned with time. A careful analysis of individual clinical cases, particularly those that do not seem to fall easily into one of the major categories of neurotic or psychotic illness, illustrates the enormous advantage of the structural approach.

An exclusive focus on the predominant descriptive characteristics of borderline patients may be misleading, for example, in cases where such symptoms do not appear at all. Several authors have described intense affect, particularly anger and/or depression, as a characteristic of borderline patients. However, patients with typical schizoid personalities and borderline personality organization may not present anger or depression at all. The same holds true for some narcissistic personalities who have a typical underlying borderline personality organization. Impulsive behavior has also been described as a frequent characteristic of borderline patients, but many typical hysterical patients with a solid neurotic — in contrast to borderline — structure may also show impulsive behavior. Clinically, therefore, a descriptive analysis alone falls short with some borderline cases. This is even more true with efforts to arrive at a diagnosis from a purely genetic viewpoint. The study of the possible genetic relation of severe personality disorders to the schizophrenic spectrum is still in an early stage, and it may be that important findings are awaiting us in this area. At present, however, the genetic history usually has very little to contribute to the clinical problem of differentiating neurotic, borderline, and psychotic symptomatology. It is possible that a structural approach may contribute to research into the relation of genetic predisposition to overt symptomatology.

A structural approach may have the additional advantage of bringing into sharper focus the mutual relation among the various symptoms of borderline disorders, particularly the predominant constellations of pathological character traits one so typically finds in this group. As I have pointed out in earlier work (1975a, 1975b, 1976a), the structural characteristics of borderline personality organization have important prognostic and therapeutic implications. The quality of object relations and the degree of superego integration are major prognostic criteria for intensive psychotherapy of borderline patients. The nature of the primitive transferences that these patients develop in psychoanalytic psychotherapy and the technique geared to deal with them stem directly from the structural characteristics of their internalized object relations. In an earlier study (Kernberg et al., 1972) the diagnosis of nonpsychotic ego weakness (corresponding to borderline personality organization) was highly related to the various outcomes of treatment by psychoanalysis, expressive (exploratory) psychotherapy, or supportive psychotherapy: patients with ego weakness responded well to expressive modalities of psychotherapy, but poorly to nonmodified psychoanalysis and to supportive psychotherapy.

In short, the addition of the structural viewpoint may enrich psychiatric diagnosis, particularly that of "transitional cases" which resist easy classification. The structural approach, which has been very helpful in the clinical diagnosis of individual patients, may add an important new dimension to this field and contribute to diagnosis, prognosis, and treatment.

Mental Structures and Personality Organization: An Overview

The concept of mental structure has various connotations. From a psychoanalytic viewpoint, it has traditionally referred to mental processes as defined by three postulated psychic structures: ego, superego, and id, first formulated in 1923 by Freud in "The Ego and the Id." Within psychoanalytic ego psychology, structural analysis has referred to the view of Hartmann, Kris, and Loewenstein (1946) and of Rapaport and Gill (1959) that the ego is a combination of (1) slowly changing "structures" or configurations which determine the channeling of mental processes, (2) the mental processes or "functions" themselves, and (3) "thresholds" of activation of these functions and structures. Structures, according to this conception, are relatively stable configurations of mental processes; superego, ego, and id are viewed as over-all organizing structures which dynamically integrate substructures, such as the cognitive and defensive structures of the ego. More recently within psychoanalytic thinking, the term "structural analysis" has been used to describe the analysis of the structural derivatives of internalized object relations (Kernberg, 1976b) and the various levels of organization of mental functioning in terms of an over-all hierarchy of motivational systems intimately linked to internalized object relations.

Finally, in recent psychoanalytic thinking, structural analysis also refers to the analysis of the permanent organization of the predominant content of unconscious conflicts, particularly to the Oedipus complex as an organizational feature of the mind that has a developmental history, is nuclear in the sense that it is more than the sum of its parts, and that incorporates early experiences and phase-specific drive organizations into a new organization (Panel, 1977). This last viewpoint of mental structures relates to the previous one with regard to the structuralization of internalized object relations: the predominant mental contents, such as the Oedipus complex, reflect an organization of internalized object relations. Both viewpoints (the object-relations approach and the last one mentioned) imply a conception of hierarchically organized motivational sequences in contrast to purely linear development, a sequence of discontinuous hierarchical organizations rather than a simple genetic (in a psychoanalytic sense) one.

I have applied all of these structural conceptions to the analysis of the predominant intrapsychic structures and instinctual conflicts of borderline patients. I propose three broad structural organizations corresponding to neurotic, borderline, and psychotic organization. Such structural organization constitutes a stabilizing function of the mental apparatus, mediating between etiological factors, on the one hand, and direct behavioral manifestations of illness, on the other. Regardless of the genetic, constitutional, biochemical, familial, psychodynamic, or psychosocial etiology of the illness, the effects of all these factors are eventually reflected in the type of over-all psychic structure. The individual stabilizes his psychological functioning in terms of this structure, which then becomes the underlying matrix from which behavioral symptoms develop.

These three structural types (neurotic, borderline, and psychotic organization) are reflected in the patient's overriding characteristics, particularly (1) identity integration versus identity diffusion and the related over-all quality of internalized object relations, (2) a constellation of advanced versus primitive defensive operations, and (3) reality testing. I propose that neurotic personality structure implies an integrated identity, in contrast to borderline and psychotic structures. Neurotic personality structure presents a defensive organization centering around repression and other advanced or high-level defensive operations. In contrast, borderline and psychotic structures are found in patients showing a predominance of primitive defensive operations centering around the mechanism of splitting. Reality testing is maintained in neurotic organization and borderline organization, but severely impaired in psychotic organization. In short, these structural criteria can supplement the ordinary behavioral or phenomenological descriptions of patients and sharpen the accuracy of the differential diagnosis of mental illness, particularly in cases difficult to classify.

Additional structural criteria helpful in the differential diagnosis of borderline personality organization from the neuroses include: the presence or absence of nonspecific manifestations of ego weakness, particularly anxiety tolerance, impulse control, and the capacity for sublimation, and — for the purpose of differential diagnosis of schizophrenia — the presence or absence in the clinical situation of primary-process thinking. Because the nonspecific manifestations of ego weakness are clinically less essential in the differentiation of borderline from neurotic conditions, and because psychological testing rather than clinical interviews may be most helpful in the differentiation of borderline from psychotic cognitive functioning, I shall not examine these criteria in detail here. The degree and quality of superego integration is an additional, prognostically important structural characteristic differentiating neurotic from borderline organization. Finally, I shall spell out the particular characteristics of the predominant organization of oedipal conflicts in borderline organization, which differentiates it from nonborderline neurotic character pathology and symptomatic neuroses.

A review of the literature on descriptive and structural characteristics of the borderline personality may be found in Kernberg (1975a).

THE STRUCTURAL INTERVIEW AS A DIAGNOSTIC METHOD

The traditional psychiatric interview was modeled after the general medical interview, separated into history taking and mental-status examination, and mostly geared to psychotic and organic patients (Gill, Newman, and Redlich, 1954). Under the influence of psychoanalytic theory and practice, the traditional psychiatric interview gradually changed, shifting the emphasis to the patient-interviewer interaction. It replaced a semistandard sequence of questions with a more flexible evaluation of the predominant problems, focused on the patient's understanding of his conflicts, and linked the study of the patient's personality to that of his present behavior in the interview. Menninger's case study (1952) is a good example of this approach.

Whitehorn (1944), Powdermaker (1948), Fromm-Reichmann (1950), and particularly Sullivan (1954) are major contributors to a modified psychiatric interview that concentrates on the patient-therapist interaction as a major source of information. Gill, Newman, and Redlich (1954) designed a new model of psychiatric interviewing that stressed a broad appraisal of the patient and a reinforcement of his desire for help. The nature of the disorder, the motivation for psychotherapy, and the capacity for psychotherapy can be evaluated in the current interaction with the interviewer. This approach to interviewing establishes an immediate link between the patient's psychopathology and the indication for psychotherapeutic treatment. It also focuses on resistances that will probably become major issues in the early stages of treatment. Because the supportive approach to the patient involved in this approach tends to highlight the patient's assets, however, it may miss certain aspects of the patient's psychopathology.

Felix Deutsch (1949) advocated a psychoanalytic method of interviewing in order to obtain the natural unconscious connections between present problems and the patient's past. From a different theoretical background, Rogers (1951) proposed an interview style that encourages the patient to explore his emotional experiences and the connections among them. These unstructured approaches have the disadvantage of minimizing objective data and do not explore the patient's psychopathology and assets in a systematic fashion.

MacKinnon and Michels (1971) discuss a psychoanalytic evaluation that stresses the patient-interviewer interaction. Clinical manifestations of the characterological patterns the patient demonstrates in the interview are used for diagnostic purposes. This approach yields sophisticated descriptive information within a psychoanalytic framework.

The clinical interviews described have become crucial tools in evaluating descriptive and dynamic features, but, in my view, do not permit the eliciting of structural criteria differentiating borderline personality organization. Bellak, Hurvich, and Gediman (1973) developed a structured clinical interview in an attempt to achieve a differential diagnosis between normal subjects, neurotic patients, and schizophrenics on the basis of a structural model of ego functioning. While this study did not seek to differentiate borderline patients, the authors found significant differences between the three groups on rating scales evaluating ego structures and functions. Their study illustrates the usefulness of a structural approach to differential diagnosis.

In collaboration with S. Bauer, R. Blumenthal, A. Carr, E. Goldstein, H. Hunt, L. Pessar, and M. Stone we have developed what Blumenthal (personal communication) suggested calling a "structural interview" to highlight the structural characteristics of the three major types of personality organization mentioned: the neurotic, borderline, and psychotic organization. This specially constructed interview focuses on: (1) symptoms, conflicts, or difficulties that the patient presents; and (2) the particular characteristics by which the patient reflects these in the present "here-and-now" interaction with the interviewer.

We assume that the interviewer's focus on the patient's main conflicts will create enough tension so that his predominant defensive or "structural" organization of mental functioning will emerge. In highlighting these defensive operations in the interview, we obtain data that permit classification into one of the three personality structures. As mentioned before, the principal structural characteristics that permit the differential diagnosis are: (1)

the presence or absence of identity integration (reflecting the degree of integration of self- and object representations), (2) the type of predominant defensive operations, and (3) the presence or absence of the capacity for reality testing. In order to activate and diagnose these structural characteristics, the interview we have developed combines: (1) the traditional mental-status examination, (2) the modified psychoanalytically oriented interview focusing on the patient-therapist interaction, and (3) the clarification, confrontation, and interpretation of the identity conflicts, defensive mechanisms, and reality distortion the patient reveals in the interaction with the interviewer, particularly as they express identifiable transference elements.

Clarification refers to the exploration, with the patient, of all the elements in his information that remain vague, unclear, puzzling, contradictory, or incomplete. Clarification is the first cognitive step in which what the patient says is clarified and discussed in a nonquestioning way in order to bring out fully all the implications of what he has been saying and the limits of his own understanding or confusion regarding what remains unclear. Clarification aims at evoking conscious and preconscious material in a nonchallenging way.

Confrontation, the second step in this process, involves presenting the patient with areas of information that seem contradictory or incongruent. In a deeper sense, confrontation means pointing out to the patient those aspects of the interaction that seem to indicate the presence of conflictual functioning and, by implication, the presence of defensive operations, contradictory self- and object representations, and decreased awareness of reality. First, the patient's attention is drawn to something in his interaction of which he has been unaware or has taken as natural and which in the interviewer's perception is inappropriate, contradictory to other aspects of the information, or confusing. Confrontation involves bringing together conscious and preconscious material that the patient presented or experienced separately. Second, the interviewer raises with the patient the question of the possible significance of this behavior for his present functioning. In this process, the patient's capacity to look at things differently without further regression, the internal relations among the various issues brought together, and particularly the integration of the concept of self and others are explored. The increase or decrease in awareness of reality reflected in the patient's response to confrontation and the ongoing empathy with the interviewer as a reflection of social awareness and reality testing are also highlighted. Third, the interviewer connects the "here-and-now" interaction with similar or related problems in other areas and thus makes a connection between descriptive issues and complaints and structural personality features.

Interpretation, in contrast to confrontation, links conscious and preconscious material with assumed or hypothesized unconscious functions or motivations in the "here and now." It explores the conflictual origins of dissociation of ego states (split self- and object representations), the nature and motives for the defensive operations activated, and the defensive abandonment of reality testing. In other words, interpretation aims at the underlying anxieties and conflicts activated. Confrontation brings together, reorganizes the observed; interpretation adds a hypothesized dimension of causality and depth to the material. In this process, the interviewer connects the present functions of a particular behavior with the underlying anxieties, motives, and conflicts, which clarifies the patient's general difficulties beyond the present interaction. For example, pointing out to a patient that he seems to behave suspiciously and exploring his awareness of this fact is a confrontation; suggesting that the patient's suspiciousness or fear is due to his attributing to the interviewer something "bad" that he is trying to get rid of within himself and which the patient has been unaware of before is an interpretation.

Transference means the presence in the diagnostic interaction of inappropriate behavior that reflects unconscious re-enactment in the present of significant pathogenic and conflictual relations with others in the patient's past. Transference reactions provide the context for interpretations linking the "here-and-now" disturbance with the patient's "there-and-then" experiences. Pointing out to the suspicious patient that he is acting in a controlling and suspicious way toward the diagnostician is a confrontation. Pointing out that he may be seeing the interviewer as controlling, strict, harsh, and suspicious — and therefore has to be on guard against him because of the patient's own struggle with such a tendency within himself — is an interpretation. Pointing out that the patient is struggling with an internal "enemy" having such characteristics (suspiciousness, etc.) because he experienced a similar interaction in the past with a parental figure is an interpretation of the transference.

In summary, *clarification* is a nonchallenging, cognitive means of exploring the limits of the patient's awareness of certain material, *confrontation* attempts to make the patient aware of potentially conflictual and incongruous aspects of that material, *interpretation* tries to resolve the conflictual nature of the material by assuming underlying unconscious motives and defenses that make the previously contradictory appear logical, and *transference interpretation* incorporates the application of all of the above to the present interaction between the patient and the diagnostician.

Structural interviews, because they focus on the confrontation and interpretation of defenses, identity conflicts, and reality testing, or distortions in internalized object relations, and on affective and cognitive conflicts, subject the patient to some stress. Instead of putting the patient at ease and reducing his "defensiveness" by tolerating or overlooking it, the interviewer tries to bring out the pathology in the patient's organization of ego functions so as to elicit information regarding the structural organization of his illness. This approach is, however, by no means a traditional "stress" interview, which attempts to induce artificial conflicts or anxiety in the patient. On the contrary, the tactful clarification of reality involved in much initial confrontation reflects respect and concern for the patient's emotional reality, an honest engagement, in contrast to what at times may be an indifferent or "superior" tolerance of the inappropriate.

After a traditional opening asking for the difficulties that bring the patient to consult, the structural interview follows a systematic search pattern, surveying the cycle of cardinal symptoms indicated by dots on the perimeter of the circle in Figure 1. These are located on the perimeter in such a way as to indicate their significance for differentiating between the various diagnostic categories. This survey completed, the interviewer focuses on the significant symptoms that have emerged in the survey, as indicated in Figure 2. This includes an exploration of the symptoms as they appear in the here-and-now interaction of the interview, followed by clarification,

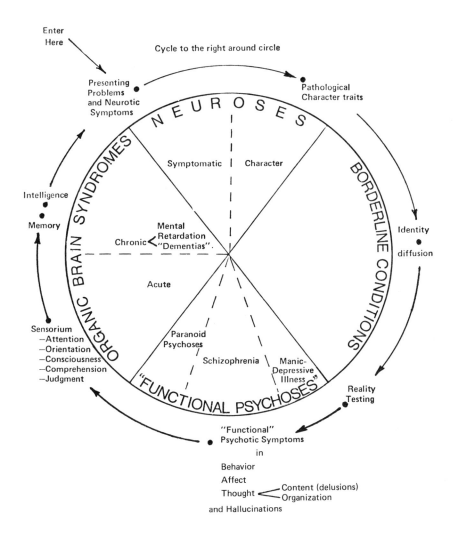

FIGURE 1. Cycling of Cardinal Symptoms

confrontation, and tentative interpretation, with careful attention given to the patient's reactions to these approaches. The patient's capacity to empathize with the interviewer's query, to further clarify issues regarding his ego identity, object relations, reality testing, and present defense-impulse configurations, gives an indication of his capacity for introspection. The structural diagnosis depends in a

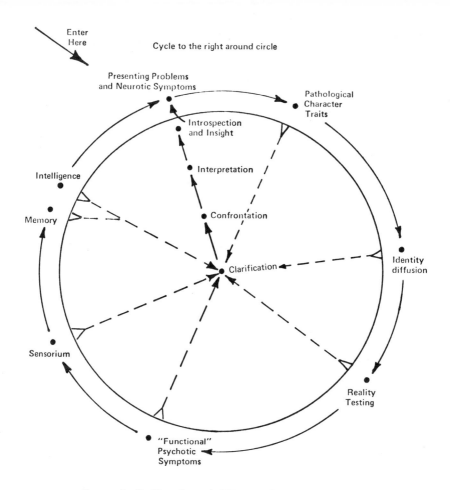

FIGURE 2. Cycling through "Here-and-Now" Interaction

major way upon how the patient handles clarifications, confrontations, and interpretations. These successive stages are indicated by steps on the pathway that traverses the middle of the circle in Figure 2.

For example, if the initial survey has revealed some evidence of identity diffusion and defects in reality testing, the interviewer first attempts to amplify the expression of these characteristics in the here-and-now interaction of the interview. Then the interviewer confronts the patient by calling attention to discrepancies in what the patient has said or to other incongruities that indicate the possible defensive nature of his behavior. In addition to this confrontation, there is tentative interpretation of the possible significance of the discrepancies that have emerged, which further challenges the patient to explore his behavior and motivations. The patient is asked how he sees these inconsistencies, how he feels about them, and what other information might clarify what has been occurring. The patient's responses to clarifications, confrontations, and interpretations are of primary importance in differentiating neurotic, borderline, and psychotic structures. Given their intact capacity for reality testing, borderline patients reveal an often surprising reorganization and improvement in functioning with these clarifications, confrontations, and interpretations. They are able to empathize with the interviewer's "confusions," clarify and correct their perceptions, and use these corrections constructively in subsequent phases of the interview. In addition, borderline patients demonstrate some capacity for introspection and insight concerning the basis for these incongruities. In contrast, patients with psychotic structures lack this ability to empathize with ordinary social criteria of reality, and, therefore, attempts to clarify may reveal further distortions in reality testing. Neurotic patients, in contrast to borderline cases, emerge with an integrative conception of themselves that, in turn, permits the interviewer to increase his empathy with various aspects of their conflicts and reality, and with their integrative conceptions of significant others, which make their interpersonal reality and past history acquire a sharp presence. Whereas borderline patients may increase their realistic behavior in the interview, they simultaneously also make plain the emptiness, chaos, and confusion in their life situation and object relations.

Some patients are inarticulate and communicate poorly so that information from sources other than the interview must be brought to bear on the diagnostic process. Inferences about cardinal symptoms can be made from previous information from these other sources. Then, the focus on the symptoms in the here and now and clarification, confrontation, and interpretation can be attempted for the significant cardinal symptoms as indicated in Figure 3. This more detailed investigation may be carried out for several of the

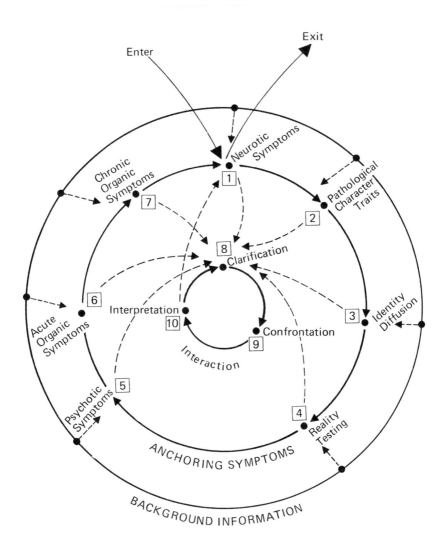

FIGURE 3. An Integrative Model of the Structural Interview

presenting cardinal symptoms until the interviewer feels comfortable with the structural diagnosis.

This diagnostic research interview, then, combines a psychoanalytic focus on the patient-interviewer interaction with a psychoanalytic technique for interpreting conflictual issues and defensive operations in this interaction in order to highlight simultaneously the classical "anchoring" symptoms of descriptive psychopathology and the underlying personality structure. In what follows, I describe the major structural characteristics of borderline conditions and how these structural characteristics should become evident in the structural interview.

THE STRUCTURAL CHARACTERISTICS OF BORDERLINE PERSONALITY ORGANIZATION

DESCRIPTIVE SYMPTOMS AS "PRESUMPTIVE" EVIDENCE

These are not structural criteria, but neurotic symptoms and pathological character traits that point the clinician's attention toward the exploration of structural criteria of borderline personality organization. Similarly, the presence of symptoms "presumptive" of a psychotic nature that do not seem to justify or correspond to a clear-cut diagnosis of manic-depressive illness, schizophrenia, or an acute organic brain syndrome should induce the clinician to focus further on structural criteria for borderline personality organization. The descriptive symptoms of borderline patients are similar to the presenting symptoms of ordinary symptomatic neuroses and character pathology; however, these symptoms usually have peculiarities that point to an underlying borderline personality organization. The following symptoms are particularly important (see Kernberg, 1975a).

1. *Anxiety*. Borderline patients tend to present chronic, diffuse, free-floating anxiety.

2. *Polysymptomatic neurosis*. Many patients present several neurotic symptoms, but here I am considering only those presenting two or more of the following neurotic symptoms:

   a. Multiple phobias, especially those imposing severe restrictions on the patient's daily life.

   b. Obsessive-compulsive symptoms that have acquired secondary ego syntonicity and therefore a quality of "overvaluated" thoughts and actions.

   c. Multiple, elaborate, or bizarre conversion symptoms, especially if they are chronic.

    d. Dissociative reactions, especially hysterical "twilight states" and fugues, and amnesia accompanied by disturbances of consciousness.

    e. Hypochondriasis.

    f. Paranoid and hypochondriacal trends with any other symptomatic neurosis: this is a typical combination indicating a presumptive diagnosis of borderline personality organization.

    3. *Polymorphous perverse sexual trends.* I refer here to patients who present a manifest sexual deviation within which several perverse trends coexist. The more chaotic and multiple the perverse fantasies and actions and the more unstable the object relations connected with these interactions, the more strongly should the presence of borderline personality organization be considered. Bizarre forms of perversion, especially those involving primitive aggressive manifestations or primitive replacement of genital aims by eliminatory ones (urination, defecation), are also indicative of an underlying borderline personality organization.

    4. *"Classical" prepsychotic personality structures.* These include:

    a. The paranoid personality (paranoid trends of such intensity that they themselves determine the main descriptive diagnosis).

    b. The schizoid personality.

    c. The hypomanic personality and the cyclothymic personality organization with strong hypomanic trends.

    5. *Impulse neurosis and addictions.* I refer here to those forms of severe character pathology wherein chronic, repetitive eruption of an impulse gratifies instinctual needs in a way that is ego dystonic outside of the "impulse-ridden" episodes, but is ego syntonic and actually highly pleasurable during the episode itself. Alcoholism, drug addiction, certain forms of psychogenic obesity, and kleptomania are all typical examples.

    6. *"Lower-level" character disorders.* I refer here to severe character pathology typically represented by the chaotic and impulse-ridden character, in contrast to the classical reaction-formation types of character structure and the milder "avoidance-trait" characters. From a clinical point of view, most typical hysterical personalities are not borderline structures; the same holds true

for most obsessive-compulsive personalities and the "depressive personality" (Laughlin, 1956) structures or better-integrated masochistic personalities. In contrast, many infantile personalities and most typical narcissistic personalities present underlying borderline organization; the as-if personalities also belong to this latter group. All clear-cut antisocial personality structures I have examined have presented a typical borderline personality organization.

All these symptoms and particular character traits may be elicited by the initial investigation of the symptoms that bring the patient into treatment and the investigation of the characteristics of his present interpersonal and social life with regard to his work, family, sexual and marital relations; interactions with close relatives, friends, acquaintances; and interactions in the area of recreation, cultural, political, religious, and other interpersonal community interests. With all patients where the diagnosis of borderline personality organization is to be evaluated, a comprehensive history of the symptomatology and the peculiarities of interpersonal interactions are therefore important initial information.

LACK OF AN INTEGRATED IDENTITY: THE SYNDROME OF IDENTITY DIFFUSION

Clinically, identity diffusion is represented by a poorly integrated concept of the self and of significant others. It is reflected in the subjective experience of chronic emptiness, contradictory self-perceptions, contradictory behavior that cannot be integrated in an emotionally meaningful way, and shallow, flat, impoverished perceptions of others. Diagnostically, identity diffusion appears in the patient's inability to convey significant interactions with others to an interviewer, who thus cannot emotionally empathize with the patient's conception of himself and others in such interactions.

Theoretically, the following assumptions underlie this lack of integration of self and of the conception of significant others (Kernberg, 1975a): (1) In borderline personality organization, there is a sufficient differentiation of self- from object representations to permit the maintenance of ego boundaries (that is, of sharp delimitation between the self and others), thus differentiating borderline personality organization from psychotic structures where a regressive refusion or lack of differentiation between self- and object representations is present. (2) However, in contrast to neurotic structures, where all self-images (both "good" and "bad") have been integrated into a comprehensive self, and where "good" and "bad" images of others can be integrated into comprehensive conceptions of others, in borderline personality organization such an integration fails, and both self- and object representations remain as multiple, contradictory, affective-cognitive representations of self and others. (3) This failure of integration of "good" and "bad" aspects of the reality of self and others is presumably due to the predominance of severe, early aggression activated in these patients: dissociation of "good" and "bad" self- and object representations protect, in essence, love and goodness from contamination by overriding hate and badness.

In the structural interview, identity diffusion is reflected in a history of grossly contradictory behavior, or alternation between emotional states implying such grossly contradictory behavior and perception of the self that the interviewer finds it very difficult to integrate them in his efforts to empathize with the patient, to see the patient as a "whole" human being. In contrast to severe neurotic character pathology, where contradictory interpersonal behavior may reflect a pathological but integrative view of the patient of himself and of significant others, in borderline personality organization it is the internal view of himself and of others that are not integrated.

For example, a neurotic patient with predominantly hysterical personality structure said that she wanted help for her sexual inhibitions, but was very reluctant to discuss these sexual difficulties in the interview. Confronted with this contradiction, she explained that she felt that the male interviewers would enjoy the humiliating effect it would have on a woman to talk about her sexual difficulties, that they might get excited sexually in the process while enjoying the depreciation of her as sexually inferior. This conception of men, and of the humiliating nature of sexual experiences and their revelation, was part of an integrative — although pathological — conception of self and others.

In contrast, a patient with predominant infantile character structure and borderline personality organization explained how disgusted she was with men who were only out to use women as sex objects, how she had to escape from the sexual advances of a previous boss, and how she avoided social contacts because of men's predatory sexual approaches. But she also said that she had worked for some time as a "bunny" in a Playboy club and she was very surprised when the interviewer confronted her with the contradictory nature of her previous assertions and this particular job.

Identity diffusion is also reflected in descriptions of significant persons in the patient's life that do not permit the interviewer "to put them together," to gain any clear picture of them. There are frequently such gross contradictions in the description of significant others that only caricaturesque or shallow images of isolated behaviors emerge through the patient's descriptions—other people sound more like caricatures than like real people. One woman who lived in a *menage à trois* could not describe the characteristics of the man and the woman she lived with or the sexual and human relations between them and, particularly, with her. Another borderline patient with masochistic personality structure described her mother at various points as warm, engaging, sensitive, and alert to the patient's needs; and cold, indifferent, insensitive, self-involved, and withdrawn. Efforts to clarify these apparent contradictions first led to an increase of anxiety as the patient acknowledged the contradictory nature of her information, and later to a sense of being attacked by the interviewer—she felt she was being criticized for having contradictory images of her mother and, implicitly, for harboring "bad" feelings toward her. The interpretation of the projection of her own guilt feelings upon the interviewer reduced the anxiety, but left the patient with the painful experience of a chaotic perception of her mother. A patient may, of course, describe someone who is truly chaotic, so that one has to differentiate a chaotic description of another person from the accurate one of somebody who is chronically contradictory; this, in practice, is simpler than it might seem.

The structural interview often allows us to obtain such information not only from the patient's relations with significant others but also from the exploration of the patient's perceptions of the interviewer and the patient's difficulty in empathizing with the interviewer's efforts to bring together what he perceives as the patient's perceptions of him. In short, the structural interview constitutes an experimental situation in which the extent of integration of self and of the perception of objects can be explored and tested.

A solid ego identity or integration of self- and object representations reflects a neurotic personality structure in a patient with intact reality testing. An abnormal, pathologically integrated identity may appear in some chronic delusional systems in both manic-depressive and schizophrenic patients. Structurally speaking, it is both integration and congruence with reality that differentiate neurotic from borderline personality organization.

An intimately related structural issue is that of *the quality of object relations* — the stability and depth of the patient's relations with significant others, as manifested by warmth, dedication, concern, and tactfulness. Additional qualitative aspects are empathy, understanding, and maintaining the relationship when it is invaded by conflict or frustration. The quality of object relations is largely dependent on identity integration, which includes not only the degree of integration, but also the temporal continuity of the patient's concept of himself and others. Normally, we experience ourselves consistently throughout time under varying circumstances and with different people, and we experience conflict when contradictions in our self-concept emerge. The same applies to our experience of others. But in borderline personality organization, this temporal continuity is lost, and these patients have little capacity for a realistic evaluation of others. The borderline patient's long-term relations with others are characterized by an increasingly distorted perception of them. He fails to achieve real empathy; his relations with others are chaotic or shallow; and intimate relations are usually contaminated by the typical condensation of genital and pregenital conflicts.

In the interview, the quality of the patient's object relations may become apparent in his interaction with the interviewer. Although brief, such diagnostic interactions with patients often permit differentiation of the neurotic personality's gradual build-up of a personal relation of an appropriate kind from the borderline personality's persistently chaotic, empty, distorted, or blocked relation.

In the case of psychotic personality organization, where reality testing is lost, even more severe distortions of the patient-diagnostician relation may ensue. It is the combination of such a distortion within an interaction in which reality testing is maintained that is so characteristic of borderline personality organization. The frequent shift of focus from the present interaction of patient and interviewer to the patient's communication about difficulties in interactions with significant others provides additional material for the evaluation of the quality of object relations.

DEFENSIVE OPERATIONS CENTERING AROUND SPLITTING

A further difference between neurotic personality structure, on the one hand, and borderline and psychotic structures, on the other, is the nature of the defensive organization. In the neurotic, this centers around the repression and other advanced or high-level defensive operations. Borderline and psychotic structures, in contrast, reveal a predominance of primitive defensive operations centering around the mechanism of splitting. Repression and related mechanisms such as reaction formation, isolation, undoing, intellectualization, and rationalization all protect the ego from intrapsychic conflicts by means of the rejection of a drive derivative or its ideational representation, or both, from the conscious ego. In contrast, splitting and other related mechanisms protect the ego from conflicts by means of dissociating or actively keeping apart contradictory experiences of the self and significant others. When splitting and other related mechanisms predominate, contradictory ego states are alternatively activated, and as long as these contradictory ego states can be kept separate from each other, anxiety related to these conflicts is prevented or controlled.

The mechanism of primitive dissociation or splitting and the associated mechanisms of primitive idealization, primitive types of projection (particularly projective identification), denial, omnipotence, and devaluation may be elicited in the clinical interaction of patient and diagnostician. These defenses protect borderline patients from intrapsychic conflict, but at the cost of weakening their ego functioning, thereby reducing the adaptive effectiveness and flexibility in the interview and in their life generally. These

same primitive defensive operations when found in psychotic organization protect the patient from further disintegration of the boundaries between self and object. The fact that the same defensive
operations can be observed in borderline and psychotic patients,
and yet serve different functions, is demonstrated by clinical evidence indicating that interpretation of splitting and other related
mechanisms in borderline personality organization integrates the
ego and improves the patient's immediate functioning. This
immediate (if only transitory) increase in social adaptation and in
reality testing can be utilized for diagnostic purposes. In contrast,
interpretation of these defenses to the psychotic patient in the
diagnostic interview brings about further regression in his functioning. Thus, whether the patient immediately improves or deter-
iorates under the effect of such interpretation contributes in a
crucial way to the diagnostic differentiation of borderline from psychotic organization.

The presence of splitting and related primitive defense mechanisms may be elicited both in the analysis of the patient's personality
as reflected in interactions with significant others (at work or school,
in social, family, and sexual life, etc.) and in the interview itself.
Because I have dealt with these defensive mechanisms in detail elsewhere (1975a), I shall only briefly summarize the conclusions
relevant to the structural diagnosis of borderline patients.

SPLITTING

Probably the clearest manifestation of splitting is the division of
external objects into "all good" and "all bad," with the concomitant
possibility of complete, abrupt shifts of an object from one extreme
compartment to the other — that is, sudden and complete reversals
of all feelings and conceptualizations about a particular person.
Extreme repetitive oscillation between contradictory self-concepts is
another manifestation of the mechanism of splitting. In the diagnostic interview, sudden shifts in the perception of the interviewer,
or complete reversals of the patient's perception of himself or a
complete separation of contradictory reactions to the same theme
may reflect splitting mechanisms in the here-and-now interaction.
The patient's increase in anxiety when contradictory aspects of his
self-image or his object representations are pointed out to him, also

reveals the mechanism of splitting. The effort to clarify, confront, and interpret such contradictory aspects of the self- and object representations activates the mechanism of splitting in the here-and-now interaction, reflects its functions regarding reality testing (increase or decrease), and the rigidity of the character traits that "fixate" splitting into stable problems.

PRIMITIVE IDEALIZATION

This mechanism complicates the tendency to see external objects as either totally good or totally bad by increasing artificially and pathologically their quality of "goodness" or "badness." Primitive idealization creates unrealistic, all good and powerful images; this may be reflected in the interaction with the diagnostician by treating him as an ideal, omnipotent, or godly figure on whom the patient depends unrealistically. The interviewer or other idealized person may be seen as a potential helper against equally powerful but unrealistic "all bad" objects.

EARLY FORMS OF PROJECTION, ESPECIALLY PROJECTIVE IDENTIFICATION

In contrast to higher levels of projection characterized by attributing to the other an impulse the patient has repressed in himself, primitive forms of projection, particularly projective identification, are characterized by (1) the tendency to continue to experience the impulse which is, at the same time, projected onto the other person; (2) fear of the other person under the influence of that projected impulse, and (3) the need to control the external object (the other person) under the influence of this mechanism. Projective identification therefore implies intrapsychic as well as behavioral interpersonal aspects of the patient's interactions, and this may be reflected dramatically in the diagnostic interview. The patient may accuse the interviewer of a certain reaction to him, a reaction that the patient actually is attempting to induce in the interviewer by means of his own behavior. For example, one patient accused the interviewer of being sadistic while he himself treated the interviewer in what might best be described as a cold, controlling, derogatory, and suspicious way. The interpretation of this defensive operation in the here and now often dramatically permits the differentiation between a paranoid personality (a typical borderline personality constellation) and paranoid schizophrenia.

DENIAL

Denial in borderline patients is typically exemplified by mutual denial of two emotionally independent areas of consciousness (a case in which we might say denial simply reinforces splitting). The patient is aware that his perceptions, thoughts, and feelings about himself or other people at one time are completely opposite to those he has had at other times, but this memory has no emotional relevance and cannot influence the way he feels now. Denial may be manifest as a complete lack of concern, anxiety, or emotional reaction about an immediate, serious, pressing need, conflict, or danger in the patient's life, so that the patient calmly conveys his cognitive awareness of the situation while denying its emotional implications. Or an entire area of the patient's subjective awareness may be shut out from his subjective experience, thus protecting him from a potential area of conflict. The diagnostician's empathic effort to evaluate the patient's life situation and the normal human reactions one would assume the patient might have to such a reality situation often provides the patient with a sharp contrast between this empathic effort and his own almost indifferent or callous attitude about himself or important others. Denial may be manifest in the patient's discussion of his present life situation and may also become evident in the contradiction between that life situation and the patient's reaction in focusing upon it in the diagnostic interview.

OMNIPOTENCE AND DEVALUATION

Both omnipotence and devaluation are derivatives of splitting operations affecting the self- and object representations and are typically represented by the activation of ego states reflecting a highly inflated, grandiose, omnipotent self relating to depreciated, devaluated, emotionally destroyed representations of others. Narcissistic personalities, a special subgroup of borderline personality organization, present these defensive operations quite strikingly. Omnipotence and devaluation may become manifest in the patient's descriptions of significant others, his interactions with them, and in his behavior during the diagnostic interview. In this connection, whatever small or subtle indications of pathological behavior can be elicited in the early diagnostic contacts with the patient need to be highlighted. If one considers that usually a patient tries to present himself at his best in a new situation (and that, when the opposite is true it represents an indication of serious character pathology), one must conclude that both grossly inappropriate behaviors, when present, and subtle deviations from otherwise "perfectly normal" behavior need to be highlighted in diagnostic interviews.

MAINTENANCE OF REALITY TESTING

Both neurotic personality organization and borderline personality organization present maintenance of reality testing, in contrast to psychotic personality structures. Therefore, while the syndrome of identity diffusion and the predominance of primitive defensive operations permit the structural differentiation of borderline from neurotic conditions, reality testing permits the differentiation of borderline personality organization from the major psychotic syndromes. Reality testing is defined by the capacity to differentiate self from nonself, intrapsychic from external origins of perceptions and stimuli, and the capacity to evaluate realistically one's own affect, behavior, and thought content in terms of ordinary social norms. Clinically, reality testing is recognized by (1) the absence of hallucinations and delusions; (2) the absence of grossly inappropriate or bizarre affect, thought content, or behavior; (3) the capacity to empathize with and clarify other people's observations of what to them seem inappropriate or puzzling aspects of the patient's affects, behavior, or thought content within the context of ordinary social interactions. Reality testing, thus defined, needs to be differentiated from alterations in the subjective experience of reality, which may be present at some time in any patient with psychological distress, and from the alteration of the relation to reality that is present in all character pathology as well as in more regressive, psychotic conditions, and is, by itself, of diagnostic value only in very extreme forms (Frosch, 1964). How is reality testing reflected in the structural diagnostic interview?

1. Reality testing is preserved in the patient's information's indicating that he has not suffered from hallucinations or delusions

in the past or in the present, or, if he has had such hallucinations or delusions in the past, in his present capacity to evaluate them fully and totally, including the presence of appropriate concern or puzzlement over such phenomena.

2. In patients who have not had hallucinations or delusions, reality testing can be evaluated by the interviewer's focusing sharply on whatever inappropriate affect, thought content, or behavior can be observed. Reality testing is reflected in the patient's capacity to empathize with the interviewer's perception of these characteristics and, in a more subtle way, in the patient's capacity to empathize with the interviewer's perception of his interaction with the patient in general. The structural interview therefore constitutes an ideal testing ground for reality testing, and thus for the differentiation of borderline from psychotic organization.

3. For reasons mentioned earlier, reality testing may also be evaluated by interpreting primitive defensive operations in the patient-interviewer interaction. An improvement in the patient's immediate functioning as a consequence of such interpretation reflects maintenance of reality testing, while an immediate deterioration of the patient's functioning as a consequence of such intervention indicates loss of reality testing.

NONSPECIFIC MANIFESTATIONS OF EGO WEAKNESS

The "nonspecific" aspects of ego weakness include lack of anxiety tolerance, lack of impulse control, and lack of developed channels for sublimation. These are to be differentiated from the "specific" aspects of ego weakness: the ego-weakening consequences of the predominance of primitive defensive mechanisms. Anxiety tolerance refers to the degree to which the patient can tolerate an additional load of tension to that habitually experienced by him without developing an increase in symptoms or in general regressive behavior; impulse control refers to the degree to which the patient can experience instinctual urges or strong emotions without having to act on them immediately against his better judgment and interest; and sublimatory effectiveness refers to the degree to which the patient can invest himself in values beyond his immediate self-interest, or beyond self-preservation—particularly the degree to which he is able to develop creative resources in some area beyond his natural background, education, or training.

These characteristics, although reflecting structural conditions, are manifest in direct behavior which may be elicited in the patient's history. Nonspecific manifestations of ego weakness differentiate both borderline personality organization and the psychoses from neurotic personality structures, but they have a less precise and clear differentiating function between borderline and neurotic structures than is true for the previously mentioned structural criteria (identity integration and levels of defensive organization). Thus, for example, many narcissistic personalities who reflect a borderline personality organization present fewer indications of nonspecific symptoms of ego weakness than one would expect.

LACK OF SUPEREGO INTEGRATION

A relatively well-integrated although excessively severe superego characterizes the neurotic types of personality organization. Borderline and psychotic organizations reflect impairments in superego integration, and are characterized by primitive sadistic and idealized object representations. Superego integration can be evaluated by studying the degree to which the patient identifies with ethical values and has normal guilt as a major regulator. Regulation of self-esteem by severe, excessive, pathological guilt feelings or depressive mood swings represent a pathological superego integration (typical of neurotic organization), in contrast to the modulated, specifically focused, self-critical functions of the normal individual in terms of ethical values. The degree to which the person is able to regulate his functioning according to ethical principles, abstaining from the exploitation, manipulation, or mistreatment of others, and his ability to maintain honesty and moral integrity in the absence of external control indicate superego integration. This criterion is diagnostically less reliable than the ones previously described. Even patients employing predominantly primitive defenses may give evidence of superego integration, although it may be sadistic in nature, and there are patients with borderline personality organization who maintain a relatively good superego integration in spite of severe pathology in the area of identity integration, object relations, and defensive organization. Also, information regarding superego integration can be elicited more effectively from the patient's history and from long-term observation than in the diagnostic interview. Nevertheless the prognostic importance of the degree of superego integration makes it an enormously important structural criterion for the indication or contraindication of long-term, intensive psychotherapy. In fact, the quality of object relations and the quality of superego functioning are probably the two most important prognostic criteria stemming from a structural analysis.

GENETIC-DYNAMIC CHARACTERISTICS OF THE PREDOMINANT CONSTELLATION OF INSTINCTUAL CONFLICTS

These structural characteristics refer to the organization of predominant mental contents; they are reflected in the vicissitudes of the instinctual life and conflicts of borderline patients and clarify the apparently bizarre and strange qualities of their object relations throughout time. Although they become highly manifest in long-term therapeutic engagements, these characteristic contents are relatively difficult to evaluate in diagnostic interviews and are described here in the interest of completeness.

Borderline personality organization presents a pathological condensation of genital and pregenital instinctual strivings, with a predominance of pregenital aggression (Kernberg, 1975a). This assumption explains the clinical characteristics of the bizarre or inappropriate condensation of sexual, dependent, and aggressive impulses found in borderline (and also psychotic) organization. What appears on the surface as a chaotic persistence of primitive drives and fears, the pansexuality of the borderline case, represents a combination of several of various pathological solutions of these conflicts.

It should be stressed here that the discrepancy between the patient's actual historical development and his internal, fixated experience of it is enormous. What we find out in psychoanalytic exploration of these cases is not what happened in external reality, but how the patient experienced his significant object relations in the past. By the same token, we cannot take the patient's initial history at face value: the more severe the character pathology, the less reliable the initial history. In severe narcissistic personality disorders, and borderline personality organization in general, the initial history of early development is frequently empty or chaotic or misleading, and only after years of treatment is it possible to reconstruct an internal genetic sequence (in the sense of intrapsychic origins) and relate it in some way to the patient's actual past experiences.

The characteristics listed here of instinctual conflicts one finds most frequently in borderline personality organization integrate the observations from the literature summarized before (Kernberg, 1975a) with my own experience in intensive psychoanalytic psychotherapy and psychoanalysis of borderline patients. First, is an excessive aggressivization of oedipal conflicts so that, typically, the image of the oedipal rival acquires terrifying, overwhelmingly dangerous, and destructive characteristics, castration anxiety and penis envy appear grossly exaggerated and overwhelming, and superego prohibitions against sexualized relations acquire a savage, primitive quality, manifested in severe masochistic tendencies or paranoid projections of superego precursors.

Second, the idealization of the heterosexual love object in the positive oedipal relation and of the homosexual love object in the negative oedipal relation are exaggerated and have marked defensive functions against primitive rage. There is thus a combination of both unrealistic idealization of and longing for such love objects, and the possibility of rapid breakdown of the idealization, with a reversal from the positive to the negative (or negative to positive) relation in a rapid, total shift of the object relation. As a consequence, the idealizations appear as both exaggerated and frail, with the additional complication of easy devaluation of idealized objects and total withdrawal in the case of narcissistic character pathology.

Third, the unrealistic nature of both the threatening oedipal rival and the idealization of the desired one reveal, on careful genetic analysis, the existence of condensed father-mother images of an unreal kind, reflecting the condensation of partial aspects of the relations with both parents. While sexual differences in the object relations are maintained, the nature of the fantasied relation with each of these objects is unrealistic and primitive and reflects the condensation of idealized or threatening relations stemming from preoedipal and oedipal developments and a rapid shift of both libidinal and aggressive relations from one to the other parental object. Each particular relation with a predominant parental object turns out to reflect a more complex developmental history than is usually the case with neurotic patients — excepting the most severely neurotic — where the transference developments are more closely related to realistic events of the past.

Fourth, the genital strivings of patients with predominant pre-oedipal conflicts serve important pregenital functions. The penis, for example, may acquire characteristics of the feeding, withhold-ing, or attacking mother (basically the feeding function of her breast), and the vagina may acquire functions of the hungry, feeding, or aggressive mouth; similar developments occur regarding anal and urinary functions. Although neurotic patients and patients with less severe character pathology also frequently present these characteristics, their existing in combination with the excessive aggressivization of all these pregenital libidinal functions is typical of patients with borderline personality organization.

Fifth, borderline patients typically show what could be described as a premature oedipalization of their preoedipal conflicts and relations, a defensive progression in their instinctual development which is reflected clinically in early oedipalization of the trans-ference. This early oedipalization of the transference often turns out to be spurious in the sense of eventually leading back to severe and chaotic preoedipal pathology, and yet is at the same time significant in terms of indicating the predominant defensive organization of oedipal conflicts that eventually, sometimes after years of treatment, predominate in the transference. In this regard, our developing knowledge about early genital awareness in both sexes and the difference in mother-infant relations in terms of the infant's sex, may provide information on early infant behavior that relates to the intrapsychic processes by which an escape from preoedipal conflicts into oedipalization of object relations takes place.

In practice, the following are the most frequent constellations of preoedipally distorted oedipal conflicts. In both sexes, the dis-placement of frustrated dependency needs from mother to father colors the positive oedipal relation of the girl and the negative oedipal relation of the boy. The displacement of oral-aggressive conflicts from mother onto father increases castration anxiety and oedipal rivalry in boys, and penis envy and related character distortions in girls. In girls, severe pregenital aggression toward the mother reinforces masochistic tendencies in their relations to men, severe superego prohibitions against genitality in general, and the negative oedipal relation to the mother, as a defensive idealization and reaction formation against the aggression. The projection of primitive conflicts around aggression onto the sexual relation between the parents increases distorting and frightening versions of the primal scene and promotes destructive envy and jealousy of the good relation between the parents which may become extended into hatred of all mutual love offered by others. More generally, the defensive displacement of impulses and conflicts from one parent to the other fosters the development of confusing, fantastic combinations of bisexual parental images condensed under the influence of a certain projected impulse.

All these characteristics of instinctual conflicts of patients with borderline personality organization may be reflected in the initial symptomatology, in their sexual behavior, fantasies, and interpersonal relations, but, as mentioned before, often do not lend themselves to an analysis in depth during the early diagnostic interviews. For practical purposes, therefore, these genetic-dynamic considerations have less relevance for the structural diagnosis than they have for the exploration, from a therapeutic viewpoint, of the patient's main conflicts, and their defensive and impulsive features.

SUMMARY, OPEN ISSUES, AND FINAL THOUGHTS

The main considerations for a differential diagnosis of borderline personality organization from a structural viewpoint are the criteria of: (1) identity integration versus identity diffusion and the related quality of object relations; (2) the predominance of constellations of defensive operations centering around repression versus those centering around splitting; and (3) the presence or absence of reality testing. Together these three criteria should permit differentiation of the vast majority of patients with borderline personality organization from neurotic personality organization, on the one hand, and psychotic organizations, on the other.

A number of issues still remain open at this time and require further clinical and experimental research. These relate to the structural diagnosis of borderline personality organization at times of temporary regression, such as the brief chaotic episodes that borderline patients have under the influence of severe emotional turmoil, alcohol, or drugs. Preliminary clinical experience indicates that the structural diagnostic interview proposed may still differentiate borderline personality organization under these conditions, in effect temporarily reducing the loss of reality testing in these patients; however, more exploration will be necessary to confirm this. The descriptive characteristics of such brief psychotic episodes and the fact that they are embedded in a personality structure typical of borderline personality organization constitute the positive diagnostic criteria at this time.

Another problem is presented by psychotic reactions under the influence of psychotomimetic drugs, which often, during their acute stage, raise the question of differential diagnosis between acute psychotic episodes in borderline personality organization and acute schizophrenic reactions. Again, preliminary evidence seems to indicate that loss of reality testing in drug-induced psychosis in borderline personality organization may transitorily improve with the structural diagnostic evaluation proposed, in contrast to the temporary increased regression when primitive defenses are interpreted in the case of schizophrenic reactions. However, this is only a preliminary impression.

A major issue is that of the structural characteristics of patients with chronic schizophrenic reactions during periods of remission. My colleagues and I have observed various types of personality organization in such patients. Some chronic schizophrenic patients seem to "seal over" and present a neurotic personality organization during periods of latency; other chronic schizophrenic reactions present a typical psychotic regression when examined with the structural approach during periods of clinical remission, thus indicating the permanence or persistence of an essentially psychotic structure; and some patients with chronic schizophrenic reactions "seal over" and present a borderline personality organization. Thus, the underlying personality structure of chronic schizophrenic patients during remission may not be uniform, and it may be possible to differentiate, with structural criteria, chronic psychotic personality organizations proper from patients with a "higher-level" "sealing-over." This may have prognostic and therapeutic implications in terms of the preconditions for and characteristics of shifts in the predominant personality organization that we observe in some schizophrenic patients during remission.

Another problem is the diagnostic examination of psychotic patients of all kinds under the influence of specific antipsychotic medication: the effect of the major tranquilizers, antidepressants, and lithium on personality organization from a structural viewpoint still needs to be evaluated. The evaluation of the structural personality characteristics in patients with manic-depressive illness in remission constitutes another area in which my and my colleagues' preliminary experience is insufficient to allow us to reach definite conclusions.

The structural criteria proposed, particularly that of reality testing, can be regarded as a powerful diagnostic tool, to be used in conjunction with an evaluation of the descriptive symptoms of the various psychotic conditions mentioned. The structural diagnostic approach to clinical psychiatry may enrich significantly the sharpness, precision, and accuracy of our differential diagnoses and add important elements to the prognostic and therapeutic considerations of each individual case. But it is quite likely that some cases will remain which, so far, defy our capacity for differential diagnosis, at least when this is attempted in a relatively brief period of time.

The structural approach to the differential diagnosis of borderline personality organization highlights the central importance of diagnosing the patient as a total individual, and his internal life of object relations in terms of his conception of himself and of significant others as integrated individuals. Paradoxically, this dynamic, object-relations-theory-based approach, which seems to run counter to a more descriptive, symptom- and behavior-oriented diagnostic focus, enriches the latter. It is not a question of either-or; both are valuable. From the viewpoint of research methodology, the breaking down of human behavior into clusters of behavioral manifestations is easier and apparently more "objective" than the effort to study the human individual in his totality. However, in spite of the methodological difficulties implied by this structural approach, such a study of the totality of the individual may in the long run provide a firmer basis for research on personality organization and personality change.

The diagnosis of borderline personality organization affects both the prognosis and the treatment. Where structural diagnosis determines the presence of borderline personality organization rather than ordinary symptomatic neurosis and character pathology; it indicates limitations to the possibility of psychoanalytic treatment; it suggests that intensive, long-term exploratory psychoanalytic psychotherapy, rather than supportive treatment would be most appropriate; it signals the need to carefully evaluate whether and how to structure the patient's external life while such intensive psychotherapy proceeds; it means that, under conditions of acute crisis, crisis intervention is indicated, and that the decision will ultimately have to be made which treatment approach to adopt — exploratory or supportive psychotherapy. It means, for those cases where exploratory psychotherapy is contraindicated and a supportive approach elected, the possibility of accepting that a patient may need support over many years or perhaps for life.

In my opinion, today this diagnosis means a better prognosis for many patients than was thought only 20 or 30 years ago. In the case of patients with chronic schizophrenic illness, the diagnosis of borderline personality organization — in contrast to psychotic structure — during periods of remission indicates the possibility of psychoanalytic psychotherapy and, implicitly, the possibility of fundamentally improving the personality structure and thus affording the patient additional protection against psychotic breakdown.

REFERENCES

Bellak, L., Hurvich, M., & Gediman, H. K. (1973), *Ego Functions in Schizophrenics, Neurotics, and Normals.* New York: Wiley-Interscience.
Deutsch, F. (1949), *Applied Psychoanalysis.* New York: Grune & Stratton.
Freud, S. (1923), The ego and the id. *Standard Edition,* 19:3-66. London: Hogarth Press, 1961.

Fromm-Reichmann, F. (1950), *Principles of Intensive Psychotherapy*. Chicago: University of Chicago Press.

Frosch, J. (1964), The psychotic character: Clinical psychiatric consideration. *Psychiat. Quart.*, 38:91-96.

Gill, M. M., Newman, R., & Redlich, F. C. (1954), *The Initial Interview in Psychiatric Practice*. New York: International Universities Press.

Hartmann, H., Kris, E., & Loewenstein, R. M. (1946), Comments on the formation of psychic structure. *The Psychoanalytic Study of the Child*, 2:11-38. New York: International Universities Press.

Kernberg, O. F., et al. (1972), Psychotherapy and psychoanalysis: Final report of the Menninger Foundation's psychotherapy research project. *Bull. Menninger Clinic*, 36(1/2).

———— (1975a), *Borderline Conditions and Pathological Narcissism*. New York: Jason Aronson.

———— (1975b), Transference and countertransference in the treatment of borderline patients. *Strecker Monograph Series*, XII. Also in: *J. Nat. Assn. Private Psychiat. Hosp.*, 7:14-24.

———— (1976a), Technical considerations in the treatment of borderline personality organization. *J. Amer. Psychoanal. Assn.*, 24:795-829.

———— (1976b), *Object Relations Theory and Clinical Psychoanalysis*. New York: Jason Aronson.

Laughlin, H. P. (1956), *The Neuroses in Clinical Practice*. Philadelphia: Saunders.

MacKinnon, R. A., & Michels, R. (1971), *The Psychiatric Interview in Clinical Practice*. Philadelphia: Saunders.

Menninger, K. A. (1952), *A Manual for Psychiatric Case Study*. New York: Grune & Stratton.

Panel (1977), Varieties of oedipal distortions in severe character pathologies. W. S. Robbins, reporter. *J. Amer. Psychoanal. Assn.*, 25:201-218.

Powdermaker, F. (1948), The techniques of the initial interview and methods of teaching them. *Amer. J. Psychiat.*, 104:642-646.

Rapaport, D., & Gill, M. M. (1959), The points of view and assumptions of metapsychology. *Internat. J. Psycho-Anal.*, 40:153-162.

Rogers, C. R. (1951), *Client-Centered Therapy*. Boston: Houghton Mifflin.

Sullivan, H. S. (1954), *The Psychiatric Interview*. New York: Norton.

Whitehorn, J. C. (1944), Guide to interviewing and clinical personality study. *Arch. Neurol. Psychiat.*, 52:197-216.

An Approach to the Understanding of Borderline Disorders

LEÓN GRINBERG, M.D.

Among the salient characteristics of borderline patients, as described in the psychoanalytic literature (Frosch, 1964; Kernberg, 1967, 1975; Knight, 1953; Mahler, 1971; Stern, 1938), I have personally observed the following: a predominance of the "psychotic part of the personality"; intolerance of frustration; preponderance of aggressive impulses; utilization of pathological splitting, narcissistic identifications, fantasies of omnipotence and omniscience, and idealization as central defense processes; identity disturbances; states of diffuse anxiety; defective contact with reality, though without complete loss of touch with it; temporary loss of control over impulses, with a tendency toward acting out; predominance of primitive object relations; depression and extreme, infantile dependence on objects; prevalence of pregenital strivings and liability to develop a transference psychosis, with a possibility of transient psychotic breakdowns.

I intend to focus on some specific aspects of the borderline personality, namely, the prevalence of a psychotic part and various types of splitting mechanisms and narcissistic identifications, and to propose a distinction between two categories or groups of borderline patients according to their characteristic symptoms, defense operations, and object relations, both internalized and external.

THE CONCEPT OF PSYCHOTIC PERSONALITY

Although I agree with those who hold the view that the pathological organization of borderline personality is a specific and

---

Faculty Member, Argentina Psychoanalytic Institute, Buenos Aires, Argentina.

stable one (Kernberg, 1967, 1975), I believe it can be described in terms of two categories, namely "schizoid borderline" and "melancholoid borderline," according to the peculiar functional modalities of certain elements that make up the borderline personality organization.[1] Before entering into a detailed discussion of the various elements that constitute the two proposed categories, however, I would like to dwell briefly on the concept of "psychotic personality."

As conceived by Bion (1957), the term "psychotic personality" does not refer to a psychiatric diagnosis, but rather, to a modality of mental functioning, which manifests itself in the person's behavior and language and in the effects it produces on the observer. This mental state coexists with another—the "nonpsychotic personality" or "neurotic personality."[2] Among the most significant components of the psychotic personality are an intolerance of frustration, a prevalence of aggressive impulses that become manifest as a hatred of internal and external reality, a fear of imminent annihilation, and premature object relations, which, though tenaciously maintained, are nonetheless precarious and fragile, as observed in the analytic transference.

Owing to heightened aggressive impulses, the psychotic personality makes use of splitting and pathological projective identification in order to attack aspects of the self, of internal as well as external objects. Such an attack on reality and on those self-aspects that make for awareness of reality causes the principal mental

[1] The classification I have just suggested is likely to have emerged from a concern similar to that of Grinker, Werble, and Drye (1968), who set up, on the basis of their observational studies, four groups within the over-all denomination of borderline patients.

[2] This approach to mental functioning harks back to Freud's article on "Fetishism" (1927), in which he shows how the ego can at times keep up two different attitudes, a more normal one through which contact with reality is preserved, and a more pathological one which tends to withdraw from or deny reality. Freud applies the term "disavowal" (*Verleugnung*) to the child's or the fetishist's rebuff of the fact that women lack a penis; such a rebuff necessarily implies a splitting of the ego. The psychotic part of the personality is also discussed by Bleger (1967) under the name of "agglutinated nucleus." He sees this as the remnant of a very primitive organization ("syncretic organization"), the essential characteristic of which is a defective discrimination between ego and non-ego, between "good" and "bad" objects, and between different identifications.

activities and the links with objects to appear torn to pieces, minute particles that are evacuated through pathological projective identification. These fragments, formed by aspects of the self and objects, are described by Bion (1959) as "bizarre objects." They are experienced as having an independent and uncontrolled existence that dangerously threatens from the outside.[3]

The psychotic personality is dominated by a primitive and sadistic superego, which opposes any kind of evolution and learning from experience, while tending to arouse, among other affects, a sense of "persecutory guilt" (Grinberg, 1964) shared by significant objects and the analyst in his countertransference. Projective identification and splitting are used as substitutes for repression, which is the central mechanism of the nonpsychotic personality.

To understand how the psychotic personality sets in and develops in a borderline patient, one has to consider constitutional factors, such as a marked intolerance of frustration and a prevalence of destructive (oral-sadistic and anal-sadistic) impulses, as well as the relationship with a mother who was unable to receive, contain, and modify the painful affects projected by the baby, because she lacked the capacity for "reverie" (Bion, 1962).

One of the fundamental factors underlying the origins of the borderline personality organization is the experience of separation from and loss of objects significant to the child — for example, loss of the mother, either in a real sense or as a result of the mother's failure to mitigate the anxiety projected onto her by the child. These experiences of separation and loss can give rise to intense depressive reactions, ulterior developmental disturbances, confusional tendencies with an impairment of the sense of identity, and defective discrimination in object relations. Faced with the mother's absence, the child falls prey to acute anxiety; he feels deserted, helpless, and terrified at the risk of falling into a void.[4]

[3] Rosenfeld (1964) describes the activity of omnipotent and destructive self-aspects belonging to a particular area of the infantile narcissistic organization, which attack any libidinal relation with the object, overrating the self while underestimating the object. The aggressive fantasies may take on an erotic character, whereas the destructive impulses are likely to give rise to perversions.

[4] Winnicott (1965) uses the term "good-enough mother" with reference to the mother who is able to meet the child's needs and to allow his real self to come to life and strengthen itself. When the environmental (mother, father, substitutes)

The two categories that I am going to describe — melancholoid and schizoid borderline patients — should not be thought of as sharply separated; in fact, a combined presence of characteristics belonging to both is usually observed, with a prevalence of one over the other.

SCHIZOID BORDERLINE PATIENTS

In this category I include those borderline patients whose psychotic personality appears heightened, who manifest an intolerance of frustration, a predominance of aggressive impulses, pathological splitting, projective identification, and some other special defense constellations, such as "reversal of perspective," the aim of which is to avoid psychic suffering and other intolerable affects. These patients are usually susceptible and egocentric. They tend to evade emotional commitments. They are frequently overwhelmed by a sense of futility, which they try to counteract by means of feelings of omnipotence and underestimation of others. They present a tendency to isolation, withdrawal, self-sufficiency, and exhibitionism, with occasional episodes of depersonalization associated with identity disturbances (Fairbairn, 1954).

Though they never regress to a fully psychotic state, their behavior in the analytic situation is characterized by a transference psychosis, which fluctuates between fantasies of idealization and persecution. Fantasies of persecution develop from a restirring of primitive persecutory links with the earliest objects (mainly the mother), fantasies or feelings stemming from projected aggressive tendencies, and fancied destructive attacks against the mother's body and its contents. These oral-sadistic fantasies, feelings, and impulses extend to the relationship with the father, and at times manifest themselves as intense hostility toward both parents. This,

---

response is not good enough, the child is unable to develop his real self. A "false self" then arises in order to cloak or protect the former, but does not succeed in preventing its impoverishment. Mahler (1971, 1972) also emphasizes the importance of the mother's libidinal availability for the development of normal object relations. Masterson and Rinsley (1975), on the basis of Mahler's views, stress the early interaction established between the borderline patient and his mother, in what they call "the rewarding and withdrawing object relations part units."

in turn, gives room to the fantasy of a "combined couple," which is a powerful source of persecutory feelings (Klein, 1948). All these experiences are relived in the transference relationship with the analyst, with periodic reinforcements of the attack against the patient-analyst link, defining a pathological form of projective identification.

These patients feel imprisoned within their own mental condition. They also feel that any sign of progress will confront them with the painful recognition of their "madness." This is why they repeatedly resort to pathological projective identification to place in the analyst the dreaded words, internalized objects, self-aspects, and dreams, just to get rid of them and of their threat.

Incidentally, these patients are barely capable of dreaming; if they do dream, their dreams acquire the peculiar characteristics that make up "evacuative" dreams (Grinberg et al., 1967). The primal aim of evacuative dreams is the immediate discharge of the anxiety aroused by threatening internalized object relations. As a rule, once the dream has been reported, the patient tries to avoid its being reintrojected; hence he resorts to varied means to stop the analyst from interpreting it.

With borderline patients, the transference is intense from the earliest stages of treatment. In relation to the positive aspects of the transference link, the patient projects his idealization and omnipotence onto the analyst's image, but minor frustrations are enough to arouse in him strong persecutory reactions and a tendency to regard the analyst as a bad object. At times, the patient exerts strong pressure and makes demands so as to make the analyst show affection for him; at others times, he tries to project anxiety, inducing the analyst, by means of projective identification, to act out and give up his analytic function.

Under normal circumstances projective identification is part and parcel of all human relations and lays the foundations for meaningful communication. It determines the empathic link with an object by enabling the person to place himself in the position of his fellow human being and so understand the other's feelings better. In pathological cases projective identification consists of an omnipotent fantasy through which unwanted parts of the personality and internalized objects, together with the attendant affects, are split off, projected, and controlled in the object toward which projection is directed. As a result, the object is equated with what is projected onto it.

The patient's pathological projective identification can bring about a specific reaction in the analyst which I have termed "projective counteridentification" (Grinberg, 1962). This reaction is not consciously perceived or registered by the analyst. As a result, he is sometimes passively "led" to play certain roles or functions, or to experience those affects (anger, depression, anxiety, boredom, drowsiness, and so on) that the patient actively, though unconsciously, "forces" onto him. I have elsewhere (Grinberg, 1963) detailed this phenomenon, which I consider to be a very specific aspect of the analyst's response, to be distinguished from countertransference reactions based on the analyst's own emotional attitudes or neurotic remnants of the past becoming reactivated by the patient's conflicts, and which would correspond to what Racker (1957) describes as "complementary countertransference." As a result of their countertransference, different analysts would react in different ways to the material reported by the same patient. However, by using his projective identification in a specific and intense way, one patient may trigger off the *same* reaction of "projective counteridentification" in different analysts (Grinberg, 1970).

From a structural point of view, one may say that what is projected by means of the psychotic mechanism of projective identification operates within the object as a parasitic superego, which omnipotently induces the analyst's ego to act or feel what the patient in his fantasy wants him to act or feel. I think that this, to some degree, bears comparison with the dynamics of hypnosis as described by Freud (1921). According to Freud, the hypnotizer places himself in the position of the ego ideal, and hypnotic submissiveness is of a masochistic nature. Freud furthermore holds that in the hypnotic relation a sort of paralysis appears as a result of the influence of an omnipotent individual upon an impotent and helpless being. I believe the same applies to the process I am discussing, in that the analyst, being unaware of what happened, may later rationalize his action, as the hypnotized person does after executing the hypnotic commands. By means of mechanisms of obsessive control, the inducing subject continues to control what he projected onto the induced object. The subject's omnipotent fantasies thus acquire some consistency, as they seem to be confirmed by the object's response. All this corresponds to an object relationship, but one of a narcissistic nature in that the projection onto the object consists of parts of the subject's self or internal objects.

Projective identification and counteridentification phenomena are frequent in the analysis of borderline patients and give rise to a pathogenic interaction between analyst and patient, which is not always possible to resolve. The patient, owing to his early personal history and to repetition compulsion, tries to play a certain role and to induce in the analyst a complementary one. He tends to take up a position in the interaction which is inversely symmetrical with the one he seeks to induce in the object; as a result, what the patient says is usually the opposite of what he does. For instance, the schizoid borderline patient will perceive himself as persecuted and ascribe the role of persecutor to the object, whereas it is he who actually acts as a persecutor (Gear and Liendo, 1974).

In view of the characteristics commonly associated with schizoid borderline patients—namely, ego weakness, an intolerance of frustration, thought disorders, narcissistic tendencies, a reliance on omnipotence, the use of pathological splitting, excessive projective identifications, and a tendency to act out—one may wonder why such patients are not actually psychotic. In spite of the severity of their symptoms, they are still capable of detecting what has happened to the object and of grasping the other's specific needs and weaknesses. One of the explanatory factors lies in the use of obsessive mechanisms of "adaptive or realistic control" (Grinberg, 1966),[5] which help him keep control over aspects projected onto the object and bestow some coherence upon the patient's ego, despite

---

[5] I differentiated between two levels of functioning of the mechanisms of obsessive control: one includes the more regressive aspects and corresponds to the widely known "omnipotent control" which is chiefly related to psychotic conditions or to a predominance of the psychotic personality; the other comprises the most highly developed aspects and corresponds to what I termed "mechanisms of adaptive or realistic control" to stress that they feature better adaptation to reality and closer contact with external objects. When the patient is under the predominance of the psychotic personality, the use of these mechanisms enables him to uphold ego coherence and contact with the projected self-aspects, and to avoid losing touch with reality (Grinberg, 1966).

the intensive functioning of projective identification. This points to the importance of obsessive mechanisms in this kind of patient. Should the operation of obsessive control mechanisms fail, the precarious self-balance may be shattered and give way to a psychotic breakdown, or to a state of depersonalization in the analytic situation.

Schizoid borderline patients are particularly prone to acting out. One of the prevailing aspects of acting out consists of the patient's need for an object in the outer world capable of containing his separation anxiety and grief (Grinberg, 1968). Within the analytic situation this role is assigned to the analyst, on whom the patient evacuates his unbearable affects, whenever his past experiences are reactivated in the present transference. The analyst's occasional absence, whether due to routine or unforeseen interruptions of treatment (weekends, vacations, illnesses), re-creates the infantile experience of a missing object when such an absence was intolerable and thus renders him into a persecutory "non-object," which has to be evacuated onto another "container-object" by means of projective identification. Even when present, if the analyst happens to frustrate a certain transference fantasy and especially if he has not been experienced as a gratifying object, he may acquire the same quality of absence and thus become a persecutory internal "non-object" which has to be eliminated. This is why absences, separations, or frustrations occurring in the course of analysis tend to trigger off episodes of acting out, through which the patient seeks the peremptory discharge of dreaded and unbearable affects onto a substitute object. On other occasions the role of "container-object" is played by the patient's own body, resulting in psychosomatic or hypochondriacal disturbances (Grinberg, 1968).

CASE 1

I now wish to refer briefly to one of my patients and describe the characteristics of his acting out at the beginning of treatment. He was an intellectually gifted individual with apparently good social adaptation and a successful career. He had a narcissistic personality with a bent for exhibitionism. His thinking was characterized by an impulsive rhythm which made meditation or profound conceptualization difficult. But his chief weakness lay in his handling of affects and in his marked intolerance of anxiety or any suffering. From the beginning he tried to reverse our respective roles and to attack the analytic relationship. He would not listen to my interpretations, interrupting me over and over to object to what I was saying or to suggest alternative interpretations which were always "better" than mine. At other times he seemed to scrutinize my way of talking or tone of voice, to later "interpret" my affects. Although markedly dependent on analysis, he was quite unwilling to admit any therapeutic dependence, which he felt as cruelly humiliating. He therefore denied it and projected it onto me. In all this, he acted out within the analytic situation.

I had to be very careful not to fall into projective counteridentification reactions; I am not quite sure I always succeeded. I occasionally realized that some of my feelings were actually those of the patient. In fact, he perceived those feelings within himself and, being unable to tolerate them, he would project them onto me. His acting out also took the form of delays in the payment of fees, through which he sought to make me feel dependent on him and on his money. In this way he actively reproduced what he had passively experienced in relation to his parents. On other occasions he would arrive before the appointed time, thus acting out the fantasy of catching the analyst in an embarrassing situation, of spying into the primal scene — all of which underlined his voyeuristic tendencies.

He used to withhold material, a fact which he himself called "attacks through silence." By keeping stubbornly silent for long periods of time, even entire sessions, he would test my tolerance for waiting and frustration. Nor was he able to tolerate his occasional positive feelings toward me, lest a primitive, cruel, and jesting internalized image sneer at those feelings and ascribe to them a passive and humiliating character. At other times he showed an apparent understanding of my interpretations; however, there was no genuine insight. He employed his "understanding" as a further equivalent of acting out, to evade recognition of what was actually going on inside himself.

In addition, this patient often engaged in acting out beyond the analytic situation, during weekends or other interruptions, when the reactivation of his separation anxiety drove him to promiscuous behavior, extra-marital sexual activities associated with oral-sadistic and anal-sadistic fantasies. These episodes of acting out alternated with somatization and hypochondriacal fears.

At a later stage of the analysis I was able to detect the strivings of the nonpsychotic part of the patient's personality to override the psychotic part. Attempts at dealing with conflicts on the level of thinking and affects, rather than on the level of action, became noticeable, as in the following dream:

> I was at your office and saw my car in the waiting room. I started the engine and realized something had gone wrong with the *head* motor valves. I got out and looked to see if there was smoke coming out of the exhaust pipe. But to my distress, what I saw oozing out of it was black oil; it smeared everything and burnt the carpet. Then I found out that some men were trying to make a scaffolding to hoist up my car to the higher part of a building. I suddenly felt like helping them, and I joined them.

The patient's associations revealed that the car stood for himself, with his disease-defect in the "head." Acting out was experienced as an unmanageable anal activity. Owing to his projective identification with the fantasied image of the analyst, he used his powerful mind-engine to produce interpretations-flatulences. As he became aware how he had "smeared" treatment, however, his omnipotence abated, and his nonpsychotic part resumed control of the situation. He was then able to help "hoist" his activities-car, thus restoring contact between his own mind and that of the analyst. He was now able to cooperate in having his conflicts dealt with and finally solved on the "higher" level of mind and thinking, rather than on the "lower" level of acting out.

At this point I should like to comment on two other related defense operations: somatization and the "reversal of perspective" (Bion, 1963), by means of which the patient tries to paralyze the dynamics of the analytic process in order to evade the specific danger of mental pain. Somatization features an unconscious displacement of mental conflict over the body by causing organic suffering, which is at times more tolerable than psychic suffering. Mental phenomena then turn into sense impressions, which as such do not have meaning. That is, they lack psychic content and therefore spare the subject the experience of intolerable affect and subject him instead to a mere physical sensation—bodily pain.

Reversal of perspective consists of an inconspicuous but steady rebuff of the interpretive tenets, which is disguised as agreement with the analyst. A patient, for example, may say he had a dream and proceed to report it; what he actually seeks is a confirmation that what he had was "just a dream" and not an anxiety-provoking experience of a hallucinatory kind. Consequently, he is not interested in the analyst's interpretation, which he does not even take into account. For other patients, interpretation is a mere antidote to anxiety, much more so when they are under the terrifying impression that everything is meaningless. Whenever the analyst interprets, they seem to hear the word "because," with the attendant connotation of causality; incomprehensible things thus take on some meaning, no matter what. Such patients will perhaps learn much about the analyst's theoretical equipment, but will not be able to use it to gain any insight.

A further example of this mechanism is afforded by the patient who regards interpretations as a hint of the analyst's mood, which in his fantasy amounts to a sort of countertransference confession. Another example is the patient who, letting himself be guided by the analyst's tone of voice, hears something other than what the analyst actually says. Attitudes of this kind, exemplifying the defensive operation of reversal of perspective, are made possible by a special kind of splitting—what Bion (1963) calls "static splitting." This is a pervasive tendency to dissociate and evade understanding in order to avoid insight and to paralyze the dynamics of the analytic process.

MELANCHOLOID BORDERLINE PATIENTS

Melancholoid borderline patients usually present rapid mental processes and a remarkable receptivity to sensorial messages coming from the body and from the outer world. However, their grasp of the mental state and affects of those with whom they come into contact, excellent as it may be, is based on fantasies of omnipotent control, rather than on genuine identification. Such persons expect others to be equally sensitive, perceiving any evidence to the contrary as proof of total and final rebuff, to which they react traumatically by developing persecutory ideas and depressive feelings. At times they obstinately seek a skin-to-skin contact with objects, thus trying to recapture the very primitive, sensory nature of a symbiotic relation.

Melancholoid patients resemble schizoid borderline patients, especially in their intolerance of frustration and reactions to separation from and absence of the object; they differ primarily in their use of splitting mechanisms. As was pointed out earlier, schizoid borderline patients not only try to separate contradictory—persecutory or idealized—objects and affects, but, due to an inherent excessive hostility, they either abandon themselves to destructive impulses and actively attack self-object ties and different self-aspects, or they seek substitutes into which to "smuggle" themselves and engage in pathological projective identification or acting out. The melancholoid patient's response to separation is more depressive in nature. And he will resort to a more passive kind of splitting, leading to what Meltzer (1975) has called object and ego "dismantling." The patient's ego functions tend to be reduced to primitive perceptual capacities, which in turn may bring about a suspension of attention and a transitory interruption of awareness of the passing of time. The patient may appear and sound dull, even though he is not dull at all. He may at times give the impression that his mental apparatus is "falling to pieces." This transient suspension of ego functions makes him seem reduced to a primitive state of "mindlessness," as if he were mentally retarded. This state of mind also makes it difficult for him to discriminate between animate and inanimate objects.[6]

Such a regressive potential establishes itself early in childhood and prevents the development of a sense of inner space in both self

[6] In my opinion, the symptomatology of melancholoid borderline patients is related, in part at least, to that of the autistic and symbiotic syndromes studied by Mahler (1958), particularly as concerns the occasionally defective discrimination between live and inanimate objects, and the vulnerability to frustrations, however trivial these may be. Meltzer (1975) considers "dismantling" and "adhesive identification" (Bick, 1968) to be characteristic of autistic children and holds that the effects of both phenomena are noticeable in postautistic personalities.

and objects, thus hindering normal introjective and projective processes. Consequently, melancholoid borderline patients continue to be extremely dependent upon objects, the attendant fantasy being that of sticking or clinging to these objects.

I should like to underline the importance of the borderline's defective notion of inner space, for it explains the shallowness of his interpersonal relations. Green (1975) describes a state of decathectization or primary depression, almost in a physical sense, with an attendant state of emptiness, a yearning for "nothing" or "not to be," with the fundamental dilemma being "to rave or die." For these states he advances the hypothesis of what he terms "blank psychosis"; i.e., a psychotic nucleus without full-blown psychosis, characterized by emptiness of thought, inhibition of representation functions, etc. The patient is under the combined effects of depression (due to object loss) and intrusion of a persecutory presence.

The lack of a maternal object capable of satisfactorily performing the function of receiving and containing the infantile evacuations and projections renders the melancholoid borderline incapable of distinguishing between being inside and outside the object. Lacking as he does the notion of an inner space within himself and in his objects, the patient cannot utilize projective identification, which is the mechanism that, above all, accounts for the establishment of an emotionally tridimensional world. Instead, he resorts to an equally primitive but less functional mechanism — "adhesive identification" (Bick, 1968). This mechanism can bring about a situation of utmost dependence, to the point that the object's separate and autonomous existence is no longer recognized. The patient fantasies himself as stuck like a stamp on the object's surface; he becomes part of the object, reproducing the other's looks and behavior and, in effect, attempting to take over. A rebuff by the object of this kind of controlling behavior can lead the subject to a depressive breakdown. Because of his marked intolerance of separation, the subject feels that to be torn away from his object means to be torn away from his own skin as well.

It is interesting to note that infant observation reveals that when left unclad, very young babies become restless as if sensing danger, or they try to cling to the mother's clothes or to whatever is within reach. Bick (1968) interprets this as an expression of the babies' fantasies of scattering or falling, as if spilling out of themselves. Fear of disintegration makes them cling to whatever is near, for they feel they do not have a "skin" (experienced as their own) capable of containing them. At times this manifests itself in adult patients as a loss of control or an incapacity to contain the body limits, as in instances of loss of sphincter control, vomiting, etc. Infant observation shows that only the nipple in the mouth, "like a cork in a bottle," or the mother's tightly holding arms can soothe the child's fear that nobody will help him keep together and stop his fragments, so precariously held together, from falling apart.

Melancholoid borderline patients seem to have had difficulties in the development of the notion of the skin as a psychic container (Bick, 1968) and the subsequent development of narcissistic organization, of which splitting and projective identifications are the central mechanisms. When the mechanisms of dismantling and adhesive identification prevail, a person develops traits such as those Deutsch (1942) describes in the "as-if personality." Although the intellectual capacity of such a patient does not seem to be severely impaired, his emotional reactions are as if suspended or disguised, as if something vague interposes itself between him and other people to make them wonder: "What is the matter with him?" With the passivity he displays in his relations to others, and because of the absence of stable object links, he often experiences identity disturbances of a very peculiar kind.[7]

CASE 2

A brief vignette illustrates the fantasy of disintegration underlying the object relations of a melancholoid borderline patient characterized by a strong dependence tie. I shall only mention those data which are strictly relevant to what I wish to emphasize.

The patient, whose treatment I supervised, was a young married woman, the mother of two children. Professional duties made her husband travel abroad quite often and, owing to her tremendous

[7] Khan (1960) points to the "passivity of the ego" in patients of the as-if type and regards such passivity as a means of side-tracking strong affects, and also of maintaining inherently contradictory and conflictual contents (affective as well as psychic) in a benign, ego-syntonic state.

difficulties in coping with separation, she went along with him whenever she could. Within the therapeutic setting, this intolerance of separation manifested itself on weekends, when the patient used rigid obsessional mechanisms in order to counteract anxiety.

The following fragment depicts the patient's dramatic reaction, an oneiroid episode of pseudo-hallucinatory nature, when her husband called her from abroad to inform her that he would be back 24 hours later than originally expected.

Patient: I'm feeling awful. Alfredo [the husband] called me up yesterday and told me he would only arrive on Wednesday, not on Tuesday as scheduled. It was very odd. His voice seemed to me so distant! I felt sad and got frightened as I became aware how far away he is. And to think I had everything so carefully planned to meet him at the airport with the kids.... Something of this sort happened before. I went to the airport, the plane landed, all the passengers came out, except him. I asked for the passenger list and he wasn't on it. I got frightened, then I tried to convince myself that nothing had happened, but I thought, "When he comes, then I'll have my turn!" Back home, I found a belated cablegram explaining that he hadn't been able to board the plane. That is why I got scared when he called me yesterday, and when I heard his voice I said, "How far away you are!" Besides, it annoyed me to see all my plans fall through: early in the morning at the hairdresser's, fetch Juanito [her son] from school and then off to the airport to meet Alfredo. I'm always planning things in anticipation; for what, I don't know.

Analyst: You need all that planning in order to fill the void left by Alfredo's absence, so as not to feel that far away from him. Planning is a sort of substitute that keeps you company.

Patient: Yes ... I remember when mother came to stay with us for some time; after she left, I started tidying up and putting things away, especially what she had used while she was here. Last night I felt like crying. I was very distressed when I went to bed; then, as I was falling asleep, I had a vision; it was horrid ... I seemed to see Juanito disintegrate, fall to pieces ... It wasn't a dream ... I got so terribly scared, restless and had palpitations. I wanted to take that image off my mind; I couldn't

at first, then it did vanish but still I was frightened. I tried to reassure myself by thinking of you, and wrapped myself up in the
blankets.

Analyst: Juanito stands for yourself as a small child in fear of
disintegration because of Alfredo's absence and that of your
mother's. You thought of me as if seeking a close contact capable of holding you together.

The fact that her husband let her know of his postponed return,
when all her plans had centered on the original date of arrival,
made the patient feel her husband as more distant and, so to speak,
much more absent. Her obsessional defenses having failed, the
hallucinatory fantasy of disintegration and dismantling emerged,
but was then projected onto her son. As a result, she recalled her
analyst as a containing object and used the blankets as a protective
and integrating "skin."

Obsessional mechanisms are among those most frequently used
by melancholoid borderline patients in order to hold omnipotent
control over their objects and to avoid the psychic suffering caused
by separation.

TREATMENT CONSIDERATIONS

Before bringing this paper to a close, I would like to make some
remarks concerning technical aspects of the psychoanalytic treatment of borderline patients. I have been so far quite disinclined to
depart from the psychoanalytic procedures customarily used with
neurotic patients. I try to oppose the patient's efforts to make me
quit the analytic position of neutrality, and I refrain from resorting
to reassurance or noninterpretive interventions. I try to interpret
systematically those fantasies connected with the transference link,
particularly negative transference and the manifestations of
transference psychosis. I pay special attention to the functioning of
pathological projective identification, keeping closely in sight my
countertransference reactions, and, above all, projective counteridentification as it specifically results from the patient's projections.
Even when confronted with episodes of acting out, which are at
times markedly intense and quite difficult to deal with, my technical
approach remains the same.

It is not easy for me to assess yet whether my approach to the problems posed by borderline patients is the best, or whether it would be advisable — as suggested by other authors — to use parameters not belonging to the classical psychoanalytic technique. To put it more broadly: Is our analytic instrument less effective than we think and, as a result, are we supposed to widen its possibilities and compensate for its limitations by incorporating additional parameters? Or does the problem really lie in ourselves, in that we have not yet learned to employ the analytic instrument in all its potentialities and make the most of it?

I personally agree with the view, advanced some time ago by Stone (1957), that further progress in psychoanalysis is likely to emerge, not only from new ideas and discoveries inherent to psychoanalysis proper, but also from an interchange of ideas with other scientific disciplines. Contributions from such an exchange must not be mistaken for contamination or a threat to our analytic identity. As I pointed out on a previous occasion (Grinberg, 1969), we should find a way to bring to light the still unexplored wealth of psychoanalysis and oppose both dogmatic attitudes or biased rejection of new ideas, on the one hand, and the tendency toward excessive superficiality and dilution of technique or theory, on the other.

REFERENCES

Bick, E. (1968), The experience of the skin in early object-relations. *Internat. J. Psycho-Anal.*, 49:484-486.

Bion, W. R. (1957), Differentiation of the psychotic from the nonpsychotic personalities. *Internat. J. Psycho-Anal.*, 38:266-275.

_____ (1959), Attacks on linking. *Internat. J. Psycho-Anal.*, 40:308-315.

_____ (1962), *Learning from Experience*. New York: Basic Books.

_____ (1963), *Elements of Psychoanalysis*. New York: Basic Books.

Bleger, J. (1967), *Simbiosis y ambigüeded. Estudio psicoanalítico*. Buenos Aires: Paidos.

Deutsch, H. (1942), Some forms of emotional disturbance and their relationship to schizophrenia. *Psychoanal. Quart.*, 11:301-321.

Fairbairn, W. R. D. (1954), Schizoid factors in the personality. In: *An Object-Relations Theory of the Personality*. New York: Basic Books, pp. 3-27.

Freud, S. (1921), Group psychology and the analysis of the ego. *Standard Edition*, 18:69-143. London: Hogarth Press, 1955.

_____ (1927), Fetishism. *Standard Edition*, 21:152-157. London: Hogarth Press, 1961.

Frosch, J. (1964), The psychotic character: Clinical psychiatric consideration. *Psychiat. Quart.*, 38:81-96.

Gear, M. D., & Liendo, E. C. (1974), *Semiologia Psichoanalítica*. Buenos Aires: Nueva Vision.

Green, A. (1975), The analyst symbolization and absence in the analytic setting (on changes in analytic practice and analytic experience). *Internat. J. Psycho-Anal.*, 56:1-22.

Grinberg, L. (1962), On a specific aspect of countertransference due to the patient's projective identification. *Internat. J. Psycho-Anal.*, 43:436-440.

_____ (1963), Psicopatología de la identificación y contraidentificación proyectivas y de la contratransferencia. *Rev. Psicoanál.*, 20:112-123.

_____ (1964), Two ﹐inds of guilt—their relations to normal and pathological aspects of mourning. *Internat. J. Psycho-Anal.*, 45:366-372.

_____ (1966), The relationship between obsessive mechanisms and a state of self disturbance: Depersonalization. *Internat. J. Psycho-Anal.*, 47:177-183.

_____ (1968), On acting out and its role in the psychoanalytic process. *Internat. J. Psycho-Anal.*, 49:171-178.

_____ (1969), New ideas: Conflict and evolution. *Internat. J. Psycho-Anal.*, 50: 517-528.

_____ (1970), The problems of supervision in psychoanalytic education. *Internat. J. Psycho-Anal.*, 51:371-383.

_____ et al. (1967), Función del soñar y clasificación clinica de los sueños en al proceso analitico. *Rev. Psicoanál.*, 24:749-789.

Grinker, R. R., Sr., Werble, B., & Drye, R. C. (1968), *The Borderline Syndrome*. New York: Basic Books.

Kernberg, O. F. (1967), Borderline personality organization. *J. Amer. Psychoanal. Assn.*, 15:641-685.

_____ (1975), *Borderline Conditions and Pathological Narcissism*. New York: Jason Aronson.

Khan, M. M. R. (1960), Clinical aspects of the schizoid personality: Affects and techniques. *Internat. J. Psycho-Anal.*, 41:430-437.

Klein, M. (1948), *Contributions to Psycho-Analysis, 1921-1945*. London: Hogarth Press.

Knight, R. P. (1953), Borderline states. *Bull. Menninger Clinic,* 17:1-12.

Mahler, M. S. (1958), Autism and symbiosis, two extreme disturbances in identity. *Internat. J. Psycho-Anal.*, 39:77-83.

_____ (1971), A study of the separation-individuation process. And its possible application to borderline phenomena in the psychoanalytic situation. *The Psychoanalytic Study of the Child,* 26:403-424. New York: Quadrangle.

_____ (1972), On the first three subphases of the separation-individuation process. *Internat. J. Psycho-Anal.*, 53:333-338.

Masterson, J. F., & Rinsley, D. B. (1975), The borderline syndrome: The role of the mother in the genesis and psychic structure of the borderline personality. *Internat. J. Psycho-Anal.*, 56:163-177.

Meltzer, D. (1975), Dimensionality as a parameter of mental functioning: Its relation to narcissistic organization. In: *Explorations in Autism*, D. Meltzer et al. London: Clunie Press.

Racker, H. (1957), The meanings and uses of countertransference. *Psychoanal. Quart.*, 26:303-357.

Rosenfeld, H. A. (1964), On the psychopathology of narcissism: A clinical approach. *Internat. J. Psycho-Anal.*, 45:332-337.

Stern, A. (1938), Psychoanalytic investigation of and therapy in the borderline group of neuroses. *Psychoanal. Quart.*, 7:467-489.

Stone, L. (1975), Some problems and potentialities of present-day psychoanalysis. *Psychoanal. Quart.*, 44:331-370.

Winnicott, D. W. (1965), *Maturational Processes and the Facilitating Environment*. New York: International Universities Press.

Borderline or Prepsychotic Conditions in Childhood— A French Point of View

COLETTE CHILAND, M.D. and SERGE LEBOVICI, M.D.

TERMINOLOGICAL PROBLEMS

Let us begin with a few remarks on terminology. The psychiatric term borderline appears in French as *états-limites* or, literally, "borderline states." In our opinion, *états-limites* is an appropriate term for describing psychopathological organizations in children, where one is dealing not with fixed structures but with evolving processes of variable potential. The avoidance of the term borderline in French child psychiatry contrasts with the popularity of both the use of the English "borderline," and its translation *états-limites* in French general psychiatry. In fact, over the past few years, a considerable number of articles and books, including a recent issue of the *Nouvelle Revue de Psychanalyse* (Gallimard, 1974), have been published on the subject of borderline disorders. Despite the variety of terms used— *états-limites* (Bergeret, 1974a, 1974b), *psychose blanche* (Donnet and Green, 1973), and *psychose froide* (Kestemberg, Kestemberg, and Decobert, 1972)—these authors hold a position analogous to that of many authors in the United States, Kernberg (1975) in particular. According to this viewpoint, borderline disorders are not transitional states between neurosis and psychosis, but rather a specific psychopathological per-

Dr. Chiland is Professor of Psychology, University of Paris; Practicing Psychiatrist, Mental Health Association of 13th District, Paris, France.

Dr. Lebovici is Director, Alfred Binet Center, Paris; Faculty Member, Psychoanalytic Institute of Paris; President, International Psychoanalytic Association, Paris, France.

sonality organization which follows from its own characteristic pattern of evolution and which lies on the frontier between neurosis and psychosis, somewhere between psychosomatic and character disorders and psychopathic organizations.

The term generally used in France to refer to borderline disorders in childhood is *prépsychose*. It was introduced by Lebovici and Diatkine (1963), who adopted it from the American psychoanalytic literature, in particular an article by Katan (1950). This term, too, has its disadvantages — one of the most obvious being that it appears to refer to a stage chronologically preceding psychosis, whereas in fact it was chosen to indicate the unfolding of mental structures with comparatively varied developmental potential and distinct characteristics of their own, apart from psychosis. Generally speaking, the term was introduced by clinicians who believe that the traditional nosological approach fails to provide an adequate description in many child cases, and who maintain that individual modes of mental functioning should be described in each case separately, with their evolving potential being recognized as precisely as possible. The term *prénevrose* has been similarly used with regard to a different category of personality organization.

CLINICAL EXPRESSION OF CHILDHOOD BORDERLINE DISORDERS

At this point we wish to underline the seriousness of those childhood borderline disorders that, while leaving open a number of different modalities of evolution, exclude total normalization in the sense of *normativité*, that is, the availability of the widest range of possible adaptations to the vicissitudes of life by means of flexible restructuralizations. Leaving aside adolescent borderline disorders, we feel that two main forms of childhood borderline pathology can be distinguished — namely, borderline disorders during early childhood and during the latency period. Attention is drawn to the very young child by severe disturbances in his appearance and the initial development of his major ego functions. In the older child the diagnosis of borderline is reached by a more subtle study of the quality and particularities of the presenting symptoms and of the child's mental functioning.

In the case of the young borderline child, psychiatric advice is often sought because of the child's agitated irritability, which can

appear as a state of manic excitement. These are extremely turbulent children, who incessantly run about and touch everything,
often with considerable dexterity and apparently quite indefati-
gably. This euphoric agitation, however, belies poor emotional
contact with the parents and the examiner. It frequently emerges
that a pediatrician has already been consulted because of particularly intense and early sleeping difficulties, and often severe
anorexia as well.

At the other end of the continuum, some children arouse anxiety
by their inhibition, which cannot really be classified as infantile
autism, whether of the early type described by Leo Kanner (1943,
1944), or of the so-called secondary type. Still other children are
brought to the attention of a psychiatrist because of retarded
speech, which contrasts with normal psychomotor development.
Certain particularities and peculiarities of speech can be observed at
this stage (de Ajuriaguerra, Diatkine, and Kalmanson, 1958).

The great variety of circumstances under which these childhood
disturbances are brought to psychiatric consultation indicates the
contrasts between one case and another. Also striking are the
irregularities of the pattern of development in the same child, as is
well illustrated by the general acceptance of the concept of "developmental dysharmony"—that is, that mental functioning is
impaired in certain areas but not in its entirety.

In the latency period we again find forms of borderline
pathology corresponding to those just described, but with the
addition of a variety of modes of pathological organization. Both
excitability and inhibition stand out more sharply. During the
earlier period, it was the parents who complained most, as the nursery school was fairly tolerant of the individual peculiarities of each
child. With entry into elementary school, however, the constraints
imposed by discipline and learning requirements make these paradoxically behaved children quite noticeable. They are agitated,
jump up in class when they are supposed to be seated, talk at any
time without having been asked to do so. (These features have to be
underlined because French schools are less liberal and easy-going
than their American counterparts.) The teachers are struck by the
insensitivity of these children to rebukes, punishment, or any other
disciplinary measures. Inhibition is often misperceived as timidity,
but even so, teachers are surprised at the intensity of the child's

rejection of any attempt at communication and his refusal to carry out assigned tasks, which alternate with moments of explosive, even destructive rage. One particular form of inhibition consists of extra-familial mutism: the child talks when he is at home and his parents are quite unaware of the silence, often accompanied by immobilization, into which the child withdraws outside of the home environment. There is no loss of contact with reality as a whole, and learning performance can be high, either in all subjects or in some—a fact that often appears surprising when seen against the behavior we have just described.

At the age of latency, developmental dysharmony is no longer shown by the lack of development of a particular function, but by the different rates of development of various functions and by the contrast between intellectual development and relational modalities. In some cases this developmental dysharmony or more accurately, "dysharmony of evolution," takes the form of a dysphasia, with backward speech and poor performance on verbal intelligence scales standing out against good psychomotor aptitude and better results in performance tests. In other cases there is a form of dyspraxia—the child's clumsiness contrasting with his over-all intellectual development, with a gap of over twenty I.Q. points between the results on verbal and performance scales, in favor of the former.

The experienced child psychiatrist is sensitive to clinical subtleties that might easily escape the attention of teachers and parents—which explains how severely disturbed or even psychotic adults are often said to have been completely normal as children.

In conversation with the borderline child one frequently observes an affected style of expression, in which the labored elegance of words used may contrast sharply with poor sentence construction. Often words are used not for efficiency of communication, but for the narcissistic pleasure afforded by their manipulation. One can also point to the paradoxical aptitudes for mental arithmetic and calendar calculation shown by some children (Lebovici et al., 1966).

Other children present masturbation-equivalent stereotypies or tics with magical meanings, which people around them mistake for insignificant habits. Some borderline children are brought for consultation because of symptoms which might be diagnosed as neurotic, if it were not for their being abnormally compelling for the subject's age, their strangeness, and the coldly detached way the child talks about them, with the interlocutor himself feeling the whole burden of anxiety involved. Although phobias are quite common at this age (Chiland, 1971), the phobias of borderline children are characteristically bizarre, as, for example, the fear of the absence of noise in falling snow (Lebovici and Diatkine, 1963). Severe school phobias, giving rise to states of terror, also depart from the neurotic register and belong with borderline disorders.

Nowadays one meets more frequently than in the past cases with a psychopathic cast whose development along this line seems to be favored rather than corrected by the liberal character of our psychiatric institutions, residential centers, and day hospitals. Striking cases of cruel behavior, particularly in certain crimes committed by borderline children, led clinicians of the past to talk of "constitutional perversity."

One thing common to almost all borderline children is the deep reaction of the psychiatrist who examines them, and the strong countertransference when he attempts to treat them. Often he experiences the anxiety of the situation on behalf of the child, who appears to be devoid of any concern or feeling. In other cases the psychiatrist finds it impossible to identify with the child.

MENTAL FUNCTIONING

The various characteristics of mental functioning one is likely to detect in borderline children are not always present simultaneously—a phenomenon that is particular to the compartmentalized pathology of the borderline disorders as opposed to the psychoses proper. The expression of conflicts through fantasy products in drawing, conversation, or play is direct and undisguised. Expression of the Oedipus complex, in particular, far from being absent in such children, is immediate and unveiled, although its presence does not prevent pregenital mechanisms from dominating the picture, especially projective identification, as described by Melanie Klein. Neurotic defense mechanisms, on the other hand, are poorly developed.

Although we do not intend to discuss here the handling of borderline children in the family, we would like to point out the remarkable fact that what is made explicit in the children's fantasies or
revealed in the parents' attitudes and casual remarks during the
consultation tends to reproduce the crude expression of the Oedipus
complex, without the benefit of neurotic elaboration through repression, displacement, or symbolization. During one consultation,
for example, an eight-year-old boy, suffering from a severe school
phobia since the death of his father, seized his father's hat, which an
older brother was wearing, dented it, put it on his head, and said in
front of his mother, "Look what the tigress did to it."

In another case, that of a typical prepsychotic ten-year-old boy,
who was far behind in school despite a normal level of intelligence
and who showed effeminate behavior, the mother's first question to
the psychiatrist was whether she should keep her hair long because
her son liked it better that way. When the father arrived, he immediately asked the same question, declaring that his son preferred
women with long hair. The mother thus set herself up as a woman
who ought to be sexually pleasing to her son, and the father assigned
to her the role of a woman who had to be attractive to his son,
instead of confirming her as the child's mother and his own wife.

One of the most striking things experienced in interviewing a
borderline child is the extent to which his spontaneous productions
are dominated by primary-process thinking. The flow of representations and affects is extremely rapid, and links are only established by
contiguity, leaving a great deal of room for condensation. Words
are hypercathected, and the linking of representations is weak or
labile. The deficiency of the preconscious allows primitive
representations to pass directly into verbal expression and behavior.

Diagnosis of Borderline Disorders
or Prepsychosis in Childhood

A number of French psychiatrists (Misès, 1966; Misès and
Moniot, 1970) reject the diagnosis of prepsychosis, although they do
accept that of dysharmony of personality evolution. These authors
see no point in distinguishing a psychotic from a prepsychotic
structure in children; they believe in two diametrically opposed

lines, a neurotic versus a psychotic one, with no intermediary area at all.

This view, however, implies enlarging the concept of psychosis in children. Although for some time now no one has denied the nosological importance of either the Kanner-type early infantile autism, or secondary autism, what Lutz (1937, 1945) calls infantile schizophrenia, and although there is no longer any argument about the existence of deficit psychosis, there is still considerable doubt about a great number of cases such as those we have described. Should they or should they not be labeled as psychoses?

If one adopts strict criteria, the rate of child psychosis is rather low. A rate of only four in 10,000 was found when applying Creak's (1968) nine criteria[1] to a sample of 76,000 Middlesex children. If cases like the ones we described are taken into account, the rate becomes much higher; eight cases out of 66 children, or 12 per cent, in a random sample of the population studied in depth and followed longitudinally for fourteen years (Chiland, 1971). This rate checks out with our own consultation data. It seems, furthermore, that the prepsychosis rate is fairly equal in both boys and girls, whereas there is a much higher rate of psychosis in boys than in girls.

The rejection of the concept of prepsychosis is understandable in the case of psychiatrists who refer to a psychotic process in which forms of expression vary according to the child's maturation, but evolve inexorably along the same line. In contrast, adoption of the concept of prepsychosis assumes that there *is* a difference between the signs observed and the developmental potential.

In conclusion, there is good reason for considering as prepsychoses, rather than as psychoses, organizations where certain areas of functioning remain intact — where, for example, the development of intelligence is good and school performance follows a normal

---

[1] These criteria, cited by Tizard (1966), are as follows: (1) the child's inability, under all circumstances, to relate himself normally to people; (2) apparent unawareness of his personal identity; (3) preoccupation with objects; (4) sustained resistance to change; (5) abnormal response to sensory experience; (6) tendency to disintegrate into utter confusion; (7) frequency of speech disorders, ranging from mutism to repetitive and echolalic speech no longer functioning as communication; (8) motor disturbance not accompanied by clear-cut demonstrable signs; (9) isolated instances of fantastic prowess against a general background of low functional achievement.

course in spite of the presence of anxiety and the bizarreness of multiple symptoms, which indisputably fall outside the neurotic register. There is also good reason for considering as prepsychotic those children whose diagnosis fluctuates, at various times and with changing conditions of observation, between psychosis and neurosis or who, at least, present some organization other than psychosis.

DEVELOPMENTAL POTENTIALS

It cannot be denied that certain prepsychoses evolve toward confirmed psychoses, even into the most distressing and classic forms of psychosis. This is not always easily predictable. However, the fact that not all prepsychoses evolve in the direction of adult psychosis justifies the optimism that has given rise to the use of the term prepsychosis, rather than psychosis, in designating organizations where certain areas of functioning remain unimpaired.

It would in fact be difficult to apply the term psychosis to the case of a child who functions well enough not to have caught the attention of his teachers and not to have given any serious cause for anxiety to his parents. This is illustrated by an eleven-year-old boy, who was well-coordinated and intelligent, interested in sports, and who enjoyed skiing and horseback riding, but who suddenly made a suicide attempt. Psychiatric examination revealed a prepsychotic organization of a depressive type.

The most favorable evolution runs toward neurotization, obsessional neurosis, and, especially in males, certain phobic conditions. In some cases, while there is no establishment of a characteristic neurosis, a process known as "obsessionalism" develops; without any obsession properly speaking, contention mechanisms develop, which represent an attempt at complete and constant control over aggressive and libidinal excitations.

Between the two extremes of development—neurosis and psychosis—lies an entire range of pathological character structures: asymptomatic character neurosis; rigid, neurotic characters, who are poorly integrated and under constant threat of a breakdown; psychotic characters; bizarre characters; collectors of strange objects; or psychopathic characters with frequent episodes of acting-out behavior. Other cases evolve toward psychic impoverishment without intellectual deficiency, or toward a characteristic intellectual deficiency.

THERAPEUTIC TACTICS

Therapeutic action should be initiated as early as possible, but this is made difficult by the very nature of the disturbances involved. As these affect only certain areas of mental functioning, the child is brought for consultation at a late stage of pathological development.

The conception of therapy has evolved greatly over the last two or three decades, with the accent placed on the importance of full-time treatment which allows the child to continue with normal schooling and to receive intensive therapy outside of his school hours (as, for example, in the evening unit of intensive care of the Alfred Binet Center).

Therapeutic action should be an over-all and continuous undertaking, and not something fragmented or sporadic. It must include work with the parents in whatever way is appropriate to each individual case: parent groups, casework, individual psychotherapy, family therapy, etc. The quality of the support given to the child by his family is of fundamental importance in his development.

It may also be recommended that the child receive psychoanalytic treatment to complement institutional action, but psychoanalysis proper as the treatment of choice is prescribed only in very rare instances as, for example, in cases of exceptionally gifted children who are capable of maintaining themselves with success in the normal school environment.

It should be underlined that prognosis for borderline children is today much more favorable than it was twenty years ago, a fact that can be legitimately attributed to an improvement in therapeutic tactics.

BORDERLINE ADULTS AND THEIR CHILDHOOD

For a long time, knowledge about the childhood of adult patients was based only on parental anamnesis—which we know to be relatively unreliable—and reconstruction during psychoanalytic treatment. Only recently have observations on adult mental patients begun to be compared against data collected during childhood, in cases where patients were examined as children in medicopedagogical services that kept these examinations on file. Spoerry (1964) has demonstrated that schizophrenics in the canton of Geneva had not, in fact, been "mute" in their childhood, and that the disorder did not simply explode into existence in adulthood like a bolt from the blue. It would be helpful to have analogous data for borderline adults.

Catamnesic studies of disturbed children, properly diagnosed and, wherever possible, subjected to treatment, have been elaborated by Cahn (1962) and Robins (1966), who show that evolution was often far less unfavorable than feared. Severely disturbed children, who today would be labeled prepsychotic, did in fact become stabilized and achieved a relatively satisfactory social adaptation, even though on a level lower than their original sociocultural background and their intellectual potential predicted.

Conversely, catamnesic studies have shown that children who have undergone frequent changes of environment during their early childhood, or who have been through various traumatic events and life vicissitudes (illnesses, difficult circumstances) during that period, seem to recover during the latency period only to decompensate in adolescence or adulthood. This was the case with some of the children Chiland (1971) studied as six-year-olds and at twenty years of age. After the latency period, a surprising reduction of symptoms, and unexpected achievement in school, these children had a breakdown during adolescence with, for example, an attempt at suicide, or social maladaptation, delinquency, and imprisonment.

It also appears that childhood depressions, which have been the subject of intensive study over the past few years, may lead to borderline disorders in adulthood.

In conclusion, we would like to reiterate our belief that one can justifiably speak of prepsychosis or borderline disorders in children who present personality organizations with varying developmental potentials. It is furthermore our impression that, apart from problems of terminology and a certain tendency among American colleagues to invoke the notion of minimal brain dysfunction, there is in fact little fundamental difference between the French and American points of view regarding childhood borderline disorders.

REFERENCES

Ajuriaguerra, J. de, Diatkine, R., & Kalmanson, D. (1958), Les troubles du développement du langage au cours des états psychotiques précoces. *Psychiat. Enfant*, 2:1-65.

Bergeret, J. (1974a), *La Personnalité normale et pathologique*. Paris: Dunod.

—————— (1974b), *La Dépression et les états-limites*. Paris: Payot.

Cahn, P. (1962), Les structures psychopathologiques des enfants inadaptés. *Psychiat. Enfant*, 5:255-316.

Chiland, C. (1971), *L'Enfant de six ans et son avenir*. Paris: Presses Universitaires de France.

Creak, M. (1968), Psychosis in childhood. In: *Foundations of Child Psychiatry*, ed. E. Miller. New York: Pergamon.

Donnet, J. L., & Green, A. (1973), *L'Enfant du ca. Psychanalyse d'un entretien: Las psychose blanche*. Paris: Editions Minuit.

Gallimard, ed. (1974), Aux limites de l'analysable. *Nouvelle Revue Psychanal.*, 10.

Kanner, L. (1943), Autistic disturbances of affective contact. *Nervous Child*, 2: 217-250.

—————— (1944), Early infantile autism. *J. Pediatrics*, 25:211-217.

Katan, M. (1950), Structural aspects of a case of schizophrenia. *The Psychoanalytic Study of the Child*, 5:175-211. New York: International Universities Press.

Kernberg, O. F. (1975), *Borderline Conditions and Pathological Narcissism*. New York: Jason Aronson.

Kestemberg, E., Kestemberg, J., & Decobert, S. (1972), *La faim et le corps*. Paris: Presses Universitaires de France.

Lebovici, S., et al. (1966), A propos des observations de calculateurs de calendrier. *Psychiat. Enfant*, 9:341-396.

—————— & Diatkine, R. (1963), Essai d'approche de la notion de prépsychose en psychiatrie infantile. *Bull. Psychol.*, 17:20-23.

Lutz, J. (1937), Uber die Schizophrenie im Kindesalter. *Schweiz. Arch. Neurol. Psychiat.*, 39:375-372.

—————— (1945), Einige Bemerkungen zur Frage der kindlichen Schizophrenie. *Zeitschr. Kinder Psychiat.*, 2:161-166.

Misès, R. (1966), Le concept de psychose chez l'enfant. *L'Evolution Psychiat.*, 31: 741-766.

—————— & Moniot, M. (1970), Les psychoses de l'enfant. *Encyclopédie Médico-Chirurgicale, Psychiatrie*, 37299:M10-M30.

Robins, L. N. (1966), *Deviant Children Grown Up*. Baltimore: Williams & Wilkins.

Spoerry, J. (1964), Les manifestations prémorbides dans la schizophrénie. *Psychiat. Enfant*, 7:299-379.

Tizard, J. (1966), Mental subnormality and child psychiatry. *J. Child Psychol. Psychiat.*, 7:1-15.

III

EMPIRICAL STUDIES

> Ought we not to consider first
> whether that which we wish to
> learn and to teach is a simple or
> multiform thing, and if simple,
> then to enquire what power it has
> of acting or being acted upon in
> relation to other things, and if
> multiform, then to number the
> forms; and see first in the case
> of one of them, and then in the
> case of all of them, what is that
> power of acting or being acted
> upon which makes each and all of
> them to be what they are?
>
> —From *Phaedrus*, by Plato

Empiricism is the trademark of the behavioral scientist. Most of the contributions in this section are based on hard-core research rather than clinical experience or naturalistic observation. They deal with statistics and the problem from the outside, describing observable phenomena rather than making inferences on the basis of what individual patients say or their therapists experience in the treatment situation.

Grinker's article is an elaboration of his well-known position on the borderline syndrome, which he and his collaborators first worked out in their monograph of the same title ten years ago. He takes the opportunity to respond to some of his critics and to criticize, in turn, the findings and methods of others—in particular,

Kernberg. Paradoxically, when it comes to the conceptualization of the origins of borderline disorders, Grinker does not seem to differ much from his fellow analysts, including Kernberg.

Gunderson takes off from the position, elaborated in his previous articles, that borderline patients can be described in terms of five areas of functioning: social adaptation, impulse-action patterns, affects, psychotic symptoms, and interpersonal relations. His findings show that these particular areas have discriminating value in differentiating borderline from schizophrenic or neurotic patients, if not from both groups at once. Even though questions concerning the adequacy of his statistics make Gunderson cautious about his results, he believes that there is enough evidence to support the idea that borderline personality disorders is a noso-logical entity of its own.

Singer covers the field as assessed by psychological testing. She gives a comprehensive review of the literature, beginning with some crucial findings of Rapaport, Gill, and Schafer more than a genera-tion ago at the Menninger Clinic, and ending up with some recent studies, including her own, confirming "the clinical impression that a goodly segment of borderline persons have a series of cognitive and communication traits well worth exploring with the Rorschach and in conjunction with other measures."

In their well-designed, prospective study, Goldstein and Jones examine personal and familial antecedents of borderline pathology as manifested in presumably "high-risk" adolescent patients. Seen in an outpatient clinic, their subjects were followed up into early adulthood at five- and ten-year intervals. Data from only the first five years are presented here. The authors attempt to integrate their findings with respect to the severity of adolescent symptomatology and the parents' communication deviance into an etiological model.

Carpenter and his co-workers describe a five-year follow-up study of similar patients. It is of interest to note that all these investi-gators, with the exception of Grinker, form a network of collabo-rators who take advantage of each other's methodology, share their knowledge of the literature, and together seek to generate hypothe-ses for new research.

Finally, Wender reviews a series of adoption studies by Kety, Rosenthal, and himself, which claim not only to help separate the respective roles of nature and nurture insofar as the origin of borderline disorders is concerned, but also to provide a unique way of specifying their phenomenological characteristics. Wender, however, cautions that what he calls "borderline" may not coincide with what other researchers designate as such. Incidentally, like Searles in a later section, Wender speaks of "borderline schizophrenia." He suggests the possibility of dividing the borderline group into homogeneous and ideological meaningful subgroups and points out that it is only then that significant data may be obtained with regard to the pathogenesis, dynamics, prognosis, and treatment response in "borderline schizophrenics." He furthermore makes the intriguing speculation that there are three groups of borderline disorders: pure borderline schizophrenia, a mixture of borderline schizophrenia with sociopathy, and a mixture of borderline schizophrenia with affective illness.

The Borderline Syndrome:
A Phenomenological View

ROY R. GRINKER, SR., M.D.

During the last several decades, experienced psychiatrists have recognized changing styles in the form and content of both neuroses and psychoses. The histrionic behaviors of the psychoses seem to have decreased in frequency, although their characteristics are sufficiently constant to insure approximate diagnosis. This is not to say that all excited manics and catatonics have disappeared, or that hysterical conversion cases no longer show up in less-sophisticated pockets of our society.

The problem of changing styles in emotional disorders became the central theme of a symposium at a meeting of the American Psychiatric Association in which I was invited to participate (Schimel et al., 1973). In an attempt to pinpoint the sources of the change, I contributed a superficial run-down of the various parts of our psychiatric classification system and concluded with the statement: "But the how and why are all unknown" (Grinker, 1973, p. 152). This is especially true of the term borderline, which includes the concept of a personality or character deviance and a relation to schizophrenia, described under the rubric of some dozen terms— depending on the describing psychiatrist's geographic location.

ASSUMPTIONS, METHODOLOGY, AND FINDINGS LEADING TO A DESCRIPTION OF BORDERLINE SYNDROME

In 1959, in the belief that a study of the "borderline" entity might be fruitful in clarifying at least one of the contents of our

Director, Schizophrenia Research Program, Michael Reese Medical Center, Chicago, Illinois.

diagnostic wastebasket, several of us undertook a lengthy investigation, which resulted in a monograph entitled *The Borderline Syndrome* (Grinker, Werble, and Drye, 1968). A review of the literature revealed that several investigators had tackled the problem before us with confusing results, but, in general, they related the syndrome to latent schizophrenia or to the borderland between neuroses and psychoses. We could not trace the primary source of the term, although we were able to find seemingly relevant statements such as the following, published almost a century ago: "The borderland of insanity is occupied by many persons who pass their whole life near that line, sometimes on one side, sometimes on the other" (Hughes, 1884).

As we began our research work, we adopted the following guiding principles:

1. Behavior can be observed, described, and quantified.

2. Behavior assessed in terms of ego functions is an index of mentation that the psychotherapist does not typically observe; hence the study of such behavior adds to the knowledge of patients' assets and liabilities and capacities for adaptation.

3. Behavioral manifestations have validity in terms of estimating the quality and quantity of internal psychological functions.

4. A large-enough time sample of the behavior of an individual patient is an adequate index of his ego functions.

5. A finer analysis of ego functions in a large-enough sample of patients designated by a specified diagnostic term can result in a sharper definition of that specific syndrome.

In our search for a better definition of the borderline syndrome, we followed a research design comprised of observations, descriptions, statistical analyses, and interpretations in various stages. Observations of patients' behaviors were made by fifteen to twenty personnel serving them over 24 hours in a psychiatric ward. Descriptions were dictated to an outside interviewer to include the five major assumptions outlined above, for which 280 variables accompanied by a set of definitions were used. Each patient's protocol was then rated by independently trained raters, who reached a high level of reliability. Complex statistical analyses were performed by independent computer scientists using cluster, discriminate, and factor analyses. The results enabled us to identify the borderline syndrome and four subgroups, later tested on individual patients not in the original sample. Family studies revealed profound disturbances but no characteristic syndrome. Two follow-up studies were made after a period of years.

Our investigation led us to the following definition of the borderline syndrome: a prevalence of anger, a defect in affectionate relations, an absence of indications of self-identity, and the presence of depressive loneliness.

With such a gestalt or gamut of symptoms, we were able to describe various groups of borderline patients, representing different pathological positions. Group I patients fail in their relationships and, at the same time, overtly, in behavior and affect; they react negatively and angrily toward other people and to their environments. Subjects in Group II are inconsistent, moving toward others for relations, which is then followed by "acted-out" repulsion —moving away into isolation, where they feel lonely and depressed. This back-and-forth movement is characteristic of Group II patients and corresponds to the fact that they are both angry and depressed, but at different times. Patients in Group III seem to have given up their search for identity and try to defend themselves against their perception of the world as empty. They do not have the angry reactions characteristic of Group I patients. Instead, they passively await cues from others to behave in complementarity—feeling, thinking, or behaving in an "as-if" way, in a way others might expect of them. In no other group are defenses as clearly or as consistently observable as in Group III. Subjects in Group IV search for lost symbiotic relations with a mother figure, relations they rarely achieve (except for females who had an exceptionally supportive marriage). In consequence, they reveal what may be called an anaclitic depression.

In a cluster analysis, Groups I and III were shown to be relatively close together; Groups II and IV were likewise close. This makes clinical sense as patients in Groups I and III have given up the hope of establishing meaningful relationships, while those in Groups II and IV are still searching. Group I patients are angry at the world, and their ego integration is endangered by this strong affect. As a result of the overwhelming rage which destroys their weak ego controls, we would expect them often to become temporarily psychotic. Those in Group III have given up even their reactions to frustration. They are compliant, passive, and relate as others wish, successfully defending themselves against angry eruptions and aggressive behavior.

Group II includes patients who are buffeted by virtue of their own ego dysfunctions. In their attempt to relate to others, they become stimulated to anger, and then withdraw and suffer loneliness. Patients in Group IV, on the other hand, are characterized by abandonment of any but dependent, clinging relationships. And when the wish to engage in such relationships is not gratified, they develop the characteristics of an anaclitic depression, weeping and feeling neglected and sorry for themselves.

The four groups elicited from our statistical analysis, when translated into clinical syndromes, coincide with clinical experience. In general, Group I appears to be closest to the psychotic border and Group IV closest to the neurotic; Group II represents the core process of borderline patients, and Group III corresponds to those who are most adaptive, compliant, and lacking in identity (the "as-if" cases).

Our findings, as reviewed above, suggest that the borderline is a specific syndrome with a considerable degree of internal consistency and stability, and not a regressive state in response to some internal or external conditions of stress. It represents a syndrome characteristic of arrested development of ego functions. Clinicians have recognized that the borderline syndrome is a confusing combination of psychotic, neurotic, and character disturbances with many normal or healthy elements. Although such symptoms are unstable, the syndrome itself as a process is recognizably stable, giving rise to the paradoxical term "stable instability."

The onset of the disorder is difficult to ascertain but, assuming that it is a developmental defect, one would expect to observe manifestations of it in early childhood. This is exactly what has been reported by a series of writers (Ekstein and Wallerstein, 1954; Pavenstedt, 1964). Retrospective information about borderline adults is difficult to obtain, but careful probing often elicits indications of failure of affection for others early in life. Information from families is well-nigh impossible since most of them reveal a high degree of disturbance, which cannot be classified in any specific way.

In our monograph (Grinker, Werble, and Drye, 1968) we had intended to include data from psychiatric residents treating individual patients in our sample under supervision. The first interviews of these therapists revealed little in the way of understandable communications. In fact, what the therapists said often led us to believe that they were describing patients whom we had not seen. Our own study of six individual patients not in the main sample indicated clearly the difficulty in describing the dynamics of the borderline syndrome. Delving into unconscious processes can only be a guessing game accompanied by a vividly based imagination simply because these patients do not develop a transference, which corresponds to their inability to attain or maintain affectionate relationships. Therapists are "things" to be used.

If a transference neurosis does not develop with this kind of patient, how can analysts make such profound interpretations as they do based on material antedating the current problem by so many years? How can psychoanalysts like Kernberg develop the formulations he has recently summarized (1975) from several previous publications on an unknown number of patients? And how many borderline patients can any psychoanalyst endure over the years? I wonder.

We have found that the borderline patient is best treated by milieu or behavioral therapy in a hospital, with advice, direction, and control. Once in the hospital, borderline patients do not like to leave; and once they leave, they are likely to pick the wrong kind of employment. Attempts at insight therapy are hindered by the basic personality structure, which obstructs not only transference but object relations with therapists.

The negative aspects of the borderline can be ascertained by their subsequent course. Placement in jobs in an isolated situation may be conducive to stability. Unfortunately, many borderline patients are bright enough to be transferred to positions requiring social interactions, in which their social awkwardness is revealed and failure ensues.

CRITICISM AND CORROBORATIVE STUDIES

Several questions have been raised regarding the validity of our conclusion that the borderline syndrome is a nonschizophrenic developmental disorder. They are italicized in the following expository statements, which attempt to meet these criticisms by elaborating on our research process and follow-up results.

1. *The sample was not random and did not include psychotic patients.* Our subjects were chosen by an experienced psychiatrist from a population of patients in the Cook County Psychopathic Hospital, a detention institution for severe psychotic and behavioral disorders brought in by the police for court hearings. The patients were chosen on the basis that diagnosis was difficult and uncertain.

2. *Although our samples were not schizophrenic at the time of the study, they were pseudoneurotic schizophrenics (Hoch and Polatin, 1949) who would at a later time reveal their schizophrenia; 40 per cent would end in a state mental hospital.* Follow-up studies up to a five-year period did not agree with this criticism (Werble, 1970). Further follow-up studies could not be made because of the high attrition rate from the study. Later psychological tests on a sample of the total patient group (Gruenewald, 1970) did not disclose schizophrenic thought disorder.

3. *No control groups were utilized.* We had a built-in group of 135 healthy or normal males (Grinker, Grinker, and Timberlake, 1962) who were in the same age distribution at the time of study and who, in a follow-up study fourteen years later, showed no evidence of schizophrenic or borderline syndrome. At present our Schizophrenic Research Program studies consecutive admissions of young (18 to 28 years of age) first-break patients including schizophrenics, borderlines, depressives, and severe behavioral disorders. Our current investigations thus enable us to compare at least fifteen borderlines with schizophrenics and they can be sharply discriminated. Two profiles of our Schizophrenic State Inventory are included to show the difference. One is that of a young schizophrenic at the end of a psychotic break (Figure 1). Note the heavily weighted ratings above 4. The other is a young "as-if" type of borderline (Figure 2) showing the pleasurable states and the failure in maintaining stable identification.

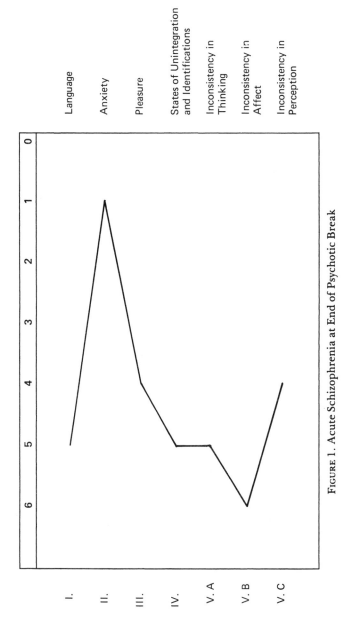

FIGURE 1. Acute Schizophrenia at End of Psychotic Break

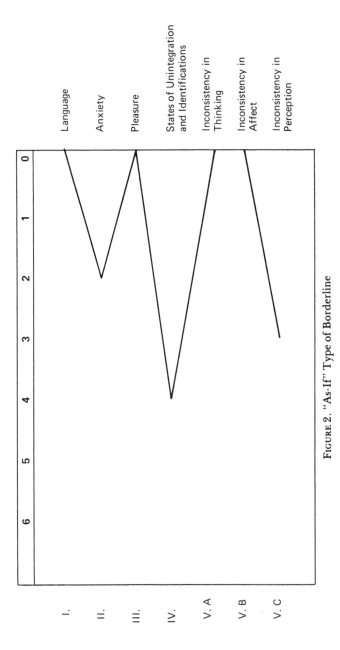

FIGURE 2. "As-If" Type of Borderline

The relation to schizophrenia, suggested by the fallacious term borderline, has been emphasized by some workers, beginning with Hoch and Polatin (1949). Let me state clearly that *there is no borderline schizophrenia.* One is or is not. There is, however, a borderline psychosis in that patients, under proper precipitating conditions, may be thrown into a temporary psychosis — what Frosch (1964) underlines in his description of "the psychotic character." This is the borderline syndrome. But what Hoch and Polatin (1949) describe is characterized by pan-anxiety, which does not appear in the borderline and has a 40 per cent occurrence of schizophrenia requiring state hospital commitment. Two successive follow-ups of our patients did not show such a development; but, as might be expected, we occasionally made the wrong diagnosis. Even later psychological tests failed to reveal a schizophrenic profile in our patients. We believe that the borderline is a *sui generis* condition and we hypothesize that it is a developmental defect, requiring precipitating circumstances from early childhood to late adulthood. It is specifically characterized by deficient self- and object constancy.

In a recent overview of the borderline, Gunderson and Singer (1975) found eight other terms that seem to be synonymous. The literature contains three types of descriptive reports: behavioral observations, psychodynamic formulations, and psychological tests. As these authors correctly point out, such results are determined by four variables: who does the describing, what methods are used in describing, in what context these methods are used, and how the sample is selected. From studying previous reports, they abstract the following six descriptive features: (1) intense affect, mainly anger; (2) impulsive behavior; (3) poor social adaptation; (4) brief psychotic episodes; (5) psychological tests revealing primitive personality organization; (6) interpersonal relations that are transient and marked by a high degree of dependency. Such conclusions are in general agreement with our own findings, including the observation that anxiety in borderline cases is not free or manifest but inferred, and depression has a lonely, affectless quality. But I would certainly disagree with their statement that psychodynamic formulations belong to the same category as descriptions, and I am wary of psychological tests since they contain a high degree of subjective bias in their interpretations. I do not contend that observations, descriptions, and statistical evaluations are free from subjective biases —only less so.

Critics of Gunderson and Singer's statements about the borderline point out that diagnosis should depend on outcome and not on some clinical pattern (Meza, 1975; Sidley, 1975). I believe that both are essential, in that outcome determines the validity of classification, but the latter is the first step. Meza (1975) questions whether anger is the only affect a borderline patient is capable of, which is what we found to be true for Group I patients. It is this anger that probably overwhelms the borderline individual, leading him at times to temporary psychosis. Loneliness and depression are often difficult to distinguish, but they are separate affects, both appearing in the borderline, depending on the subgroup and the ultimate degree of his social isolation.

Mack (1975) has edited a volume on what he refers to as "borderline states" in psychiatry. Clearly this term has been used to designate a vast wasteland of diagnoses and, although it encompasses many conditions, these are similar character types described in various languages and called by different names. All of them seem to share a developmental defect (biological, experiential, or both) associated with a defect in object relations in that internalized representations and reality are not fused but irreparably split into "good" and "bad."

THE PROBLEM WITH THE PSYCHOANALYTIC LITERATURE

Psychoanalysts and psychoanalytically oriented writers (Atkin, 1975; Kernberg, 1967; Mahler, 1971; Masterson and Rinsley, 1975) have offered "explanations" as to the derivation of the borderline syndrome. They postulate, for example, a constitutional excess of oral aggression, a deficient neutralization of aggression, a lack of anxiety tolerance with fixation at four to twelve months of age, and so on. They write of a defective ego synthesis, attributing it to a rewarding and withdrawing maternal object or to an inability to internalize the representation of the maternal object. Not one indicates how many patients were investigated, by what methods, with what controls, and how reliability and validation were studied.

As I have stated before, the era of the Freudian "Grand Theory" is over and individual cases are not sufficient to support new theory. Empirical research with all its difficulties is necessary to verify "explanations."

Let me quote Kernberg (1973) who has written prolifically on the subject of the borderline:

> . . . In patients with borderline character pathology and in the psychoses, there exists a lack of integration of the ego, lack of integration of the superego (with projection of personified superego nuclei), and an "infiltration" of ego functions with primitive instinctual derivatives. This infiltration derives from the predominance of a different set of defense mechanisms from those centering around repression in better integrated patients. At the level of borderline personality organization and in the psychoses, there is a predominance of splitting and other re-lated, primitive defensive operations (such as projection, projective identification, primitive idealization, denial, omnipo-tence, and devaluation), all of which have in common their defense of the psychic apparatus against conflict by mutual dissociation of contradictory, primitive ego states. Each of these mutually dissociated, primitive ego states reflects a primitive, internalized object-relationship, a basic unit of self- and object-image, and a corresponding primitive affect-disposition, rela-tively unintegrated and hence easily activated in the interperson-al field [p. 366].

As I read this excerpt, I cannot help thinking that its seemingly significant words and sentences would require years before any group of psychoanalysts could reach a consensus regarding their meaning. This is one of those statements about the "borderline" we read or hear about frequently these days; one that makes me feel as if the whole is less than the sum of its parts and not the other way around.

The bulk of published psychoanalytic reports are based on one or a few patients, for whom treatment represents the only method of observation. Conclusions are couched in the form of psychoanalytic interpretations. The raw data are skimpy, "metapsychological" theory is directly applied, and conclusions are inferences as to meanings rather than definitions of processes. Such reports are carried through the literature as "findings," monotonously confirmed in continuity.

To gain any credence for psychodynamic formulations the psychoanalyst needs to know the phenomenology of the condition under study as derived from empirical data from large numbers of cases statistically isolated from other conditions. The "what" or diagnosis includes and excludes by adequate clinical descriptions. By including multiple groups of phenomena in the syndrome, Kernberg's "what" is everything not included under depressions and schizophrenias; his "borderline" is not empirically recognized but is nevertheless imaginatively "explained."

Psychoanalytic theory designates the concept of ego as a border function filtering and controlling inner impulses and outer reality. This concept has become reified, described in quantitative terms as weak or strong, brittle or flexible, as are so many other psychoanalytic terms. Many functions have been attributed to the "ego," and its versatility in satisfying the psychoanalysts' needs for explanations is amazing. Yet logically, objectively, and according to behavioral scientists (Elkes, 1963; Kantor, 1963; Kaufer and Saslow, 1966; Skinner, 1957), what goes on internally, within the mental "black box," can only be determined by behaviors in action. Behavior represents functions allocated to the hypothetical ego. Behaviors are the final common pathway of psychic processes.

In recent years there have been several attempts to shift psychology from an overemphasis on the contents within the "black box" and internally derived "psychodynamics," to action models of communications and behavior (Fuqua, 1975; Schafer, 1975; Wittgenstein, 1953). Perhaps the modern approach in psychiatry, oriented toward systems or unified theories of human behavior, is best outlined by Ruesch (1967). The transition is difficult and has met many obstacles. If carried too far, it may extend beyond man's capacity to endure the dominance of our current computerized world. As my co-workers and I have stated:

> Operationally we may observe behaviors under various headings and subheadings and then utilize well-defined scales with which to rate them numerically. These headings correspond to the allocated functions of the ego translated into operational

terms. . . . it is sufficient to indicate the close connection between ego-functions and behaviors by referring to such large categories as *outward behavior* (to people, environment, and tasks), *perception* (awareness, differentiation, assessment), *messages* (verbal, nonverbal, reception), *affects and defenses* (relations with people, control of affect and behavior, defense mechanisms and situational mastery) and *synthesis* (integration, capacity to resist disintegration and to carry on usual life processes) [Grinker, Werble, and Drye, 1968, p. 34].

It is indeed about time that in the development of our primitive nosology we recognize the need for accurate descriptions of clinical typologies and address ourselves to the question of "what," so that we may attain a handle on etiology. At present, we can only generalize by stating that the neuroses are designated by their types of defense against anxiety, the psychoses by various defects in affect and cognition (acquired, constitutional, or both), and the character neuroses, including the borderlines (at least Group IV in our study), by developmental defects in ego function.

REFERENCES

Atkin, S. (1975), A borderline case: Ego synthesis and cognition: A reply to the discussion by Janice de Saussure. *Internat. J. Psycho-Anal.*, 56:221-223.

Ekstein, R., & Wallerstein, J. (1954), Observations on the psychology of borderline and psychotic children. *The Psychoanalytic Study of the Child*, 9:344-369. New York: International Universities Press.

Elkes, J. (1963), Subjective and objective observations in psychiatry. *The Harvey Lecture Series*, 58:63-92. New York: Academic Press.

Frosch, J. (1964), The psychotic character: Clinical psychiatric consideration. *Psychiat. Quart.*, 38:81-96.

Fuqua, P. (1975), Freud and Wittgenstein. (Unpublished.)

Grinker, R. R., Sr. (1973), Changing styles in psychoses and borderline states. *Amer. J. Psychiat.*, 130:151-152.

———— Grinker, R. R., Jr., & Timberlake, J. (1962), Mentally healthy young males (homoclites). *Arch. Gen. Psychiat.*, 6:405-453.

———— Werble, B., & Drye, R. C. (1968), *The Borderline Syndrome.* New York: Basic Books.

Gruenewald, D. (1970), A psychologist's view of the borderline syndrome. *Arch. Gen. Psychiat.*, 23:180-184.

Gunderson, J. G., & Singer, M. (1975), Defining borderline patients: An overview. *Amer. J. Psychiat.*, 132:1-10.

Hoch, P., & Polatin, P. (1949), Pseudoneurotic forms of schizophrenia. *Psychiat. Quart.*, 23:248-276.

Hughes, C. (1884), Borderline psychiatric records—pro-dromal symptoms of physical impairments. *Alienist & Neurol.*, 5:85-90.

Kantor, J. R. (1963), Behaviorism: Whose image? *Psychol. Record*, 13:499-512.

Kaufer, F. H., & Saslow, G. (1966), Behavior analyses. *Arch. Gen. Psychiat.*, 12:529-538.

Kernberg, O. F. (1967), Borderline personality organization. *J. Amer. Psychoanal. Assn.*, 15:641-685.

———— (1973), Psychoanalytic object-relations theory, group processes, and administration: Toward an integrative theory of hospital treatment. In: *The Annual of Psychoanalysis*, 1:363-388. New York: Quadrangle.

———— (1975), *Borderline Conditions and Pathological Narcissism*. New York: Jason Aronson.

Mack, J. E., ed. (1975), *Borderline States in Psychiatry*. New York: Grune & Stratton.

Mahler, M. S. (1971), A study of the separation-individuation process: And its possible application to borderline phenomena in the psychoanalytic situation. *The Psychoanalytic Study of the Child*, 26:403-424. New York: Quadrangle.

Masterson, J. F., & Rinsley, D. B. (1975), The borderline syndrome: The role of the mother in the genesis and psychic structure of the borderline personality. *Internat. J. Psycho-Anal.*, 56:163-177.

Meza, C. (1975), Anger in the borderline syndrome. *Amer. J. Psychiat.*, 132:875.

Pavenstedt, E. (1964), Environments that fail to support certain areas of early ego development. In: *Ego Development and Differentiation*. Des Plaines, Ill.: Forest Hospital.

Ruesch, J. (1967), Epilogue. In: *Toward a Unified Theory of Human Behavior*, 2nd Ed., ed. R. R. Grinker, Sr. New York: Basic Books, pp. 376-390.

Schafer, R. (1975), Psychoanalysis without psychodynamics. *Internat. J. Psycho-Anal.*, 56:41-56.

Schimel, J. R., et al. (1973), Changing styles in psychiatric syndromes: A symposium. *Amer. J. Psychiat.*, 130:146-155.

Sidley, N. T. (1975), What is the real test of a diagnostic category? *Amer. J. Psychiat.*, 132:876.

Skinner, B. F. (1957), *Verbal Behavior*. New York: Appleton-Century-Crofts.

Werble, B. (1970), Second follow-up study of borderline patients. *Arch. Gen. Psychiat.*, 23:3-7.

Wittgenstein, L. (1953), *Philosophical Investigations*. New York: Macmillan.

Characteristics of Borderlines

JOHN G. GUNDERSON, M.D.

This study systematically assesses the psychopathology of borderline patients in five areas of functioning: social adaptation, impulse-action patterns, affects, psychotic symptoms, and interpersonal relations. These areas were selected from a systematic review of the literature for clinical descriptive characteristics (Gunderson and Singer, 1975). The data are analyzed to determine whether the literature accurately describes borderline patients' characteristics and whether these characteristics have discriminant value when compared to patients of other diagnostic groups.

The long-standing diagnostic confusion over borderlines is due to many factors including the problems of defining enduring personality traits as pathological in the absence of specific symptoms and of overcoming strongly entrenched beliefs about a discontinuity between psychosis and neurosis. As Guze (1975) points out, the diagnostic confusion also arises from the paucity of systematic studies.

In a previous study we utilized an operational definition of borderline to sort out a sample largely given other diagnoses and then examined how this sample compared to a matched sample of schizophrenics on prognostic variables, symptoms, and two-year outcome (Gunderson, Carpenter, and Strauss, 1975). We (Carpenter, Gunderson, and Strauss, 1977) have now presented five-year-outcome data from this study. Although the study utilized reliable and systematically collected data, it did not assess many areas

Assistant Professor of Psychiatry, Harvard Medical School; Assistant Psychiatrist, McLean Hospital, Belmont, Massachusetts.

The author acknowledges the major contributions of Jonathan Kolb, M.D., and Rick Jentens, Research Assistant. This research was partly supported by NIMH contract PLD 10405-73.

considered important for diagnosing borderlines. Moreover, the method of selecting the sample made it difficult to generalize to borderlines clinically diagnosed as such. The other major effort to study borderlines systematically utilized a sample clinically diagnosed as borderline but did not use a structured means of data collection or involve comparison groups (Grinker, Werble, and Drye, 1968).

The current study attempts to build upon and compensate for some of the limitations of previous research by selecting a sample clinically diagnosed as "certain borderline," by utilizing a semi-structured interview which targets those areas of functioning considered most typical for borderlines, and by having both psychotic and neurotic comparison groups.

METHODS

All patients were screened and given "certain" clinical diagnoses by the admitting physicians at McLean Hospital between October 1973 and November 1975. Patients admitted to McLean represent a broad spectrum of social class with a wide geographical distribution. The sample, however, mainly consists of white middle-class people from the Boston metropolitan area.

General selection criteria for all patients included were: (1) hospitalized, (2) age 16 to 35, (3) independent clinical diagnosis considered "certain," and (4) no evidence of organicity (including effects of recurrent ECT).

Clinical diagnoses were made by a staff psychiatrist experienced in psychiatric evaluation in consultation with other members of the admitting unit team. Patients given a primary diagnosis of alcoholism or drug habituation, even if considered borderline, were not included. Patients were then interviewed within one week of the admission date by one of two research psychiatrists utilizing the Diagnostic Interview for Borderlines (DIB). This interview is designed to assess psychopathology in the five areas of functioning considered characteristic for borderlines: social adaptation, impulse-action patterns, affects, psychosis, and interpersonal relations. A description of this instrument and the satisfactory reliability obtained on it is reported elsewhere (Gunderson and Kolb, 1976). A further check on the diagnostic validity of the samples utilizes research diagnostic criteria developed for schizophrenia (Carpenter, Strauss, and Bartko, 1973) and primary depression (Feighner et al., 1972). Validity checks comparing these criteria with the clinical admitting diagnosis, the research interviewer's diagnosis, and a final diagnosis made after completing the clinical evaluations are reported elsewhere (Kolb and Gunderson, 1976). A recent report suggests the need for such validity checks on structured interview diagnoses (Carpenter et al., 1976).

To retain the clinical "feel" for the data, a one-way analysis of variance was employed for all items in the interview. Because this is a nonorthogonal method and because of the large number of variables (161) for the number of subjects (72), the results cannot be reported conclusively as findings. It is reassuring, however, that of the statistically significant t-test results an exceptionally large fraction were found at p values less than .01 (59 per cent) or less than .001 (32 per cent). Nevertheless, the only findings reported in detail here are those obtained from the summarizing statements in the interview. Each of the 29 statements describes a characteristic of borderlines relevant to one of the five sections—social adaptation, impulse-action patterns, affects, psychosis, and interpersonal relations. The scoring of these statements is based on a series of previous, more specific inquiries. These statements are thus synthesizing items with especially high reliability, minimizing the possibility that differences between groups could be due to chance. I shall also briefly report the scores derived by scaling the totals of each section.

RESULTS

The sample in each of the three groups was compared on demographic variables (see Table 1). No significant differences were found between the samples on age, sex, race, and marital status.

The following results are presented by sections. Characteristics of the borderline sample are described, followed by a comparison with the two comparison groups. The mean score for the borderline sample on each of the 29 statements and the comparisons with the control groups are summarized in Table 2.

TABLE 1
DEMOGRAPHIC VARIABLES

	N[a]	Age	Sex		Marital Status	
			M	F	Ever	Never
Borderline	31	23.7	9	22	11	20
Schizophrenic	22	23.7	8	14	4	18
Neurotic	11	25.5	4	7	2	9

[a] All subjects were white except one black who was in the borderline group.

SOCIAL ADAPTATION

The borderline patients are generally quite aware of social conventions—even if in defiance of them. Although past literature suggests that many borderlines are unusually attractive, appealing, or talented people, this impression is not confirmed here. The patients lead active social lives outside of their families and generally feel they get along well in social groups. Most of the borderlines were steadily but nonprogressively employed during the five years prior to admission. They do not indicate any particular capacity to work effectively despite personal distress or report that their work seems dependent upon structured situations.

This section contains some statements that clearly discriminate borderlines from each of the two groups but none that discriminates both groups (see Figure 1). The neurotic depressives are significantly more stable ($p = .002$) in their work history over the past two years and are more likely to have areas or periods of special achievement ($p = .01$). The schizophrenics are less likely to have an active social life involving groups of people ($p = .001$) and are judged more likely to appear inappropriate or nonconventional with their socioeconomic peers ($p = .011$) than the borderlines. In sum, the borderlines look socially more like the neurotics, but they behave vocationally more like the schizophrenics. The scaled total for this section is higher for the borderlines than the schizophrenics ($p < .001$).

TABLE 2
RESULTS

Section	Areas Assessed (statements)	Borderline (Mean score)	Schizophrenic (Comparison of means[a])	Neurotic
Social Adaptation	School/Work Achievement	.807	.594	.002
	Special Abilities/Talent	.677	.199	.010
	Social Activities	1.548	.001	.719
	Appearance/Manners	1.677	.011	.471
	Scaled section total	1.871	.000	.486
Impulse-Action Patterns	Self-mutilation	.710	.015	.024
	Manipulative Suicide[b]	2.226	.001	.020
	Drug Abuse	1.516	.000	.001
	Sexual Deviance	.839	.003	.286
	Antisocial	.613	.352	.565
	Scaled section total	1.484	.000	.002
Affects	Depression	1.613	.149	.422
	Hostility	1.516	.135	.131
	Demanding/Entitled	.936	.399	.336
	Dysphoria/Anhedonia	1.097	.124	.127
	Flat/Elated (−)[c]	.226	.000	.264
	Scaled section total	1.677	.000	.241
Psychosis	Derealization[b]	.355	.023	.567
	Depersonalization[b]	.871	.376	.346
	Depressive	.871	.181	.216
	Paranoid	.774	.097	.014
	Drug-induced	.387	.083	.336
	Hallucinations/Bizarre, Nihilistic, Grandiose Delusions (−)[c]	.290	.000	.379
	Mania/Widespread Delusions (−)[c]	.065	.000	.922
	Past-therapy Regressions	.871	.003	.004
	Scaled section total	1.194	.105	.012
Interpersonal Relations	Aloneness	1.452	.010	.525
	Isolation (−)[c]	.290	.000	.520
	Anaclitic	1.742	.006	.029
	Instability	1.200	.001	.020
	Devaluation/Manipulation	1.452	.000	.000
	Dependency/Masochism	1.581	.006	.060
	Past-therapy Relations	.774	.000	.018
	Scaled section total	1.774	.000	.005

[a] Probability of t-test results.
[b] These statements had a possible score range of 0-4; all others were 0-2.
[c] (−) refers to negative weight given statement if scored as present.

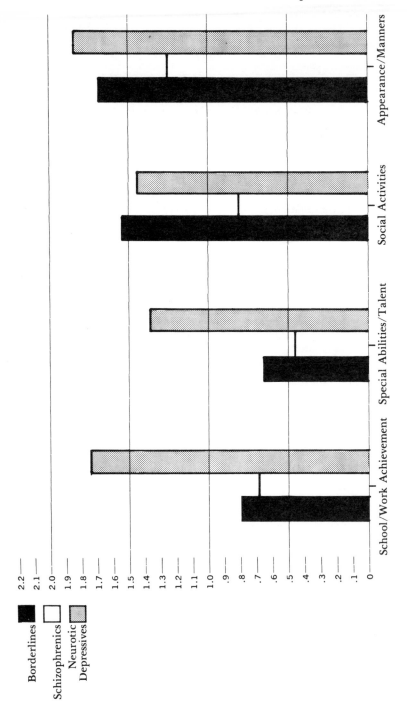

FIGURE 1. Social Adaptation

IMPULSE-ACTION PATTERNS

No single type of impulse or action pattern is so prevalent as to be considered characteristic. Yet virtually every borderline patient is involved in considerable acting out in a variety of ways within the areas inquired about, i.e., self-destructive acts, destructive acts toward others, antisocial behavior, and drug or alcohol abuse. Considerably more self-directed destructive behavior appears than that done or threatened to others. Borderlines frequently overdose, threaten suicide, and mutilate themselves (usually by slashing but also by head-banging and burning). Although many of the females report promiscuity, few borderlines report deviant sexual habits or preferences—in contrast to the emphasis on this in the literature.[1]

Figure 2 shows that a number of summary statements clearly discriminate the borderlines from *both* of the comparison groups. The borderlines are significantly more likely to report having slashed their wrists or otherwise mutilated themselves than either the depressives ($p = .024$) or schizophrenics ($p = .015$). The borderlines are judged to have made manipulative suicide threats or efforts more frequently than either depressives ($p = .02$) or schizophrenics ($p = .001$). "Manipulative" suicide threats are those judged to occur under circumstances where someone is likely to know about it and can be expected to make a preventative response. In fact, in this hospitalized sample, the borderlines often had made such suicide efforts repeatedly. The serious and repeated abuse of illicit drugs is far more common in the borderlines than either control group ($p < .001$). The sexual practices of the borderlines differ from those of the schizophrenics ($p = .003$) largely in their extensiveness. There is no significant difference between groups in terms of trouble with the law, assaultiveness, or other antisocial impulse-action patterns. The summation section score discriminates borderlines from both the schizophrenics ($p < .001$) and neurotics ($p = .002$).

AFFECTS

The borderlines frequently report depression, anger, and anxiety. In the interview itself, however, depression was much more

[1] The discrepancy may be due to the understandable reluctance of patients to provide reliable information about an area so confidential in the context of a research interview with a relative stranger.

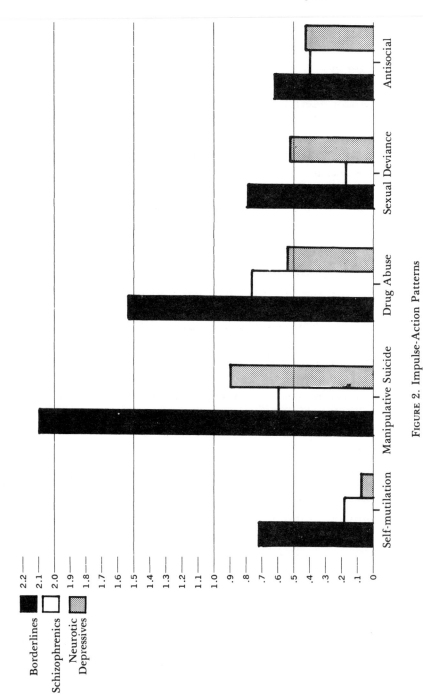

FIGURE 2. Impulse-Action Patterns

frequently observed than was hostility. Many seemed anxious and restless to the interviewer, but they were less likely to report this than either depression or anger.

The depression is accompanied by some crying and sleep disturbance but the vegetative signs of weight change, early morning awakening, or diurnal mood swings are the exception. Although the borderlines deny brooding over death, they do report frequently feeling life isn't worth living. No clear pattern emerges with respect to whether the depression relates to loneliness, loss, or guilt. Many patients have had previous episodes of depression, and they relate this to chronic feelings of loneliness or emptiness. Nevertheless, many recall some occasions when they felt satisfied or self-fulfilled.

The affect of anger is characteristically expressed in irritability or sarcasm but not by losing one's temper or being argumentative. A significant percentage report that their impatience or demand-ingness has created problems for them in the months prior to admission.

The summary statements are not particularly discriminating in this section (see Figure 3). The borderlines, for example, do not differ significantly from either the schizophrenics or neurotic depressives in reporting or appearing depressed, angry, sarcastic, or demanding. Nor do they give a different over-all impression with respect to chronic feelings of dysphoria or anhedonia. Only in the area of flat affect does a significant difference appear—as predicted the schizophrenics are much more likely to be flat ($p < .001$), as evidenced in both an expressionless face and absent emotion during the interview. Despite this flatness of observed affect, the schizo-phrenics often report significant depression and hostility. The section over-all scores discriminate the borderlines from the schizo-phrenics ($p < .001$) but not from the neurotics.

PSYCHOSIS

The survey of a wide variety of psychotic symptoms reveals that the borderlines do not have any continuous or severe psychotic ex-periences. Some of the borderlines report possible hallucinatory ex-periences of both auditory and visual types. These are unrelated to

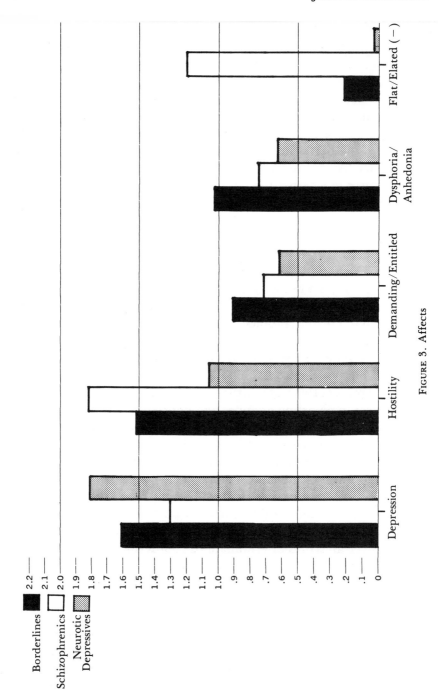

FIGURE 3. Affects

drug usage and prove difficult to evaluate clinically. Most commonly the borderlines report psychotic ideation in the depressed area —
namely, extended periods of feeling worthless or hopeless. It is rare
to find a more outright delusional depressive percept such as the
belief of having hurt someone or committed a crime. The only other
psychotic symptom reported with frequency is ideas of reference.
Many patients have had periods when they felt unduly suspicious of
others' intentions. They characteristically feel uncertain or uncomfortable about any psychotic experience. The interviewers generally
noted that the psychotic percept is at least not bizarre and totally
unfeasible. There are virtually no nihilistic or religious delusions,
delusions of thought-insertion, interference, or broadcasting, or
delusions of somatic passivity. Many borderline patients had been
hospitalized or treated in individual psychotherapy. As predicted,
they often report that these experiences made them worse. Contrary
to expectations, these patients rarely experience severe or continuous dissociative experiences of any kind. Depersonalization
experiences are somewhat more likely than derealization. The least
common dissociative experience is feeling things are changing size
or shape and the most common is feeling physically separated from
one's feelings.

Figure 4 shows that, in addition to their surprisingly low frequency, derealization experiences actually discriminate the schizophrenics, who experience them more frequently ($p = .023$). No significant differences are apparent for depersonalization. Nor does
any difference appear for psychotic depressive symptoms. The
borderline sample has more brief paranoid experiences than the
neurotic group ($p = .014$) but not than the schizophrenics. The
latter group, however, is much more likely to have widespread delusional beliefs in other areas ($p < .001$), which makes clinical discrimination quite easy. Although borderlines are slightly more likely
to report psychotic experiences from marijuana or alcohol or persisting psychotic symptoms after psychotomimetics, this occurs too
infrequently in these samples for any significant differences to
surface. As expected, the schizophrenic sample presents significantly more of those psychotic symptoms specifically felt to be
unlikely in borderlines, i.e., hallucinations, nihilistic and grandiose
delusions, and patently absurd or bizarre delusional content

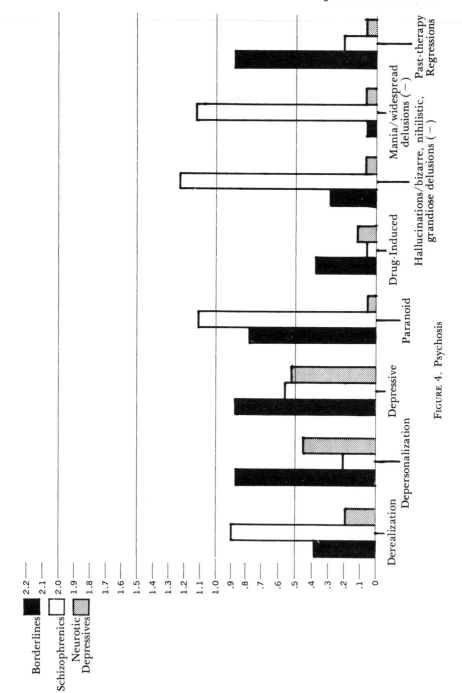

FIGURE 4. Psychosis

(p <.001). In hearing about past psychiatric contacts, the interviewers judged that the borderlines develop transient psychotic experiences within psychotherapy or have had a behavioral regression after hospitalization with much more frequency than either the schizophrenics ($p = .003$) or the neurotic depressives ($p = .004$). The section total score is significantly higher for the borderlines than for the neurotics ($p = .012$) but not than for the schizophrenics.

INTERPERSONAL RELATIONS

Borderlines associate with many people and spend most of their time in the presence of others. They feel a need to have people around and report being bothered when alone. They consider that they have close friends and manage to keep in touch with these people. Almost all of them tend to feel sorry for and make efforts to take care of others. Yet they decidedly do not like having others take care of them and find this uncomfortable when it occurs. This apparent paradox continues in their commonly describing having someone in their lives whom they feel they need but less often having someone who they feel needs them. They usually find it uncomfortable to live with their families of origin and yet they often long to be with their parents when they are away from home.

Their most intense current relationships are frequently troubled by breakups. Their relationships are strongly dependent, masochistic, and marked by devaluation and conscious manipulative efforts. The interviewers could frequently see similarities between these interactional patterns and those described in the patient's relation to one of his parents — usually the mother. The current interactions seem to serve a substitutive function.

During the research interviews, the borderlines are often quite suspicious and problems in rapport are common. Their past psychiatric hospitalizations often include a history of presenting special problems for the staff.

The summary statements *all* discriminate between one or both groups in this section (see Figure 5). The borderlines differ from schizophrenics both in their disinclination to and their difficulty in being alone ($p = .01$). The schizophrenics are more often judged to be socially isolated "loners" (p <.001). The borderlines seek

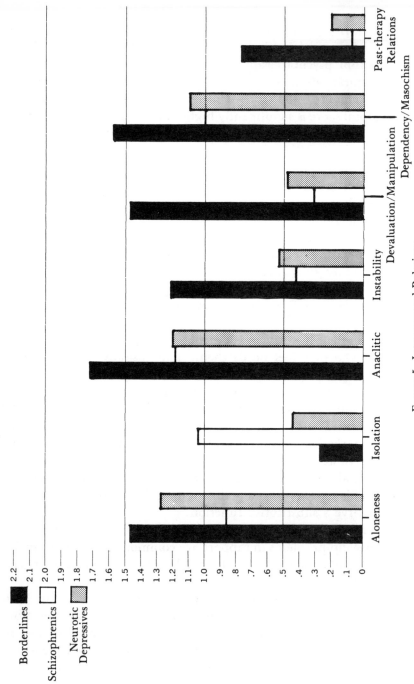

FIGURE 5. Interpersonal Relations

anaclitic relations in which they act as care givers, yet they are in active conflict about giving and receiving care. These patterns are less common for both the schizophrenics ($p = .006$) and the neurotics ($p = .029$). The quality of borderlines' close relationships are more intense and unstable than for either the schizophrenic ($p = .001$) or neurotic sample ($p = .02$). Problems with devaluation, manipulation, and hostility are so characteristic and discriminatory that they contrast with both comparison groups ($p < .001$). Problems with dependency and masochism are also highly characteristic but only differ significantly from the schizophrenic sample ($p = .006$). After reviewing past relations with therapy persons, the interviewers concluded that the borderline patients have almost always been involved in some problem with staff splitting, countertransference problems, or "special" relations to their past therapist ($p < .001$ with the schizophrenics, $p = .005$ with the neurotic depressives). This section is highly discriminatory over-all between borderlines and both schizophrenics ($p < .001$) and neurotics ($p = .005$).

COMPARISON WITH OTHER STUDIES

This study offers considerable confirmation for the results of our previous comparison between borderlines and schizophrenics (Gunderson, Carpenter, and Strauss, 1975). Given that the two studies clearly differ in selection criteria, age, and economic status of the two samples, the areas of agreement seem especially likely to be generalizable. Both studies agree on the similarities between borderlines and schizophrenics in their past work or school history, the different quality of their psychotic experiences, and the similar degree of depression. The past literature on borderlines seems to have overestimated their work or school achievements and skills. Moreover, I feel confident that the degree or type of depression will not help to discriminate between borderlines, neurotic depressives, and schizophrenics. With respect to dissociative experiences, the schizophrenic sample in both studies had more frequent derealization experiences than the borderlines. However, the frequency is considerably reduced for both samples in the present study and no differences in severity were measured. This discrepancy in frequency can be accounted for by the selection criteria and differing interview formats.[2]

The current study also affords some interesting contrasts with the previous study. The discriminating value of angry affect is not confirmed except as it is manifest in close relationships. Another area on which the two studies disagree concerns social function. The present study indicates that the consistently more active social histories of borderline patients (e.g., frequency of contacts, degree of group participation, active sexual lives, more intimate friendships, and the intense quality of their personal contacts) discriminates them in each instance from the schizophrenics. These results are more convincing both because of their impressive consistency and because the data were more extensively and carefully obtained in these areas. This finds some confirmation in our five-year follow-up on the earlier study, which grudgingly shows a better quality of social relations in the borderline sample than the schizophrenic (Carpenter, Gunderson, and Strauss, 1977). Because of the advantages in the methodology employed in the present study (cited earlier), the results reported here are more likely to be valid and generalizable to the range of people diagnosed as borderline. Thus, with respect to schizophrenia, I do not believe severe dissociative experiences are a particularly helpful differential diagnostic criterion, and, conversely, I propose that the degree and kind of social interaction and interpersonal relations can provide very helpful differential diagnostic clues indeed.

Grinker, Werble, and Drye (1968) specify four defining characteristics of borderlines: the predominance of anger as an affect, a type of depression based on loneliness, lack of coherent self-identity, and anaclitic dependent relationships. My results generally confirm their conclusions. The affect of anger and depressive loneliness were frequently found in our borderline sample, but these qualities offer no significant discrimination from either control group. Although the results do not bear directly on issues of identity, the clinical impression leaves little doubt about the validity of this observation.

[2] The first study was derived from patients specifically selected with a possible schizophrenic symptomatology in mind and more stringent criteria (actual perceptual changes) were required for a positive scoring on the DIB than on the Psychiatric Status Examination (PSE).

The clearly disturbed, anaclitic relationships noted by Grinker, Werble, and Drye are clearly evident and discriminate the borderlines from both the schizophrenic and neurotic control groups. In short, the results clarify the potential discriminatory power of three of their four characteristics. I have the impression that our sample contained fewer schizoid or as-if characters with their attendant social isolation than did Grinker, Werble, and Drye's sample (their Group III). Our patients were generally object hungry, and they also had more overt psychotic symptomatology and self-destructive behavior as we selected patients only after psychiatric hospitalization was considered necessary (like their Groups I and II). I believe our sample may be more restricted than that of Grinker, Werble, and Drye, which contained some patients who would not ordinarily be hospitalized.

It is more difficult to compare our sample with those employed by other investigators. Both Wender (1977) and Klein (1975) have approached borderline disorders by first utilizing a validating criterion and then locating a sample which is described secondarily. For Wender the validating criterion is a genetic predisposition in common with some schizophrenics. He and his co-workers have shown that a nonpsychotic group of people living outside the hospital share a common genetic predisposition with chronic schizophrenics. He notes that such patients have: (1) a chronic history of disturbed interpersonal relations, (2) anhedonia, and (3) a thought disturbance (irrelevancy or vagueness) which is more evident in unstructured interviews. Our results confirm the first characteristic but give more specificity as to the nature of the disturbance. Although most of our borderlines complained about varying degrees of chronic loneliness, emptiness, and dysphoria, these qualities were also common in both of the control populations. We have not reported data directly bearing on the issue of thought disorder. Within the semistructured interview, I have the clinical impression that our borderline patients became increasingly affective but not more cognitively disturbed over time and in the context of less structured questioning. I would judge that some fraction of our sample conform to Wender's characteristics but that most of them do not.

Klein (1975) attempts to discriminate borderline patients by utilizing drug responsivity as the validity criterion. There is a group similar to Grinker, Werble, and Drye's Group II which he believes is lithium-responsive. He also sorts out subgroups of borderlines similar to pseudoneurotic schizophrenics as responsive to anti-depressants. These drug responses, Klein believes, implicate an affective component of borderline "illness." I believe our sample includes such patients and, despite a clinical impression of over-all drug nonresponsiveness in borderlines, there is a need for more systematic studies. I especially have had very little experience with lithium in this group. Klein's other subgroups (the fickle, vain, manipulators, and the severely phobic) do not appear to resemble our patients. Clearly, more work integrating his observations would be beneficial.

DISCUSSION

The present study indicates that each of the five sections of the Diagnostic Interview for Borderlines can be utilized to discriminate borderlines from the comparison groups. Over-all, only eight of the 29 scored statements fail to reveal discriminating differences with at least one control group. In some instances this failure is attributable to the statements being too global in nature, while in others it may be attributable to the relatively infrequent occurrence of the behavior being characterized. Nineteen of the statements significantly discriminate the borderlines from the neurotics. Most unexpected is that nine statements discriminate the borderlines from both groups at once. While these results are encouraging, one should recall that the inquiries were directed only toward areas considered to be highly characteristic of borderlines. Hence the areas in which the discrepancies do *not* emerge are as interesting and occasionally surprising as those in which they do.

Until further efforts are made to study the intercorrelational relations among the items, it is not advisable to write off the possibility that other and different factors than those reported here will have discriminating power. Moreover, it's my impression that some of the most clinically useful and relevant results are in the more detailed inquiries which depend for statistical validity on these further data analyses. Further efforts can then be made to define criteria for a diagnostic form that is reliably and easily utilizable in psychiatric evaluation for borderline disorders.

The neurotics are clearly distinguishable from the borderlines despite the fact that any hospitalized sample of neurotic patients is bound to be considerably sicker than those found in outpatient practice. The areas which most clearly set them apart from the borderlines are the relative absence of: repetitive self-destructive behaviors and drug abuse, brief paranoid experiences, severe devaluation or manipulation in close relationships, and highly troubled past therapy experiences. They are most similar to the borderlines in the areas of social function and affects. The similarities of sign and symptom profiles between depressives and the earlier sample of borderlines (Carpenter, Gunderson, and Strauss, 1977) overlook those areas where clear distinction between neurotic depressives and borderlines occurs in the present study.

Generally, I feel the discriminating power of the interpersonal and action-pattern sections of the interview with respect to both comparison groups draws attention to how the more enduring, characterological traits have stronger diagnostic power than the relatively transient and multidetermined sign and symptom data popularly emphasized in diagnostic systems. In this sense, it is likely that the affects and psychoses sections are least likely to provide information predictive of future course.

In sum, the design and methods of this study intended to localize those characteristics of clinically diagnosed borderline patients which occur frequently and to test whether these characteristics could be used to differentiate borderlines from comparison groups of psychotic and neurotic patients. The fact that the results clearly indicate that such differentiation is possible argues for the survival of borderlines as a nosological entity. Further studies about etiology, course, and treatment responsiveness are needed to demonstrate whether these patients have other homogeneous and discriminating characteristics. We need to test whether the diagnosis of borderline as defined in this study is acceptably representative of how the diagnosis is used elsewhere. This seems likely both because of the widespread sources upon which the criteria were based and because borderlines I have interviewed from other institutions have scored very typically. If a reliable and acceptable means of defining hospitalized borderlines is thus available, clinicians can begin to examine whether the treatment preferences, psychodynamic concepts, and family characteristics attributed to borderlines have specificity or apply to subtypes.

REFERENCES

Carpenter, W. T., et al. (1976), Evaluating signs and symptoms: Comparisons of structured interview and clinical approaches. *Brit. J. Psychiat.,* 128:397-403.

———— Gunderson, J. G., & Strauss, J. S. (1977), Considerations of the border-line syndrome: A longitudinal comparative study of borderline and schizo-phrenic patients. *This Volume,* pp. 231-253.

———— Strauss, J. S., & Bartko, J. J. (1973), Flexible system for the diagnosis of schizophrenia: Report from the WHO International Pilot Study of Schizo-phrenia. *Science,* 182:1275-1278.

Feighner, J. P., Robins, E., Guze, S. B., et al. (1972), Diagnostic criteria for use in psychiatric research. *Arch. Gen. Psychiat.,* 26:57-63.

Grinker, R. R., Sr., Werble, B., & Drye, R. C. (1968), *The Borderline Syndrome.* New York: Basic Books.

Gunderson, J. G., Carpenter, W. T., & Strauss, J. S. (1975), Borderline and schizophrenic patients: A comparative study. *Amer. J. Psychiat.,* 132:1257-1264.

———— & Kolb, J. E. (1976), Diagnosing borderlines: A semi-structured inter-view. Presented at the 129th Annual Meeting of the American Psychiatric Association, Miami, Florida, May 8.

———— & Singer, M. T. (1975), Defining borderline patients: An overview. *Amer. J. Psychiat.,* 132: 1-10.

Guze, S. B. (1975), Differential diagnosis of the borderline personality syndrome. In: *Borderline States in Psychiatry,* ed. J. E. Mack. New York: Grune & Stratton, pp. 69-74.

Klein, D. F. (1975), Psychopharmacology and the borderline patient. In: *Borderline States in Psychiatry,* ed. J. E. Mack. New York: Grune & Stratton, pp. 75-91.

Kolb, J. E., & Gunderson, J. G. (1976), A validity check for the diagnostic interview for borderlines. (In preparation.)

Wender, P. H. (1977), The contribution of the adoption studies to an understand-ing of the phenomenology and etiology of the borderline schizophrenias. *This Volume,* pp. 255-269.

The Borderline Diagnosis and Psychological Tests: Review and Research

MARGARET THALER SINGER, PH.D.

The first section of this paper is a review and comment on the body of literature that describes the use of psychological tests to assess borderline persons. The second section presents a brief overview of a series of related studies conducted with colleagues. The studies focus upon issues involved in the assessment of the cognitive, affective, and communication styles of borderline persons, and the results are discussed in relation to issues in the literature.

REVIEW OF THE TEST LITERATURE

The psychological test literature devoted to the diagnosis of the borderline personality is much less extensive than the clinical literature (Gunderson and Singer, 1975). Yet it is at approximately the same level of development — primarily case reports and impressionistic descriptions. In contrast to the clinical literature, however, there is rather clear-cut agreement about test patterns of persons who should be diagnosed as borderline, namely, those persons who show ordinary reasoning and communication in highly structured test situations such as the Wechsler Adult Intelligence Scale (WAIS), but who on projective techniques such as the Rorschach, where structure is low, demonstrate flamboyantly deviant reasoning and thought processes. In fact, the projective test responses of most

---

Professor, University of Rochester, Rochester, New York; Lecturer, University of California at Berkeley and University of California at Los Angeles.

borderline persons are noted for being far more openly filled with "primary-process" associations and "schizophrenic" thinking than are the Rorschach records of most schizophrenics. If a rule evolves from the test literature on borderline persons, it is that when a person performs adequately and displays almost no deviant reasoning on the structured WAIS, but on the less structured Rorschach shows highly elaborated, idiosyncratic associative content and peculiar reasoning, then it is almost axiomatic that a borderline diagnosis should follow. Why such seeming agreement? A historical overview of the literature gives some explanation.

HISTORY OF THE BORDERLINE DIAGNOSIS

In tracing the history of the psychological test literature on the diagnosis of borderline, or its seeming equivalents — overideational preschizophrenia (Rapaport, Gill, and Schafer, 1945-1946), latent schizophrenia (Rorschach, 1942), schizophrenic character (Schafer, 1948), ambulatory schizophrenia, pseudoneurotic schizophrenia (Frank, 1970; Gunderson and Singer, 1975), pseudocharacterological schizophrenia (Stone and Dellis, 1960), subclinical schizophrenia (Peterson, 1954), narcissistic neurosis (Freud, 1917), and neuropsychosis (Myerson, 1936-1937) — the continuity of findings and opinions suggests that a number of the authors have detected similar cognitive problems among a group of persons variously labeled over time. Where unanimity occurs, the persons studied tend to be age sixteen to 40 years, upper middle class or high social status, with the younger ones in school and older ones having two to four years of college, some with professional training beyond college. On the whole these persons were seen by private psychiatrists (De Sluttitel and Sorribas, 1972; Fisher, 1955; Knight, 1953; Rapaport, Gill, and Schafer, 1945-1946). Yet some reports are based on Veterans Administration and state hospital patients (McCully, 1962; Mercer and Wright, 1950; Stone and Dellis, 1960), which suggests that high social class and educational status are not necessary criteria, but are probably artifacts related to where the earlier observations were made.

The research reports, however, are few. Most articles are impressionistic and merely add confirmatory ideas and examples to those of earlier seminal contributors (Rorschach, 1942; Rapaport, Gill, and Schafer, 1945-1946; Schafer, 1948, 1954). Such papers present useful descriptions of borderline persons and attempt to relate various personality theories to over-all impressions of tests. This seems a necessary stage preliminary to more stringent research. These clinical papers present a composite picture suggesting that even though there may be several subgroups of borderline persons, there is at least a core borderline group which can be detected from test features. This core group consists of those with flamboyant, peculiarly expressed, elaborate, odd associations to the Rorschach blots. These patients' Rorschach responses are more bizarre and unusual than those generally found among openly schizophrenic persons. Yet these borderline persons are purported to function adequately on the WAIS, showing little or none of the ideational deviances there which they display on the far less structured Rorschach procedure.

Fabulized Combinations and Circumstantiality

It might be well to discuss certain features noted on the Rorschach of the seemingly core group of borderline persons. Rorschach (1942) and Rapaport, Gill, and Schafer (1945-1946) use the terms fabulizing, combinatory, and confabulated thinking to label these persons' propensities to overspecify secondary elaborations of their associations and to combine and reason oddly. The borderlines' affective elaboration of ideas cannot be consensually validated by others, and their separate perceptions tend to become intermingled and related simply because the responses are close together in time or space. Borderline persons, as seen by testers, tend to add too much and too specific affect to simple perceptions. Other persons have trouble accepting the projected, unsupportable affective implications assigned to percepts, although they might accept the same basic idea the borderline person offers. In addition, the listener is unlikely to accept the frequent circumstantiality present in the borderline's reasoning which renders his logic unacceptable to a listener.

A second central point made in the psychological test literature is that as long as a verbal interchange with borderline persons is structured, either by social convention or by another person, the thought qualities described above do not appear. Those writing from a test standpoint also point out that these thought qualities are ego syntonic and do not bother the borderline person. He expresses his affectively toned and logically quaint notions without concern or embarrassment, whereas a person in an acute schizophrenic episode saying approximately the same things would probably indicate being bothered by the emergence of such thoughts and feel his thinking or perception had in some way changed.

Borderline persons function well on tasks where there is an obvious and stable structure to guide their thinking and communication. They appear to demonstrate their odd reasoning and peculiar notions only when the guiding structure in a transaction is minimal. The widely accepted meaning of this imputed pattern is that when another person or the rules of the transaction do not patently regulate the length and type of communication and do not constrain the borderline's communication, the odd thought processes erupt. When structure is high and guidelines continually present for directing discourse, the borderline is likely to limit his remarks to the tasks set by the other person or the job at hand. The WAIS, for example, is an interchange in which the tester controls both the topics and the length of responses. The tester asks specific, direct questions which have relatively right or wrong answers. As soon as a sufficient answer is given, the tester moves on to the next topic. This controls for the borderline person the length and general content of remarks and thus prevents loose drifting. In contrast, the Rorschach task administered by the same tester is a far less structured situation. Here the borderline person is left to his own devices, for the tester merely asks him what a blot resembles or looks like. The borderline must then structure his own performance. It is in such a situation with low external structure that the borderline person displays his inimitable ideational loosening, and his propensity to construct, combine, and elaborate on his associations emerges. Since the amount of external structure is so important to the borderline person, it behooves a tester to use several tests, especially the less structured Rorschach in combination with the more structured Wechsler, to assess the borderline person.

Varying Labels over Time

Before reviewing in more detail borderline thought quality as described in the test literature, it is well to trace the development of the concept of borderline in the test literature.

Herman Rorschach was the first to call attention to persons who seem to be functioning adequately (normal colleagues and patients with surface-level neurotic complaints) but whose responses to his inkblots resemble those given by schizophrenic patients. He believes schizophrenia appears in three forms: manifest, dormant, and latent. The latter term he applies to those persons with average surface behavior, but with test features in common with schizophrenics such as self-references, belief in the reality of the cards, scattered attention, variability in quality of ideas, absurd and abstract associations. Rorschach concludes that there is an "inadequacy of the test in estimating the quantitative importance of the findings" (1942, p. 121). He further comments that some of the tests he labels latent-schizophrenic productions came from persons who had schizophrenic parents and siblings. Some 40 years later Singer and Wynne (1966) and Wynne et al. (1977) report finding a large number of borderline persons among the parents of young schizophrenics. In addition, Lidz, Fleck, and Cornelison (1965) comment on similar persons found among the siblings of schizophrenic patients.

Rorschach (1942) gives a case example of a 45-year-old woman who had held a responsible job for many years. Clinically she suffered from "nervous exhaustion," but her disordered, bizarre responses to the inkblots surprised him. To him, her thinking indicated latent schizophrenia as she felt that the cards referred to her and were real pictures at times. Her ideas were scattered, variable, self-centered, and occasionally absurd and abstract. Rorschach emphasizes how much more floridly deviant her associations were than those of many manifestly schizophrenic persons. In passing, he adds that her father had been schizophrenic for years.

Rapaport, Gill, and Schafer (1945-1946) were the next to describe the test behavior of borderline persons. They use the term preschizophrenic, and divide 33 patients into two subgroups: seventeen overideational and sixteen coarctated preschizophrenics. Each patient was given seven tests, the Wechsler-Bellevue Intelligence Scale, the Babcock Mental Efficiency Test, the Sorting Test, the Hanfmann-Kasanin Block, the Rorschach, the TAT, and a Word-Association Test.

The overideational preschizophrenics are characterized by "an enormous wealth of fantasy, obsessive ideation, and preoccupation with themselves and their bodies" (Vol. 1, p. 21). Furthermore, they have unstable, fluctuating, odd mental contents and show "a relative lack of experiencing these ideas as 'ego alien' " (p. 22). The overideational preschizophrenics give many responses to the Rorschach, responding rapidly, often to space and unusual areas. They elaborate and extend their ideas. While giving nearly the average amount of popular, conventional content, this group's ideas on the whole are fairly original. Their most outstanding features, however, are their tendencies to append vivid affective elaborations to their ideas, to combine and relate associations, and to use language peculiarly.

In contrast, the coarctated preschizophrenics are a taciturn, ideationally constricted, slow-responding group who give few associations and rarely embroider on their ideas. They are characterized by "blocking, withdrawal, marked anxiety, feelings of strangeness, extreme inhibition of affect, and some kind of sexual preoccupation" (p. 21). They occasionally fail to respond, have less than average popular content, and neither give as original responses nor use language as oddly as do the overideational preschizophrenics. Their ideas seem to just not properly fit the blot shapes, being neither as idiosyncratic, affectively embroidered, nor couched in as odd terms as those of the other group. Their thoughts are merely off-beat, constricted, and dull. Whereas the overideational group produces garish, affectively toned ideas, oddly worded and laced together circumstantially, this group seems to slowly, dully, and inhibitedly just miss the point much of the time and seems off-beat only in their mistakes about what they are viewing.

Rapaport, Gill, and Schafer (1945-1946) summarize the results of these various tests from the two groups of preschizophrenics: In distinguishing preschizophrenics from other conditions, the examiner will "rely on a relatively well-preserved Bellevue Scale, with loose sortings on the Sorting Test, and typical Rorschach records, whether coarctated or dilated" (Vol. 2, p. 465). By typical Rorschach records they mean ones filled with peculiar verbalizations, but with no concern about the emergence and expression of such ideas. Note that Rapaport, Gill, and Schafer were the first to introduce the formulation of an intact performance on the WAIS combined with a pervasively odd Rorschach record. This has been used as an almost axiomatic diagnostic rule by later writers presenting single case studies or impressionistic formulations.

These 33 patients remain the largest and most extensively tested group of borderline persons reported in the literature. The two divergent thought styles, one expansive, one constricted, bear further consideration even though the constricted type does not again receive attention in the test literature on borderline persons or ambulatory schizophrenics.

Two years after the appearance of the Rapaport, Gill, and Schafer volumes, Schafer (1948) extended his own ideas about diagnosis based on his subsequent experience with the Menninger Clinic patients. He drops the term preschizophrenic and divides the sample into three groups: incipient schizophrenics, schizoid characters, and schizophrenic characters. The incipient schizophrenics are those patients in the previous study who later experienced acute psychotic breaks. The schizoid characters are those who are chronically withdrawn, superficially bland, unable to form or sustain attachments, and whose peculiarities of behavior or fantasy are neither pervasive nor dramatic.

Under schizophrenic character, Schafer classes only extremely schizoid persons whose schizophrenic mechanisms are integrated into their character makeup. He believes they are "neither going downhill rapidly nor already 'burned out'" (p. 87). Primary disorders of thinking and affect are evident upon clinical examination, but the classical secondary symptoms of hallucinations and delusions are absent. These schizophrenic characters, or as he terms them parenthetically, ambulatory schizophrenics (the term prominent in the clinical literature at the time), are not overwhelmed by schizophrenic symptoms but their "schizophrenic style of thinking is comfortably established and ... used blandly, indiscriminately, and with confidence" (p. 87). Their test results often indicate concomitant acting out or intellectualizing problems.

Schafer presents a case study based on a battery of tests to illustrate each of the three groups. The schizophrenic character casually accepts his own bizarre ideas, elaborates on them fantastically, and has fluid associations, memories, and reasoning. Besides these general qualities, there are a series of secondary features: self-references, intellectual pretentiousness, fabulizing, associative rather than directed reasoning, syncretistic ideas, clang associations, confabulations, defective reality testing, and absurd percepts. Often affect and symbolism connect ideas. Schafer also calls attention to adequate functioning on the Wechsler Intelligence Scale.

A series of impressionistic case reports and review papers follows. Each essentially reiterates and attests to what Rorschach, Rapaport, Gill, and Schafer noted earlier. First, Fisher (1955) describes ten "ambulatory schizophrenics" referred for testing by a private psychiatrist. The tests were accrued over a two-year period and were evaluated "blindly" by Fisher at the time of testing. He states it was extremely difficult to secure a larger sample who had been strictly diagnosed by both clinical and test criteria. Testing had been requested for these patients because clinically they seemed to lack genuine social warmth, communicated in tangential ways, and seemed "basically psychotic . . . [at] a 'distance' . . . [with] a 'lack of content' " (Fisher, 1955, p. 82).

Like his predecessors, Fisher emphasizes the bizarreness of many of the responses: " 'Two unborn mice attached to a human uterus and being helped to birth by gentle hands' "; "Two statues with a growth on their head and electricity passing between them"; " 'Two embryos with dwarf's heads being bitten by a mosquito' " (p. 83). Fisher concludes that the unique feature of these persons is their tolerance for and acceptance of the pathology present in their own thinking.

Stone and Dellis (1960) write that for a number of years they were puzzled over the lack of direct relation between the amount of pathology noted in the Rorschach protocols of "pseudoneurotic schizophrenics" and "pseudocharacterological schizophrenics" and their clinical status. Stone and Dellis confirm the impressions of earlier writers in their findings of dramatically schizophrenic features on the Rorschach and Draw-a-Person Test, with good performance on the Wechsler. On the Rorschach these patients give bizarre associations and confabulations in which the content assigned to several blot areas is laced together into a relation sheerly because the blot areas touch each other. The final product violates the laws of reasoning and reality. Clinically, however, these persons are neither manifest schizophrenics, nor grossly impaired intellectually or emotionally. Stone and Dellis's impression from their experience with over 200 schizophrenics is that a "levels" hypothesis, as they term it, is confirmed. That is, whenever thinking is bizarre on a "surface-level" test such as the Wechsler, it is also bizarre on the "depth-level" Rorschach. But the obverse can also be true: the "depth-level" Rorschach may be bizarre, while the "surface-level" Wechsler is free of pathological thinking. Stone and Dellis test this hypothesis using twenty hospitalized pseudoneurotic and pseudo-characterological schizophrenics and find that the extent of personality pathology predicted from the Wechslers is less than the extent of pathology predicted from the Rorschachs of these same patients by other raters.

De Sluttitel and Sorribas (1972) compare normals', borderlines', and creative artists' Rorschach records. They find the unpleasant content within the "fabulized combination" responses of the borderline persons distinguishes them from the creative combinatory responses of the artists who have positive content within such responses.

Wynne and I have reported the study of 25 borderline young adults among a group of 114 young adult persons who were studied extensively clinically and with various psychological tests (Wynne et al., 1977; Wynne and Singer, 1968). We have also studied the parents and siblings of the entire group of normal, borderline, and schizophrenic young adults. Each parent was given a clinical diagnosis independently of the psychological tests. An interesting finding is that among the parents of twenty nonremitting schizophrenics, 35 per cent had one parent who had been diagnosed as a borderline, and an additional 40 per cent had both parents diagnosed as borderline or psychotic. Among 24 remitting schizophrenics, only 21 per cent had one parent who had been diagnosed as borderline and none had parents with psychotic diagnoses. This study is of particular interest because there were clinical and test materials on all members of the families, and the clinical diagnoses were made without knowledge of test findings. Further studies are being made of the various test findings and their clinical correlates.

OVERVIEW OF THE LITERATURE

What conclusions can be drawn? Obviously over the years varying labels have been applied to the groups studied. In each instance the term schizophrenic is included by those writing from a test vantage point. These writers feel less hesitant than those writing from a purely clinical position about the schizophrenia-like thought qualities they see in the tests of these persons. It is easy, however, to see why these writers include the term schizophrenia. All of them note various attributes of schizophrenic thinking in open and flamboyant form in the tests of the borderline persons they describe. In reviewing the psychiatric literature, Gunderson and I (1975) conclude that almost everyone now agrees on using the term borderline, but they disagree on whether the term should be followed by the word patient, state, personality, schizophrenic, condition, or syndrome.

Taken together, what do the clinical and test literature indicate about borderline persons? First, there is not a single entity, but several subgroups, the number of subgroups depending upon the criteria used (e.g., clinical symptoms, interactional traits, or cognitive styles). Grinker, Werble, and Drye (1968), for example, find four subgroups, Millon (1969) three, and Rapaport, Gill, and Schafer (1945-1946) two. Knight (1953) refers to the borderline states. Those utilizing psychological tests are likely to favor analyzing cognitive- and relationship-style groupings. The two subgroups described as ideationally constricted and ideationally loose by Rapaport, Gill, and Schafer (1945-1946) thus need further study. For instance, attempts should be made to delineate the dimensions that make up the ideational constriction or expansiveness.

Second, psychologists have written more about the expansive than the constricted borderline. Clinicians are more likely to refer for testing those borderline persons who are verbally expressive and demonstrate touches of loose reasoning in interviews, than those who are more laconic. Thus, many of the impressionistic papers based upon patients referred for diagnostic testing report upon the more flamboyantly thought-disordered persons. Future efforts should be made to study through test research the reasoning and communication style of the less verbally productive borderline persons.

Third, it would be well to consider the purported absence of odd reasoning and combinative thinking on the more structured WAIS or the object-sorting test in contrast to that displayed on the less structured Rorschach. Since testers traditionally have been trained to secure relatively more verbatim Rorschach than WAIS responses (often drastically shortening what is recorded on the WAIS because the printed form encourages brevity), research should be based upon tape-recorded transcripts of both tests to insure that the issue of differences in structure is being studied and that differences are not merely the results of two different levels of adequacy of verbatim hand-recording of subjects' responses, as may have occurred in past impressionistic reports.

Fourth, borderline persons present features challenging any definition of psychological tests as simplistic thermometers or yardsticks for gauging the vague construct of "mental health." When some psychologists "discovered" what Rorschach said 50 years ago, and what clinicians have been saying for nearly a century — namely, that certain persons who function adequately in everyday life demonstrate in clinical interviews reasoning and language deviances which are often more dramatic and captivating than those seen in many nonacutely disturbed schizophrenics — those psychologists wanted to discard the Rorschach and other procedures because they were not direct measures of total behavior. Nowhere else in medicine is any one "test" expected to directly mirror total status. If anything, the Rorschach seems to confirm the clinical impressions that a goodly segment of borderline persons have a series of cognitive and communication traits well worth exploring with the Rorschach and in conjunction with other measures. Because of this, a group of us have been systematically studying some borderline adults, their parents and siblings. Our findings are presented below.

RESEARCH FINDINGS

This section briefly outlines selected findings from five studies in which Rorschach data were used to conceptualize certain cognitive, affective, and communication behaviors of borderline persons. These studies are presented in the sequence in which our progressive interest in the borderline personality features evolved.

First, in a study of 114 young adults along with their parents and siblings (Wynne and Singer, 1968; Wynne et al., 1977), it was found that a large portion of the parents of nonremitting schizophrenics had been diagnosed as borderline by clinicians. The young adult index persons were almost equally divided among five diagnostic groups: normal, neurotic, borderline, remitting and nonremitting schizophrenics. The nearly 500 persons who comprised these 114 families had been studied extensively clinically, as well as with various psychological tests. The clinical diagnoses were made without knowledge of test findings, and the test data were analyzed blind to the clinical diagnoses.

Table 1 presents a comparison of the parental diagnoses with that of the severity of illness of the index offspring in each family. The feature to which we wish to call attention is that of the role of the diagnosis of borderline-syndrome personality style among parents. Note that the horizontal axis is the parental diagnosis and the vertical axis the index offspring's diagnosis. It is the bottom right-hand corner of the table to which we wish to direct attention. Note that among the nonremitting schizophrenics, 35 per cent had *one* parent who had been diagnosed as borderline, and an additional 40 per cent had *both* parents diagnosed as borderline or psychotic. Among the remitting schizophrenics, only 21 per cent had one parent who had been diagnosed as borderline, and none had both parents with such diagnoses.

Certain features of the language and reasoning styles of those parents who themselves were classed as borderline or psychotic by clinicians can be inferred from Table 2. This table presents the means for the parents as pairs on a measure we term "communication deviances." These are the anomalies or deviances in conversations which distract and confuse a listener (Singer and Wynne, 1966; Singer, 1973, 1974, 1975, 1976; Singer and Larson, 1976a,

TABLE 1
PARENTAL DIAGNOSIS

Severity of Illness of Index Offspring	Both Parents Normal or Neurotic (Severity 1-3)	One Parent Normal or Neurotic, One Borderline or Psychotic	Both Parents Borderline or Psychotic (Severity 4-7)	N
Normal 1-2	19 (95%)	1 (5%)	0	20
Neurotic 3	23 (92%)	2 (8%)	0	25
Borderline 4	21 (84%)	4 (16%)	0	25
Remitting Schizophrenic 5	19 (79.2%)	5 (21%)	0	24
Nonremitting Schizophrenic 6-7	5 (25%)	7 (35%)	8 (40%)	20

1976b; Wynne et al., 1977; Wynne and Singer, 1968). Note the parents of borderlines clearly have more communication deviances than parents of normals or neurotics, but less as a couple than do the parents of either of the schizophrenic groups.

Figure 1 graphically portrays the data. The severity of illness of the young adult offspring is presented across the horizontal axis, while the vertical axis represents the communication-deviance scores for parental pairs for each group. The midline of each bar is the group mean and the length of the bar indicates one standard deviation above and below the mean. The dots are group medians. The parents of normals and neurotics are vividly distinguished from the parents of both remitting and nonremitting schizophrenics. The borderline young adults' parents form a group whose spread of scores overlaps those of the schizophrenic and nonschizophrenic parents' scores. Another way of summarizing these scores is to say

TABLE 2
COMMUNICATION-DEVIANCE SCORES OF PARENTAL PAIRS

Severity of Index Disorder	Parental Pairs N	Unadjusted Mean Deviance Score	Adjusted Mean Deviance Score and Standard Error
Normal	20	.54	.63± .14
Neurotic	25	.70	.83± .10
Borderline	25	1.35	1.38± .10
Remitting Schizophrenic	24	2.26	2.13± .11
Nonremitting Schizophrenic	20	2.50	2.37± .14

The parental-pair deviance score is the midpoint between the deviance (D/T) scores of the father and the mother in each pair. These pair scores were compared across diagnostic groups, classified by the severity of disorder of the index offspring in each family. In an analysis of covariance the effects of covariates on the parental-pair deviance scores has been taken into account. The covariates were: (1) family social class, Hollingshead Index of Social Position 15; (2) mean year of education for each parental pair; (3) mean severity of disorder for each parental pair on seven-point global mental health rating scale; (4) mean age of each parental pair; (5) mean total Rorschach work count of each pair. Analysis of covariance after adjusting covariates: $F_{(4/104)} = 25.51$.

that for this sample the normals and neurotics tend to have both parents with low communication-deviance scores while borderline young adults tend to have one parent with a high and one with a low communication-deviance score. With young adult schizophrenics both parents tend to have high scores. There is thus a progressive increase in mean scores for parental groups in relation to the increasing severity of illness of their index offspring. However, it is well to note the prominent role of the parents of borderline patients. Had the diagnosis of these borderline offspring been forced, as is often done, into either the schizophrenic or nonschizophrenic category of a twofold statistical table, some valuable distinctions would have been lost.

Callenbach (1973) has studied the affective implications and

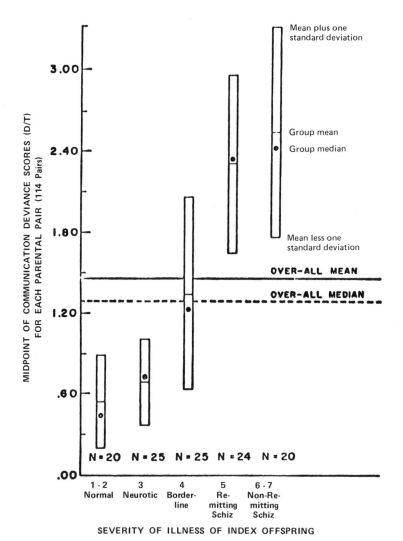

FIGURE 1. Parental Communication Deviances and
Severity of Illness of Index Offspring

elaborations of the Rorschach responses of these same groups. The
affective implications in each response were scored by two raters
using my modification of the De Vos system (Callenbach, 1973;
Singer, 1975). This scoring method classes each response as either
neutral or as having affective connotation. If the latter is deemed

present, any number from among 56 specific categories of affective connotations can be assigned a response. The 56 scores are classed under six large categories: hostile, anxious, body concern, dependent, positive, or miscellaneous affect. The sum of the hostile, anxious, and body-content categories is designated as the unpleasant content in the record.

To summarize a lengthy study, three major distinguishing features were found. The parents of borderline young adults, when compared with the four other groups of parents (parents of normals, neurotics, remitting and nonremitting schizophrenics), have more affective connotations tied to their Rorschach responses than all the other parent groups. Second, the parents of borderlines have the largest amount of "miscellaneous" affect implied within their responses. This category is assigned when content is obviously affect-laden, but the specific quality of feeling is not clear, as in the response: "an excited person, a woman yelling." Third, the parents of borderline patients have the greatest increase in affect scores from the first to the second viewing of the Rorschach cards. They are more inclined than other parents in this sample to append and imply affective connotations to their percepts, to elaborate associatively upon their ideas as they go along, and to leave the affect implications somewhat nonspecific but ever-present. The chaotic, difficult-to-classify behavior and affective states of these borderline young persons thus seem to reflect in part the affective intensity of their families. Inspection of their clinical histories suggests they collapse into brief episodes of delapidation following periods of stormy affective turmoil in their lives. The young index borderline patients themselves stand out from the other groups in the amount of hostile, anxious, and total unpleasant content they give in their responses.

Larson and I (Larson, 1973; Singer and Larson, 1976a, 1976b) next focused on the question of how best to study the articulation and integration of the borderline index patients' percepts. We wanted to follow up the leads cited earlier to see if it is possible to differentiate borderline persons' Rorschach records from those of remitting and nonremitting schizophrenics, in particular to study the reported tendencies toward unrealistic linking of ideas and circumstantial reasoning.

Again, to summarize a lengthy study, we found we could significantly discriminate borderlines, and remitting schizophrenics' from chronic young adult schizophrenics' records on thirteen of 30 items using the Developmental Level Scoring System (Goldfried, Stricker, and Weiner, 1971) plus a few selected formal scores. But we found the borderlines and the remitting schizophrenics difficult to differentiate on many items. However, as the literature has reported, the presence of fabulized combination responses is a highly significant marker of borderline persons' Rorschach records. Sixty-four per cent of the borderline group gave two or more fabulized combination responses, while only 33 and 20 per cent respectively of the remitting and nonremitting schizophrenics gave such content.

A further study of the components that make up the fabulized combinations is revealing. The remitting schizophrenics tend to combine more realistic, better-fitting percepts on the Rorschach than do the borderlines. That is, 61 per cent of the remitting schizophrenics, compared to only 36 per cent of the borderline patients, had fabulized combinations composed of all parts which were by Rorschach criteria appropriate, realistic percepts for the blot areas to which they were assigned. In their efforts to add structure to these ambiguous blots, borderline persons are more likely to circumstantially lace together rather poorly defined, unrealistic percepts than are the remitting schizophrenics. This appears to reflect the usual clinical impression that remitting schizophrenics, after their disordered episodes, often return to quite good levels of cognitive functioning and communication, while borderline persons are more likely to have islands of low-level, unrealistic ideas mixed among their thoughts on an enduring basis.

In another project, Smith (1975) found that borderline persons with obsessive traits did best, while borderline persons with hysteroid traits did least well in a therapy where the therapist prized emotional expressiveness during therapy.

Conclusions

From a review of both the clinical and the test literature on borderline personalities, and from the research just cited, the role of structure in transactions appears a central issue for the borderline person. Those associative, reasoning, and communication features said to be cognitive diagnostic features appear in the conversations of borderline persons during interactions when structure is low and another person or social role does not regulate and constrain the amount and kind of verbal responses indicated. Clinicians, even before Knight's (1953) well-received paper, were calling attention to those persons whose thinking seems to disperse in interviews when they are asked open-ended questions, or when prolonged, unguided periods occur in therapy. Grinker, Werble, and Drye (1968) also emphatically note the need for structure in the lives of borderline persons.

Further research using psychological tests of both structured and unstructured types in combination is indicated to continue to explore the associative and communication styles of borderline persons. There is a need to consider test behavior from subgroups of borderline persons. Less attention has been paid in the test litera-ture to the more constrained, less verbally flamboyant borderline persons and their cognitive and communication styles. Finally, the borderline person especially and clearly illustrates the need for careful, early clinical assessment in order to plan therapy ju-diciously.

REFERENCES

Callenbach, E. R. W. (1973), The affective characteristics of the parents of schizophrenics: A Rorschach study. Unpublished dissertation, University of California.

De Sluttitel, S. I., & Sorribas, E. (1972), The Rorschach test in a research on art-ists. (Unpublished.)

Fisher, S. (1955), Some observations suggested by the Rorschach test concerning the "ambulatory schizophrenic." *Psychiat. Quart. Suppl.*, 29:81-89.

Frank, G. H. (1970), On the nature of borderline psychopathology: A review. *J. Gen. Psychol.*, 83:61-77.

Freud, S. (1917), The common neurotic state. *Standard Edition*, 16:378-391. London: Hogarth Press, 1963.

Goldfried, M. R., Stricker, G., & Weiner, I. (1971), *Rorschach Handbook of Clinical Research Applications*. Englewood Cliffs, N.J.: Prentice-Hall.

Grinker, R. R., Sr., Werble, B., & Drye, R. C. (1968), *The Borderline Syndrome*. New York: Basic Books.

Gruenewald, D. (1970), A psychologist's view of the borderline syndrome. *Arch. Gen. Psychiat.*, 23:180-184.

Gunderson, J. G., & Singer, M. T. (1975), Defining borderline patients: An overview. *Amer. J. Psychiat.*, 132:1-10.

Knight, R. P. (1953), Borderline states. *Bull. Menninger Clinic*, 17:1-12.

Larson, D. (1973), The borderline syndrome in the Rorschach: A comparison with acute and chronic schizophrenics. Unpublished thesis, University of California.

Lidz, T., Fleck, S., & Cornelison, A. R. (1965), *Schizophrenia and the Family*. New York: International Universities Press.

McCully, R. S. (1962), Certain theoretical considerations in relation to borderline schizophrenia and the Rorschach. *J. Proj. Tech.*, 26:404-418.

Mercer, M., & Wright, S. C. (1950), Diagnostic testing in a case of latent schizophrenia. *J. Proj. Tech.*, 14:287-296.

Millon, T. (1969), Pathological personalities of moderate severity: Borderline patterns. In: *Modern Psychopathology*. Philadelphia: Saunders, Chapter 8.

Myerson, A. (1936-1937), Neuroses and psychoneuroses. *Amer. J. Psychiat.*, 93: 263-302.

Peterson, D. R. (1954), The diagnosis of sub-clinical schizophrenia. *J. Consult. Psychol.*, 18:198-199.

Rapaport, D., Gill, M. M., & Schafer, R. (1945-1946), *Diagnostic Psychological Testing*, 2 vols. Chicago: Year Book.

Rorschach, H. (1942), *Psychodiagnostics*. New York: Grune & Stratton.

Schafer, R. (1948), *The Clinical Application of Psychological Tests*. New York: International Universities Press.

—————— (1954), *Psychoanalytic Interpretation in Rorschach Testing*. New York: Grune & Stratton.

Singer, M. T. (1973), Scoring manual for communication deviances seen in individually administered Rorschachs. (Mimeographed.)

—————— (1974), Impact versus diagnosis: A new approach to the assessment techniques in family research and therapy. Presented at Family Process Meeting, Cumana, Venezuela.

—————— (1975), A revision of the DeVos affective inference scoring method for use with the Rorschach. (Mimeographed.)

—————— (1976), Stanley R. Dean Award Lecture. (Unpublished).

—————— & Larson, D. (1976a), The borderline syndrome in the Rorschach. A comparison with acute and chronic schizophrenics. (In preparation.)

—————— —————— (1976b), A Rorschach comparison of five groups: Normal, neurotics, borderline, remitting and nonremitting schizophrenics. (In preparation.)

—————— & Wynne, L. C. (1966), Principles for scoring communication defects and deviances in parents of schizophrenics: Rorschach and TAT scoring manuals. *Psychiatry*, 29:260-288.

Smith, A. C. (1975), Identity in transformation: A study of the Fischer-Hoffman process of psychotherapy. Unpublished dissertation, Wright Institute, Berkeley, Calif.

Stone, H. K., & Dellis, N. P. (1960), An exploratory investigation into the levels hypothesis. *J. Proj. Tech.*, 24:333-340.

Wynne, L. C., & Singer, M. T. (1968), Schizophrenics and their families: Recent research methods and findings. Mental Science Research Fund Lecture, London.

———— ———— Bartko, J. J., & Toohey, M. (1977), Schizophrenics and their families: Recent research on parental communication. In: *Developments in Psychiatric Research,* ed. J. M. Tanner. Sevenoakes, Kent: Hodder & Stoughton.

Adolescent and Familial Precursors of Borderline and Schizophrenic Conditions

MICHAEL J. GOLDSTEIN, PH.D.

and

JAMES E. JONES, PH.D.

A number of converging trends have focused attention on the developmental precursors of adult psychopathological conditions. As our methods for describing these conditions have grown more sophisticated, it is inevitable that we consider their natural history. This interest, however, is not purely theoretical, for a practical interest in prevention requires that we have effective means for identifying individuals at risk before the onset of the adult disorder in question. This has resulted in a surge of interest in prospective studies of the type which have come to be termed "high-risk research" (Garmezy and Streitman, 1974; Mednick and McNeil, 1968)—prospective studies of groups selected because they are believed to be at greater than normal risk for some particular psychopathological condition. Research on high-risk samples can serve two major functions: (1) to provide evidence regarding precursors of a psychopathological condition which can aid in early identification of groups at risk, and (2) to permit evaluation of

Dr. Goldstein is Professor of Psychology, University of California, Los Angeles, California.

Dr. Jones is Assistant Professor, Department of Psychiatry, University of Rochester School of Medicine and Dentistry, Rochester, New York.

The authors would like to express their deep appreciation to Eliot H. Rodnick, Co-Principal Investigator of the UCLA Family Project, and to Sigrid McPherson and Kathryn West who have been vital members of the project. Special thanks are due Margaret Thaler Singer for her generous assistance in the development of the Communication Disorder Index.

The research reported here was supported by NIMH Grant MH-08744.

etiological hypotheses which are difficult to test once the full-blown psychopathological condition is manifest.

In the present paper we present preliminary data from such a prospective study which relate to factors associated with the subsequent development of schizophrenia-spectrum disorders in which borderline cases were quite common. The data presented deal with adolescent behavioral patterns, and familial factors, associated with the subsequent development of schizophrenia and borderline disorders in early adulthood.

THE UCLA FAMILY PROJECT

The UCLA Family Project (Rodnick and Goldstein, 1974) was designed specifically to study intrafamilial relations in groups believed to vary in their degree of risk for subsequent schizophrenia and schizophrenia-like conditions. The subjects selected for study were nonpsychotic disturbed adolescents seen at an outpatient clinic for emotional difficulties. It was hoped that the level of disturbance, being moderate in nature, would not be as severe in its impact on the family system as that probably caused by a psychotic offspring. The basis for defining at least some of these adolescents as being at risk for schizophrenia was derived from the general hypothesis that adolescence is a critical period in personality adaptation and that failures at this point increase the probability of subsequent difficulties. The expectation that such a sample would contain a sufficient number of preschizophrenics is supported by the findings of Nameche, Waring, and Ricks (1964) and Robins (1966) who followed up comparable clinic populations. More specifically the design involved the contrast of disturbed adolescents believed at greater than normal risk for schizophrenia-type disorders, with other disturbed teenagers probably at risk for other adult problems, but not for schizophrenia.

We felt the critical issue at this point was whether families of preschizophrenics are distinctively different from families of other disturbed adolescent groups and not whether they can be differentiated from normal family groups. While normal families are important in such research, their introduction often involves issues of establishing comparability of motivation for participation in intensive studies of family relations. By working within the psycho-pathological spectrum one can assume equal motivation across groups in terms of anxiety over the adolescent, desire for help, and willingness to reveal intimate details of family life.

DEFINITION OF RISK

Defining risk in this project was an iterative process beginning with the manifest disturbance of the adolescent and including other variables as they became available. The initial task involved defining groups within the disturbed adolescent range (excluding psychotic adolescents). These groups were defined purely empirically from the presenting problems of the disturbed adolescents.

GROUP I. AGGRESSIVE-ANTISOCIAL

This group is characterized by poorly controlled, impulsive, acting-out behavior. Some degree of inner tension or subjective distress may be present, but it is clearly subordinate to the aggressive patterns which appear in many areas of functioning, i.e., family, school, peer relations, the law.

GROUP II. ACTIVE FAMILY CONFLICT

These adolescents are characterized by a defiant, disrespectful stance toward their parents and belligerence and antagonism in the family setting. They often exhibit signs of inner distress and turmoil, such as tension, anxiety, and somatic complaints. Few manifestations of aggression or rebelliousness appear outside of the family.

GROUP III. PASSIVE-NEGATIVE

These teenagers are characterized by negativism, sullenness, and indirect forms of hostility or defiance toward parents and other authorities. In contrast to Group II, overt defiance and temper outbursts are infrequent and there is a superficial compliance to adults' wishes. School difficulties are frequent, typically described as underachievement, although there is little evidence of disruptive behavior.

GROUP IV. WITHDRAWN-SOCIALLY ISOLATED

These adolescents are characterized by marked isolation, general uncommunicativeness, few, if any, friends, and excessive dependence on one or both parents. Gross fears or signs of marked anxiety and tension are often present. Much of their unstructured time is spent in solitary pursuits.

Subsequent to the definitions of the four groups, an attempt was made to establish working hypotheses concerning risk level from the literature on adult schizophrenia (Rodnick and Garmezy, 1957). This work suggests that the poor premorbid patient demonstrates an adolescent history of extreme social withdrawal and low involvement with the opposite sex. The parallel between the description of the poor premorbid pattern and the withdrawn, socially isolated teenager was close enough for the project to define this as a group with greater than normal risk for schizophrenia.

Other writers (Arieti, 1955; Nameche, Waring, and Ricks, 1964; Robins, 1966) suggest another preschizophrenic pattern among adolescents characterized by stormy, acting-out behavior confined largely to the family group. Their descriptions resemble the active family-conflict group in the UCLA sample and this group was therefore designated as a second high-risk group. These two groups, the active family-conflict and withdrawn, were tentatively defined as at greater than normal risk, while the other two groups, based on the literature, were not.

The definition of risk on the basis of the adolescent's presenting problem fulfilled a need for a preliminary indicator of risk. In order to establish continuity with the literature on adult schizophrenia, however, we felt that a criterion of risk derived from family studies of schizophrenics would be useful. The transactional-style-deviance concept of Singer and Wynne (1965), which has proven useful in discriminating parents of schizophrenics from other groups, appeared highly relevant for use with the UCLA-project families. Application of the Singer and Wynne measures to the data from the UCLA project permitted an estimate of risk for schizophrenia based on the degree to which parents manifested communication deviance of the type and frequency found by these investigators in parents of schizophrenics. The project was designed to obtain projective-test data, using the Thematic Apperception Test (TAT), on each member of the family. A scoring system for the TAT was developed by one of the authors, Jones et al. (1977), with the help of Singer. This assesses the communication deviance along the lines specified by the Singer and Wynne hypothesis. Using factor score patterns that have been found, on a blind basis, to discriminate parents of schizophrenics from those of other patients, Jones has established three categories of risk for schizophrenia — high, intermediate, and low — based on his findings regarding the probability of a schizophrenic diagnosis in the offspring.

A key aspect of our project is the follow-up of the index cases into early adulthood at five- and ten-year intervals to trace their subsequent histories of positive and negative adaptation. At the present time we are presenting data concerning the psychiatric status at five-year follow-up of 23 male index cases in relation to: (1) their behavior as teenagers (problem group and initial severity), and (2) the presence or absence of transactional-style deviance in their parents observed five years previously.

THE FIVE-YEAR-ASSESSMENT PROCEDURE

All cases seen initially were contacted five years later for a follow-up series. The series consisted of: (1) a private interview with the parents which focused upon the social adjustment of the offspring, (2) a separate interview with the young adult which covered many aspects of personality and social development as well as psychiatric symptomatology, (3) psychological testing of the young adult using the Minnesota Multiphasic Personality Inventory (MMPI), the Zulliger Test (a three-card, Rorschach-type test), a Word-Association Test, and two questionnaires filled out by the young adult which covered history of drug usage and sexual activities. All interviews and testing are tape-recorded.

Tapes of the interviews with the young adult were given to two psychologists (the authors), who were blind as to the prior history of the case and had never worked with the person or family as researchers or clinicians. Each psychologist reviewed a tape, abstracted the significant material on it, and attempted to summarize his findings using two diagnostic instruments: the Research Diagnostic Criteria (RDC) developed by Spitzer, Endicott, and Robins (1975), and the Borderline Evaluation Schedule, developed by Gunderson (1975). He then reviewed an abstract of the parental interview and the psychological-test protocol to determine if additional data might modify the diagnostic impression. No major diagnostic changes resulted from review of this supplemental material, but some small modifications did occur. Parents, for example, were more likely to report the full extent of acting-out behavior than was the target child himself. In one case this additional information made the diagnosis of antisocial personality definite instead of just probable. In each case a current diagnosis was assigned to reflect the present adjustment of the target child, and a past diagnosis was assigned to reflect the most severe psychopathology reported for the five-year interval since the family was seen in the project. Most of the analyses presented in this paper reflect the current-state diagnoses as they are based on the most comprehensive and directly observable behavior. The past diagnoses, however, will be contrasted with the current ones as an index of change in functioning from midadolescence to early adulthood.

After one psychologist had reviewed a tape, he presented an abstract of the material on it to the other psychologist who made an independent evaluation utilizing the same supplemental data. In all instances, both psychologists agreed on their major RDC and Borderline diagnoses. In a few instances the first listener reported difficulty in forming a clear diagnosis, and in these cases the second psychologist listened to the entire tape and made an independent evaluation. In all cases the second evaluation was close to the first, and a consensus of diagnostic impression was formed by discussion.

The final diagnoses were then used to assign subjects to a position on a seven-category system originally used by Wender, Rosenthal, and Kety (1968) in their adoption studies. The diagnoses assigned to each of the categories are presented in Table 1. It can be seen that definite borderlines were assigned to category 6, probable borderlines to category 5. In keeping with previous analyses of Wender, Rosenthal, and Kety, categories 5-7 are considered to cover the extended schizophrenia spectrum.

TABLE 1
SCALING OF DIAGNOSES

Categories	Definitions from Wender, Rosenthal, and Kety (1968)	RDC, Borderline, and Schizoid Diagnoses
1	Normal with no disorder traits	Not currently mentally ill: definite
2	Normal with minor psycho-neurotic traits	Not currently mentally ill: probable
3	Psychoneurosis or mild character neuroses	Drug abuse: probable Minor depressive disorder: definite Antisocial personality: probable No mental illness: probable with suggestions of psychotic-type experiences
4	Moderate to marked character neuroses	Drug abuse: definite Antisocial personality: definite Drug abuse plus antisocial personality: probable
5	Severe character neuroses, moderate to marked cyclo-thymic character, schizoid character, paranoid character	Drug abuse plus antisocial personality: definite Drug abuse: definite with secondary major depressive disorder Borderline: probable Schizoid personality: definite
6	Borderline schizophrenia, other functional psychoses	Borderline: definite Schizophrenia: probable Schizo-affective: probable Drug abuse: definite plus probable borderline
7	Schizophrenic psychosis	Schizo-affective: definite Schizophrenia: definite

RESULTS

The data presented here relate to two general issues. First, what relation exists between the form and severity of adolescent psychopathology and the incidence of borderline and schizophrenic symptomatology in early adulthood? Second, are parental attributes of the type identified by Wynne et al. (1977) in their analysis of parental communication disorders present prior to the onset of schizophrenia-spectrum disorders and are they predictive of those disorders?

ADOLESCENT PSYCHOPATHOLOGY AND EARLY ADULT DIAGNOSIS

Table 2 presents the relation between the behavior problem manifest in adolescence and the placement on the seven-point diagnostic scale for early adulthood. Because of the small number of cases, the data in Table 2 are collapsed into diagnostic categories 1-4 and 5-7, with the latter considered the extended schizophrenia spectrum. Here we see that one group, the passive-negative group, stands out in the small number of cases in the 5-7 category. They

TABLE 2
ADOLESCENT SYMPTOM GROUP AS A PREDICTOR

Symptom Group		Follow-up Current Diagnosis						
		1	2	3	4	5	6	7
I	Aggressive-Antisocial	0	0	1	1	1	1	0
II	Active Family Conflict	1	1	1	0	2	0	2
III	Passive-Negative	2	2	0	1	0	1	0
IV	Withdrawn-Isolated	1	0	1	0	2	2	0

Summary of Data

	1-4	5-7
I	2	2
II	3	4
III	5	1
IV	2	4

appear at low risk for schizophrenia and borderline disorders in early adulthood. It is difficult to see marked differences between the other three diagnostic groups, although there is a suggestion that Group 4 (withdrawn) adolescents appear more frequently in the extended schizophrenia spectrum and most commonly in the definite or probable borderline group. A pattern of withdrawal and severe isolation in adolescence appears to be one potential developmental route to borderline symptomatology as a young adult.

F. H. Jones (1974) has carried out blind ratings of the severity of psychopathology manifest in adolescence regardless of its formal nature. He uses a three-point scale with *3* representing extreme bizarre behavior.[1] In Table 3 we see the relation between the dichotomy $1 + 2$ vs. 3 on Jones's scale and the seven-category diagnostic assignment. In the summary of Table 3 we see that cases with

TABLE 3
SEVERITY OF INITIAL BEHAVIOR AS A PREDICTOR

	Follow-up Current Diagnosis						
	1	2	3	4	5	6	7
Initially Extreme and Bizarre Behavior	0	0	0	0	1	3	1
No Extreme Initial Behavior	4	3	3	2	4	1	0

Summary of Data

	1-4	5-7
Initially extreme and bizarre behavior	0	5
No extreme initial behavior	12	5

$p < .005$ (one-tailed)

[1] Jones (1974) defines extreme and bizarre behavior as including such things as extreme anxiety reactions in realms of everyday functioning, feelings of inadequacy

initial ratings of extreme and bizarre behavior uniformly fall into the schizophrenia spectrum ($p < .005$). A rating of less severity predicted a modal diagnosis outside the schizophrenia spectrum; however, it did not exclude the possibility that a minority of low-rated cases could appear there. The presence of extreme and bizarre behavior in adolescence is thus a positive predictor of subsequent borderline and schizophrenia diagnosis but does not represent the only developmental precursor of extended schizophrenia-spectrum disorders.

PARENTAL TRANSACTIONAL-STYLE DEVIANCE AND EARLY ADULT PSYCHOPATHOLOGY

Earlier we indicated that risk of schizophrenia can be derived from parental attributes related to clarity of communication. This procedure requires verbatim transcripts of projective-test data which were available in only sixteen of the 23 cases reported. Table 4 presents the relation between the risk for schizophrenia (high, intermediate, or low) based on parent TAT behavior and the early adult diagnosis. There was only one low-risk case in this sample; therefore the most meaningful contrast is between high-risk cases and combined low and intermediate cases. Table 4 indicates a strong association between this blind rating of parental communication style and diagnosis of their offspring in early adulthood. Parents who manifested transactional communication deviance of the sort reported by others to be present in parents of adult schizophrenics—the high-risk parent—do indeed show a marked prevalence of offspring who receive extended schizophrenia-spectrum diagnoses as young adults ($p < .03$, one-tailed). Note that the only two cases receiving level-7 diagnoses (definite schizophrenia or definite schizo-affective) are found in high-risk parental groups.

---

and worthlessness such that suicide is seriously or repeatedly contemplated, marked problems in heterosexual adjustment to the point of exhibiting bizarre sex-role behavior, or multiple problems signifying a gross deficit in maturity. Poor impulse control and acting out may also be classified in this category if they are extreme to the point of involving life-threatening behavior. Although these subjects may show areas of adequacy, these are overshadowed by serious problems of coping in other areas of sufficient magnitude to yield extreme or bizarre behavior.

When a comparison is made of past and current diagnoses, it can be seen from Table 5 that those target cases that appear to be

TABLE 4
PREDICTION WITH RISK BASED ON PARENTAL COMMUNICATION

	Follow-up Current Diagnosis						
	1	2	3	4	5	6	7
High Risk for Schizophrenia	1	0	1	0	3	1	2
Intermediate Risk for Schizophrenia	0	2	2	1	1	1	0
Low Risk for Schizophrenia	1	0	0	0	0	0	0

Summary of Data

	1-4	5-7
High Risk	2	6
Intermediate and Low Risk	6	2

$p = .03$ (one-tailed)

TABLE 5
IMPROVEMENT IN DIAGNOSIS

	Improvement in past to present diagnosis	No change in past to present diagnosis
High Risk for Schizophrenia	0	8
Intermediate-Low Risk for Schizophrenia	4	4

$p = .04$ (two-tailed)

on an improving developmental course all come from families free of severe communication deviance. The communication-deviance measure thus not only predicts borderline conditions or schizophrenia but indicates (at lower levels) latent strengths for growth in the adolescent and his family which may not be apparent during the adolescent turmoil.

PREDICTIVE VALUE OF THE COMBINED INDEX OF PROBLEM SEVERITY AND PARENTAL COMMUNICATION DISORDER

Since the severity and bizarreness of adolescent behavior and parental attributes both predict presence on the extended schizophrenia spectrum, it is natural to consider the relation between these two factors and whether a combined index would predict more effectively. In Table 6 we see that there is a relation between parental communication deviance and rated severity of adolescent behavior; all high severity cases fall in families with marked communication deviance. Not all high-communication-deviance cases, however, are rated as high in severity—the group seems evenly split on this factor. This relation permits the formation of three groups: (1) low-intermediate risk with no initial symptom severity, (2) high risk with no initial symptom severity, (3) high risk with severe initial symptoms. In Table 6 we see that cases with both indices uniformly in the pathological range are diagnosed as falling within the extended schizophrenia spectrum. When only parental communication deviance is present, the picture is mixed with two cases in the extended schizophrenia spectrum and two not. Finally, the absence of both attributes relates primarily, but not exclusively to mild and minimal symptomatology.

Interestingly, there are suggestions of an additional distinction between the two samples rated as high risk based on parental communication. Where both symptom severity and communication deviance are present, the early adult diagnoses are more extreme (6 [borderline and probable schizophrenia] or 7 [definite schizophrenia]), while the two cases in the group with parental communication deviance whose initial symptoms are not rated severe both received level-5 diagnoses. The combined attributes are thus not only more uniformly predictive of placement in the extended schizophrenia spectrum, but also predict diagnoses closer to traditional conceptions of schizophrenia. One instance which spoils the symmetry is an intermediate-risk case which fell in category 6 (probable schizophrenia); this suggests caution until more cases are considered.

Interestingly, if we look at the lower half of Table 6, the parental communication-deviance measure does predict improvement in symptomatology from the peak disturbance in adolescence

TABLE 6
RELATION BETWEEN SEVERITY OF INITIAL SYMPTOMS,
PARENTAL COMMUNICATION DISORDER, AND
EARLY ADULT DIAGNOSES AND IMPROVEMENT

Early Adult Diagnosis (Current State)

| | Group Combinations | |
	1-4	5-7
Parental communication deviance and marked initial severity	0	3[a]
Parental communication deviance without initial severity	2	2
Neither	6	2

Improvement (Past to Current Diagnosis)

	Some Improvement	No Change
Parental Communication deviance and marked initial severity	0	3
Parental communication deviance without initial severity	0	4
Neither	4	4

[a] It was not possible to rate initial severity for one case in this group.

to the current diagnostic picture. Here the severity factor tells us little, as it is only in the families lacking marked communication deviance that we see some positive signs of growth. This suggests that attributes such as severity of behavior and parental communication may be sensitive to somewhat different components of psychopathological development, the former to the ultimate severity and the latter to factors which may enhance or retard the working out of acute adolescent turmoil.

DISCUSSION

The data presented here must be interpreted with caution as there are more cases in the sample to be followed and a longer period of follow-up is necessary to estimate the stability of these diagnostic appraisals. Despite these limitations, certain trends appear in the data. First, there is a modest relation between the form of the adolescent psychopathology and early adult diagnoses of borderline and schizophrenia-spectrum disorders. The best predictor is a negative one, as passive negativism seems inversely related to these diagnoses.

Second, the severity of psychopathology noted in adolescents is a positive predictor of extended schizophrenia-spectrum diagnosis, suggesting that for some groups there is continuity in the severity of psychopathology from adolescence to early adulthood. The absence of severe symptomatology does not exclude subsequent schizophrenia-spectrum disorders, although the likelihood is less than in the more extreme adolescent group. Some patterns of severe early adult psychopathology thus appear discontinuous with adolescent adjustment, as some cases with spectrum diagnoses did not have extreme or bizarre adolescent precursors.

Third, there is a strong relation between parental communication deviance and the probability of extended schizophrenia-spectrum disorders in early adulthood. The high-risk adolescent appears as likely to manifest borderline symptoms as definite schizophrenia, supporting those theories emphasizing common precursors of these two conditions.

Fourth, the absence of parental communication deviance not only tends to predict diagnoses outside the extended spectrum, but also appears to be associated with a life course of improving adjustment.

Attempts to discriminate, on a post hoc basis, between parents of borderlines and parents of schizophrenics using TAT data analysis have proved fruitless to date. This may suggest that the intrafamilial communication disorder present in the environment of borderlines does not differ qualitatively from that associated with subsequent clinical schizophrenia. Other factors within the family may be necessary to account for the different life courses, or the ultimate symptom formation may well relate to nonfamilial factors not yet clearly defined.

The presence of parental communication disorder in 50 per cent of the cases of disturbed nonpsychotic adolescents permits us to reject arguments that these parental behaviors are merely reactive to *psychosis* in the offspring. We cannot, however, reject the hypothesis that these deviant-communication styles are reactive to severe nonpsychotic adolescent psychopathology, since those adolescents with extreme symptoms uniformly had parents with high communication deviance.

How might the predictive value of the severity of adolescent symptomatology and parents' communication style be integrated into the same etiological model? When the two factors are considered together, there are a number of alternative explanations worthy of consideration. First, parental communication disorder may be a necessary condition for the development of both extreme and bizarre adolescent symptoms and also of subsequent schizophrenia-spectrum disorders. Once expressed, the deviant intrafamilial environment supports such extreme deviance and prevents the growth toward more adaptive solutions in adulthood. We are obviously not in a position to test this very appealing hypothesis directly.

Second, extreme pathological reactions in adolescence and parental communication disorder may be independent factors which only relate after the emergence of adolescent psychopathology. Then, given a disturbed adolescent of indeterminate etiology, residence in a family with confused and blurred communication inhibits any movement toward problem solution and adaptation to subsequent life stress. The data on improvement in symptomatology support this hypothesis, as absence of parental communication disorder appears to predict movement regardless of the initial severity of the adolescent problem.

Third, parental communication may be completely reactive to some subtle characteristic of the child, possibly related to temperamental or genetic factors. In this case, the bizarre behavior noted in the high-risk cases may be merely an extreme form of a characteristic seen in attenuated subclinical form in those high-risk children without bizarre symptoms. From this view, parental communication is a useful reflection of important characteristics of the adolescent but may not be etiologically related to either adolescent or early adult psychopathology.

Fourth, extreme symptoms and parental communication deviance may form a mutually enhancing, positive-feedback loop which predicts a steadily deteriorating course. In this model, each factor is seen as reactive to and amplifying the other. Extreme behavior would deteriorate in an environment of parental communication deviance and would also induce still higher levels of parental communication disorder. Conversely, parental communication deviance would both foster spectrum symptomatology and itself increase in reaction to extreme child behavior above a certain threshold of bizarreness. Obviously, a quite complex design would be required to test this model.

Clearly, further data are needed from prospective studies which begin earlier in life to determine the temporal links between parental communication disorder and adolescent psychopathology before we can choose between these etiological hypotheses.

REFERENCES

Arieti, S. (1955), *Interpretation of Schizophrenia.* New York: Basic Books, 1974.
Garmezy, N., & Streitman, S. (1974), Children-at-risk: The search for the antecedents of schizophrenia. I: Conceptual models and research methods. *Schizophrenia Bull.,* 8:14-90.
Gunderson, J. G. (1975), Borderline evaluation schedule. *Differential Diagnosis of Borderline Disorders and Schizophrenia.* (Unpublished.)
Jones, F. H. (1974), A four-year follow-up of vulnerable adolescents. *J. Nerv. Ment. Dis.,* 159:20-39.
Jones, J. E., et al. (1977), Parental transactional style deviance in families of

disturbed adolescents as a possible indicator of risk for schizophrenia. *Arch. Gen. Psychiat.*, 34:71-74.

Mednick, S. A., & McNeil, T. F. (1968), Current methodology in research on the etiology of schizophrenia: Serious difficulties which suggest the use of the high-risk-group method. *Psychol. Bull.*, 70:681-693.

Nameche, G., Waring, M., & Ricks, D. (1964), Early indicators of outcome in schizophrenia. *J. Nerv. Ment. Dis.*, 139:232-240.

Robins, L. N. (1966), *Deviant Children Grow Up*. Baltimore: Williams and Wilkins.

Rodnick, E. H., & Garmezy, N. (1957), An experimental approach to the study of motivation in schizophrenia. In: *Nebraska Symposium on Motivation,* ed. M. R. Jones. Lincoln, Neb.: University of Nebraska Press, pp. 109-184.

—————— & Goldstein, M. J. (1974), A research strategy for studying risk for schizophrenia during adolescence and early childhood. In: *Children at Psychiatric Risk,* ed. E. J. Anthony & C. Koupernik. New York: Wiley, pp. 507-526.

Singer, M. T., & Wynne, L. C. (1965), Thought disorder and family relations of schizophrenics. IV: Results and implications. *Arch. Gen. Psychiat.,* 12: 201-212.

Spitzer, R. L., Endicott, J., & Robins, E. (1975), Research diagnostic criteria RDC for a selected group of functional disorders, 2nd ed. (Unpublished.)

Wender, P. H., Rosenthal, D., & Kety, S. S. (1968), A psychiatric assessment of the adoptive parents of schizophrenics. In: *Transmission of Schizophrenia,* ed. D. Rosenthal & S. S. Kety. New York: Pergamon, pp. 235-250.

Wynne, L. C., Singer, M. T., Bartko, J. J., & Toohey, M. (1977), Schizophrenics and their families: Recent research on parental communication. In: *Developments in Psychiatric Research,* ed. J. M. Tanner. Sevenoakes, Kent: Hodden & Stoughton.

Considerations of the Borderline Syndrome: A Longitudinal Comparative Study of Borderline and Schizophrenic Patients

WILLIAM T. CARPENTER, JR., M.D.,

JOHN G. GUNDERSON, M.D.,

and JOHN S. STRAUSS, M.D.

Confusion over the use of the term borderline as a psychiatric diagnosis is almost axiomatic, but this has neither hindered the term's rapid acceptance and wide application, nor led to a systematic delineation of the syndrome. The literature on the borderline patient is growing rapidly, but so far not a single investigation has been undertaken to reveal the extent to which clinicians agree on the definition of borderline or achieve consensus when making this diagnosis. The question of whether "borderline" merits a place in psychopathologic nosology can hardly be debated intelligently before we resolve these basic points. Before beginning this process, however, it is necessary to review the several models of psychopathology that can be applied to the concept of the borderline patient. These models have remarkably different implications.

The most common concept of borderline is based on a continuum or dimensional model of psychopathology, as is represented in Figure 1. In simplest terms, behavior or psychological functioning is viewed as ranging from normal to severely psychotic. Menninger has used this model exclusively in classifying

Dr. Carpenter is Professor of Psychiatry, University of Maryland School of Medicine; Director, Maryland Psychiatric Research Center, Baltimore, Maryland.

Dr. Gunderson is Assistant Professor, Harvard Medical School, Cambridge, Massachusetts; Assistant Psychiatrist, McLean Hospital, Belmont, Massachusetts.

Dr. Strauss is Professor of Psychiatry, University of Rochester School of Medicine and Dentistry, Rochester, New York.

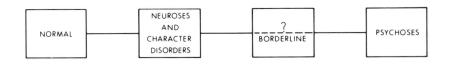

FIGURE 1. Continuous Model of Psychopathology

mental disorders in his book *The Vital Balance* (Menninger, Mayman, and Pruyser, 1963). Neuroses and character disorder are placed toward the normal end of this continuum. Borderline refers to a disorder with greater severity than neurosis and character disorder but less severity than psychosis. This concept is used by Grinker, Werble, and Drye (1968). Their four subgroups can be considered as defining subsections on a segment of this continuum, with their Group I on the border with psychoses and Group IV on the border with neuroses.

A second model — the typological model — suggests that psychopathology can best be organized into discrete groups not representing a continuum or having any other specific relation to each other (see Figure 2). In this model, nosologic groups are delineated from each other and from normals on the basis of a supposedly qualitative unique characteristic feature. Any pathologic manifestation could range from mild to marked within the group, but the presence of distinguishing features rather than their severity is critical to diagnosis. This model does not imply that no similar psychopathologic features are to be found between groups (e.g., anxiety is almost ubiquitous across diagnostic classes), only that distinguishing features identify patients as belonging to a discrete class.

The theoretical implications of these two concepts are quite different. The first model encourages a search for points on the continuum which can usefully be defined and distinguished from other points. One assumes there will be confusing cases at the interface between any two defined points, and that locating such a boundary case in either group would not be entirely misleading. In contrast, a typologic or discontinuous model of psychopathology does not allow for the intermediate case, and hence the implications are more drastic. An incorrect classification would be entirely misleading, rather than simply underestimating or overestimating the severity of psychopathology. There could be confusing cases, however, either because the disease is only partially manifest or because the patient was simultaneously afflicted with two illnesses.

Considerable evidence has now emerged suggesting some discrete classes of psychopathology. Genetic studies (adoptive, cross-fostering, and family-tree) document that manic-depressive and schizophrenic illness are discrete, and this distinction is supported by differential psychopharmacologic responsivity. On the other hand, if one looks at these two illnesses from a descriptive or an ego-psychologic point of view, phenomenologic and ontogenetic observations can be readily conceptualized on a continuum. The concept of schizophrenia spectrum (Kety et al., 1968), derived from genetic investigations, lends support to a continuous model of psychopathology.

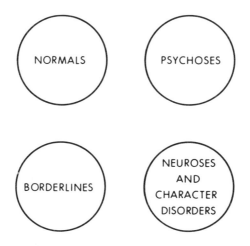

FIGURE 2. Discrete Model of Psychopathology

In the continuum model the question is whether borderline is a useful segment to delineate. There is no question about the existence of a borderline as there is a border between any two sequential points. The question is pragmatic: Does defining the characteristics of the border provide useful information in terms of etiology, course, or treatment? Is assigning a borderline diagnosis more helpful than diagnosing these patients as either neurotic or psychotic, or relegating them to an uncertain diagnostic status?

If we use a discontinuous model, on the other hand, then we must prove that such a group exists. Nosology implies a capacity to generalize from group membership. Assignment to an invalid class would be totally misleading.

The use of borderline as a diagnosis if this category is inadequately defined has different implications in the two models discussed. On a continuum model, a poorly defined point would lead to sloppy diagnostic practices reducing the usefulness of the better-defined surrounding points. In the discontinuous model a poorly defined entity would have little chance of being validated, hence its existence as well as usefulness would be in question.

A third model for classification combines the properties of the continuum and typological approaches. Such a combined or mixed model provides the means for integrating the presently available conflicting data relevant to psychiatric nosology. A mixed model can define two levels — a continuous and a discrete level — allowing one to conceptualize disordered ego functioning and character development along a severity continuum but hypothesizing that at certain segments of this continuum psychopathologic manifestations (e.g., highly distinguishing signs and symptoms) may arise to identify discrete nosologic classes.

Currently we favor a mixed model in our project, as do most of the workers in the field. In simplest terms, we are dealing with the proposition that there is a group of patients less well put together than neurotic or character-disorder patients, yet not so sick or disorganized as schizophrenic or other psychotic patients. The basic hypothesis is that such a group of patients can be defined with clinical criteria, and that a group so delineated will prove to be different from neurotic and character-disorder patients on the one hand, and schizophrenic patients on the other, in terms of manifest psychopathology, past history, course and outcome, pharmacologic responsivity, and genetic loading. We thus use a continuous model in identifying patients as borderline, but we then examine the proposition that patients so diagnosed will, in fact, comprise a discrete nosologic class.

METHODOLOGIC CONSIDERATIONS

As long as we lack external criteria for establishing psychiatric nosology, clinical diagnostic studies are necessarily bootstrap operations. We use clinical criteria for assigning a diagnosis to the individual case. We then look at groups of patients assigned to various classes and determine their clinical characteristics. We must therefore be explicit about what is circular and what represents new findings. Gunderson and Singer (1975) note this by pointing out how selection of borderline patients with initial psychotic symptoms (Hoch et al., 1962) or absence of psychotic symptoms (Grinker, Werble, and Drye, 1968) predetermines the later respective conclusions that borderlines are preschizophrenic or not preschizophrenic.

Any investigation of borderline patients requires a series of fundamental methodologic decisions. These decisions shape the data, and clarify the limits for interpreting results. Some crucial choices to be made in the study of borderlines are:

1. Will borderline patients be defined by a clinical diagnosis of borderline without explicit rules governing the diagnostic process? Or will the study group be selected by a set of criteria that can be systematically applied and communicated to others? If the first option is chosen (as it virtually always is), then the first task of study is to discover what constitutes the clinical syndrome so identified. Gunderson and Singer (1975) survey the descriptive literature and suggest several clinical features shared by most patients diagnosed as borderline.

In the alternative approach, some explicit criteria are applied in order to identify borderline patients. This approach lends itself to an investigation of clinical features (other than those used as diagnostic criteria) with the hope of testing clinical hypotheses. If patients are selected according to intense and unstable relationships, for example, will they in fact have a predilection for micropsychotic episodes?

2. How will the research data be collected? Much of the diagnostic confusion attached to the borderline concept results from a lack of systematic study. Guze (1975) could still only point to the work of Grinker, Werble, and Drye (1968) as providing systematic data. In most studies one cannot assume that any particular set of

observations is made in a similar manner for all patients. In the absence of systematic observations, reliability cannot be ascertained. Systematic observations may be made with structured or unstructured psychiatric interview techniques. There are advantages to each method, but with one exception (Gunderson, Carpenter, and Strauss, 1975), only nonstructured approaches to psychiatric assessment have been carried out.

3. Should systematic comparison with other diagnostic groups be undertaken? And what comparison groups are most appropriate? The concept of borderline was originated and developed without direct comparison to other patient groups. It is not sufficient to define a new nosologic class in terms of differences from other classes that are only assumed — these differences must be empirically established. Such direct comparisons are atypical in the borderline literature (Gunderson, Carpenter, and Strauss, 1975). Without systematic comparisons, characteristic features of a group may be mistakenly considered as distinguishing. For example, some of the distinguishing clinical features noted by Grinker, Werble, and Drye (1968) in their borderline patients have more recently been found to also characterize young adult schizophrenic patients (Grinker and Holzman, 1973). There is no merit to avoiding direct comparison of borderline and other diagnostic groups. Clearly more work of this kind is required.

4. Although cross-sectional studies are important for the reasons described, prospective longitudinal studies are required if course and outcome are central to the borderline concept. Robins and Guze (1970) point out that follow-up studies can reveal whether the initial clinical picture can be accounted for by some other disorder which has emerged more clearly over time.

5. In addition to considerations of course and outcome, psychiatric syndromes may be validated by psychological tests, genetic studies, and differential pharmacologic responsivity (see Klein, 1977; Singer, 1977; Wender, 1977). Future investigators must decide which of these (and other) potential validating criteria can be reasonably assessed in the context of their study design.

Unfortunately, the literature on borderlines has so far focused almost exclusively on clinical descriptions, theoretical constructs, and etiologic assumptions. Investigations of borderline patients have leaned too heavily on anecdotal evidence and failed to use methodologic approaches that could result in a clearer delineation of the syndrome. Investigative tools enhancing clinical observation have only occasionally been employed. Borderline remains a confusing diagnostic entity for which few reliable observations have been established, where presumed differences from other diagnostic classes have not been empirically tested, and where validation of the syndrome itself is lacking. Validation of the widely quoted theoretical constructs and the various etiological claims depends simply on a clearer delineation of the syndrome.

The project reviewed below is of interest since it was conducted with a methodology quite distinct (for better and worse!) from that used in previous investigations of the borderline syndrome. As such, it is illustrative of the issues discussed above.

BACKGROUND AND METHODS

In this project we used the continuous model of psychopathology to select patients for study. This selection process does not preclude the application of any paradigm (typological, continuous, or mixed) to the analysis of data and testing of hypotheses. We selected major assumptions from the clinical literature and attempted to operationalize these into clinical propositions testable over time and in comparison with another diagnostic category.

We accept the view of borderline disorders as located between neuroses and some character disorders (broadly defined) on the one side, and schizophrenia on the other. It is schizophrenia, and not other psychoses, which is described across the border and hence schizophrenics are the natural choice for our comparison group. Since all patients in the study were recent admissions to a hospital and most were thought to have some indication of psychosis, we assume that our attempt to delineate the borderline syndrome is focused at the psychotic border—similar to Grinker's Group I (Grinker, Werble, and Drye, 1968).

Methods for selecting and studying patients in our project have been detailed elsewhere (Gunderson, Carpenter, and Strauss, 1975) and will only be summarized here. Distinctive features of our project include: (1) Explicit criteria for sample selection were defined so that they could be replicated by other workers. (2) Clinical evaluations were done with semistructured techniques to assure systematic data collection. Data were collected in the context of a nontherapeutic psychiatric assessment rather than in an ongoing treatment context. Evaluation techniques have proved to be reliable (World Health Organization, 1973). (3) The borderline sample and the schizophrenic sample were evaluated in the same time period, and prior to planning this specific project. The two groups were matched on age, sex, race, and socioeconomic variables, making direct comparison over time meaningful. (4) Prognostic variables as well as present clinical status data were assessed initially, and two-year and five-year follow-up studies were subsequently conducted.

Our investigation was carried out using data collected from the 131 patients evaluated in the U.S. Center of the International Pilot Study of Schizophrenia (IPSS). Details of the methodology employed in this nine-nation investigation are presented elsewhere (World Health Organization, 1973). From the original group of 131 patients we selected 24 borderline and 29 schizophrenic patients matched by age, sex, race, and socioeconomic status, but sharply divergent in psychotic symptomatology. Schizophrenic patients were included only if they had one or more of Schneider's (1959) first-rank symptoms, met other stringent, specified criteria for a schizophrenic diagnosis (Carpenter, Strauss, and Bartko, 1973), and were considered as "certain" schizophrenic diagnosis by the research psychiatrist conducting the evaluation. The borderline patients were chosen for the presence of brief psychotic experiences which were neither severe nor long-lasting, for diagnostic uncertainty, and for the absence of nuclear schizophrenic symptoms. That these selection criteria succeeded in establishing clinically distinct groups was demonstrated with a profile analysis of variance across 27 psychopathologic dimensions (Gunderson, Carpenter, and Strauss, 1975).

As part of the IPSS, five-year follow-up evaluations were completed on 80 of the original 131 patients. Methods and results of the five-year follow-up study have been reported, including an analysis demonstrating that the patients seen at follow-up were representative of the entire cohort (Hawk, Carpenter, and Strauss,

1975). Fourteen of 24 borderline and twenty of 29 schizophrenic patients were evaluated at five years. This report is based on ratings of nine areas of outcome functioning (see Figure 4 below for items and reliability). Ratings were based on an interview carried out shortly after admission by a psychiatrist using semistructured interview schedules for systematic collection of sign and symptom data (the Present State Examination), social- and work-function information, and general inquiries into the quality and nature of the patient's living experience over the past year. These instruments have been described and their reliability evaluated elsewhere (Hawk, Carpenter, and Strauss, 1975; World Health Organization, 1973).

Using these procedures, relevant ratings of pre-episode functioning and presenting psychopathology were recorded. Patients were reassessed two and five years later with similar structured interviews to determine follow-up adjustment and symptom status. This provided a matched sample for comparison of premorbid and outcome functioning in borderline and schizophrenic patients.

RESULTS

A series of comparisons have been made between the borderline and schizophrenic patients selected by the above criteria. Some of these findings have been previously reported (Gunderson, Carpenter, and Strauss, 1975).

1. Presenting signs and symptoms at the initial research evaluation were compared. Marked differences were found in psychotic symptomatology, but this was due to selection criteria. The profile in Figure 3 reveals these differences—items in dimensions 10 and 13-20 were used in defining the groups. When these dimensions are dropped from the profile analysis of variance comparisons, the profile patterns are not significantly different ($p = .11$). The schizophrenic patients do show a higher level of psychopathology ($p = .47$ x 10^{-5}), however, indicating that they are a more symptomatically disturbed patient group, independent of defining criteria.

At the time of first evaluation, affective (anger, depression, and anxiety) and dissociative symptoms were common and frequently severe in the borderline patients. This is consistent with usual

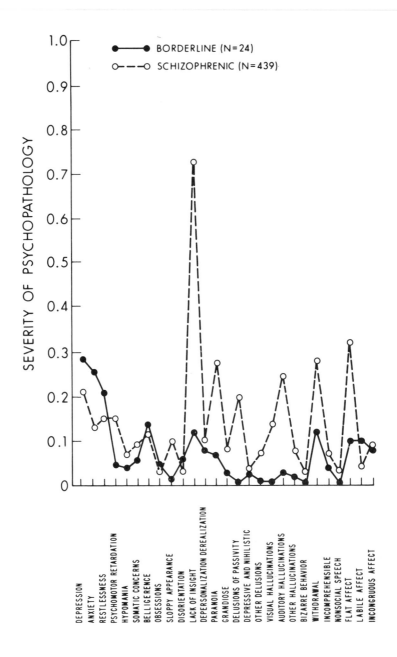

FIGURE 3. Profile of Borderline vs. Schizophrenic

descriptions of borderline patients. Schizophrenic patients, however, also had high scores on these dimensions and were not readily
distinguished from borderlines on these symptoms.

2. Prognostic status was determined in all patients on admission
to the study. It was defined by prior functioning rather than current
psychopathological manifestations. Previous work and social functioning were assessed and the Phillips scale of premorbid adjustment
was rated. History of previous hospitalizations, precipitating events,
and other relevant variables were recorded. This process has been
described in detail elsewhere (Strauss and Carpenter, 1974). No significant difference between the two diagnostic groups was found.

3. Four areas of functioning were assessed two years after the
initial evaluations: duration of hospitalization, social contacts,
employment, and symptom status. Ratings for the borderline and
schizophrenic groups were identical (see Figure 4).

4. Five-year follow-up evaluations were carried out on fourteen
of the 24 borderline and twenty of the 29 schizophrenic patients
using an expanded set of outcome ratings (see Figure 4). The total
outcome score (sum of the nine items), a global clinical judgment of
over-all outcome (item 9), and most of the individual outcome areas
reveal no statistical difference between the two diagnostic groups.
The one exception is *quality of social contacts* where the borderline
group is significantly less impaired ($t = 2.13$, $p < .05$). There is also a
trend suggesting that borderline patients spend more time usefully
employed ($t = 1.72$, $p < .1$).

Four of the nine outcome measures were also assessed at
two-year follow-up in eleven of the fourteen borderline and nineteen
of the twenty schizophrenic patients. There is no significant change
between two- and five-year evaluations in either group on extent of
hospitalization, frequency of social contacts, amount of useful work,
and symptom level ($p > .1$ in all instances, paired t-test).

5. By the selection criteria, all 29 patients in the schizophrenic
cohort were given a "certain" clinical diagnosis of schizophrenia.
This contrasts with the initial evaluations of the borderline cohort
where diagnostic uncertainty was ubiquitous. During the five-year
follow-up period the diagnosis of the borderline patients frequently
changed and was considered "certain" in only five of fourteen
patients at five-year follow-up evaluation. This continues to contrast

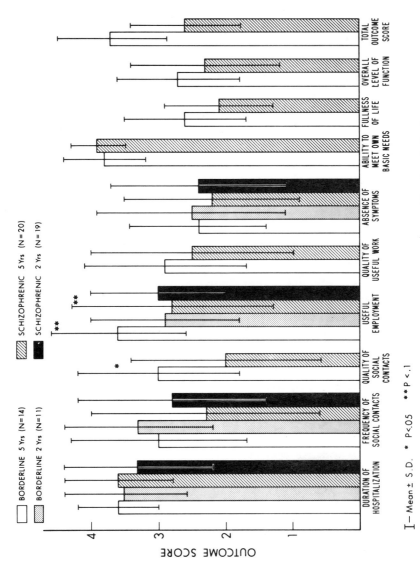

FIGURE 4. Outcome Measures in Borderline and Schizophrenic Patients

with the schizophrenic patients where all retained a schizophrenic diagnosis at five years, and uncertainty was noted in only five. In each instance of uncertainty, the second-choice diagnosis was another schizophrenic subtype.

Since certainty of diagnosis was used in selecting the study groups, the continued clarity of diagnosis in schizophrenia and confusion in borderline patients is not surprising. It does, however, illustrate the difficulties in fitting borderline patients into any of the standard diagnostic groups. This patient cohort did not neatly fit into existing nosologic classes even with the benefit of hindsight!

Psychopharmacologic treatment was used for thirteen of the fourteen borderline patients during the five-year follow-up period. We were able to identify the type of drugs used for ten patients. Six patients received neuroleptics, six antianxiety drugs, and five antidepressants. Six of the ten patients received drugs from two classes. Pharmacotherapy was more consistent in the twenty schizophrenic patients. Four received no medicine during follow-up, thirteen received only neuroleptics, and one received an antianxiety drug. Three patients received neuroleptic drugs plus another drug — lithium carbonate in one instance, amitryptamine in another, and diazepam in the third.

6. Drug abuse, antisocial behavior, and other impulse-action problems including suicidal behavior have been associated with the borderline syndrome by several writers (Gunderson and Singer, 1975). Using only patients seen at five years, we found three borderline and one schizophrenic patient with a serious drug-abuse problem. Nine of fourteen borderline patients had evidence of other action problems, including five who had been charged with a crime or involved with police. This contrasts with seven of the twenty schizophrenic patients with action problems, two of whom were charged with a crime ($X^2 = 2.8$, $df = 2$, $p > .1$).

7. Grinker, Werble, and Drye (1968) found that their borderline patients had consistent work patterns, but at a level lower than would have been expected had they not been ill. Examining our narrative material regarding employment, we were impressed that the jobs held by borderline patients were at a lower level of competence than anticipated from their social-class distribution. Jobs as busboy, cleaning lady, cocktail waitress, and errand boy seemed

typical. Examination of the job descriptions of schizophrenic patients left a similar impression, however. For example, only one borderline patient and three schizophrenic patients had jobs that involved supervising the work of others.

8. One final result involves a series of comparisons of psycho-pathologic profiles. These profiles are based on 27 sign and symptom dimensions (see Figure 3). As noted above and in Figure 3, the borderline and schizophrenic cohorts are quite different in both the pattern and level of their symptoms. The borderline profiles have to differ from the schizophrenic comparison group because of the selection criteria. Profile analysis of variance also demonstrates significant differences between the borderline and the subtypes of schizophrenia which we have described elsewhere (Carpenter et al., 1976). The pattern and level of presenting symptomatology for borderlines is significantly different from mania (Figure 5) and psychotic depression (Figure 6).

Only one comparison reveals considerable similarity, the com-parison of borderlines with patients diagnosed as having psycho-neurotic-depressive disorder (Figure 7). Aspects of the selection criteria may be one factor contributing to this surprising similarity. Borderline patients could not have severe or continuous psychotic symptoms, hence they had a low profile on PSE psychotic dimen-sions similar to neurotic depressives. Furthermore, our neurotic-depressive patients were drawn from the severe end of that spec-trum in that they were admitted to a hospital; some were even thought to have an indication of psychosis at screening. A less severely ill group of neurotic depressives might have lower ratings on lack of insight and social withdrawal, but even so considerable similarity would remain.

Discussion and Summary

We have called attention to some of the methodologic problems which should be taken into account in current studies of the borderline syndrome. The lack of systematic and comparative studies has led to confusion and has failed to clarify whether a nosologic class called borderline is scientifically justified and useful.

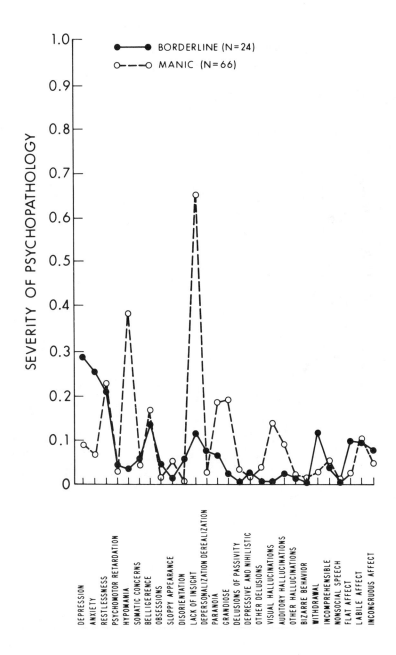

FIGURE 5. Profile of Borderline vs. Manic

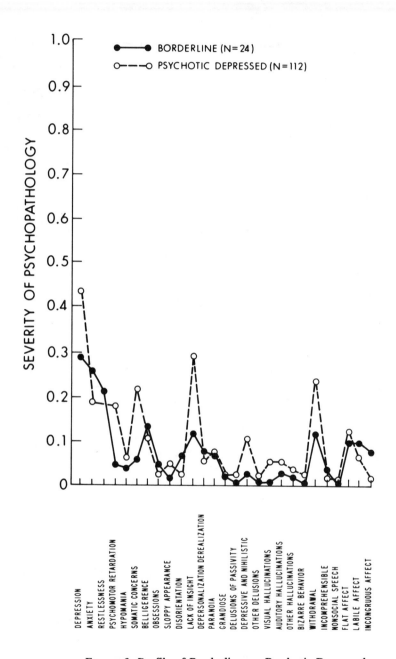

FIGURE 6. Profile of Borderline vs. Psychotic Depressed

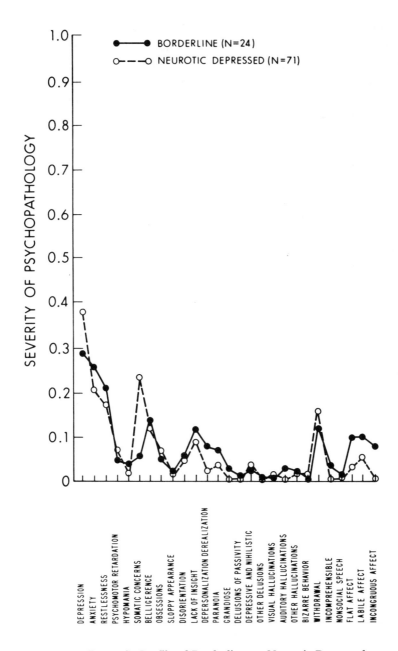

FIGURE 7. Profile of Borderline vs. Neurotic Depressed

Our discussion of methodologic issues was, to some extent, self-serving in that it highlighted the advantages of the approach used in this study. The reader will have to decide whether to agree that these issues are important and relevant to the borderline syndrome. In any case, methods used in this study are different from those usually employed in investigating borderline patients.

Although we have discussed the strengths of this type of systematic and comparative longitudinal study, the reader should also be mindful of the important limitations to our approach. Since our study relied on essentially cross-sectional clinical evaluations, we do not have the extensive and rich material that can be obtained in the course of psychotherapy and psychoanalysis. Moreover, since our criteria for borderline did not rest on an evaluation of character structure or patterns of ego functioning, we have no satisfactory means of assuring that the borderline patients described here fairly represent the usual concept of borderline syndrome. This criticism can be raised with other studies as well, of course, since reliable, agreed-upon criteria for borderline do not exist. Nonetheless, we have leaned heavily on the issue of partial reality distortion, micropsychotic episodes, and diagnostic confusion in identifying our group. It was therefore important to find that the borderline patients defined by our criteria do have independent clinical features consistent with other descriptions of the borderline syndrome. These characteristics include: (1) presence of intense affects; (2) frequency of dissociative experiences; (3) noteworthy impulse difficulty as reflected in drug use, suicidal behavior, run-ins with police, etc. Furthermore, borderline patients in our study appear to have the "stable instability" described elsewhere (Schmideberg, 1959). They hold jobs most of the time but are underemployed. Their social adjustment is stable (not deteriorating), but it is often marked by chaotic interpersonal relating.

If we accept this sample as representative of borderlines, we must attempt to account for two surprising findings. First, borderline patients are similar to schizophrenic patients in many aspects of course and outcome functioning. The only important difference noted is that the schizophrenic group showed some deterioration in the quality of their social relating over time, while the borderline group remained constant. Second, on presenting symptomatology the borderline patients were readily distinguished from other hospitalized groups with the exception of psychoneurotic-depressive patients.

These findings are worrisome since there is no point in identifying a borderline group unless differences can be found from the diagnostic groups on each side of the borderline spectrum. Failure to find the schizophrenic group readily distinguishable from the borderline (except where differences were by definition) could be explained if our schizophrenic patients were actually borderline, but the evidence for the schizophrenic and borderline groups being different seems exceptionally strong when one considers the selection criteria, the psychopathologic profile, and the pattern of diagnosis over time. It is also unreasonable to argue that the borderline patients were simply misdiagnosed schizophrenics in face of the psychopathologic profile similarity with neurotic-depressive patients.

On the other side of the border, we face the vexing problem of similarity between neurotic-depressive and borderline disorders. Could the neurotic-depressive group be misdiagnosed borderlines? Perhaps, but their pattern of sign and symptom psychopathology fits with a clinical concept of depressive disease. Since these patients were from the several centers of the IPSS, the neurotic-depressive group cannot be dismissed as reflecting the diagnostic bias of any one school.[1] It appears more reasonable to ask if the borderline patients were misdiagnosed, severe neurotic-depressive patients. We can argue against this proposition by citing the diagnostic confusion that persisted through the follow-up period, by noting the extensive similarity to schizophrenic patients in prognostic and outcome variables, and by citing the chaotic quality of borderline patients' interpersonal relations. Gunderson (1977) systematically compares neurotic-depressive and borderline patients and finds them to be distinctly different in many clinical features.

If the borderline patients in our report are severe neurotic depressives, or if the neurotic depressives are actually borderline

---

[1] The borderline patients and comparison schizophrenic patients were all from the Washington Center of the IPSS. The other profile comparisons use patients from all nine centers. The detailed comparison on variables other than presenting psychopathology was feasible only with the matched schizophrenic cohort.

cases, the implications are major. Borderline syndrome would then best be regarded as a primary affective disorder located on a continuum between neurotic and psychotic affect disorders. If the distinguishing features of the borderline are maladaptive interpersonal tactics, as suggested by Klein (1975), then a mixed typologic-continuous model would best describe the concept.

Can we rule out this proposition from data presently available? In the first place, what can be considered reliable data at this point are not sufficient to rule any meaningful hypothesis in or out. If the schizophrenia-spectrum concept overlaps with the borderline concept, then the adoptive studies suggest a genetic kinship with schizophrenia (see Wender, 1977). A relation with schizophrenia is suggested by clinical observations focused on disordered ego functioning. On the other hand, depression and other affect symptoms are almost uniformly observed in borderline patients. In addition, these patients may respond to antidepressant medication. Klein (1975) notes that even pseudoneurotic schizophrenics respond better to antidepressives than to neuroleptics.

This discussion has now come full circle. What is still needed is evidence that will clarify the nosologic status of borderline. Our study agrees with others in suggesting that borderline patients are diagnostically confusing. We find them similar in many ways to acute and subacute schizophrenic patients, but their over-all presenting signs and symptoms most resemble neurotic depression. Course and outcome studies have serious shortcomings when used to provide validating evidence for psychiatric syndromes, and biochemical tools are still wanting in this regard. Genetic family studies, psychological-test procedures, and investigations of pharmacologic responsivity are currently the most promising tools for syndrome validation (see Wender, 1977; Singer, 1977; Goldstein and Jones, 1977; Klein, 1977). Early findings from these investigations suggest that the borderline syndrome may be genetically related to schizophrenia, pharmacologically related to primary affect disorders, and psychologically and developmentally similar to, but distinguishable from, schizophrenia.

It is not always clear whether descriptive and analytic psychiatry is developing scientifically (accumulating knowledge and enhancing perspectives) or proceeding circularly (reobserving and reformulating without a steady acquisition of new knowledge). Grinker, Werble, and Drye (1968) have properly pointed out that the borderline patient is often conceptualized in terms that do not lend themselves to reliable usage among colleagues. It is also fair to note that more explicit methods (e.g., mathematical) do not necessarily result in more accurate or more reproducible results. For example, had different cluster analytic methods been utilized in the study by Grinker, Werble, and Drye (1968), then quite different results might have been obtained (Bartko, Strauss, and Carpenter, 1971). Stability, replicability, and validity of the four borderline subgroups are still to be ascertained. Likewise, in the psychopathologic profiles we presented, it cannot be said to what extent they are sensitive to describing those aspects of borderline patients peculiar to the syndrome. The observed similarity between neurotic depression and borderline personality disorders may reflect the inadequacies of our methods.

Based on the above considerations and findings, three recommendations for priorities in future research on the borderline syndrome can be made:

1. Investigators utilizing the therapeutic situation for observations should apply presently available techniques to enhance the data collection and to determine what observations and inferences can be reliably made.

2. Direct comparative studies are required to identify the distinguishing features of the borderline. It does not suffice simply to describe characteristic features, without ever empirically determining which characteristics are unique. Furthermore, comparison groups from the several borders should be utilized. Schizophrenia, neurotic and psychotic affect disorders, and some personality disorders need to be empirically distinguished from the borderline syndrome (see Gunderson, 1977).

3. Validation studies are needed, and the clinician-investigator needs to work collaboratively with the behavioral geneticist, psychopharmacologist, biochemist, and phenomenologist in an effort to determine which model of psychopathology is best suited for the borderline, and to affirm (or reject) the usefulness of the borderline concept.

REFERENCES

Bartko, J., Strauss, J. S., & Carpenter, W. T. (1971), An evaluation of taxometric techniques for psychiatric data. *Bull. Class. Soc.,* 2:2-28.

Carpenter, W. T., Jr., Bartko, J. J., Langsner, C. A., & Strauss, J. S. (1976), Another view of schizophrenia subtypes: A report from the International Pilot Study of Schizophrenia. *Arch. Gen. Psychiat.,* 33:508-516.

———, Strauss, J. S., & Bartko, J. (1973), Flexible system for the diagnosis of schizophrenia: Report from the WHO International Pilot Study of Schizophrenia. *Science,* 182:1275-1278.

Goldstein, M. J., & Jones, J. E. (1977), Adolescent and familial precursors of borderline and schizophrenic conditions. *This Volume,* pp. 213-229.

Grinker, R. R., Sr., & Holzman, P. S. (1973), Schizophrenic pathology in young adults. *Arch. Gen. Psychiat.,* 28:168-175.

———, Werble, B., & Drye, R. C. (1968), *The Borderline Syndrome.* New York: Basic Books.

Gunderson, J. G. (1977), Characteristics of borderlines. *This Volume,* pp. 173-192.

———, Carpenter, W. T., Jr., & Strauss, J. S. (1975), Borderline and schizophrenic patients: A comparative study. *Amer. J. Psychiat.,* 132:1257-1264.

——— & Singer, M. T. (1975), Defining borderline patients: An overview. *Amer. J. Psychiat.,* 132:1-10.

Guze, S. B. (1975), Differential diagnosis of the borderline personality syndrome. In: *Borderline States in Psychiatry,* ed. J. E. Mack. New York: Grune & Stratton, pp. 69-74.

Hawk, A. B., Carpenter, W. T., Jr., & Strauss, J. S. (1975), Diagnostic criteria and five-year outcome in schizophrenia: A report from the International Pilot Study of Schizophrenia. *Arch. Gen. Psychiat.,* 32:343-356.

Hoch, P. H., Cattell, J. P., Strahl, M. O., & Pennes, H. H. (1962), The course and outcome of pseudoneurotic schizophrenia. *Amer. J. Psychiat.,* 119:106-115.

Kety, S. S., Rosenthal, D., Wender, P. H., & Schulsinger, F. (1968), The types and prevalence of mental illness in the biological and adoptive families of adopted schizophrenics. In: *The Transmission of Schizophrenia,* ed. D. Rosenthal & S. S. Kety. New York: Pergamon, pp. 345-362.

Klein, D. F. (1975), Pharmacology and the borderline patient. In: *Borderline States in Psychiatry,* ed. J. E. Mack. New York: Grune & Stratton, pp. 75-91.

——— (1977), Pharmacological treatment and delineation of borderline disorders. *This Volume,* pp. 365-383.

Menninger, K. A., Mayman, M., & Pruyser, P. W. (1963), *The Vital Balance.* New York: Viking Press.

Robins, E., & Guze, S. B. (1970), Establishment of diagnostic validity in psychiatric illness: Its application to schizophrenia. *Amer. J. Psychiat.,* 126:983-987.

Schmideberg, M. (1959), The borderline patient. In: *American Handbook of Psychiatry,* 1:398-416, ed. S. Arieti. New York: Basic Books.

Schneider, K. (1959), *Clinical Psychopathology,* trans. M. W. Hamilton. New York: Grune & Stratton.

Singer, M. T. (1977), The borderline diagnosis and psychological tests: Review and research. *This Volume,* pp. 193-212.

Strauss, J. S., & Carpenter, W. T., Jr. (1974), The prediction of outcome in schizo-phrenia: II. Relationships between predictor and outcome variables: A report from the WHO International Pilot Study of Schizophrenia. *Arch. Gen. Psychiat.*, 31:37-42.

Wender, P. H. (1977), The contribution of the adoption studies to an understand-ing of the phenomenology and etiology of borderline schizophrenics. *This Volume*, pp. 255-269.

World Health Organization, eds. (1973), *International Pilot Study of Schizo-phrenia*, Vol. I. Geneva: World Health Organization.

The Contribution of the Adoption Studies to an Understanding of the Phenomenology and Etiology of Borderline Schizophrenias

PAUL H. WENDER, M.D.

The "adoption studies" of schizophrenia (Kety et al., 1968; Rosenthal et al., 1968; Wender, Rosenthal, and Kety, 1968) have shed considerable light not only on the etiology of the borderline schizophrenias, but also—and this is less well known—on the boundaries and characteristics of this syndrome. This paper reviews the data obtained from the adoption studies and discusses the consequences of these data for our understanding of the borderline schizophrenias. Notice that I use the plural. It is most cautious to employ the plural, as did Bleuler, and avoid the self-made trap of prejudging the issue and concluding that there is only one object of study.

ETIOLOGY: NATURE AND NURTURE

Most people acquainted with the adoption studies realize that they have helped piece apart the respective roles of nature and nurture in the etiology of the schizophrenias. What many people have not reflected on is that they have helped us to define the phenomenology of the borderline schizophrenias. In fact, at present, they may provide the only way for specifying the disorders

Professor of Psychiatry, University of Utah College of Medicine, Salt Lake City, Utah.

The research described in this paper was supported in part by NIMH Grant MH255-15.

whose attributes we are considering. Needless to say, if we cannot accurately specify what we are talking about, we may anticipate further confusion. Both the etiological and the phenomenological evidence have been generated by the same methods and, as will be seen, the phenomenological characterization is part of a logical bootstrap operation in the etiological study.

The purpose of the adoption studies we undertook was to separate the roles of nature and nurture in the etiology of the schizophrenias. Previous studies of the schizophrenias, undertaken by traditional geneticists on the one hand, and by family psychodynamicists on the other, had both demonstrated an increased frequency of psychiatric disturbance among the relatives of chronic schizophrenics. From these data, however, the two schools of thought reached opposite conclusions. The genetic or biological school thought that the increased frequency of psychopathology in the family was a manifestation of the same genetic tendency that had manifested itself in the full-blown illness of the schizophrenic patient, while the psychodynamic school interpreted the same psychopathology as an important cause of the patient's schizophrenic illness.

The Problem of Interpreting Early Genetic Research

To digress for a moment. Genetic psychiatrists have characterized some of these relatives as having schizophrenia-like characteristics. Kretschmer (1934) groups them under the heading "schizothymes," while Kallmann (1938) groups them under the heading "schizoidia." Both used these terms to characterize people manifesting schizophrenic tendencies, many of whom later would be called borderlines. The attributes of persons manifesting this putative genetic tendency are variously described. The scope of Kretschmer's term may be seen in his (1921) description of the relatives of a chronic schizophrenic, all of whom manifested the basic trait, "schizothymia." This patient had three brothers: one was shy, conscientious, competent; another was quiet, serious, logical and sociable, and desired to "get away"; the third was an inventor who is described as stormy and depressed, passionate, restless, with an equal desire to "get away." The patient's mother had had a short period of paranoia when she had been alcoholic. She is described as sensitive, humorless, pedantic, and depressed with a now familiar desire to "get away." The patient's father was chronically paranoid, eccentric, anxious, misanthropic, and depressed. Which of these attributes are the essential manifestation of the putative gene is unclear; the cluster appears to be more important than the individual traits.

Similar attributes—and the same problem in defining the essential symptoms—are found in Kallmann's descriptions. His schizophrenia-like personalities (persons having "schizoidia") are characterized as either "abnormal types ... with schizophrenic deficits following a usually mild or hidden psychotic episode ... [or as showing] autistic introversion, emotional inadequacy, sudden surges of temperament and inappropriate motor response to emotional stimuli, and in whom such symptoms ... as bigotry, pietism, avarice, superstition, obstinacy or crankiness" strongly color the personality (1938, pp. 102-103).

As noted, American psychodynamicists studying the familial characteristics of schizophrenics have noticed the same attributes in their relatives, but they focus on the transactional consequences of being exposed to such schizophrenia-like attributes in parenting figures. From these data they draw the equally rational conclusion that the abnormalities in the parents are the cause, not—so to speak—the consequence of schizophrenia in the patient.

The reason these data cannot help us to sort out the relative contributions of nature and nurture is that nature and nurture are completely confounded: The same parents supply both genes and rearing environment, and one cannot be certain whether their aberrant child-rearing practices are the cause of the disorder in the offspring or a manifestation of the same disorder in themselves. The same problem prevents us, of course, from interpreting the meaning of psychopathology in the patients' siblings. What the study of adopted individuals does is to separate the roles of nature and nurture by studying two sets of parents: one set supplies nature, the putative genetic load, while the other set supplies nurture, the psychological environment in which the schizophrenic has been raised.

The Adoption Strategy

A number of studies have been conducted using the adoption strategy. In the first group of studies (Kety et al., 1968), we identified adopted individuals who were schizophrenic, matched them with adopted individuals who were not schizophrenic, and studied the types and amount of psychopathology in the biological and adopted relatives of both groups.

The genetic and psychosocial theories of the etiology of schizophrenia make two contrary and testable predictions regarding psychopathology in the relatives of these adopted schizophrenics. The genetic hypothesis predicts that an increased level of schizophrenic and schizophrenic-like psychopathology will be found in the biological relatives of the schizophrenic adoptees as opposed to the control adoptees. It also predicts that the frequency of psychopathology in the adoptive relatives of the schizophrenic adoptees will be no greater than that found in the adoptive relatives of the adopted controls. The psychosocial hypothesis makes a mirror-image prediction. It predicts that the biological relatives of the schizophrenic adoptees will have no more schizophrenia and schizophrenia-like conditions than the biological relatives of the control adoptees. Similarly, it predicts an increased frequency of psychopathology among the adoptive relatives of the adopted schizophrenics as opposed to the adoptive relatives of the adopted controls.

Now let me backtrack for a moment. In order to locate a population of adopted schizophrenics, it was necessary to inspect the psychiatric hospitalization records of a population of adopted adults. Inspection revealed that some suffered from true process schizophrenia, others suffered from clear-cut acute or reactive schizophrenia, and that a remainder of patients had symptoms similar to those discussed by Kretschmer and Kallmann. We elected to call this group "borderline schizophrenics." We did not know what borderline schizophrenia "really" was, but chose this term for those patients who clinically manifested the type and degree of psychopathology described by Hoch and Polatin (1949). Our study is therefore of the relatives of Hoch and Polatin's "pseudoneurotic schizophrenics," and consequently sheds light only on the etiology of that group of disorders. Obviously, it does not shed light on the etiology of and cannot be generalized to other disorders variously called "borderline."

Findings: The Genetic Transmission of Borderline Schizophrenia

What did we find? Focusing on the borderline adoptees, we found an increase of both certain and doubtful process and border-line schizophrenia psychopathology only among their biological relatives. No other psychiatric disorder was differentially distributed among the biological or the adoptive relatives of either the index cases or the controls. We did not find an increase of schizophrenic psychopathology in the adoptive relatives of the adopted borderline schizophrenics. Remember that the borderline adoptees were not raised among their biological relatives; hence, these data fit the genetic and not the psychosocial hypothesis.

A second important question is: In what fraction of borderline adoptees did we find family histories of certain and borderline schizophrenia and could we therefore infer that genetic factors were playing a role? The answer is 44 per cent. Does that mean then that in 56 per cent of the instances borderline schizophrenia did not have genetic components? No, it does not. The reason we cannot come to that simple conclusion is that we have no knowledge of the genetic mechanisms of the transmission of borderline schizophrenias. If we were certain that the disorder — or some forms of the disorder — were transmitted by a dominant genetic mechanism, then we could assert that those instances in which the disorder did not occur in the parents were not genetically produced. If, to use a medical ex-ample, the genetic mechanisms were recessive, we would anticipate finding instances in which no relatives had the same disorder. Consider phenylketonuria. This disease is transmitted as an auto-somal recessive and usually is produced in offspring both of whose parents are carriers of the PKU gene but neither of whom has the disease. Since the genetic mechanism is recessive, approximately three fourths of the siblings of a PKU sibling will not have PKU themselves. This means that in studying families of PKU children we will rarely, if ever, find that a parent has the disorder and that in small families we will find many instances in which no sibling is affected. Not knowing the mechanisms of transmission of borderline schizophrenia, we can only place a *lower* limit on that fraction of instances in which the disorder is genetically produced. From this study we may assert that at least one half of borderline schizophrenias, *as defined by us,* have a genetic contribution. Whether the true figure is 50, 60, or 95 per cent, we cannot say.

Our study not only provides evidence for the role of genetic factors in the etiology of borderline schizophrenia, as defined by us, but it also suggests the validity of the borderline concept as so defined. First, it is an entity that "breeds true biologically." Second, it is an entity linked to only one diagnostic group, the "schizophrenic spectrum." This is so because only schizophrenic-spectrum disorders, and no other psychiatric illness, are increased among the biological relatives of the adopted borderline schizophrenic. Similar support for the concept has been generated by a further group of studies.

THE INHERITANCE OF DOUBTFUL PSYCHOPATHOLOGY

As mentioned, an increase was found not only in certain schizophrenic and borderline schizophrenic pathology in the relatives, but also in doubtful schizophrenic and doubtful borderline psychopathology. That is, we found an increase of not only "hard," but also "softer" schizophrenia-like psychopathology. The implication is that there may be genetic contributions to milder forms of the disorder. Whether this can be statistically detected depends on the definition of control adoptees. Let me explain.

The control adoptees were selected on the basis of having no record of psychiatric hospitalization. When interviews were conducted, it was found that some of the adoptees refused to participate, some had emigrated or died since the study had been initiated and could therefore not be interviewed, and that some, when interviewed, manifested schizophrenic-like disorders or other psychiatric disorders. We therefore elected to study the relatives of the controls utilizing three groups: the total initial group; the group that could be interviewed, minus those who had schizophrenic-spectrum disorder; and the "super pure," those who were interviewed and found to have no psychiatric disorder whatsoever. Statistically, the

increased prevalence of psychopathology among the biological
relatives of the adopted doubtful schizophrenics holds true not only
for probable and for borderline schizophrenic states, but for
schizoid states as well, *if* one confines one's attentions to the "super-
pure" controls. Since this is a post hoc analysis, it must be viewed
with caution. The fact that it is consonant with data obtained from
other adoption studies makes it tenable. The conservative conclusion seems to be that there is, as we have named it, a "schizophrenic
spectrum" which contains certain and doubtful, chronic and
borderline schizophrenias, and whose lower boundaries are, at the
moment, uncertain.

A Second Adoption Strategy

A second group of studies using the adoption strategy sheds
additional light on the borderline issue both by virtue of their design
and the different definition of borderline schizophrenia employed.
In these studies our initial analysis was based on the diagnostic
decision of the interviewing psychiatrist. As in the other studies, he
was blind as to the biological heritage of the patients he interviewed
and so avoided bias. This interviewer, who was psychoanalytically
trained, applied the term borderline to persons whose disturbance
was less severe, both qualitatively and quantitatively, than that of
those in the first study. I shall later characterize the symptoms he
used in making the diagnosis and which form the operational
criteria for borderline schizophrenia in this study.

First, however, let me discuss the methodology of this second
group of studies and the information they provided. In this second
group of studies, called the "adoptee studies," we investigated the
type and severity of psychopathology in four groups of subjects:
(1) persons born to schizophrenics and adopted by parents who had
never been psychiatrically diagnosed—the index group; (2) persons
whose biological parents had never had a psychiatric hospitalization and who were reared by adoptive parents who had likewise
never had a psychiatric hospitalization—the control group; (3) persons whose biological parents had never had a psychiatric hospitalization and who were adopted by parents who had had a psychiatric
hospitalization with a diagnosis of certain or possible borderline

schizophrenia or schizoid personality disorder — the cross-fostering group; and (4) persons born to and reared by their own schizophrenic parents — the nonadoptees group.

The first question asked was whether genetic factors play any role in the genesis of borderline schizophrenia. To answer this question we compared the frequency of such disorders in the index and control groups. If genetic factors do play a role, we would expect to find an increased frequency of borderline schizophrenia in the index as opposed to the control group. This is what we found. The distinctions between the groups were somewhat blurred by the high prevalence of psychopathology in the control group. After conducting the study and armed with the power of hindsight, we realized that only a small fraction of borderline patients ever receive psychiatric care and that, accordingly, it might be the case that some of the biological parents of the controls had undetected psychiatric illness. Some preliminary data have indicated that this may be the case and it is our intention to interview the biological parents of the controls in order to exclude those control adoptees whose biological parents had undetected psychiatric illness and thus perhaps "purify" the control group and decrease the frequency of pathology in that group. Parenthetically, the same issue arises in regard to the adoptive parents and, accordingly, we are undertaking a study to investigate undetected psychopathology in that group as well.

THE EFFECT OF CHILD-REARING ON BORDERLINE SCHIZOPHRENIA

A second question this design permitted us to investigate is: What is the contribution of child-rearing factors to the development of borderline schizophrenic psychopathology? We could explore this in two ways: (1) by investigating psychopathology among the cross-fostering group (Wender et al., 1974) in whom borderline schizophrenic psychopathology would (since their biological parents were not schizophrenic) have to be the product of the deviant rearing to which they had been exposed; and (2) by investigating the nonadoptees group in whom we could investigate the contribution of rearing to genetic factors. A psychosocial hypothesis would predict increased psychopathology among the cross-fostered group as compared to the controls and would likewise predict increased psychopathology among the nonadoptees group as compared with the index group (since both had the schizophrenic genes, but only one had deviant rearing as well).

Again, what did we find? First, we found that in the cross-fostering subgroup the prevalence of borderline psychopathology was no greater than in the control group. In other words, it did not appear that deviant rearing alone played any role in the genesis of borderline schizophrenia as defined in the study. Second, we found no increase in psychopathology among the nonadoptees as compared to the index group; in other words, deviant rearing did not interact with schizophrenic genes to produce more borderline schizophrenia. These studies corroborated the evidence derived from the first studies: borderline schizophrenia was associated with schizophrenic genes but not with schizophrenic rearing.

Establishing Criteria for Borderline Schizophrenia: The Technique of Ostensive Definition

As I mentioned earlier, the diagnoses in the second group of studies were first made by a psychiatrist other than ourselves. (We are currently rediagnosing these subjects employing our previous criteria.) Since his implicit diagnostic methods distinguished among the four groups and since his definition of borderline schizophrenia was similar to what we had called "doubtful schizophrenia," we chose to abstract the criteria that both he and we had employed and use these criteria to form operational criteria for the diagnosis of schizophrenia. What we have done is to take part of the sample, abstract the attributes we employed, and see how many of which sort were necessary for us to make the diagnosis of borderline schizophrenia. This technique is what in logic is called an "ostensive definition." One specifies a number of exemplars of the type in question and then goes back to abstract the characteristics of the group so designated.

In order to determine if our abstracting is correct, we must subject it to a test. In collaboration with Spitzer and Endicott, we are submitting other cases—not the ones we used for our ostensive definition—to raters who will note the number and patterns of symptoms in these other case histories. They will then employ decision rules which we have provided to designate a person as borderline schizophrenic or not, depending on the number and distribution of his symptoms.

If this operational method works, that is, if the same persons are picked by these raters on the basis of their decision rules as were picked by the clinicians on the basis of their global judgment, we will know that we have specified the cluster of signs and symptoms tacitly employed. We will then have found a disorder which is neither process nor acute schizophrenia, but which is markedly increased among the biological relatives of schizophrenics and whose signs and symptoms can be specified accurately. As in the family study, the validity of the concept is again supported by the results. It is important to realize that in both studies the disorder we call borderline schizophrenia may not bear any relation to what many clinicians call borderline states or borderline schizophrenias. This brings us to an important nosological point.

"Borderline Disorders": The Problems of Definition

We have already clinically identified a group of individuals whom we designate as borderline schizophrenics and whom we hope to be able to define in less impressionistic ways. But what if our group of individuals does not coincide with other groups designated borderline schizophrenic by others? Who is correct? It is obvious that anyone is entitled to list a group of signs and symptoms which he believes cluster together and designate them as a syndrome. He is also entitled to call them by any name he chooses. He may, however, be misleading if he calls them by a name implying a relation to disorders to which they actually bear no relation. He may, for example, notice that impulsivity, affect lability, and fluctuating reality testing seem to cluster together. If he calls persons possessing these attributes "borderlines" and if the term borderline is regarded by many as a shorthand for borderline schizophrenia, he is implying to many that these persons share both a superficial resemblance and a causal relation to true schizophrenia.

At this point the data from the adoption studies become relevant. These data tell us which signs and symptoms do cluster together and do bear a genetic relation to true process schizophrenia. The data from the adoption studies, therefore, not only document an etiological relation between borderline and process schizophrenia, but they also help us to define what borderline schizophrenia really is. What if we have not found this cluster of symptoms? The adoption studies in no way prevent, nor should they prevent, clinicians from studying interesting symptom clusters. What they should do, however, is — for the moment — form the basic criteria for defining borderline schizophrenia. If these criteria do not include affective lability, then affective lability may not be clustered with the other defining symptoms of borderline schizophrenia.

The symptomatic cluster of impulsivity, affect lability, and fluctuating reality testing might form a statistically recognizable group, but if it is not increased among the biological relatives of process or borderline schizophrenics, it is not appropriate to designate it as borderline schizophrenia. To demonstrate the nosological validity of this syndrome, one would have to employ additional data. One might, for example, find that the symptoms clustered together with greater-than-chance frequency or that similar symptom clusters were found in genetically related individuals. If the adoption studies indicate that some symptomatic and behavioral clusters which had been designated as borderline in the past do not occur with increased frequency among the separately reared relatives of borderline schizophrenics or only overlap borderline schizophrenia, as defined by us, then the re‾ ₁on of these clusters to borderline schizophrenia may be at best partial.

I said "may at best be partial." The only caveat in interpreting the adoption studies is that they are based on interview data which are far less extensive than data obtained in a therapeutic situation. Although the interviews were detailed, lasting anywhere from two to six hours, it *might* be the case that the method was less sensitive and that a number of important clinical attributes were missed. The only way to investigate this question would be to subject borderlines diagnosed in the therapeutic setting to our structured interviews. With this warning, let me proceed.

THE POSSIBILITY OF PARTIAL OR MIXED
BORDERLINE SCHIZOPHRENIC STATES

There is a logical difficulty which has been alluded to above. It is that many syndromes designated as borderline may bear a partial but incomplete relation to borderline schizophrenia as defined by these studies. It may be that these syndromes exist even though, as stated above, they are not found among the relatives of process schizophrenics.

Can genetic research aid in the understanding of these possible "partial" borderline states? Although there are, to date, no "hard" data that can directly answer this question, there are hard data that have a bearing on this question and provide a logical basis for the possible existence of other, borderline-schizophrenia-like syndromes. These data come from studies of assortative mating and the genetic transmission of other psychiatric disorders. The adoption strategy lends itself to the study of any reliably diagnosable psychiatric disorder. To date, it has been used to study sociopathy (Schulsinger, 1972), criminality (Hutchings and Mednick, 1975), and alcoholism (Goodwin et al., 1974). These studies have revealed the existence of genetic contributions to all three of these disorders. For example, starting with adopted sociopaths, one finds an increased frequency of sociopathy only among their biological relatives. In the instances of criminality and alcoholism, similar results are obtained, although with the not-surprising evidence that in criminality experiential factors as well as genetic factors play a role.

Now let us ask the seemingly simple question of what happens to the adopted-away offspring of parents, one of whom is schizophrenic and the other of whom is sociopathic? Will they, on a genetic basis, manifest abnormalities characteristic of both syndromes? We do not know the answer but we are in possession of data that may provide an answer. In the adoptee studies we began by investigating the adopted-away offspring of schizophrenic individuals and only subsequently looked at the psychiatric status of the co-parent or mate. In many instances, the co-parent was not psychiatrically healthy and in some of these instances was sociopathic. We now plan to look at the adopted-away offspring not only in terms of their schizophrenic diagnoses, but also in terms of their possession of sociopathic attributes. If we find — as seems plausible — that some of these individuals have admixtures of sociopathic and schizophrenic symptoms, we will have provided a rational basis for the observation of the clustering of sociopathic and schizophrenic characteristics. We would be able to assert that there are indeed persons who manifest two sets of syndromal characteristics, and that they do so on a genetic basis. There would thus be a rational — etiological — basis for describing persons with a cluster of mixed schizophrenic and sociopathic characteristics. They would not constitute pure borderline schizophrenics, but they might constitute pure borderline schizo-sociopaths or socio-schizopaths. As such, they would form a discrete group to study.

But why should such a syndrome occur frequently enough to be described? If sociopathy occurs in, say, five per cent of the population, only five per cent of schizophrenics would mate with sociopaths and, since schizophrenic-spectrum disorders occur roughly in five to ten per cent of the population, only five to ten per cent of sociopaths would be mated with schizophrenics. The combination of attributes would thus occur far more infrequently than the "pure" borderline state, say one tenth to one twentieth of the prevalence of pure borderline schizophrenia — that is, if assortative mating did not take place.

Assortative mating simply means nonrandom mating. In many genetic studies and analyses it is hypothesized that people mate at random since this makes the mathematical analyses easier. The hypothesis of random mating contradicts not only common sense, but data that have been collected. Black people tend to marry black people, high IQ people marry high IQ people, and so forth. If assortative mating does exist, then sociopaths might mate with schizophrenics with a greater-than-chance expectancy. On the basis of such reasoning, Rosenthal (1975) has investigated the psychiatric status of the co-parents of our schizophrenic parent probands. The results demonstrated considerable assortative mating. Of the female schizophrenics, approximately 30 per cent had mated with sociopaths and 30 per cent had mated with schizophrenic-spectrum disorders. Of the male schizophrenic fathers, slightly more than 40 per cent had mated with schizophrenic-spectrum females; the number mating with sociopaths was not above expectancy. The number mating with affective disorders remains to be explored. If the genetic studies do — and it is very likely they will — demonstrate a genetic contribution to the primary affective disorders, and if assortative mating with schizophrenics occurs, we might anticipate seeing not only persons who manifest severe mixed psychopathology — and who would be labeled as schizo-affective psychotics — but we would also anticipate seeing persons with mild to moderate pathology, i.e., borderline affective schizophrenia.

The suggestion then is that there are a priori reasons for believing that three groups of borderlines may exist: the pure and the mixed — the latter being constituted of admixtures of sociopathy and affective illness. Perhaps these as yet hypothetical conditions bear some similarity to symptom clusters other than those designated borderline schizophrenia. This speculation suggests the possibility of dividing those various disorders designated as borderlines into homogeneous and etiologically meaningful subgroups.

In conclusion, the adoption studies of schizophrenia have not only granted us some understanding of the etiology of one clearly specifiable illness which we have labeled "borderline schizophrenia," but they have also provided a logical basis for positing the existence of other syndromes, which have been labeled "borderline schizophrenia" by others. One type of borderline schizophrenia has been delineated. Others may exist. It is only by breaking down this muddled mass of humanity into relatively pure components that we can hope to obtain meaningful data in regard to the pathogenesis, dynamics, prognosis, and treatment response of borderline schizophrenics.

REFERENCES

Goodwin, D. W., et al. (1974), Drinking problems in adopted and nonadopted sons of alcoholics. *Arch. Gen. Psychiat.,* 31:164-169.

Hoch, P. H., & Polatin, P. (1949), Pseudoneurotic forms of schizophrenia. *Psychiat. Quart.,* 23:248-276.

Hutchings, B., & Mednick, S. A. (1975), Registered criminality in the adoptive and biological parents of registered male criminal adoptees. In: *Genetic Research in Psychiatry,* ed. R. R. Fieve, D. Rosenthal, & H. Brill. Baltimore: Johns Hopkins University Press, pp. 105-116.

Kallmann, F. J. (1938), *The Genetics of Schizophrenia: A Study of Heredity and Reproduction in the Families of 1,087 Schizophrenics.* New York: Augustin.

Kety, S. S., Rosenthal, D., Wender, P. H., & Schulsinger, F. (1968), The types and prevalence of mental illness in the biological and adoptive families of adopted schizophrenics. In: *The Transmission of Schizophrenia,* ed. D. Rosenthal & S. S. Kety. New York: Pergamon, pp. 345-362.

—— et al. (1975), Mental illness in the biological and adoptive families of adopted individuals who have become schizophrenic: A preliminary report based upon psychiatric interview. In: *Genetics and Psychopathology,* ed. R. R. Fieve, D. Rosenthal, & H. Brill. Baltimore: Johns Hopkins University Press.

Kretschmer, E. (1921), *Physique and Character; An Investigation of the Nature of Constitution and of the Theory of Temperament,* trans. W. J. H. Sprott. New York: Harcourt, Brace, 1925.

—— (1934), *A Text-Book of Medical Psychology,* trans. E. B. Strauss. London: Hogarth Press, 1952.

Rosenthal, D. (1975), The concept of subschizophrenic disorders. In: *Genetic Research in Psychiatry,* ed. R. R. Fieve, D. Rosenthal, & H. Brill. Baltimore: Johns Hopkins University Press, pp. 199-215.

—— et al. (1968), Schizophrenics' offspring reared in adoptive homes. In: *The Transmission of Schizophrenia,* ed. D. Rosenthal & S. S. Kety. New York: Pergamon, pp. 377-391.

Schulsinger, F. (1972), Psychopathy, heredity and environment. *Internat. J. Ment. Health,* 1:190-206.

Wender, P. H., Rosenthal, D., & Kety, S. S. (1968), A psychiatric assessment of the adoptive parents of schizophrenics. In: *The Transmission of Schizophrenia,* ed. D. Rosenthal & S. S. Kety. New York: Pergamon, pp. 235-250.

—— —— et al. (1974), Cross fostering: A research strategy for clarifying the role of genetic and experiential factors in the etiology of schizophrenia. *Arch. Gen. Psychiat.,* 30:121-128.

IV

TREATMENT APPROACHES

You are very impetuous, Mr. Chamberlayne.
There are several kinds of sanatoria
For several kinds of patients.
And there are also patients for whom
A sanatorium is the worst place possible.
We must first find out what is wrong with you
Before we decide what to do with you.
        —From *The Cocktail Party,* by T. S. Eliot

    The question of diagnosis looms large when it comes to treating a patient, any patient. With borderline cases, however, it is not merely a question of correct diagnosis — who is diagnosed as borderline and who is not — but what kind of borderline patient he is to begin with. It is not too different perhaps in schizophrenia or the neuroses, if one thinks of them as global psychopathological entities, composed of several subgroups of different degrees of pathology. The problem with the borderline group is that patients are often described or understood as all more-or-less alike.

    There is general agreement that borderline patients are most difficult to treat. As Searles pointed out in one of the workshops of the conference, in treating frankly psychotic patients a therapist may take refuge in the conviction that he is very different from his patient. Borderline patients are altogether too much like ourselves. It is easy to identify ourselves with their healthy aspects; and when they become irrational, we fear that we may go mad also. We feel ruefully envious of their ability to have the best of both worlds — the pleasures of health and the irresponsibility of madness. Incidentally, when Searles was asked what he thought of Winnicott's idea that borderline patients sometimes need to be hated, he replied that patients inevitably evoke in their helpers the same feelings they previously aroused in their parents. Not to experience these feelings would be ungenuine and confusing to the patient and, indeed, frightening. As a therapist, the point is not to act out the hateful feelings while being aware of them.

The use of treatment parameters is advocated by almost all therapists, including psychoanalysts. Such parameters include the active use of confrontation, or the interpretation of the here and now in the analytic situation rather than the classical, genetic type of interpretation; the use of medication, primarily for target symptoms and moments of maniclike anxiety rather than for maintenance purposes; the understanding that the patient can call the therapist at home any time, up to a certain hour, when anxious; and periodic brief hospitalizations, sometimes no longer than a few hours.

Kernberg exemplifies the kind of psychoanalytic psychotherapy that has developed recently, largely under his impact, around the diagnosis of borderline personality. His approach is rather intrusive, underlining the negative aspects of transference and making bold use of the therapist's own countertransference. By putting pressure on the patient's inner resources and activating his potential for reality testing, the patient is said to become more accessible to effective psychotherapy.

Adler writes about the hospital as a therapeutic modality for borderline patients. He examines the indications for hospitalization and problems encountered during such treatment. He advocates the use of brief hospitalization, periodically, in support of outpatient psychotherapy. He warns against the tendency to make a "dumping place" of the hospital after treatment has gone sour, or to set it up as a refuge, as an omnipotent shrine, in a situation where therapy has failed.

The article by Hunt, written by a professional researcher and offering a theoretical discourse on research methodology, is about treatment from a behavioral point of view. But Hunt feels equally at home with psychoanalysis. Suggesting that the behavioral and psychodynamic points of view should supplement or complement each other, rather than compete, he argues that out of the confrontation of these two theoretical views, a creative synthesis is likely to emerge, which may be applicable to the study and treatment of borderline patients.

A rather lengthy hospital treatment, with supportive use of psychotropic drugs, would be ideal for severely disturbed borderline patients, according to Sarwer-Foner, a psychoanalyst with expertise in psychopharmacology. Klein, on the other hand, is critical of psychoanalytic constructions and psychoanalytic psychotherapy and advocates the use of drugs in relation to the borderline patient's predominant affective state. His psychopharmacological approach offers an intriguing formulation of borderline disorders, while his chemotherapeutic recommendations, based as they are on extensive clinical experience with psychotropic drugs and knowledge of the psychopharmacological literature, may prove useful to the psychiatric practitioner.

Group psychotherapy, including family therapy, is found to be particularly helpful for some borderline patients. Horwitz deals with psychoanalytically oriented group therapy, as either a primary or adjunctive treatment modality; Mandelbaum's concern with family therapy is influenced by Minuchin's structural theory of family. Both modalities are based on the authors' experience with borderline patients at the Menninger Clinic.

Structural Change and Its Impediments

OTTO F. KERNBERG, M.D.

STRUCTURAL CHANGE

In this paper I shall focus on issues related to structural intra-psychic change in borderline patients, that is, on the fundamental modification of personality organization which is the specific goal of psychoanalysis and psychoanalytic psychotherapy (Eissler, 1950). "Psychoanalytic psychotherapy" here refers only to the so-called expressive or exploratory type of psychotherapy within the broad spectrum of psychoanalytically oriented psychotherapies. This type of psychotherapy is derived from and closely linked to psycho-analytic theory and technique and centers on transference interpre-tation with limited genetic reconstructions; the therapist's position of or ongoing movement toward technical neutrality; and the introduction of parameters of technique into an essentially psycho-analytic approach (Eissler, 1953; Kernberg, 1975b). Research findings from the Psychotherapy Research Project of the Menninger Foundation (Kernberg et al., 1972) and my earlier work (Kernberg, 1975a, 1975b, 1976a) stress the advisability of such a modified psychoanalytic procedure or psychoanalytic psychotherapy as the treatment of choice for borderline disorders. This paper focuses on the nature of change in patients with borderline personality organi-zation undergoing such modified psychoanalytic procedures. I have proposed in earlier work that structural intrapsychic change is, in effect, the aim of this kind of treatment for borderline disorders.

The psychoanalytic theory of structural intrapsychic change implies that the resolution of unconscious conflicts by interpretation —mainly by interpretation of the defenses (including the trans-

Medical Director, The New York Hospital-Cornell University Medical Center, Westchester Division; Professor of Psychiatry, Cornell University Medical College.

ference) reflected in the patient's resistances—brings about a change in the impulse-defense configurations, so that previously repressed impulses become freer, more directly available in consciousness, and are integrated with the patient's ego-regulated functioning (Eissler, 1950; Gill, 1954; Wallerstein, 1965). An expansion of ego potentials and functions goes hand in hand with the reduction of the restrictions on the ego, and on the personality in general, imposed by the previous, excessive repression and other defenses. The most important area of this structural change is in the transference. Instinctual impulses directed toward infantile objects become evident in the transference, and both the impulse and the infantile object relation are modified by transference interpretation. The earlier psychoanalytic formulation of "making the unconscious conscious" is replaced by the formulation "resolving the resistances" and thus bringing about the ultimate aim "where id was there ego shall be."

Contemporary ego psychology has broadened the analysis of resistances (including not only those of the ego, but those of the superego and id) and has emphasized the analysis of pathological character structures as compromise formations of defense and impulse. The study of ego defects and disorders related to structural intrapsychic conflicts has focused on the adaptive as well as maladaptive expression of impulse-defense configurations and stressed that, insofar as impulse-defense configurations are deeply anchored in the character structure (in repetitive, rigid, or persistent inappropriate behavior patterns), change in impulse-defense configurations may be evaluated by change in character structure.

I think that the study of borderline disorders has further expanded our understanding of impulse-defense configurations by focusing on the existence of primitive, "nonmetabolized" object relations as a major structural characteristic of borderline personality organization. In these patients, ego, superego, and id as overall intrapsychic structures have redissolved—or never evolved from—their constituent substructures of units of internalized object relations. I have previously proposed (1976b) that the essential units of internalized object relations consist of a self-image, an object image, and an affect disposition linking them. I have suggested that the study of the vicissitudes of internalized object relations may make it possible to explore simultaneously (1) the nature of the patient's drive organization; (2) the nature of the patient's ego organization; (3) the predominant level of developmental fixation or regression; and (4) the general level of severity of the pathology.

Let me elaborate a little. (1) The predominant level of drive organization is reflected in the degree to which the patient can integrate libidinally and aggressively invested internalized object relations, thereby allowing him to tolerate ambivalence. Within such an integration, his affect dispositions are modulated and become deeper and more sophisticated. The implication is that the study of the affect dispositions involved in the units of internalized object relations tells us something about the over-all organization of drives. (2) Regarding the predominant levels of ego organization: the degree to which the internalized object relations are dissociated or split off, as opposed to integrated into major hierarchical organizations, reflects the extent to which primitive levels of defensive organization (centering around splitting), in contrast to advanced organizational levels (centering around repression and its related mechanisms) predominate. By the same token, the integration of object relations reflects the integration of the ego, the degree to which there are nonspecific manifestations of ego strength, the degree of superego integration, and the stability of the repressive barrier separating ego, superego, and id. (3) Regarding the predominant level of developmental fixation or regression, I have described (1976b) stages in the development of the differentiation and integration of internalized object relations which coincide with the developmental stages described by Mahler (1968, 1971, 1972). Mahler relates these stages to certain periods of infantile development, which permits a diagnosis of the predominant developmental level at which the patient's pathology has been consolidated. Briefly, the autistic, symbiotic, borderline, neurotic, and normal levels of organization of internalized object relations reflect such a developmental viewpoint. (4) Regarding the general level of severity of psychopathology: the predominant developmental level of internalized object relations, the predominant drive organization, and particularly the predominant organization of ego and superego permit a classification of character pathology which has diagnostic, prognostic, and therapeutic value (Kernberg, 1976b).

According to the proposed model, pathogenic intrapsychic conflicts are expressed in the relationship between self- and object images, which reflect intrapsychically the predominant pathogenic conflicts with significant others. Thus, in contrast to the classical definition of unconscious conflict in terms of impulse and defense, object-relations theory proposes that the impulse-defense organization always involves an object relation; both the impulsive and the defensive sides reflect aspects of internalized object relations. In addition, when primitive dissociation or splitting predominates over repression and related mechanisms, whether intrapsychic conflicts are conscious or unconscious is less important than the extent to which the mutually opposed aspects of such conflicts are split or integrated. In other words, the quality of unconsciousness has less relevance at primitive levels of organization, that is, before ego, superego, and id have consolidated as over-all intrapsychic structures.

The main structural characteristic of borderline patients, therefore, is the presence of persistent patterns of behavior and intrapsychic functioning which reflect the dissociation of contradictory, potentially severely conflictual and anxiety-raising object relations. These object relations are primitive, fantastic, and unrealistic in nature, and these characteristics become manifest as the internal object relations are re-enacted with the therapist in the transference. What becomes crucial is the extent to which the patient presents himself as an integrated or dissociated self in the transference, the extent to which his major object representations are integrated (total) or dissociated (part objects), and the extent to which projection of self- and object images in rapid succession and alternation brings about chaos, meaninglessness, or a generally fantastic quality to the transference. I have suggested in earlier work (1975b, 1976a) that the diagnosis, interpretation, and resolution of primitive transferences reflecting primitive internalized object relations are major technical requirements in the treatment of borderline patients. Structural intrapsychic change in these patients has to be evaluated in terms of the occurrence of fundamental change in the predominant constellation of pathological internalized object relations manifest in the transference. This change consists of the transformation of the predominant internalized object relations from primitive and dissociated into advanced and integrated ones. Clinically, this process coincides with the resolution of primitive object relations in the transference.

The theoretical and research problems posed by this approach may appear overwhelming. Fortunately, however, in clinical practice, any borderline patient seen in intensive psychoanalytic psychotherapy over an extended period of time expresses his major psychopathology with a limited repertoire of predominant primitive internalized object relations, so that, in the midst of the chaos and confusion, repetitive patterns of his predominant object relations become activated and, indeed, highly perduring in the transference (Lester Luborsky, personal communication, 1974). The diagnosis of the predominant structuring of internalized object relations is not in itself a major difficulty, although it may take time for these structures to reveal their persistence in the transference.

I propose, therefore, that the clinical problem is less complex if and when the patient's psychopathology is studied after the transference has stabilized. This, however, may take varying periods of time. For some patients, the initial mode of relating to the therapist stabilizes after a few weeks and then remains constant over years of treatment — sometimes so constant that any minor change becomes very evident indeed, if and when it occurs. With other patients, various transformations of internalized object relations may occur over an extended period of time and manifest themselves in various changes in the transference and in the patient's external life. In these cases, general improvement of functioning may coincide with relatively rapid shifts in the predominant constellation of internalized object relations (in many ways these are our ideal treatment cases). Finally, there are patients who achieve relatively nonspecific shifts in their functioning and some improvements in their over-all life, without any significant deepening of the predominant transference paradigm, and where gradually, after periods varying from a few months up to two or three years, a major over-all internalized object relation crystallizes in the transference and then maintains itself totally, while the improvement achieved stubbornly remains at the same level.

In these latter cases, it may take a long time to diagnose the predominant constellation of transference resistances, which reflects, at the same time, the predominant internalized object relation active in the transference. The diagnosis of this pattern and its resolution may bring about significant changes which transform not only the psychopathology but the patient's life. I do not doubt that the late and protracted nature of structural change in these patients—who are often regarded as almost hopeless over many months or years of treatment—constitutes a major challenge to our evaluation of structural intrapsychic change.

It might be argued that my emphasis on structural intrapsychic change and on formulating it in terms of transformations of the predominant constellation of internal object relations creates more problems for research purposes than it solves. However, the clinician who works with both severely ill patients who do eventually change in dramatic ways, and with patients who seem quite similar and yet never change, cannot help but have an interest in research on these issues. Luborsky (1974, personal communication) has stressed the value of studying improvement in terms of significant change in the predominant repertoires of patients' interactions with the therapist. The fact is that after varying periods of time the predominant constellation of internal object relations, which simultaneously constitutes a major expression of the patient's problems and the major obstacle to change, reveals itself painfully clearly in the transference. Clinically, we cannot escape the need to focus on these persistent structural transferences, and therefore our research as well as our therapeutic efforts will have to explore further the pathology of internalized object relations.

In what follows, I shall focus on the clinical issues concerning transformations in the basic constellations of internal object relations reflected in the transference, and attempt to illustrate the usefulness of conceptualizing structural intrapsychic change in terms of change in the predominant constellation of internal object relations of patients with borderline personality organization.

I have proposed that structural intrapsychic change is reflected in the transformation of predominant internalized object relations, so that change occurs simultaneously in the area of self-integration, object integration, and affect integration around a particular object relation activated in the transference. Insofar as shifts in transference patterns within primitive transferences are often simply repetitive sequences which represent alternative enactments of self- and object images of an essentially unchanged transference relation, or represent mutually dissociated or split-off complementary object relations, true structural intrapsychic change has to be differentiated from repetitive cycles of what is basically one stable transference paradigm. Rapid shifts in transference patterns and the endless recycling of such shifts are the background against which significant transformations in such constellations have to be diagnosed. Such transformations appear fleetingly at first, in the context of interpretations of a certain transference disposition, and then reappear periodically with an ever-growing and deepening quality, until the transformation has incorporated the entire constellation of the sequence of part-object relations involved. Insofar as the transformations involve integration of part-object relations into total object relations, previous sequences gradually become transformed into the simultaneous availability of all the different components of a certain constellation. Under extreme circumstances, certain contents, fantasies, emotions, and identificatory processes that have been separated from each other over various sessions or even over a period of months become part of an integrated pattern, which, retrospectively, permits a better understanding of the significance of each component and its interaction with the others.

In the process of transformation, a gradual simplification of the material usually occurs, so that eventually years of treatment are circumscribed by a few major transference paradigms. The sequences mentioned in the development of the transference in Case 1 summarize such a set of essential transference paradigms. Transformations in the predominant object-relations structures in the transference also allow one to begin to formulate genetic reconstructions. The relationship among (1) the developmental history as observational data, (2) the intrapsychic elaboration of these experiences, and (3) the dynamic organization of the internal world of object relations is not linear, but hierarchical and systemic. There is a regrettable tendency to confuse developmental issues with genetic and intrapsychic transformational ones: the relationship between development and intrapsychic genetics is quite complex, and never on a one-to-one basis (William Grossman, personal communication, 1976).

CASE 1

The following case illustrates the development of significant structural intrapsychic change over a period of four years of psycho-analytic psychotherapy, four sessions a week, and details a stage during the fourth year in which further change seemed extremely difficult. At that point, a certain constellation of internal object relations became a major chronic transference resistance in the treatment. I shall first summarize the developments in the trans-ference over the four years and then re-examine them in terms of significant change and its limitations in the patient's external life.

The patient, a Latin American artist in her early thirties, presented a borderline personality organization with predominant masochistic and schizoid features, and severe sexual inhibition to the extent that she was unable to reach orgasm in masturbation. Her sexual fantasies were of mutilation of her own and her fantasied male partner's genitals in sexual intercourse, and she had been studiously avoiding any real opportunity of involvement with men whom she had found attractive.

In the transference, the following major paradigms developed sequentially over the four-year period. First she wished that the therapist would rape her and kill her in intercourse because only in hatred and the infliction of death could true love and commitment be found. A sadistic, primitive oedipal father image lay at the core of these fantasies. Later she fantasied being the dependent child of a motherly father and believed that if she were permitted to suck the therapist's penis, all her needs for warmth, love, sex, and protection would be met. She now wished that the therapist would hold her as a mother holds a baby while she sucked his penis with its never-ending flow of semen or milk. It became clear that a major reason for her incapacity to engage in relations in depth with men was her terror over the confusion of these two contradictory attitudes, her terror over her love and hatred coming together in an unbearable situation of danger: she was afraid that her hatred would destroy both of them.

In a later stage of her treatment, when sexual fantasies toward men acquired more integrative qualities, her fears of orgasm emerged as "fears of uncontrollable wetness." She could not show sadness in the hours because crying also meant uncontrollable wetness. Crying, orgasm, and urinating at points of sexual excitement represented the threat of loss of control, with dangerous dependency on an unreliable object — her cold and frustrating mother. She also feared that orgasm meant a frightening dissolution of her personality into impersonal fragments. In summary, the predominance of splitting mechanisms, the fear over conflicts related to severe oral frustration, and the regressive dangers of the oedipal situation, all blocked sexual excitement and orgasm.

At a still later time the patient was able to fantasize more elaborate sexual experiences with men, and the therapist in particular, which centered upon "letting herself go," urinating during orgasm, and which expressed her longings for dependency and sexual gratification in more synthetic ways. She now began to date men more freely, became engaged in heavy petting with one of them, and at this time, three and one-half years after the beginning of treatment, developed severe blockings in the hours, with long periods of silence; she also became aware of internal prohibitions against any further improvement or good experiences with the therapist or men in general. This could be traced back to a primitive maternal superego introject of an extremely sadistic nature. A primitive type of negative therapeutic reaction now developed, in the course of which emerged her submission to a sadistic superego constellation combining the hated and hateful pregenital mother with the feared oedipal rival. It turned out that the earlier fantasy of a sadistic father represented a displacement onto him of this very mother image. Only after a prolonged working through of her primitive superego pressures was the patient finally able, for the first time in her life, to establish a sexual relation with an appropriate love object.

Now to an examination of the implications of these transference developments for the diagnosis of significant structural intrapsychic change: The shift from the first transference disposition (the wish for the therapist to rape her and kill her) to the transference pattern of wishing to be the dependent child of the motherly father actually reflected a permanent feature of the patient's conflicts, namely, her terror over the confusion of her two contradictory attitudes and fears regarding men. This sequence, then, reflected only one pattern of internalized object relations, a pattern that changed only when she became aware that her hatred, death wishes, and fear of being destroyed were directed toward the same object on whom she wished to depend, and when she could tolerate this frightening contradiction. In the transference she became able to both fear and hate the therapist, to express criticism, attack, and suspicion toward him in that mood, and yet also to express longing and experiences of warmth and dependency upon him. The gradual increase in tolerating the integration of these contradictory experiences permitted her to overcome this major transference constellation and represented the first transformation in her predominant transference paradigm—reflecting a transformation in a predominant internalized object relation.

This transformation was reflected behaviorally in an impressive decrease in the patient's experiences of confusion regarding all object relations in her life and a remarkable decrease of anxiety, suspiciousness, and fearfulness without use of medication. (In the past, the patient had been massively medicated for her panic attacks, without satisfactory response.) The patient could now talk more coherently, consistently, and thoughtfully in the sessions, and began to take the first steps toward more objective and less fear-provoking relations with other people.

A second major transformation occurred when the patient began to describe her sexual fantasies and fears in more detail in the hours; this occurred in connection with her increased tolerance for enjoying genital, urinary, and dependent longings in fantasied relations with the therapist and other men. At this point, she started to have sexual experiences with men. She also improved in her creative activities and work, and only now did it emerge that one major reason for her blocking in her artistic work had been the uncontrollable sexual fantasies that were triggered off by various subjects she was attempting to explore. For example, a reference to the differences between men and women immediately evoked pervasive sexual fantasies of penises and urinating. This difficulty now subsided.

A third major transformation occurred at the time of the severe blockings in the hour and the negative therapeutic reaction related to the activation of a primitive maternal superego introject. The overcoming of this major transference pattern, again reflecting a primitive object relation, permitted this patient to become objectively more independent from her parents, to separate from her mother's values, and to become more self-affirming in her daily life.

I should stress that very little information about these issues was available at the beginning of treatment. The patient had consulted for severe and chronic anxiety and depression, breakdown in her social functioning, inability to perform in her artistic work, severe suicidal attempts, and failure in previous psychotherapeutic efforts, reflected in long-lasting, stubborn silences in the hours with previous therapists (all of them men). Only in hindsight was it possible to diagnose the nature of the blocking in the previous therapeutic experiences; it was related to the activation of the same primitive sexual fantasies that terrorized the patient. Her negativistic behavior toward her previous therapists reflected the wish to induce sexual attacks and punishment from men and to punish herself for her efforts to overcome her problems, that is, for rebelling against the primitive mother introject. These needs had motivated severe suicidal attempts which interfered with and complicated previous treatment efforts.

To stress again my principal point: in this case it took considerable time with several transference developments to diagnose the significant sequence of internalized object relations which jointly constituted a persistent constellation in the transference. It took even more time to bring about a significant transformation of these major constellations in the transference. This transformation was a precondition for bringing about change in other areas of the patient's life. It needs to be underlined that the changes that occurred in this case were not derived from the therapist's supportive, suggestive, or manipulative efforts, but followed naturally, spontaneously, and unpredictably the transformations in significant object relations in the transference.

CASE 2

The patient was a businessman in his late thirties, diagnosed as a narcissistic personality structure with overt borderline features. He was in psychoanalytic treatment. In the beginning of his treatment, he characterized his mother as a sadistic, overwhelming, hypocritical, and manipulative woman whom he had hated all his life, and his father as a warm, gentle, giving person who, however, had not been sufficiently available to him. He had a history of several relations with women in his early adulthood, affairs in which he would attempt gratification of both sexual and dependent wishes while escaping immediately from the relationship whenever a woman made any demand on him. He also had had several idealized relations with men whom he perceived as protective, warm, and giving father figures. This patient had recently married, and he perceived his wife as being very similar to his mother. The major difference was that he could dominate his wife fully, and he actually treated her at times as a slave to provide him with dependent and sexual gratifications and then he contemptuously dismissed her from his mind.

In the transference, a set of alternating constellations did not change over a period of over two years. At times the patient saw the analyst as a warm, giving, idealized father figure with certain maternal attributes, and he was aware of his sexual attraction to this father figure. At other times he became angry, suspicious, controlling, practically paranoid toward the analyst whom he perceived as his controlling and manipulative mother. These two opposing transference dispositions (the idealized-sexualized and the sadistic-depreciatory one) alternated without significantly influencing each other. When he was feeling positive and warm toward the analyst, the patient looked for dependent relations with others (idealized men) and simultaneously devalued and depreciated his wife while searching for sexual relations with slavelike prostitutes to caress him in a motherly fashion. Times of distrust and rage toward the analyst were concomitant with attacks of rage against his wife and a tendency to withdraw from all relationships in a haughty and yet depressed aloofness.

This patient could not experience any feelings of concern or guilt over his relentless attacks on the analyst during times of manifest negative transference, and the shift from the negative to the positive transference occurred almost abruptly. Only very gradually did he become able to acknowledge, at times of positive transference, an awareness of the inappropriateness of the aggression that he experienced and expressed toward the analyst at other times. This gradual recognition of his contradictory reactions to the analyst was followed by an increasing awareness of his identification with his sadistic mother and of the need to project his own aggressive and derogatory behavior onto the analyst in order to protect himself from severe guilt about his behavior. The gradual tolerance of guilt over his aggression to the analyst then expanded into a growing awareness of the similarity of this relation to that with his wife, and, for the first time in his married life, he felt concern and guilt, mixed with tenderness and appreciation, for his wife's patience with him, and regret at his having missed those loving aspects of her he now began to perceive. In short, a basic transformation in the sequence of related transference dispositions developed, reflecting a structural intrapsychic change in the organization of his internalized object relations. This structural change brought about important changes in his attitude toward his wife, and significant maturation in his general outlook on his work, social life, and family.

IMPEDIMENTS TO CHANGE

ABSENCE OF CHANGE AND THE THERAPIST'S REACTION TO IT

Many borderline patients do not change significantly over years of treatment, despite the efforts of skilled therapists of various orientations. Because of my particular interest in these patients, I have had the opportunity of acting as a consultant in the treatment of many such cases. What follows are some general considerations regarding the issues frequently involved in lack of change in the treatment situation and some general requirements for the therapist which have seemed helpful to me in facilitating significant change in some of the more difficult cases.

The problem merges with that of the development of severe negative therapeutic reactions in the treatment of borderline cases.

In fact, negative therapeutic reactions are a major cause of lack of significant change. However, in order to avoid an excessive broadening of the term negative therapeutic reaction, I think it preferable to discuss these issues in terms of lack of significant change.

I would restrict the meaning of negative therapeutic reaction to the worsening of the patient's condition, particularly as reflected in the transference, at times when he is consciously or unconsciously perceiving the therapist as a good object who is attempting to provide him with significant help. Such negative therapeutic reactions derive from (1) an unconscious sense of guilt (as in masochistic character structures); (2) the need to destroy what is received from the therapist because of unconscious envy of him (as is typical in narcissistic personalities); and (3) the need to destroy the therapist as a good object because of the patient's unconscious identification with a primitive, sadistic object which requires submission and suffering as a minimal precondition for maintaining any significant object relation (as in some borderline and many schizophrenic patients who severely confuse love and sadism [Kernberg, 1975a]). My findings seem consonant with those of other recent contributions to the psychoanalytic study of negative therapeutic reaction (Olinick, 1964; Rosenfeld, 1971, 1975; Valenstein, 1973; Asch, 1976).

These contributions, although from very different clinical and theoretical standpoints, stress the importance of preoedipal conflicts, severe aggression, and structural issues involving early self- and object representations (rather than later superego-ego conflicts). These dynamics are highly relevant to the issue of why borderline patients fail to change significantly in treatment. The stubborn persistence of pathological behavior and the lack of response to intensive psychotherapy on the part of patients who apparently were appropriately selected for intensive psychotherapy —and in whom one at first expected significant change—may be considered a form of negative therapeutic reaction and may infiltrate the entire treatment situation over months—and unfortunately, even years—of treatment.

As mentioned before, chronic lack of change may occur from the beginning of treatment, or it may make its appearance after years of treatment that had produced some significant change (as illustrated in Case 1). In spite of the fact that the therapist is naturally more optimistic when a therapeutic stalemate develops after years of treatment which has already achieved some significant change, the severity of such late stalemates is often of such an intensity as to cause the therapist to doubt whether his appreciation of previous change was realistic. The nature of the deterioration in the transference and in the patient's entire life may be such that all previous change seems to have been annulled. The situation may therefore be difficult and even dramatic both in cases where no change occurs from the beginning of the treatment, and in those where this complication develops after many months or years of treatment.

I would like to focus on some common features of such stalemates in treatment. The situations most frequently met with are: (1) Unchanged grandiosity in severe narcissistic structures. Dehumanization of the treatment situation, amounting to a complete denial of any emotional reality in the transference, may appear even in narcissistic patients who seem to be functioning at a nonborderline level. (2) Severe masochistic acting out, related to the submission to and triumphant identification with a relentless, sadistic superego formation — the stalemate in the fourth year of treatment of Case 1 had these characteristics. (3) The even more primitive identification with a sadistic, "mad" object which provides love only under the aegis of suffering and hatred. Any satisfactory relation is thus equivalent to killing — and being killed by — the needed parental image, and, therefore, losing it, while the triumph over all those who do not suffer from such a horrible human destiny is the only protection from a sense of total psychic disaster.

(4) The need, derived from all these situations, to neutralize or defeat the therapist's efforts may evolve into a malignant vicious circle. As the therapist persists in helping the patient in the face of obvious lack of response or even worsening of the patient's condition, the patient's envy and resentment of the therapist's commitment and dedication may reinforce the need to escape from what would otherwise be unbearable guilt. This guilt is caused by the mistreatment the patient feels he has given to the therapist (who, in contrast to the patient's experiences, does not respond to hatred with hatred). Severely regressed patients may have a sense of relief when their therapist loses his patience and "counterattacks" them.

Although this temporarily induces relaxation in the patient, he may rationalize this in terms of his sense that the therapist is "human after all"; usually, on a deeper level, there is an increase in the defenses against guilt feelings, an acting out of sadistic triumph over the therapist, and the danger of the reconfirmation of the pathological vicious circles of interactions the patient has engaged in with significant others in the past.

Sometimes, under conditions of chronic therapeutic stalemate, one may observe the apparently strange occurrence of some improvement in the patient's functioning outside the hours, while the psychotherapeutic work itself seems to be at a complete standstill. Or the patient may appear increasingly willing to continue an impossible therapeutic situation endlessly. At some point it is as if the treatment had replaced life and as if the patient were expressing in his behavior an urgent wish and magic command that the treatment continue forever (therefore without any change), that reality be left aside in an unconscious collusion between the therapist and the patient. The therapist may feel intuitively that the patient will experience any challenge to this stable equilibrium as an unbelievable act of cruelty, as if the therapist were throwing him to the lions.

In the middle of this situation of chronic therapeutic stalemate, patients may formulate quite directly the angry, revengeful request that the therapist compensate them for their past suffering by dedicating his life totally to them. But, regardless of the extent to which the therapist might go out of his way to accommodate the patient's desires, eventually the following issues tend to become prominent. First, the patient may destroy time in the sense of losing his perspective on time; that is, he focuses on each session as if time had come to a halt in between the sessions, and, in a deeper sense, as if both patient and therapist would live forever.

Second, this destruction of time may be accompanied by a specific neglect and rejection of what otherwise would have to be perceived as manifestations of the therapist's concern for and dedication to the patient. It is as if the patient's suspiciousness and destructive disqualification of the therapist were geared to destroying love with cruelty, while projecting this cruelty onto the therapist. Relentless accusations implying that the therapist does not love the patient enough are the most frequent, but not the most severe, manifestation of this tendency. Uncannily, at times when the therapist may in fact be internally exhausted and withdraw passively from active attempts to work with the patient, the patient's accusations may decrease, and an eerie unconscious collusion fostering paralysis and emptiness in the psychotherapeutic situation ensue.

Third, the patient may attempt to convince the therapist that the patient is really not human, that ordinary psychological understanding and empathy have no place in this situation, and the therapist may be induced to replace his concrete understanding of the dynamics of the transference by more general formulations of ego arrests, lack of capacity for emotional understanding, cognitive deficits, and the like. There are, of course, cases with such limits in their ego functioning—for example, an incapacity for symbolic communication as part of minimal organic brain damage. However, what is striking in these cases is that a careful initial study or review of the case does not reveal such deficits, and that often, to the contrary, early interactions in the treatment had given some evidence of the patient's capacity for psychological understanding. Sometimes even very experienced therapists may have to ask for help at points when ordinary human understanding no longer seems to work, only to find from the observation of others that the patient has been giving evidence of much more understanding of what has been going on than he has revealed to the therapist (this has been a dramatic feature of consultation work with such cases).

In short, something very active in the patient attempts to destroy time, love and concern, honesty, and cognitive understanding. I think that under these circumstances the therapist is facing the activation of the deepest levels of human aggression—sometimes hopelessly so. However, it is sometimes possible to resolve these severe treatment stalemates with an essentially analytic approach, and it seems to me that certain of the therapist's general characteristics and attitudes now become crucial. I shall attempt to spell out these attitudes.

IMPATIENCE IN THE "HERE AND NOW"

First of all, it is helpful to combine an attitude of patience over an extended period of time with an attitude of impatience, of not accepting passively the destruction of concrete psychotherapeutic work in each hour. This approach is in contrast to a gradual giving up reflected in a passive "wait-and-see" attitude in each hour, while the therapist actually becomes more and more impatient and discouraged as time passes; he may even reach a sudden explosion point. The implication is that the acting out of severe aggression needs to be actively countered by the therapist. "Activity" does not mean abandoning the position of technical neutrality, a point I have explored in detail elsewhere (1976a).

There are times when the therapist may feel exhausted, unable to think or say anything, and there is nothing wrong with that — so long as the therapist is aware of what is going on in him and is using it to further understand and overcome his reaction. Outside such transitory periods, however, the therapist needs to confront the patient very actively with his undermining of the therapeutic relation. Under these circumstances, the patient may react with anger and suspicion to the therapist's penetrating efforts to examine and resolve a therapeutic stalemate. It is as if the patient were actively involved in attempting to convince the therapist that what the therapist sees as his concern and interest is really anger and aggression. This active distortion by the patient of what the therapist is doing needs to be interpreted.

For example, one patient in analysis fell asleep immediately every time the analyst focused on the transference; he never fell asleep at other times. The patient gradually extended his falling asleep to all comments by the analyst that the patient suspected were indirectly related to the analyst's effort to focus on the transference, including all comments related to the patient's falling asleep and to his falling asleep when the analyst commented about the danger of his immediately falling asleep, and so on. Retrospectively, this may seem an extreme, almost amusing case of repression, but while it was going on in the treatment, it reflected an extremely serious, unconscious effort to defeat the analyst perceived as a sadistic father image. The analyst began to focus more and more on the patient's extraordinary tranquility and lack of concern in the face of this development which had brought about a therapeutic stalemate lasting for months, and in the process, the interpretive focus broadened until the patient's entire life seemed to center on his tendency to fall asleep during the analytic hours.

It hardly needs to be stressed that the therapist should intervene only when he is not under the sway of negative, hostile affects toward the patient. Such aggression toward the patient may be a "normal" reaction under such extreme circumstances, but it usually becomes condensed with whatever potential for aggressive counter-transference reactions exist in the therapist, and the therapist must contain this reaction in terms of utilizing it for his understanding rather than transferring it into action. The patient may become alarmed at what he perceives as the therapist's aggressive, confronting attitude, and the interpretation of the patient's fears that the therapist is about to stop the treatment as retaliation against the patient's unconscious efforts to undermine it may be an important help in clarifying the nature of this transference situation.

FOCUS ON TIME AND TREATMENT GOALS

A second major attitude of the therapist that might be helpful under conditions of therapeutic stalemate is to focus sharply on the patient's omnipotent destruction of time. The therapist needs to remind the patient of the lack of progress in treatment, to bring into focus again and again the over-all treatment goals established at the initiation of treatment, and how the patient appears to neglect such goals completely while assuming an attitude that the treatment should and could go on forever. In this connection, the establishment of realistic treatment goals and their differentiation from the patient's life goals, as stressed by E. Ticho (1972), become crucial.

For example, a 45-year-old woman who had divorced her husband as the latest re-enactment of a long series of sadomasochistic relationships with men (all of which ended up in frustrating and disappointing abandonments of her by them) developed a prolonged rage reaction with the therapist because the therapist would not consider responding to her amorous advances toward him. Careful and fairly full interpretation of the transference implications of this pattern over an extended period of time had not led to its solution. When the therapist finally realized that the patient had maintained the secret fantasy of marrying him as part of her initial decision to enter treatment, he confronted her with this information. Faced with this unrealistic confusion of her life goals and her treatment goals, the patient angrily terminated the treatment and refused to either continue or reinitiate her treatment with somebody else. This issue should have been explored from the beginning of her treatment.

FOCUS ON DESTRUCTION OF EXTERNAL REALITY

The focus on the broad goals of the treatment needs to be complemented by a sharp focus on the patient's immediate reality. Usually, under conditions of extreme, prolonged stalemate, the patient also neglects his immediate reality situation and reveals what at times amounts to an almost conscious sense of triumph in defeating his own efforts, a triumph over the therapist, whose impotence is reconfirmed every day as impossible situations develop and disaster is courted. It is essential that the therapist interpret the unconscious (and sometimes conscious) rage at him expressed in the patient's playing Russian roulette in his daily life.

The patient will, in the process, have to reassume responsibility for his immediate life situation as well as for his long-range plans. This is a responsibility that I think we expect any patient who undergoes psychoanalytic psychotherapy on an outpatient basis to be able to assume, and it constitutes the reality baseline against which transference acting out can be evaluated and interpreted. In other words, acting out may take the form of burning all bridges with the present external life and with the future, with the implicit expectation that the therapist will assume full responsibility for these; this must be interpreted consistently.

All of which points to the crucial need for a careful initial evaluation of the indications and contraindications for psychoanalysis or intensive psychoanalytic psychotherapy of borderline (and other) patients. It illustrates what I have suggested elsewhere (1976a) are the three issues that codetermine the priorities for interpretive work in each session with borderline patients: first, the predominant transference paradigm at any particular moment; second, the patient's immediate life situation; and third, the over-all goals of the treatment.

INTERPRETATIONS OF DISSOCIATED LOVE AND CONCERN

One important way the therapist can be helpful under the conditions described is by consistently interpreting the splitting between the patient's angry, demanding, and self-defeating attitudes in the transference, on the one hand, and his periods of calm, friendly, and even warm, relaxed, and unconcerned behavior toward the therapist, on the other. There is a need to bring together such islands of potentially observing ego and, particularly, of remaining self-concern, with the major area of his personality where aggression dominates unbound and unchecked. Although this point may seem rather obvious in theory, in practice one cannot underestimate the relief a therapist may experience when there are at least a few quiet, relaxed, "good" moments in his interactions with a patient whose treatment is becoming more and more a nightmare.

There may be a temptation for the therapist to collude with splitting mechanisms in the patient as one way of preserving his good feelings about the patient in the face of his unrelenting aggression. But the therapist needs to maintain faith in the patient's capacity to work on his problems, faith that some area of humanity which is still potentially available does exist. This faith in a potentially "good" aspect of the patient should permit the therapist to actively confront him without colluding in defensive islands of friendliness, and without letting himself drown in guilty feelings stemming from the patient's accusations that the therapist is attacking him.

In other words, confidence in what the patient potentially is or might become is the basis of strength from which confrontation may be carried out without punitive implications, in contrast to the temporary participation in or enjoyment of quiet moments dissociated from or as an expression of defense against the patient's awareness of his own aggression. Paradoxically, the therapist who can maintain this kind of confidence and trust in the patient's potential without denying the defensive aspect of the patient's temporary "friendliness" in the face of all-encompassing aggression will be freer and more effective in dealing with the negative transference than a therapist who attempts to maintain an image of the patient's "nice qualities" dissociated from the unpleasant or frightening aspects of his behavior.

A corollary of this attitude is to expect nothing in terms of immediate, short-range change in the hours, to maintain a consistent attitude of concerned challenge from hour to hour, while expecting that any change will take a very long time indeed. The patient may be willing to "improve" for the therapist's sake, and thus tempt the therapist to feed into his efforts to replace life with the treatment situation. The therapist has to interpret this aspect as well. In the long run, the combination of sublimated impatience in each hour, a questioning and concerned attitude, a lack of expectation of immediate change and yet a maintenance of hopefulness regarding long-term change, may provide a very strong, supportive aspect to the treatment in terms of implicit communication of such confidence and hope.

The opposite extreme is a quiet, almost masochistic submission to the patient's omnipotent control in the hours, an effort on the therapist's part to maintain a picture of the patient as a "nice person," a gradual development of pity for the patient (a quite frequent, complex manifestation of counteraggression toward him), and the tendency to "suddenly give up" at some point, in what might be called a quiet temper tantrum. A realistic giving up should involve an ongoing process in which patient and therapist share the growing conviction that not much more can be accomplished in a given treatment situation.

LACK OF PROGRESS AS A CATASTROPHIC SITUATION

When treatment remains at a stalemate for a long period of time, the therapist may sometimes feel that not only is nothing going on in the session, but he has nothing new to offer. He is, as it were, completely paralyzed in terms of any thought, feeling, or intervention that might influence the situation. I think it is realistic to consider sessions during which "nothing happens" in patients with chronic therapeutic stalemate as an expression of a catastrophic situation. For the therapist to be forced into a subjective sense of paralysis reflects the destruction or denial of the present human interaction's significance—such a situation cannot but evoke anxiety in the therapist.

The therapist may experience a sense of helplessness, a feeling that he needs a new beginning without knowing where to start, a sense of responsibility and of tasks unfilled, and a sense of guilt for permitting the patient to continue in a situation that is, as far as the therapist can see, not helpful. Such anxiety will also activate whatever countertransference potential exists in the therapist at this point, and it may be very helpful for the therapist to explore this fully within himself, utilizing bad moments in the patient's treatment for learning more about himself.

If and when the therapist can reassure himself that his intervention will not be determined by his own countertransference needs, but by the real needs of the patient, he should then confront the patient actively with the fact that nothing is happening and that both patient and therapist have the urgent, unfulfilled task of exploring why this is so. Indeed, this may be the major task for both participants, and to begin carrying it out in ignorance of its meaning should become a concern to the patient as well as the therapist.

In short, the therapist now raises a major issue for which he has no answer, except his concern about the lack of progress in the treatment. My point is that it is better to become a "bull in the china shop" than to remain paralyzed in situations of chronic stalemate, to be lulled into a passive collusion with the patient's destruction of time. At the very least, such an approach reconfirms for the patient the therapist's concern, his determined intolerance for chronic impossible situations, and his faith in the possibility of change. Particularly with patients who have been in treatment over years, it may become more and more difficult for the therapist to face in any one session his impatience with his growing awareness of lack of change. To cut through months and even years of a sterile, repetitive process which only imitates significant human interaction may become very difficult for the therapist. The accumulation of guilt for having tolerated an impossible situation over such an extended period of time, realistic or unrealistic as it may be, is one more impediment to change: this one stemming from the therapist.

SECONDARY GAIN OF TREATMENT

One other attitude of the therapist that may be of great help under conditions of chronic stalemate is his re-evaluation of whether the patient, realistically speaking, has anything better to look forward to than the eternal maintenance of the present life and treatment situation. The implication is that, at times, the patient with chronic therapeutic stalemate or negative therapeutic reaction may manage to infiltrate the therapist's mind with a growing conviction that the patient cannot expect anything better from life than what he has right now, and that the patient really would not be able to have a more satisfactory life if he were functioning more on his own.

This problem becomes particularly important with middle-age and older patients where the therapeutic illusion that, if everything else fails, youth holds its own promises for the future, must break down. It is, of course, important to evaluate at the beginning of treatment whether the patient — if and when treatment goals are accomplished — will have anything better to look forward to than his present life situation. If the therapist is convinced, for example, that the patient's life has passed by, that the amount of destruction the patient has incurred in terms of the possibility of love, family life, work or creativity, and sources of gratification in general is such that there is really not much hope, then perhaps there is no reason for subjecting the patient to intensive psychoanalytic psychotherapy. It is true that at times a change in the internal attitude toward life may be what is aimed at, but then this needs to be a clearly understood, shared treatment goal.

As an illustration, one patient came to treatment because his wife had abandoned him for another man. His initial treatment goal was to become healthy psychologically so that he could get his wife back. Only after some time of preliminary discussion of treatment and life goals was the patient able to become fully aware that psychological treatment would not only not give him any guarantee of getting his wife back, but would not even assure him of the possibility of obtaining another satisfactory relationship with a woman, and that the most he could expect was that whatever internal attitudes of his interfered with the potential of a good relationship might change. The decreasing possibility of obtaining a satisfactory sexual, particularly a marital, partner as life goes on has to be part of the discussion of treatment and life goals. These preconditions then permit the therapist, at periods of lengthy stalemate, to reconfirm internally his confidence that the patient has potentially something better to look forward to than to an eternal psychotherapeutic situation such as the present one.

THE THERAPIST'S OWN REACTIONS TO LIFE CRISES AND
TOLERANCE OF AGGRESSION

Considering that borderline patients, struggling against a terrifying past and incapable of projecting into the future any illusion of a better life situation than they had before, have few inner resources for expecting things to get better, the therapist's conviction that one can live a meaningful life independently and, in a deep sense, become an adult, and that loss, severe illness, and failure can be tolerated and worked through if not fully surmounted, becomes very important. The therapist's conviction that it is possible to "start all over again" may become a powerful instrument in the interpretation and working through of the transference.

Realistic treatment goals involve the acceptance not only of unresolved shortcomings but of the unavoidability of aggression in ordinary life. The therapist's tolerance of his own aggression and that of the people he loves may make it easier for him to interpret the patient's aggression without being sucked into the patient's conviction that his aggression is dangerous because it will inevitably destroy love, concern, meaning, and creativity. Therefore, the therapist's thoroughly understood awareness of the aggressive components of all love relations, of the essentially ambivalent quality of human interactions, may be a helpful asset in the treatment of extremely difficult cases.

The fact that the therapist can accept truths about himself and his own life may permit him to express in his behavior the conviction that the patient might also be able to accept truths about himself and his own life. Such uncompromising honesty in facing the most turbulent and painful of life's prospects may become part of very concrete interventions with patients having long-term stalemates in the treatment. The confidence that the patient can take and accept the truth about himself expresses at the same time a confidence in the patient's potential resources. For example, in working with older patients, where the therapist has to struggle with his own fantasies that for such patients the needs for sex, companionship, and social effectiveness will be hard to satisfy and achieve, and that death and illness are too close for comfort, the therapist's resolution of these anxieties may permit him to cut through the defensive use of old age as a device for potentially raising guilt in the therapist, or as a rationalization for self-destructive giving up on the part of the patient.

One additional issue regarding the therapist's attitude toward chronic therapeutic stalemate concerns his function as a "holding" object, his providing a function akin to basic mothering for patients for whom, for whatever reason, normal mothering did not exist. I have observed periods in the analysis or psychoanalytic psychotherapy of borderline patients where, as Winnicott suggests (1958, 1965), a silent regression takes place to what amounts to a primitive form of dependency on the analyst experienced as a "holding mother." At such times, the analyst's intuitive, empathically understanding presence may be sufficient, in contrast to the disturbing, intrusively experienced effects of verbal interpretations. However, such periods of quiet togetherness and intimacy, in which the patient's "true self" may emerge beyond his "false self" (his artificial, pseudoadaptive efforts), differ dramatically from the situation in chronic states of stalemate where the patient's sense of not being understood, of not being loved by the therapist, and of the therapist's intrusiveness are a product of the patient's defensive negation of his own destructive needs and efforts.

It is true that at such chronic periods of acting out of destructiveness in the transference the therapist's remaining silent and sitting back may temporarily relieve the patient's anxiety and rage. But this relief often turns out to reflect the fantasied satisfaction of the patient's aggression — for example, his fantasy that his envious attacks have destroyed the therapist's creative processes, particularly the therapist's capacity for independent, creative thinking. Thus what on the surface may resemble the therapist's tolerating the patient as he is, on a deeper level may reflect the patient's experience of the therapist as giving in to his demands and destructiveness — a situation radically different from that in which moments of silent concern and empathy on the part of the therapist are met by the patient's awareness of these characteristics of the therapist. There is, however, another "holding" function exercised by the therapist at times of chronic therapeutic stalemate, namely, that provided by his ongoing faith in the possibility of the patient's change, his concern for the passage of time, and his intolerance for chronic impossible situations.

Further Observations on the Psychoanalytic Attitude in the Psychotherapy of Borderline Patients, and the Therapist's "Holding" Function

My main point here is that an essentially analytic attitude, reflected in a position of—or ongoing movement toward—technical neutrality, provides an optimal background for an interpretive approach to borderline patients. Such "holding," "mothering," or "emotionally corrective" functions as are implicit in this context (Winnicott, 1958, 1965; Modell, 1976) have an important therapeutic value, but for reasons that are more complex than a simple re-creation or compensating re-enactment of a normal mother-child (infant) relation.

I think Mahler's (1971) proposal that borderline pathology is related specifically to the rapprochement subphase of the separation-individuation process, and my proposal that the problem with borderline patients is not the lack of differentiation of self from nonself but the lack of integration of "good" and "bad" self- and object representations, coincide in stressing that these patients' main problem is their failure to achieve a satisfactory loving relation with an object that can be trusted and relied upon in spite of the patient's aggression toward it, in spite of the awareness of the shortcomings of and frustrations stemming from that object, and in the context of tolerance of painful guilt, concern, and gratitude toward that loved object. For the patient to accept closeness and being understood and to rely on the therapist requires acceptance of his own aggression and the trust that this aggression will not destroy the therapist or the love for the therapist. For the therapist to be able to "hold" the patient means to accept the reality of the patient's aggression without being overwhelmed by it, to trust in some loving potential of the patient in spite of his present limitations in expressing it, and to trust the possibility that life has something to offer the patient in spite of a realistic awareness of his limitations.

For example, one patient with severe hypochondriacal tendencies became aware that he was no longer constantly preoccupied with illness and death when he could experience a capacity to express love and care for his wife and children. He felt that he was now able to give, and this made it possible to accept the idea of future illness and death without the terrible thought of dying and not having left anything of value to those who were important to him. Before that, unconsciously, death was the final condemnation of being swallowed up by his own "evil nature" in a world that was empty and devoid of love. Another patient, a woman with a narcissistic personality whose life centered largely around keeping up an artificial semblance of youthfulness and carefully disguising all manifestations of the aging process, could accept "letting go," in the sense of looking her age and accepting the aging process, when her fear over the terrible envy of the young decreased, and when, in spite of her envy, she was able to invest interest in the young people who surrounded her in her daily life and work.

For the patient to be able to accept being "held," to rely on another person, also means he accepts the possibility of "letting go," of abandoning his self in a relation with the knowledge that all relations are limited, and over a long time, uncertain. The essential precondition for accepting this possibility is a toning down, a decrease in the predominance and fears about his own aggression. The achievement of this capacity in treatment is reflected in the patient's becoming able to accept closeness to the therapist in spite of the time limitations of the hours, and to accept that the therapist has a life of his own beyond the patient and the hours with him.

It is essential that the therapist come to terms with and tolerate aggression, both in himself and in others. To squarely face the existence of aggression and to maintain a realistic attitude about the limits and limitations of the therapeutic relationship is in contradistinction to such antitherapeutic attitudes as obsessive coldness, narcissistic withdrawal, "messianic oneness" with the patient, and above all, a naïve, Pollyannaish neglect of the ambivalence of all human relations.

There are areas in which the therapist must let patients know that he can not or will not do for them what they can not or will not do for themselves. The intense and deepening object relation involved in each psychotherapy hour, and throughout weeks, months, and even years of treatment has a totally different quality from an ongoing real life relation, and this is something the patient must eventually accept. The empathic attitude of the therapist, derived from his emotional understanding of himself and from his transitory identification with and his concern for the patient, has elements in common with the empathy of the "good-enough mother" with her infant. There is, however, also a totally rational, cognitive, almost ascetic, aspect to the therapist's work with the patient which gives their relation a completely different quality from that of a mother-infant one.

Because patients with good ego strength frequently use either intellectualization or excessive affective reactions as a defense (obsessive-compulsive versus hysterical pathology), we tend to overlook the intimate connection between affects and cognition at the earlier levels of development and in the more pathological or primitive psychological functioning that retains modes of such early development. In addition, the traditional focus on "catharsis" in psychoanalytic psychotherapies (and the distortion of this concept in some currently employed psychotherapeutic modalities that naïvely assume that affective discharge will produce, by itself, fundamental psychological change) has prevented us from recognizing to what extent cognitive clarification and integration is a basic and potent psychotherapeutic tool.

In psychoanalysis as well as in the psychoanalytic psychotherapies, the therapist's cognitive formulations strengthen or broaden the patient's integration of affects and internalized object relations. What Winnicott (1965) has described as the "holding" environment — the provision of functioning akin to early mothering by the therapist who empathically "holds" the patient under certain regressive conditions — involves not only the therapist's affective disposition, but also, and fundamentally, his cognitive integration of fragmented, dissociated, or chaotic information from the total patient-therapist interaction. To formulate interpretations with patients in a state of severe regression is to interpret primitive defensive splitting, to integrate defensively dissociated affects and object relations, and to increase the patient's cognitive capacities, all in one. Not all intellectual knowledge is "intellectualization," and authentic knowledge both fosters and is a concomitant of any emotional growth.

The therapist who carries out an interpretive psychotherapy with borderline patients will necessarily frustrate the patient's wishes by carefully avoiding making decisions for him. The patient may for a long time remain unaware that what he is receiving is consistent

alertness, interest, and concern in the face of the many temptations
for the therapist, under the onslaught of the patient's aggression, to
become angry, sleepy, withdrawn, indifferent, impatient, and the
like.

I have stressed that it is not enough for the therapist to be emotionally available, warm, and sympathetic and to tolerate aggression without responding in counteraggressive ways, that he must
maintain at all times an intellectual clarity expressed in good
reasons explaining why he does or does not carry out certain interventions. He must also maintain an awareness of the realistic limits
of the effectiveness of his interventions.

Returning once more to the beginning of change, what I have
said implies that in the treatment of borderline patients, rather than
experiences of sudden discovery or cathartic awareness, there is
usually a slow, uncertain, and repetitive process of exploration of
meanings, confrontation, testing of interpretive hypotheses, and
working through of self-defeating character patterns. The first,
usually weak, signs of change in any rigid character pattern (such as
in malignant grandiosity, self-defeating narcissism, chronically triumphant masochism, total denial of emotional reality, or the self-
perpetuating trickery of antisocial exploitation) may be so brief and
transitory that any hope originally triggered by such early changes is
soon dashed.

The realistic perception of change in the predominant constellation of internalized object relations is a long and slow process.
This is one more reason why consistent impatience in every session
should be coupled with great patience for lack of change (while
remaining aware of this lack) over a long period of time. In addition, the manifestations of the growth of the capacity for love,
concern, and gratitude are usually complex, turbulent, and unclear
at first; in contrast, hatred often has a clarifying, precise, boundary-
drawing quality to it. While the patient may experience hatred of
the therapist and in the process become precise, clear, excited, or
even elated, the therapist's concern for his patient at that time may
have a confusing and even somewhat disorganizing effect on his own
thinking. And yet this confusion and turbulence within the therapist
is the raw material for his growing understanding of the patient.
The early stages of "humanization" of the patient may take the form

of confusion and chaos, depression and suffering. There is no easy way in the long, expecting, waiting, and groping road toward understanding.

In summary, I have attempted to draw attention to similarities and differences between the therapist's attitude to the borderline patient in intensive psychotherapy and that of ordinary mothering. The expectation that, with increasing knowledge, psychological treatment of severe character pathology and the borderline disorders will become shorter may represent one more illusion about the process, the technique, and the outcome of psychotherapy. But the possibility of diagnosing the major transference constellations reflecting the predominant conflicts in the area of borderline patients' object relations after a limited period of treatment seems a realistic consequence of our growing knowledge about these patients. Such an earlier diagnosis should provide the possibility of defining more concretely, after an initial period of psychotherapy, what significant changes one might expect in such constellations and their respective sequences: here may be an area for new, sophisticated research on the process and outcome of intensive psychotherapy.

REFERENCES

Asch, S. S. (1976), Varieties of negative therapeutic reaction and problems of technique. *J. Amer. Psychoanal. Assn.*, 24:383-407.

Eissler, K. R. (1950), The Chicago Institute of Psychoanalysis and the sixth period of the development of psychoanalytic technique. *J. Gen. Psychol.*, 42:103-157.

———— (1953), The effect of the structure of the ego on psychoanalytic technique. *J. Amer. Psychoanal. Assn.*, 1:104-143.

Gill, M. M. (1954), Psychoanalysis and exploratory psychotherapy. *J. Amer. Psychoanal. Assn.*, 2:771-797.

Kernberg, O. F., et al. (1972), Psychotherapy and psychoanalysis: Final report of the Menninger Foundation's psychotherapy research project. *Bull. Menninger Clinic*, 36(1/2).

———— (1975a), *Borderline Conditions and Pathological Narcissism.* New York: Jason Aronson.

———— (1975b), Transference and countertransference in the treatment of borderline patients. *Strecker Monograph Series*, XII. Also in: *J. Nat. Assn. Private Psychiat. Hosp.*, 7:14-24.

———— (1976a), Technical considerations in the treatment of borderline personality organization. *J. Amer. Psychoanal. Assn.*, 24:795-829.

_____ (1976b), *Object Relations Theory and Clinical Psychoanalysis.* New York: Jason Aronson.

Mahler, M. S. (1968), *On Human Symbiosis and the Vicissitudes of Individuation.* Vol. I. *Infantile Psychosis.* New York: International Universities Press.

_____ (1971), A study of the separation-individuation process: And its possible application to borderline phenomena in the psychoanalytic situation. *The Psychoanalytic Study of the Child,* 26:403-424. New York: Quadrangle.

_____ (1972), Rapprochement subphase of the separation-individuation process. *Psychoanal. Quart.,* 41:487-506.

Modell, A. H. (1976), "The holding environment" and the therapeutic action of psychoanalysis. *J. Amer. Psychoanal. Assn.,* 24:285-307.

Olinick, S. L. (1964), The negative therapeutic reaction. *Internat. J. Psycho-Anal.,* 45:540-548.

Rosenfeld, H. (1971), A clinical approach to the psychoanalytic theory of the life and death instincts: An investigation into the aggressive aspects of narcissism. *Internat. J. Psycho-Anal.,* 52:169-178.

_____ (1975), Negative therapeutic reaction. In: *Tactics and Techniques in Psychoanalytic Therapy,* Vol. II. *Countertransference,* ed. P. L. Giovacchini. New York: Jason Aronson, pp. 217-228.

Ticho, E. A. (1972), Termination of psychoanalysis: Treatment goals, life goals. *Psychoanal. Quart.,* 41:315-333.

Valenstein, A. F. (1973), On attachment to painful feelings and the negative therapeutic reaction. *The Psychoanalytic Study of the Child,* 28:365-392. New Haven: Yale University Press.

Wallerstein, R. S. (1965), The goals of psychoanalysis: A survey of analytic viewpoints. *J. Amer. Psychoanal. Assn.,* 13:748-770.

Winnicott, D. W. (1958), *Collected Papers.* New York: Basic Books.

_____ (1965), *The Maturational Processes and the Facilitating Environment.* New York: International Universities Press.

Hospital Management of Borderline Patients and Its Relation to Psychotherapy

GERALD ADLER, M.D.

Hospital treatment for borderline patients may be indicated during regressions manifested by increasingly destructive or self-destructive behavior. The regression may be precipitated by a loss of support from important people in their lives, disappointments in attaining their often unrealistic goals, or increasing primitive rage in the transference as early childhood abandonment issues appear in the course of treatment.

In the present essay I shall deal with aspects of the hospital treatment of all borderline patients, but shall emphasize those patients already in therapy who require hospitalization during ongoing treatment. I shall stress: (1) unresolved developmental issues that emerge in therapy requiring more support than that available to the patient outside of the hospital; (2) useful functions hospitalization can perform for both patient and therapist; (3) the therapist's countertransference difficulties and vulnerabilities which may become more manifest when the patient is hospitalized; (4) hospital-staff countertransference difficulties that promote destructive, regressive patient behavior, and may often impede the therapist's work with the patient; and (5) administrative and staff problems within the hospital setting that can facilitate or impede the resolution of issues that led to hospitalization.

THE BORDERLINE'S DILEMMA

The borderline patient's vulnerability consists of latent, desperate aloneness and panic, which he may experience when his prim-

Professor of Psychiatry, Tufts University School of Medicine; Director of Training in Adult Psychiatry, Tufts Psychiatric Residency Training Program, Boston, Massachusetts.

itive rage begins to emerge in his relations with important people.
This rage may appear in therapy when equally primitive longings to
be held and nurtured surface and are frustrated by the realities of
the therapeutic situation. The fact that this fury arises early in
treatment, even in an empathic, supportive psychotherapeutic
setting, helps to distinguish most borderline patients from narcissistic character disorders, who form stable idealizing or mirror
transferences. The borderline patient's experience of his rage is
often overwhelming and leads to an increasing sense of destructiveness, panic, or both. The panic stems from the feeling that he has
destroyed any image or fantasy of good, nurturing figures, as well as
his conviction that the outside world is malevolent and retaliatory
(Adler, 1973, 1975; Adler and Buie, 1976).

Developmentally, the furious borderline patient has regressed to
a period where a sense of object constancy is not solidly established
and the capacity to evoke the sustaining image of nurturing figures
is transiently lost (Adler, 1975; Adler and Buie, 1976). At the height
of the regression, the patient's ability to recognize the previously
valued aspects of the therapist, even though he is in the same room
with the patient, may disappear. These frightening experiences
derive partly from failures in the resolution of developmental issues
of the second year of life, including the development of object constancy, increasing separateness from parents, and continuing
individuation. Relatively prolonged lack of empathic "good-enough
mothering" or specific unbearable traumatic losses may contribute
significantly to the vulnerability of the future borderline adult
(Adler, 1975; Adler and Buie, 1976). The emergence of this vulnerability is to be expected in any psychotherapy with borderline
patients, even though the therapist may utilize an approach that
discourages dependency and regression.

This brief formulation of the borderline patient's dilemma complements the major contributions of Kernberg (1967, 1968, 1973a),
as well as the formulations of Guntrip (1971), Balint (1968), and
Frosch (1970). A focus on developmental issues must also include
further elaboration of the borderline patient's primitive defenses
and other aspects of ego weakness. Kernberg's work does not require
detailed restatement; it will be utilized below in understanding the
hospital treatment issues of borderline patients.

INDICATIONS FOR HOSPITALIZATION

Hospitalization has to be considered for borderline patients who are experiencing intense panic and emptiness, either because of the emergence of destructive fury in the transference or because of a desperate reaction to relative or total loss of important people or other disappointments in their current lives. Implicit in this desperation is an inability to experience the therapist as someone who constantly exists, who is available and supportive. The fragile, unstable working alliance, characteristic of borderline patients, readily breaks down under stress. The patient's desperation may include destructive and self-destructive preoccupations and present a serious danger of suicide and other destructive or self-destructive behavior.

Treatment of borderline patients within a hospital setting provides the patient and treatment team, including the patient's therapist, with a series of opportunities to formulate and implement a treatment plan leading to a productive use of hospitalization, rather than one that supports and continues the regressive behavior with its real dangers. Whether the borderline patient requires and can benefit from hospitalization depends upon an evaluation of several factors: the patient's basic ego strengths and ego weaknesses, the type or types of precipitating stress, the support systems available to the patient outside the hospital, the patient's relation to his therapist, the intensity of the transference feelings, and the therapist's awareness of his countertransference feelings and responses. Also important are the quality and availability of an appropriate hospital, the patient's and family's willingness to participate in the hospitalization, and the financial resources of the patient and family, including the adequacy of hospitalization insurance.

Since hospitalization may be the first stable situation in a long time for a desperate, disorganized borderline patient, it may also provide the first opportunity for the patient to collaborate in a thorough evaluation. This evaluation should include participation of the family and a careful look at the patient's work with his therapist. Even though the therapist who hospitalizes the patient has attempted to evaluate the needs and usefulness of hospitalization, this outpatient evaluation may, of necessity, be brief and sketchy because of the chaos of the patient's life and the dangers the patient is facing. On the other hand, patients who decompensate during long-term therapy may have been thoroughly evaluated by their therapist. Hospitalization for this group offers a chance for the therapist to obtain an impartial evaluation of his work with the patient and assistance with the family, if indicated, and a safe setting to begin the resolution of transference issues that overwhelm the patient.

Once the decision to hospitalize the patient is made, the choice of the hospital is important. Sometimes there is no choice in areas that have no hospital where the staff has a dynamic understanding of programs for the borderline patient. Or there may be one such hospital, thereby making the decision simple. When there are several suitable hospitals, considerations include the need for short- or long-term hospitalization, whether the therapist can continue with the patient while the patient is in the hospital, whether the hospital's policy supports this continued psychotherapeutic work, and whether, in cases where it is indicated, the hospital emphasizes family involvement.

THE HOSPITAL SETTING: A GOOD-ENOUGH MOTHERING AND HOLDING ENVIRONMENT

The borderline patient's developmental vulnerabilities must be addressed in the hospital setting. The regressed suicidal or destructive patient requires a protective environment that fulfills many aspects of Winnicott's (1965) "holding environment" and has a staff with the characteristics of his "good-enough mothering" concept. The abandoned-child feelings of the enraged, regressed borderline are accompanied by distrust, panic, and a feeling of nonsupport and desperation. The transient loss of an evocative-memory capacity for important sustaining people contributes significantly to feelings of being "dropped," alone, abandoned, and isolated, and the panic these feelings induce (Adler, 1975; Adler and Buie, 1976).

When borderline patients require hospitalization, the ward structure must provide holding qualities that offer the needed soothing and security. A sufficient empathic staff response to the patient's rage, despair, and aloneness provides the potential for relationships with new people who can communicate their grasp of the patient's experience with them and be physically present and empathically available often enough. Holding and good-enough mothering imply a genuine flexibility; the child at different ages and with different experiences and stresses needs a varying response from caring parental figures. The highest level of expression of these functions by a hospital staff includes the understanding that the borderline patient is an adult who may be transiently overwhelmed; the adult aspects require nurturance, support, and respect at the same time that the childhood vulnerabilities which have unfolded need an empathic, and when necessary, a protective response.

The "good-enough mothering" and "holding environment" concepts are often misinterpreted by the staff to mean a position that offers only a constant warm, nurturing response to all patients all the time. Such a staff response may increase the patient's regressive feelings and behavior. This misunderstanding highlights problems of utilizing early child-development concepts for adult patients with difficulties that include regressions or fixations to issues related to these early years. Winnicott's concepts, when applied to hospitalized adult borderline patients, must specifically include an empathic awareness and response to adult strengths and self-esteem issues. A misunderstanding of these concepts may be part of a countertransference response that includes an omnipotent wish to rescue the patient. The correct utilization of these concepts helps support the formation of alliances and an observing ego through staff attempts to clarify and share with the patient their assessment of his complex feelings, the fluctuations of these feelings, and the patient's varying capacity to collaborate with the staff to control them over time.

The newly hospitalized borderline patient requires a rapid evaluation on admission that assesses his needs for protection. This initial evaluation investigates the suicidal and destructive dangers, and reviews the patient's history of dangerous actions in the recent and more distant past. It also includes a beginning understanding of the precipitants that led to hospitalization, as well as an evaluation of the patient's work with his therapist, if he is in therapy. A history of recent losses, whether fantasied or real, including the transient or permanent loss of a therapist, is particularly important, even though some losses may ultimately be understood as fantasied distortions or aspects of projective identification. The staff evaluation makes use of the patient's capacity to relate and to give a history to staff members, his ability to share fears and fantasies, and the degree to which he can collaborate with the staff to determine a useful hospital treatment plan. Obviously, the early assessment is very tentative, since some borderline patients have a capacity, even when regressed, to present a "false-self" picture that minimizes current desperation and dangers. A staff experienced in handling borderline patients will utilize its empathically based countertransference fantasies and feelings as part of the assessment.

The protective and supportive measures a hospital and its staff formulate and implement, in which the patient's needs are assessed correctly, can provide the most supportive holding response to an overwhelmed, regressed borderline patient. A patient may respond with a dramatic decrease in panic when his frightening suicidal feelings are evaluated to be nearly out of control and appropriate measures are instituted. These may range from assignment to a locked ward, frequent staff checks, a special nurse, to the use of antipsychotic medication when there is evidence of disorganization or fragmentation as a manifestation of the patient's anxiety. Again, the frequent collaborative attempts with the patient to reassess his status support the patient as someone who has strengths and the capacity to relate and form alliances, even though these may be transiently lost.

Once the basic protective needs of the patient are met, a more intensive, thorough evaluation of the patient and family can occur, and a treatment plan developed that includes milieu, family, and individual treatment decisions. This assessment leads to a more definitive treatment plan and helps determine whether short- or long-term hospitalization is indicated.

In the past decade many general hospitals have opened short-term intensive treatment units capable of providing excellent brief therapeutic intervention with borderline patients and their families. Such units sometimes believe they have failed when they cannot discharge a borderline patient as "improved" within weeks. They do not recognize that some borderline patients require long-term hospitalization because of long-standing ego weaknesses, overwhelming recent loss, or a family situation that has become increasingly chaotic. Kernberg (1973b) has defined characteristics of patients who require long-term hospitalization. These include low motivation for treatment, severe ego weakness as manifested by lack of anxiety tolerance and impulse control, and poor object relations. In addition, long-term inpatient hospitalization sometimes becomes a necessity because of the lack of alternatives to such hospitalization, such as day or night hospitals, or a halfway house.

There are advantages and disadvantages to both short- and long-term units. A short-term hospital presents the expectation to the patient that he can resolve his regressive behavior rapidly. It also discourages new regressive behavior as an attempt to relieve distress because the patient knows he cannot expect a long stay. Often short-term units discharge or threaten to discharge or transfer to long-term facilities those patients who regress after brief hospitalization. The knowledge of this discharge or transfer policy tends to discourage regressions; the patient may, however, utilize it for: (1) a sadomasochistic struggle with the staff, or (2) as a way of confirming projections of rage which are then experienced as angry rejections by the staff. In addition, the patient described by Kernberg as needing long-term hospitalization may feel more misunderstood and abandoned in a setting that expects him to accomplish something beyond his capacity. The policy of discharging patients who regress is especially potentially destructive if it is part of a staff's countertransference, angry, rejecting response to the projective identifications used by the enraged, regressed borderline patient (Hartocollis, 1969). When such a policy is an aspect of supportive limit setting that acknowledges realistic expectations and limits, it can be useful for those patients who can benefit from brief hospitalization. These latter patients may make good use of a short-term unit after discharge through a later readmission that carefully defines workable guidelines, including limits, and patient and staff expectations.

Although a long-term hospital may tend to prolong hospitalization unnecessarily for some patients, it can present a safe supportive structure for the appropriate patient to do important work on issues of vulnerability or the precipitating stresses that led to hospitalization. For some patients it provides the required safety for the beginning resolution of the life-and-death issues that have emerged in the transference in psychotherapy. Long-term hospitalization also allows milieu aspects to be utilized more creatively than is possible in short-term settings. For example, a variety of therapy groups can flourish when the patient population is relatively stable, in contrast to the disorganizing effect of rapid group-member turnover in brief hospitalization.

As Bion (1961) and Kernberg (1973a) have indicated, open-ended groups that offer little task structure tend to be regressive experiences for the participants. These regressive phenomena occur whether we are describing hospitalized borderline patients or a normal population in situations where group tasks are left vague or undefined. This knowledge can be utilized in planning group experiences for a hospitalized borderline patient. A program of specific task groups, such as community and ward meetings and occupational therapy, and less structured experiences, such as psychotherapy groups, can be defined to fulfill the needs of each patient. It may be that a hospital staff that is sufficiently firm and supportive can "contain" the regressive features of an unstructured ward group. In such a setting the patient program may benefit from the mobilization of negative transference affects that gravitate to the surface and are subject to group transference interpretations (Boris, 1973). These negative feelings then may not need to be acted on to sabotage other parts of the program.

Limit setting is a much discussed aspect of the borderline patient's treatment. When limit setting is too firm and is utilized too rapidly and readily in a treatment program, the unfolding of the patient's psychopathology, both in action and in words, may be seriously impeded. Among the results of such an approach may be lost opportunities to understand the patient's fears, since they may not be permitted to emerge. On the other hand, when limit setting is so lax that patients can act out issues to a degree that frightens them, their increasing individual chaos can spread to the entire ward structure and involve other patients and staff (Adler, 1973). A major aspect of a successful limit setting depends upon whether it is utilized as part of a caring, concerned, protective, and collaborative intervention with a patient (Adler, 1973) or as a rejecting response and manifestation of countertransference hate (Maltsberger and Buie, 1974).

Therapist-Patient Issues in Hospital Treatment

If the therapist decides that hospitalization is indicated, a setting that allows him to continue regular appointments with his patient is crucial. The "abandoned-child" theme, which emerges with intense rage and panic, remains among the major issues to be resolved. A hospital that encourages the therapist to continue with his patient during the hospitalization can offer the supportive structure in which this rage can be safely experienced and analyzed. For many borderline patients, hospitalization itself seems to threaten the loss of or abandonment by their therapist. The therapist's willingness to continue with the patient, in spite of the patient's conviction that he will be abandoned because of the dangerous, provocative behavior that necessitated hospitalization, also presents an opportunity for a corrective emotional experience.

Case 1

A borderline patient in intensive psychotherapy required her first hospitalization after one year of therapy when she became acutely suicidal. She was convinced that her therapist wanted to end treatment with her; his suggestion that she be hospitalized confirmed this conviction. She reluctantly agreed, however, to enter the hospital. Her therapist's continuing sessions while she was in the hospital not only permitted her to become aware of her fury at him, but helped her see that this fury was projected onto him as part of her belief in being abandoned. The continued appointments helped the patient clarify her anger, become aware that she was projecting it, and separate it from the basic caring, reliable position of her therapist. During further recurrences of this theme in later years, it was easier for the patient, with the therapist's help, to recall this earlier hospital experience. The memory of her therapist's reliability throughout the hospitalization and its relation to her anger helped her maintain a relationship and relative alliance with her therapist, thus minimizing the need for further hospitalization.

Since it is common for a borderline patient's hospitalization to be precipitated by the emergence of intense rage in the transference, we can expect an intense countertransference response in which the therapist may ultimately feel overwhelmed, helpless, frightened, exhausted, and wish to terminate his work with the patient. These countertransference feelings occur in part as a response to the patient's projections and projective identifications and may impede the therapist's accurate assessment of the patient's suicidal risk or prognosis. The therapist may not be aware of his wish to get rid of the patient, or he may acknowledge it to himself and be able to share it with a supportive hospital staff after the patient's hospitalization. Occasionally the therapist may only become aware of it after the hospital staff finds tactful ways to confront and support the therapist to acknowledge, for example, his avoidance of his commitment to participate in his patient's evaluation and treatment. When the therapist's rejecting anger remains unconscious and unavailable to his scrutiny, suicidal danger is particularly great (Maltsberger and Buie, 1974).

Case 2

A therapist admitted a chronically anxious, acutely suicidal borderline patient to a hospital and stated to the ward administrator that he wanted to participate actively in the evaluation and treatment of his patient. He missed a meeting with the resident and the resident's supervisor, phoning to say he had to bring his car in for servicing. Although it was apparent to the staff that the therapist had been doing similar things with his patient, e.g., missing appointments for a variety of reasons, the therapist could not acknowledge his anger at the patient and his wish to reject him. In spite of tactful, supportive consultation with the therapist, different staff members were unsuccessful in helping him become aware of and modify his unconscious countertransference anger, which the staff felt was largely responsible for the suicidal behavior of his patient.

A major aspect of the patient's hospital evaluation consists of the clarification of the patient's therapy, including the transference-countertransference issues. Under optimal circumstances, the hospital unit can function as a consultant for the therapist and clarify treatment issues that facilitate continuing work. The therapist who hospitalizes a regressed borderline patient may feel devalued, defensive, guilty, or ashamed as he relates to the hospital staff. In part, these feelings are his countertransference responses to the patient's intense fury, devaluation, and projection of worthlessness which the therapist may experience as a part of himself through projective identification. Earlier there may have been a reactivation in the therapist of primitive omnipotent and grandiose feelings followed by shame for his "failure" with the patient. When these countertransference feelings are coupled with the hospital staff's own omnipotent and grandiose responses, which include devaluation of the therapist and a wish to rescue the patient from him, the therapist and patient are placed in a situation that can accentuate the defensive splitting borderline patients tend to act out with any hospital unit. The experienced hospital unit always keeps in mind its own propensity for certain countertransference responses to therapist and patient as it evaluates and treats the patient.

An important task for the hospital staff is the development of a safe environment for the patient to experience and put into words his overwhelming feelings with his therapist. The borderline patient's readiness to use splitting as a defense can easily keep these feelings, especially anger, outside of the therapist's domain. The traditional use of separate therapists and administrators in many hospitals, both of whom are on the hospital staff, tends to support the splitting process in borderline patients. The patient may be angry at the administrator for decisions which limit his activities or privileges, and idealize the therapist as the caring person who would not allow such things to happen if he had the power. When the therapist is a member of the hospital staff, it is sometimes possible for him to be both administrator and therapist. If the therapist cannot assume both roles, he can, in collaboration with the administrator, ally himself with administrative decisions — assuming that he is consulted and agrees with them. He can present to the patient his agreement with the administrator, especially when the patient attempts to avoid his anger with the therapist by devaluing the administrator for some management decision.

The hospital staff that excludes the outside or staff therapist from collaborative work with treatment planning may foster a continuation of pathological splitting and lose an opportunity to help the patient develop the capacity to love and hate the same person, an obvious important step in emotional growth. It also tends to perpetuate the unit's devaluation of the therapist and his work with the patient and further intensifies another aspect of the splitting process: the patient views the therapist as weak and worthless and idealizes the hospital or hospital administrator as the omnipotent, rescuing parent. The borderline patient's defensive use of splitting is supported whether the therapist is idealized or devalued; the hospital is then less able to help the patient and his therapist continue the work of reconciling murderous fury toward a therapist who is felt as an abandoning as well as a beloved, caring, holding parent.

Of course the hospital administration can only work collaboratively with a therapist if its assessment of the therapist's work is largely positive. Often the process of evaluation helps the therapist clarify issues for himself. Sometimes the staff can formulate issues that help the therapist think through countertransference difficulties that were interfering with therapy. Such countertransference issues that can be clarified through staff consultation usually are not deeply rooted psychopathological problems in the therapist, but transient, overwhelming countertransference feelings that emerge in the heat of the treatment of regressed borderline patients. The hospital setting that protects the patient and takes the pressure off the survival issues in therapy often automatically allows the therapist to get his own perspective on countertransference issues. Sometimes a supportive, tactful consultation by an appropriate staff member helps complete the outside therapist's understanding of his work with his patient and helps him resume a useful therapeutic stance that focuses on the issues formulated.

The question may be raised: How does the hospital staff proceed when it feels that there are serious, perhaps unresolvable difficulties in the therapist's work with his patient? The staff's obligation to the therapist and patient includes a careful assessment of its own possible devaluing countertransference responses to the therapist as part of the already defined splitting processes. When the staff feels increasingly certain that pathological countertransference difficulties exist which are not modified through consultation, it must carefully review the data obtained from patient and family and the therapist's work as presented in conferences and consultations that are tactful and supportive of him. The staff may, after this review, feel that countertransference difficulties or empathic failures based upon limitations in the therapist's personality have led to an unresolvable impasse. This impasse may also continue to threaten the life of the patient, and often is the major manifestation of countertransference hate which remains unmodified and largely unconscious. At such times, the staff has little choice but to help the patient and therapist end their work. Goals then include: (1) protecting the patient while helping him understand that there is an impasse and supporting him not to see this impasse in terms of his own badness or failure, and (2) helping the therapist maintain his self-esteem in the termination process, while attempting to allow him to learn from it. Ideally, both patient and therapist should be supported to learn as much as possible, maintain their self-esteem, and say good-bye appropriately.

The therapist described above who could not be helped to become aware of his anger and rejection of the patient was relieved when the ward administrator suggested that he terminate with his patient. The decision to terminate was presented to the therapist as part of the patient's need for more intensive therapy and the difficulty the therapist was having in fitting the patient into his busy, overcommitted schedule. Once termination was decided upon and accepted by the therapist and patient, the therapist's countertransference difficulties were no longer evident. Instead, he helped the patient effectively acknowledge and bear the sadness and disappointment of ending therapy with him. I may add that the therapist did not spontaneously discuss with any staff member his role in the suicidal impasse with his patient. Although his termination work was excellent, staff members could not tell how much he became aware of the countertransference difficulties that led to the decision to terminate.

Staff Countertransference Issues within the Hospital Milieu

The borderline patient presents special challenges to any hospital staff. His use of primitive defenses—projection, projective identification, and splitting—becomes especially manifest during the regression that leads to hospitalization, and may quickly involve the hospital staff (Adler, 1973; Main, 1957). Some staff members may become recipients of aspects of the patient's projected positive, previously internalized self- and object representations, while negative self- and object representations are projected onto other staff members. This description is not meant in a literal sense, but as a way of conceptualizing the intense, confusing affects and fantasies in the patient and staff. Often these projections coincide with similar but repressed affects, fantasies, and self- and object representations in specific staff members. These staff members may have achieved much higher levels of integration and maturity; however, primitive aspects that were repressed can readily become reactivated in work with borderline patients, most of whom intuitively choose a staff member to project aspects of themselves that reverberate with similar but repressed aspects in that staff member. When these projected aspects are projective identifications, the patient's need then to control the staff member, and the latter's countertransference need to control the patient, compound the chaos of the splitting phenomena. The disagreements, fury, and often totally opposite views and fantasies staff members have about a specific borderline patient are manifestations of the splitting and projective identification process.

Another aspect of the staff's countertransference difficulties with borderline patients involves a process in which the patient is labeled as "manipulative." Manipulation for many borderlines is largely unconscious and characterological, has important adaptive elements, and helps keep some of them from feeling and being totally alone. When the patient, however, is seen predominantly as a conscious, deliberate manipulator in the negative sense, the staff feels entitled to make unrealistic demands, punish the patient, and even threaten him with discharge (Hartocollis, 1972). An observer who is not part of this ward process is often impressed with the almost total lack of empathy for the patient's pain or distress. It is as if the patient had succeeded in convincing the staff that only his negative aspects exist; at such times the staff may find it impossible to see any other part.

As stated, borderline patients use manipulation in their relations with people. Their primitive narcissism, which is part of their entitlement to survive, and the neediness associated with it, as well as the voracious oral quality of their hunger and rage, are often accompanied by a manipulative attitude when this neediness is most manifest (Buie and Adler, 1972). To miss the patient's pain, desperation, and distress, however, is to allow the splitting and projective identifications to become the staff's only view of the patient. This image of the patient as manipulator is also evidence of the patient's success in getting himself punished and devalued, which may involve projections of his primitive, archaic superego. Often the patient is seen by the staff as manipulative when he is most suicidal and desperate. At these times, staff countertransference hate is potentially lethal (Maltsberger and Buie, 1974).

A hospital staff working with borderline patients has the responsibility to itself and its patients to be alert to the described countertransference danger signals. There is no simple prescription or solution for them. Obviously, the quality of the professional staff, in particular, their achievement of higher levels of ego functioning and a solid capacity for object relations without ready utilization of primitive projective defenses, is important. In spite of the maturity of the staff, however, regressive group phenomena, especially in work with borderline patients, are inevitable (Hartocollis, 1972).

The structure of the hospital unit becomes important in the resolution of these regressive staff responses. Ongoing, regular staff meetings where patient and patient-staff issues are open for scrutiny in a nonthreatening environment are particularly useful. Staff members who know each other well are less likely to respond regressively to a borderline patient's projections, i.e., staff members' reality-testing capacities are enhanced when they have prolonged contact with other staff members in settings where they can learn clearly the reliable, consistent responses and personality characteristics of their co-workers (Adler, 1973).

A hospital administrative hierarchy that values the varying contributions of different disciplines and workers and clearly defines staff responsibilities and skills aids in minimizing projections. Such an administration also understands the importance of establishing sufficient task-oriented groups for both patient and staff needs to protect against a staff regressive pull (Garza-Guerrero, 1975). The ability of the hospital or unit director to maintain equanimity in the face of the regressive propensities of staff and patients may be a crucial ingredient in successful hospital treatment. The administrator who respects staff and patients, can tolerate their anger without retaliating, and yet be firm when necessary, and who can delegate power unambivalently can provide the mature "holding environment" and a model for identification for the staff that facilitates a similar experience for the patients.

REFERENCES

Adler, G. (1973), Hospital treatment of borderline patients. *Amer. J. Psychiat.*, 130:32-36.

———— (1975), The usefulness of the "borderline" concept in psychotherapy. In: *Borderline States in Psychiatry*, ed. J. E. Mack. New York: Grune & Stratton, pp. 29-40.

———— & Buie, D. H., Jr. (1976), The process of psychotherapy in the treatment of borderline patients. Presented at 11th Annual Tufts Symposium on Psychotherapy, Boston, April 19.

Balint, M. (1968), *The Basic Fault: Therapeutic Aspects of Regression.* London: Tavistock.

Bion, W. R. (1961), *Experiences in Groups and Other Papers.* New York: Basic Books.

Boris, H. N. (1973), Group therapy in an inpatient setting. (Unpublished.)

Buie, D. H., Jr., & Adler, G. (1972), The uses of confrontation with borderline patients. *Internat. J. Psychoanal. Psychother.*, 1:90-108.

Frosch, J. (1970), Psychoanalytic considerations of the psychotic character. *J. Amer. Psychoanal. Assn.*, 18:24-50.

Garza-Guerrero, A. C. (1975), Therapeutic use of social subsystems in a hospital setting. *J. Nat. Assn. Private Psychiat. Hosp.*, 7:23-30.

Guntrip, H. (1971), *Psychoanalytic Theory, Therapy, and the Self.* New York: Basic Books.

Hartocollis, P. (1969), Young rebels in a mental hospital. *Bull. Menninger Clinic*, 33:215-232.

———— (1972), Aggressive behavior and the fear of violence. *Adolescence*, 7:479-490.

Kernberg, O. F. (1967), Borderline personality organization. *J. Amer. Psychoanal. Assn.*, 15:641-685.

———— (1968), The treatment of patients with borderline personality organization. *Internat. J. Psycho-Anal.*, 49:600-619.

———— (1973a), Psychoanalytic object-relations theory, group processes, and administration: Toward an integrative theory of hospital treatment. In: *The Annual of Psychoanalysis*, 1:363-388. New York: Quadrangle.

———— (1973b), Discussion of: Hospital treatment of borderline patients by G. Adler. *Amer. J. Psychiat.*, 130:35-36.

Main, T. F. (1957), The ailment. *Brit. J. Med. Psychol.*, 30:129-145.

Maltsberger, J. T., & Buie, D. H., Jr. (1974), Countertransference hate in the treatment of suicidal patients. *Arch. Gen. Psychiat.*, 30:625-633.
Winnicott, D. W. (1965), Ego distortions in terms of true and false self. In: *The Maturational Processes and the Facilitating Environment.* New York: International Universities Press, pp. 140-152.

Behavioral Perspectives in the Treatment of Borderline Patients

HOWARD F. HUNT, PH.D.

When we speak of structural characteristics of the borderline patient, we use a metaphor. The structures we speak of are not really things, like the frame of a house or the steel skeleton of a skyscraper. Rather, we are using an abstraction that refers to configured collections of psychological functions. In the last analysis these psychological functions represent functional relations between behaviors and the contexts that control them. These contexts include present stimuli impinging on the subject, his past, insofar as it is recapitulated in the present, and other intercurrent behaviors.

The psychodynamic and the behavioristic approaches have much in common, but also important differences. Ultimately, both are tested at the same endpoint — what the person does — but the two approaches follow very different routes to get there. Psychoanalysis is fundamentally mentalistic. This statement is not intended to be disparaging, but rather recognizes that psychoanalysis is about wishes, thoughts, fantasies, impulses, fears, internalized objects, psychic energies, and other internal events that produce and are reflected in overt behavior. Only through an understanding of these internal events and how they are configured can overt behavior be understood and predicted. In contrast, radical behaviorism, which I prefer for analytic purposes because of the discipline it imposes, has little to say about such covert matters (Hilgard and Bower, 1966). It treats behavior as an output that is a function of input, as an output controlled by the environmental context. As with modern ego psy-

Professor of Psychology, Columbia University; Chief of Research Psychology, New York State Psychiatric Institute, New York City, New York.

chology, the behavior is controlled in the here and now, with the subject's conditioning history contributing only insofar as it is represented in the present (Hunt, 1968). Only recently, however, has serious consideration extended to the special ways in which self-referential verbal behavior may participate in this control. Even then conceptualization has remained largely in terms of cognition and self-perception, which are generally seen as behavior within the realm of the rationalistic secondary process (Hunt, 1975, 1976).

The structural, psychodynamic view seeks to identify borderline patients and to deal with them in terms of such covert pathologies as poor object relations, primitive defensive operations, identity diffusion, nonspecific ego weakness, and the like. These all reflect the substantial intrusion of the illogic and affect of primary process and transferential distortion, and the consequences of developmental vicissitudes, into everyday interpersonal interactions in the here and now. What, then, has a behavioristic approach to offer this enterprise when behaviorism is so aphasic on these covert matters?

Behaviorism can probably help in three major overlapping respects: methodological, conceptual, and organizational. The contributions flow both ways, of course, and behavioristic approaches should be substantially enriched by the challenges posed by the intrapsychic pathology of borderline patients. This may not cure the aphasia, but it should extend fluency.

SOME METHODOLOGICAL CONSIDERATIONS

As to methodology, the operational contributions of behaviorism (or better, experimental psychology) are familiar to all of us. The Watsonian revolution has been won on the methodological front in psychology, most of psychiatry, and across a broad expanse of the social sciences in general. "Right-thinking" investigators expect and are expected to define variables explicitly and in terms of operations, be concerned with reliability and validity, use statistical inference, and so on, or at least to appear to be doing so.

A brief quotation from Skinner's *Beyond Freedom and Dignity* (1971) gives a taste of the differences between ordinary clinical description and behavioral description:

Consider a young man whose world has suddenly changed. He has graduated from college and is going to work, let us say, or has been inducted into the armed services. Most of the behavior he has acquired up to this point proves useless in his new environment. The behavior he actually exhibits can be described, and the description translated, as follows: he lacks assurance or feels insecure or is unsure of himself (*his behavior is weak and inappropriate*); he is dissatisfied or discouraged (*he is seldom reinforced, and as a result his behavior undergoes extinction*); he is frustrated (*extinction is accompanied by emotional responses*); he feels uneasy or anxious (*his behavior frequently has unavoidable aversive consequences which have emotional effects*); there is nothing he wants to do or enjoys doing well, he has no feeling of craftsmanship, no sense of leading a purposeful life, no sense of accomplishment (*he is rarely reinforced for doing anything*); he feels guilty or ashamed (*he has previously been punished for idleness or failure, which now evokes emotional responses*); he is disappointed in himself or disgusted with himself (*he is no longer reinforced by the admiration of others, and the extinction which follows has emotional effects*); he becomes hypochondriacal (*he concludes that he is ill*) or neurotic (*he engages in a variety of ineffective modes of escape*); and he experiences an identity crisis (*he does not recognize the person he once called "I"*) [pp. 146-147].

Skinner recognizes the imprecision of the paraphrasing, but emphasizes that the alternate wording suggests effective action. In other words, a behavioral language may help in two ways: it identifies what needs to be done and suggests ways of doing it. In effect, behavioral analysis of an apparent impasse often helps us discover alternative modes of action that might not even be conceived otherwise. What the subject tells us about his feelings permits us to make some informed guesses about what is wrong. But we must go directly to the contingencies of reinforcement if we want to verify the guesses. And we must change those contingencies if we want to change the subject's behavior.

Even so, one runs into curious discontinuities. Clinical data, for example, usually represent a mixture of descriptions of events and interpretations. Special inquiry usually is required to find out what happened, as opposed to general statements such as "patient was depressed, had a bad night, became uncontrollably aggressive or obstructive," or whatever. A behavioristic approach is interested in who said or did what, to whom, and when, and what happened then. But if you ask for the "facts," you are suddenly reminded that a "fact" is really an inference about an event, within a particular conceptual framework. A single event may turn into very different "facts" when seen from the vantage point of different conceptual frameworks. This is an operational problem in our study of hospital treatment at the Psychiatric Institute at Columbia University Presbyterian Hospital as we attempt to define and identify instances of confrontation in the diagnostic interviews. While it may be easy to agree, for example, on defienda for confrontation so we can identify it reliably, what about validity? Does this discrimination, however reliable, tell us something we want and need to know about a patient? The conceptual framework is critical.

Here we begin to touch on more fundamental conceptual matters. In distinguishing between neurotic, borderline, and psychotic patients, are we dealing with a typology, a set of mutually exclusive categories, or are we distinguishing broad bands along some continuous, underlying dimensions of quantitative variation? If the latter, confrontations probably should be arranged in some graded series of force or severity, and patients' reactions to them evaluated relativistically. Then, confrontations and responses to them would be susceptible to some kind of scaling. From a practical point of view, as long as borderline patients are defined largely by exclusion, or just descriptively, finer conceptual details can stay in the background. We can stumble along, determining empirically how to cope with borderline patients. But the point of the structural approach to the borderline syndrome, as I understand it, is to provide a conceptual basis for developing maximally effective treatment (Kernberg, 1975). This requires more fundamental inquiry into psychopathology.

By analogy, I am reminded of the three phases of matter—solid, liquid, and gaseous—which differ quantitatively in terms of heat and which change from one phase to another with addition or subtraction of heat, with trade-offs between heat and pressure. To be sure, men knew about shoveling snow, chipping ice, distilling water, and so on long before Count Rumford and Carnot did their fundamental work in thermodynamics, but only afterwards were men able to take real advantage of latent heat to do useful work efficiently. Without getting lost in this analogy and without speculating on what might be equivalent to the "latent heat" therapy must add or remove to change a borderline patient into a neurotic or characterological problem I think we can agree that sooner or later we have to consider, as hypotheses, whether we are dealing with a collection of discrete categories or with dimensions of quantitative variation. If the former, we can accomplish the diagnostic classification by discovery and accumulation of qualitative signs. If the latter, diagnostic distinctions should ultimately rest on titration and adjustment of parameters in confrontation and other diagnostic probes.

Radical behaviorism stresses the functional analysis of behavior (Hunt, 1975). Among other things, it sees confrontations as a graded series of challenges or probes acting as stimuli. A patient's behavioral repertoire (here, ego functioning) would be indexed by his response relative to several levels of intensity of challenge. In passing, it should be noted that in functional analysis a behavior class is identified not by its form (topography), but by what controls it — by what contexts are the occasion for its occurrence and what consequences it has. Similarly, stimuli (or contexts) are classified in terms of their effects on behavior, not in terms of their qualitative characteristics (topography). Patients, particularly borderline patients, are highly idiosyncratic, so what constitutes a challenge for each probably should be defined within the contexts of that patient's history and, particularly, his behavior and content emerging during the interview. In effect, it is possible that we will have to see each patient as an experiment unto himself, with generalizations or "scientific laws" developing out of replications of the experiment over successive cases.

Such a possibility has profound implications for experimental design and research in this area. Case studies and experimentation based on careful observation have a long and distinguished history, but the rush toward scientific respectability lately has produced lapses into simplistic dogma. Ordinarily, I would not comment much on general considerations of method, but just recently I heard it proclaimed that only randomized control-group designs have scientific merit. This requires a rejoinder.

If so, how did the sciences of astronomy and geology develop? Where were the control groups? Obviously, control *comparisons* are critical if one is going to demonstrate functional covariation between independent and dependent variables, but the randomized control-group procedure is not the only way to achieve this (Fiske et al., 1970). Indeed, these procedures are sometimes wasteful or downright bad insofar as they treat systematic variation idiosyncratic to individual cases as noise or error (Sidman, 1960). Sometimes they are so reactive (Webb et al., 1966) that they obscure important changes. And sometimes they are impossible in those field settings in which validating studies must be carried out to show that a particular approach to diagnosis and treatment has practical value. The experiment may so distort the situation that the test loses its ecological validity (Campbell and Stanley, 1966).

There is more than one way to "do science," to ask important questions in ways that can produce solid answers. Sometimes comparisons across groups are appropriate; sometimes comparisons across situations within single cases are more powerful. It all depends on the question one is asking and the answer one hopes to get. In my laboratory we use both, depending on the problem, and we certainly do not adhere rigidly to the same experimental design over and over again just because it once conferred success and respectability.

Procedures for demonstrating functional covariation among variables, and the effects of manipulating parameters, using very small numbers of cases, have been spelled out most elegantly by Sidman (1960) (see also Kazdin, 1973, 1976). These designs emphasize large numbers of repeated observations of a particular behavioral effect, replicated over a small number of subjects studied intensively, to demonstrate functional relations. In one of the most rigorous and scientific doctoral dissertations I ever supervised (Gibbon, 1967), six rats were run over a period of about three years. As another example, Ferster and Skinner (1957) did their classical work on schedules of operant reinforcement on a handful of pigeons.

Such own-control designs for one or a few cases have been a staple of clinical research in psychoanalysis. I find it intriguing indeed to note how importantly these designs have figured in rigorous basic research in operant conditioning, too. The difficulty in psychoanalytic research, however, has rested less with the over-all own-control design than with problems in execution. Clinical researchers often fail to define variables and procedures explicitly enough to permit decisive replication. Often they have employed explanatory constructs with only elusive operational referents (e.g., motivation). Finally, clinicians often have been confronted with processes that are essentially irreversible. The reversal design is a major feature of operant research. Here, the effect of a variable on some baseline behavior can be determined and verified by introducing the variable and then removing it, often alternating repeatedly, to permit observation of changes in the baseline behaviors that accompany these maneuvers. Some variables and some effects of clinical and theoretical interest, however, particularly those related to development and to biological change, cannot be reversed easily (e.g., a child learning that everything has a name, an adolescent discovering that he is not just a piece of dirt). Even so, observationally oriented experimental designs for scientific research with single (or a few) cases are achieving increased recognition (see Davidson and Costello, 1969; Edgar and Billingsley, 1974; Hunt, 1975; Kazdin, 1973, 1976). Own-control designs may be particularly important for evaluating treatment and outcome, given the range and kind of idiosyncratic variation characteristic of borderline patients.

BEHAVIORAL ASPECTS OF TREATMENT

A behavioristic view of treatment highlights the importance of the interface between the milieu and the individual treatment session, particularly for the borderline patient. Dyrud (1972), a psychoanalyst writing about treating these patients, stresses the importance of improving their performance in relation to reality and their sense of reality. He sees interpretation as a way of helping the patient develop a sharper discrimination of both inner and outer stimuli, with the emotional interaction between patient and analyst as a way of shaping the patient's behavior not only in the session, but in the milieu outside. He goes on to say: ". . . the patient will display in his words and actions a manifest form of behavior in which a variety of themes can be distinguished. If then the therapist gives an interpretation, that is, points out a theme and approves its expression, then the subsequent material will contain the approved theme or related material in greater abundance" (p. 167). In this connection, he sees that interpretation, provided it takes account of the transference and current life situation, produces a greater "congruence between the patient's witting and unwitting behaviors [with a] move toward a higher degree of appropriateness in the here and now" (p. 168). Dyrud has also emphasized the importance of overt behavior, an expression of executive function, in enhancing the synthetic functions of the ego which are so defective in borderline patients (Dyrud and Donnelly, 1969). What goes on in the session, and what goes on outside it, provide grist for the therapeutic mill, provided the therapist is skillful and the milieu is prosocially responsive and appropriate.

Elsewhere, writing in a more behavioristic vein about both psychotic and borderline patients, I have suggested specific procedures for both milieu and individual therapy that can facilitate these changes (Hunt, 1975).

[In moving to individualized programs and beyond the concretistic token economy] . . . patients should have as much responsibility as they can manage for choosing what behaviors to change and for monitoring their progress. They will differ considerably in their capacities here, and the actual program arrived at requires the exercise of good clinical judgment. Details can be worked out . . . between patient and therapist, leading to a specific agreement as to what is expected, what is to be done, and how it is to be judged and rewarded. The agreement may be as formalized as a "contingency contract," or less formidable, but it must be specific and push the patient into contact with reality issues. The agreement provides a basis for commitment, but it should not be rewarded as such. To do so may short-circuit the therapeutic process by rewarding promises, however empty. Rather, reinforcement should be for realistic action toward fulfilling the agreement. The patient should play as major a role as he can in record keeping, so he may be rewarded not only for performance but also for accuracy, perceptiveness, faithfulness, and other pro-social aspects of his performance.... Some things should be left out of the program as discretionary matters up to the patient or as performances that are to be expected of ordinary functioning people. (After all, the activities of half or more of the 24 hour day are discretionary for most of us. Contingent access to these options powerfully reinforces our pro-social behavior on the job.) Further, maximum use of metaphors implying trust, autonomy, and self-control helps to avoid infantilizing the patient and blocking his growing capacity to exercise these virtues, as long as the metaphors contain a substantial element of realism and truthfulness.

Some form of patient diary, that can be discussed with the therapist in connection with awarding points and back-up amenities, often provides the basis for differentially reinforcing progress to more subtle, self-regulating social functioning, including fantasy. Within this flexible format, and with this much material, a sensitive therapist (in consultation with the patient) usually can discern easily what behaviors are causing difficulty, when and in what regard escalation of the social level of the program is advisable, and even when all or part of the program as such can be discontinued. In effect, the therapist not only differentially reinforces overt behavior, but also what the patient says (writes) to himself about his own behavior, in effect producing a kind of behavioral control over intra-psychic events.

Interestingly enough, patients reaching and going beyond these advanced stages often continue to keep diaries and use the language of points and rewards, long after transactions with the therapist have become largely cognitive and verbal. The concrete rhetoric, based on shared experience between the two people, seems to furnish a vocabulary for referring to things the patient finds it hard to verbalize abstractly.... By this time, the patient often has developed what might be thought of as a theory about his own behavior and its control. Indeed, workable approaches to self-control often emerge from these experiences, with the "theories reinforced because they worked." [These formulations] can be of immense value in active mastery and self-control... [pp. 303-304].

The Borderline Patient, the Role of Theories, and the Problem of Self-Control

The borderline patient, with his deficiencies in ego functioning and pathology in object relations, presents a most interesting challenge to a behavioral formulation of treatment. The passage above quickly skims the high spots in moving from the concretely structured, *quid pro quo* world of token economy, useful for managing chronically and severely regressed psychotic patients, to the world of individual treatment and of cognitively managed self-control more characteristic of neurotic patients. As presented, the progression only glances at a few of the innumerable problems in clinical inference, psychopathology, and behavioral technology. To conduct such a progression successfully with a real patient is, at present, largely an art form, a clinical *tour de force*.

As they move on this trajectory, patients often show disconcerting reversals—changes in direction of movement, redefinition of objectives and of what a reward consists—and other transformations, particularly in their statements about themselves and their feelings. These shifts and transformations are difficult to accommodate within the rationalistic framework of cognitive social-learning theory (e.g., Mischel, 1973) or within a behavioral analysis derived entirely from observing environmental events outside the person. As the passage implies, the therapist often has to come to terms with what would ordinarily be called the "meaning" or "significance" of actions and events to the behaving person, using diaries and other devices to evoke self-reports for these purposes. These reports usually cannot be taken singly or at face value; rather they exist in configurations and usually show a repetitive patterning.

In the conventional behavioral experiment in the laboratory we manipulate independent variables, as "causes," and observe changes in isolated behaviors, as "effects." In the clinical situation, however, the situation and the logic are reversed. We observe behaviors, as effects (usually not conveniently isolated or marked off), and have to guess what might have caused them (Hunt, 1976). To anyone with any clinical experience, the content of these self-reports bears an important functional relation to what the person actually does, and to perturbations in his behavioral career, but the data are not accommodated easily within a strict behavioristic or cognitive (rational) framework. They do fall within the purview of psychodynamics, however, and, I think, will turn out to be clarified substantially by the structural approach Kernberg (1975) proposes. They seem to reflect shifts in internalized object relations, defensive splitting, projective identification, superego functioning, and the like which are so much at issue in the diagnosis and treatment of borderline patients.

I suggest that behavioral and psychodynamic views supplement or complement each other, rather than compete. This does not imply any interest in developing a loose eclecticism that blithely lumps apples and axes together, but it does suggest that out of the confrontation of two converging theoretical views, at the level of the borderline patient, a creative synthesis may emerge. Of more immediate importance, to a behaviorist at least, each of these different views may help illuminate dark corners in the other (Hunt and Dyrud, 1968).

Let us, for the moment, agree that the main function of a theory is to help us think about a domain. (It would be nice if theories could be true, but probably those we have now are not.) Complementary theories may give the therapist something of a three-dimensional view of the patient's problem, revealing facts which might be missed if one metaphor were used exclusively, but only if they are used consistently (just as a holograph requires coherent light from two laser sources to generate a three-dimensional image [Hunt, 1976]).

Whether a creative synthesis will emerge, or just better illumination cannot be foreseen. Either approach—psychodynamic or behavioral—can use all the help it can get in understanding such a momentous human problem as self-control. Perhaps the behavioral emphasis will furnish ego psychologists with better techniques for developing, in patients, more stable and less frightening internalized objects and higher-level defenses. On the other hand, the behavioral approach, which knows so much about situational control and, consequently, about the *controlled self,* can be helped by psychodynamic insights to a better understanding of the *controlling self*. In situational control the subject manipulates circumstances so that he is more likely to emit the desired behavior, or less likely to emit undesired behavior, judges his performance against some standard (often one of his subjective making), and rewards or punishes himself accordingly. The technology for this has been pretty well worked out (Skinner, 1953; Goldiamond and Dyrud, 1968; Stuart, 1972; Kanfer and Karoly, 1972). But what remains to be dealt with is the matter of the *controlling* self, the self that decides to produce a particular effect. Such a decision is as determined as any other, but so far I have not been able to carry the analysis much beyond the point of specifying *commitment* as an important descriptive ingredient (Hunt, 1975). (My current thinking suggests that commitment is produced as a function of the nature of the reinforcer, coming at the end of that chained sequence of behavior we call self-controlled, in interaction with the subject's self-concept and internalized objects.)

That man visualizes a future, sees himself in it, makes plans, and the like appears given by his ethology (Hunt and Dyrud, 1968). But how this process is mobilized or aroused, how it gets changed, what holds a man to it, and how hard are poorly understood, if at all. The answer seems to rest in some relation to what are called internalized object relations. If the form and function of these are given ethologically in interaction with experience, so also will their form and function constrain and interfere with some kinds of learning and facilitate other kinds — just as the ethology of other species makes some things easy and some things almost impossible to learn (Breland and Breland, 1961; Hinde and Stevenson-Hinde, 1973; Schwartz, 1974).

The intrusion of structural considerations into behavioral theory from ethology is paralleled by the intrusion of structural considerations into psychodynamic theory from ego psychology. In a way, psychodynamic theory (including ego psychology) summarizes extensive field experience with man as a species. It thus has a lot to suggest about human ethology, about species-specific characteristics that may limit, impair, channel, or facilitate behavioral changes to be produced in man through learning. The interface between dynamic theory and behavioral theory, as they join forces to cope with the borderline patient, should generate productive new models for the scientific understanding of man in his most human, existential manifestations.

THE RESPONSIVE MILIEU AND ITS VICISSITUDES

The above discussion assumes not only close and noncompetitive coordination between the individual psychotherapist and the staff managing the hospital milieu, but also a milieu that is both reasonably structured and prosocially responsive. Reasonably structured means only that it provides prosocial ways that all its denizens can use to get things done with a minimum of bureaucratic doublebinds and "catch-22's." Prosocially responsive means that the milieu is designed to respond positively to prosocial behavior, to enhance functioning rather than just to contain the patients. Finally, the milieu must be flexible enough to accommodate the different needs of different patients and to handle the difficult paradox which the Cummings (1962) put into clear relief: To facilitate learning and problem solving, the situation must be structured initially to lower anxiety, but ultimately it must face the patient with the necessity of problem solving which is, itself, anxiety-producing.

Such an environment is easy to ask for but hard to produce. I have yet to see any hospital (or other) milieu that arrived at this environment naturally or stayed this way without continual tinkering. The problem is particularly acute with respect to the borderline patient, who is often an interpersonal "porcupine" (Dyrud, 1972) and whose transferential storms place major demands on the therapist's ego strength (Kernberg, 1975). Indeed, from a behavioral point of view, most of these patients appear to have developed interpersonal repertoires or scenarios, probably shaped through a history of differential reinforcement, which seem almost designed to obstruct smooth operation of the ward and which provoke countertransferential reactions from the therapist which the patient then uses to justify further acting out. Or, as Otto Will suggests in discussing ego psychology and hospital care, milieu therapists often simply seem to wear out, exhausted, as it were, from trying to pump motivation into reluctant and recalcitrant patients (in Eldred and Vanderpol, 1968). Whatever the arrangements for the therapeutic milieu, however, those used with borderline patients need to be "well sprung" and to have good "shock absorbers."

The therapeutic milieu is of course a complex social system, with formal, structural characteristics and its own dynamic (Cumming and Cumming, 1962; Brown, 1973). A great deal has been written about it at high levels of abstraction. As others are more competent than I to discuss these matters, I'll confine my consideration to a few of the larger chunks of existential grit that have turned up in my behavioral filter.

First, behavioral control is a two-way street. While the staff controls the patients, patients exercise powerful control over the staff. The higher levels of administration control both, particularly the staff, but again the control is reciprocal. When patients misbehave, one should look at what the staff might be doing to provoke or support the behavior. When the staff misbehaves, though it is usually blamed on the patients, one should look at what the administration is doing (Skinner, 1971; Hunt, 1971, 1975, 1976).

Second, a distressingly large fraction of the behavioral control exerted around a hospital is aversive. This is easy to understand because punishment rapidly terminates undesired behavior. Such fast action is rewarding for those who engineer the controls. In aversive control, the negative reinforcement in the conditioning evokes escape. Escape is usually incompatible with the behavior you want to stop, leading to its prompt cessation. The subject learns to terminate the signal that indicates a punishment is coming, with this termination serving as a reward (Gibbon and Hunt, 1972). Finally, following new views of behavioral control (see Gibbon, Berryman, and Thompson, 1974), the subject learns to behave in such a way as to maintain a "safe signal"—to remain in a context that implies immunity from punishment. This is reminiscent of superego control.

Several complications detract from the apparent "efficiency" of aversive control. It often has unintended and untoward affective byproducts that may interfere with constructive behavioral change. Indeed, most of the borderline patients we see are the result, at least in part, of chronic overuse of aversive control. Further, if the behavior being prevented is under the control of strong positive reinforcement, the punishment contingency must remain in force continuously. If not, the subject will be tempted to, and will try to "taste the forbidden fruit." Even if the punishment contingency remains in force, many subjects eventually find a way to circumvent or minimize it. In psychopathology, these circumventions are known as symptoms. Finally, and most important from the standpoint of chronic behavioral control, behavior rewarded because it keeps the safety signal "on" is precariously poised (Neffinger and Gibbon, 1975). This safety-reward system is easily weakened (degraded) by occasional mistakes, such as accidental shocks to the rat or the unavoidable occasional misadventures to which patients fall heir.

From the standpoint of organizational behavior, aversive control leads to conservatism, a reluctance to take risks that might get the subject out of his safety conditions, and to bureaucratic routinization. These characteristics are incompatible with flexible innovation and a differentiated individualized approach to patients (Brown, 1973). Everybody tends to keep hunkered down, presenting as small a target area as possible, keeping out of sight, and generally maintaining a low profile until his time has been served. Further, aversive control produces the subjective experience of being coerced (Skinner, 1971). Given human inventiveness, surreptitious arrangements for achieving the forbidden gratification usually develop to run invisibly alongside official arrangements that prohibit it, as any prison demonstrates! Aversive control should be reserved for emergencies, or when nothing else can work.

Control by appetitive rewards, in contrast, is more dependable and robust (Gibbon, 1976). Occasional failures in the system do not degrade its effectiveness as much or as rapidly as in the aversive case. Moreover, appetitive control generates the subjective experiences of freedom and exercise of choice (Skinner, 1971). By all odds it is to be preferred for chronic use, even though it requires more ingenuity to devise, more flexibility, and, usually, more disposable resources to maintain than an aversive scheme.

Simply enriching the environment by increasing the amenities available to all, unconditionally and as a matter of right, does not necessarily produce a responsive environment that will have therapeutic effects. Even an impoverished milieu can be responsive if prosocial behavior gets prompt and sincere support from the staff and is backed up by preferential access to whatever amenities are available (Hunt, 1971, 1975). Such a milieu cannot be artificial; the rewards must be real, not just a game, and must be delivered only for real performance, not just for expressions of good intentions. Even psychotic patients respond well to honest appreciation for a difficult job well done.

The borderline patient presents particularly tricky social-engineering problems. His capacity to provoke aggression makes what is positive about his behavior difficult to appreciate honestly. He can, through interpersonal manipulation, turn what should be a self-rewarding, pleasurable activity into a task for which he expects extrinsic reward in payment. Even learning that some previously enjoyed activity is viewed as "good for him" awakens enough transferential opposition to rob it of its pleasurable aspects. One is tempted to enter into a power struggle in which controls are tightened, behavior requirements escalated; the therapist then finds himself buying good behavior from the patient. These *quid pro quo* arrangements fail, of course, as soon as the patient gets away from the control schedules. The experience has taught him only how to beat the system. The therapist has come to stand *in loco parentis*. This sequence is familiar to therapists, of course; it is our old friend transference, beefed up with a little behavioral rhetoric.

Both psychotherapists and staff need substantial social/behavioral support to maintain a responsive milieu. They, too, must be in a responsive environment: one not so laced with aversive control that it promotes regression into bureaucratic routine; one that positively supports a problem-solving approach and small gains without emphasizing the negative consequences of the inevitable failures; and one that supports closer collaborative cooperation between psychotherapists and staff than usually obtains (see Brown, 1973). While many of the difficulties to be encountered in maintaining such arrangements have psychodynamic roots, the problems also take place within a social reality and have to be dealt with at that level. Therapists and staff usually are normal/neurotic, but even if they are high-level borderline types, they are not patients and do not have that relation to colleagues and supervisors. Accordingly, a perfectly good (and true) dynamic confrontation or interpretation may only cause trouble, while handling the problem as presented within its purported reality frame often produces positive results.

Indeed, the same comment applies to handling patient complaints. Psychiatric institutions too often cope with reality problems, and complaints about them, as if they were symptoms; it is easier that way. For a patient to have his most reasonable and justified prosocial behaviors discounted as being symptomatic is antitherapeutic, profoundly dehumanizing, and insulting. Over the years, I have become convinced that most patients can tell the difference, at some level of self-awareness, between their symptomatic maneuvers and "honest coping." By looking first to the environment and its controlling contingencies, the behavioral approach can imply ways to meet such "reality challenges," ways that closely track external events to avoid falling into interpretive traps too easily (Hunt, 1971).

REFERENCES

Breland, K. B., & Breland, M. (1961), The misbehavior of organisms. *Amer. Psychol.,* 16:681-684.

Brown, G. W. (1973), The mental hospital as an institution. *Soc. Sci. Med.,* 7:407-424.

Campbell, D. T., & Stanley, J. C. (1966), *Experimental and Quasi-Experimental Designs.* Chicago: Rand McNally.

Cumming, J., & Cumming, E. (1962), *Ego and Milieu.* New York: Atherton Press.

Davidson, P. O., & Costello, C. G., eds. (1969), *N Equals One: Experimental Studies of Single Cases.* New York: Van Nostrand Reinhold.

Dyrud, J. E. (1972), The treatment of the borderline syndrome. In: *Modern Psychiatry and Clinical Research,* ed. D. Offer & D. X. Freedman. New York: Basic Books, pp. 159-173.

_____ & Donnelly, C. (1969), Executive functions of the ego. Clinical and procedural relevance. *Arch. Gen. Psychiat.,* 20:257-261.

Edgar, E., & Billingsley, F. (1974), Believability when N = 1. *Psychol. Rec.,* 24:147-160.

Eldred, S. H., & Vanderpol, M., eds. (1968), *Psychotherapy in the Designed Therapeutic Milieu.* Boston: Little, Brown.

Ferster, C., & Skinner, B. F. (1957), *Schedules of Reinforcement.* New York: Appleton-Century-Crofts.

Fiske, D. W., et al. (1970), Planning of research on the effectiveness of psychotherapy. *Arch. Gen. Psychiat.,* 22:22-32.

Gibbon, J. (1967), Discriminated punishment: Avoidable and unavoidable shock. *J. Exper. Anal. Behav.,* 10:451-460.

_____ (1976), Scalar expectancy theory and Weber's law in animal timing. (Unpublished.)

_____ Berryman, R., & Thompson, R. L. (1974), Contingency spaces and measures in classical and instrumental conditioning. *J. Exper. Anal. Behav.,* 21:585-605.

_____ & Hunt, H. F. (1972), Post-shock discriminations in the acquisition of free-operant avoidance in the rat. *Psychol. Rec.,* 22:151-159.

Goldiamond, I., & Dyrud, J. E. (1968), Some applications and implications of behavioral analysis for psychotherapy. In: *Research in Psychotherapy,* Vol. III, ed. J. M. Schlien et al. Washington, D.C.: American Psychological Association.

Hilgard, E. R., & Bower, G. H. (1966), *Theories of Learning,* 3rd Ed. New York: Appleton-Century-Crofts.

Hinde, R. A., & Stevenson-Hinde, J., eds. (1973), *Constraints on Learning.* New York: Academic Press.

Hunt, H. F. (1968), Prospects and possibilities in the development of behaviour therapy. In: *The Role of Learning in Psychotherapy,* ed. R. Porter. London: Churchill.

_____ (1971), Behavioral considerations in psychiatric treatment. In: *Science and Psychoanalysis,* Vol. 18: *Techniques of Therapy,* ed. J. H. Masserman. New York: Grune & Stratton, pp. 51-62.

_____ (1975), Behavioral therapy for adults. In: *American Handbook of Psychiatry,* 2nd Ed., Vol. V., ed. D. X. Freedman & J. E. Dyrud. New York: Basic Books.

_____ (1976), Recurrent dilemmas in behavioral therapy. In: *Psychopathology of Human Adaptation,* ed. G. Serban. New York: Plenum.

_____ & Dyrud, J. E. (1968), Commentary: Perspective in behavior therapy. In: *Research in Psychotherapy,* Vol. III, ed. J. M. Schlien et al., Washington, D.C.: American Psychological Association.

Kanfer, F. H., & Karoly, P. (1972), Self-control: A behavioristic excursion into the lion's den. *Behav. Ther.,* 3:398-416.

Kazdin, A. E. (1973), Methodological and assessment considerations in evaluating reinforcement programs in applied settings. *J. Appl. Behav. Anal.,* 6:517-531.

_____ (1976), Statistical analysis for single-case experimental designs. In: *Single-Case Experimental Designs,* ed. M. Herson & D. H. Barlow. Oxford: Pergamon.

Kernberg, O. F. (1975), *Borderline Conditions and Pathological Narcissism.* New York: Jason Aronson.

Mischel, W. (1973), Toward a cognitive social learning reconceptualization of personality. *Psychol. Rev.,* 80:252-283.

Neffinger, G. G., & Gibbon, J. (1975), Partial avoidance contingencies. *J. Exper. Anal. Behav.,* 23:437-450.

Schwartz, B. (1974), On going back to nature: A review of Seligman and Hager's "Biological boundaries of learning." *J. Exper. Anal. Behav.,* 21:183-198.

Sidman, M. (1960), *Tactics of Scientific Research.* New York: Basic Books.

Skinner, B. F. (1953), *Science and Human Behavior.* New York: Macmillan.

_____ (1971), *Beyond Freedom and Dignity.* New York: Knopf.

Stuart, R. B. (1972), Situational versus self-control. In: *Advances in Behavior Therapy,* ed. R. D. Rubin et al. New York: Academic Press.

Webb, E. J., Campbell, D. T., Schwartz, R. D., & Sechrist, L. (1966), *Unobtrusive Measures: Nonreactive Research in the Social Sciences*. Chicago: Rand McNally.

An Approach to the Global Treatment of the Borderline Patient: Psychoanalytic, Psychotherapeutic, and Psychopharmacological Considerations

G. J. SARWER-FONER, M.D.

If one has had many years experience in treating all kinds of patients at all levels of psychiatric illness; if one has seen all levels of recovery toward health; and if one has been trained and worked both as a psychoanalyst and as a pioneer psychopharmacologist in open, university, and general hospital psychiatric settings; then one has seen a vast range of patients who could be included under the rubric borderline. While a classification schema becomes necessary (Grinker, Werble, and Drye, 1968; Kernberg, 1975; Knight, 1953a; Mack, 1975; Schmideberg, 1947), one sees the differences in approach, technique, and the limits of what can be achieved by the various therapeutic techniques in different circumstances and with different patients. One also becomes preoccupied with the necessary training to properly equip physicians to care, at the appropriate levels, for different patient needs with individually different treatment goals.

The usefulness of the rubric borderline varies with the sense it is given (Deutsch, 1942; Ekstein and Wallerstein, 1954; Federn, 1947; Geleerd, 1958; Grinker, Werble, and Drye, 1968; Hoch and Polatin, 1949; Kernberg, 1967, 1968, 1970, 1975; Knight, 1953a, 1953b; Kohut, 1971; Mack, 1975; Masterson, 1971, 1972, 1975; Modell, 1963, 1968; Panel, 1956; Schmideberg, 1947, 1959; Stengel, 1945;

Director, Department of Psychiatry, Ottawa General Hospital; Professor and Chairman, Department of Psychiatry, University of Ottawa Faculty of Medicine, Ottawa, Ontario, Canada.

Stern, 1945; Tartakoff et al., 1966; Zetzel, 1971; Zilboorg, 1941).
Is it a classificatory phenomenological summation? Is it a psychoanalytic or psychodynamic visualization of a series of regressions
and particular character defenses and thus helpful in determining
which technical approaches should be used in intensive treatment
of a particular patient? Is it employed as a heuristically useful,
but overly general classificatory categorization of the broad spectrum of cases whose psychopathology and general clinical course
cause them to oscillate symptomatically between the neuroses
and the psychoses? Is it used by a particular school of thought to
allude only to those patients who, always on the brink of psychosis,
never regress into overt psychosis? Or does it include those who
oscillate occasionally into an acute psychotic decompensation and
then show good recovery, but never progress much further into
being an integrated person? And what about the psychopathic,
impulse-ridden character disorders (Sarwer-Foner, 1969), do they
belong here? What about those patients with ego-syntonic sexual
deviations, such as certain transvestites, who are in symbiotic fusion
with symbolic parental representations, and who oscillate throughout their entire life about this point, but do not often come to
treatment for this condition, although they are sometimes seen in
consultation? Should some or all of these patients be classified under
this rubric (Deutsch, 1942; Fraiberg, 1969; M. Sim, personal communication, 1976)?

The answer to these questions relates partly to at least three
factors: (1) the setting in which one works and thus the opportunities one has had to study all or some of these numerous groups of
patients; (2) one's training and therefore technical expertise in
being able to approach psychotherapeutically the individual patient
—this has to be coupled with a setting (Alexander, 1944; Sarwer-
Foner, Ogle, and Dancey, 1960) that permits sufficient time to
explore the varied and multiple defenses, progressions and regressions, and, above all, the repetitive patterns of ego defensive oscillation around psychosexual developmental arrests or fixations; and
(3) whether one has training and expertise in modern techniques of
controlling and treating acute crisis, both psychotherapeutically
and with other behaviorally influencing techniques, such as hospitalization, psychopharmacology, electric shock, subcoma insulin,

and anaclitic therapies (sleep, time-regressive therapies followed by time-progressive therapies, etc.). Here again, the setting in which one works, or has gained past experience, is of determinant value. (In my use of the term setting, I am of course including office practice, both psychoanalysis and outpatient psychotherapy, as being one kind of "setting.")

The role of the clinician, trained in the above-mentioned techniques, as a teacher and as an identification model for students is important. Such a physician often handles cases as a consultant or teacher, teaching, supervising, and directing others in short-term (time-limited) therapy (Sifneos, 1972) and showing what might be the best treatment approach for the individual patient, given the vast spectrum of diverse patients one sees in such settings.

Basic Characteristics of the Borderline Patient

The borderline rubric includes those patients who cannot function with an integrated concept of self, and yet who have progressed enough in their psychosexual development to have object-relation capacities with neurotic and characterologic defenses which hold well enough to ward off acute psychotic disintegration. Their symptoms illustrate this in that they are in ongoing intrapsychic *symbolic* fusion with another person in which "the other person plus the patient" form a whole. These patients cannot function independently over time; they cannot function alone. They must always symbolically to re-create this symbiotic fusion (Sarwer-Foner, 1967, 1972-1973).

The symptoms of such patients are protean in their manifestations. They present with multiple pathological defenses, particularly of the obsessive-compulsive kind (Grunberger, 1960; Reich, 1949; Sarwer-Foner, 1972-1973; Stengel, 1945). Passivity (Brody, 1964; Parens and Saul, 1971; Sarwer-Foner, 1970, 1972-1973), dependency (Brody, 1964; Mahler, 1968; Parens and Saul, 1971; Sarwer-Foner, 1972-1973), fatigue, hypochondriasis, self-depreciation, and depression are well to the fore. Hidden doubts as to the adequacy of their body image, and therefore their intrapsychic unconscious concept of self, are linked to their dependency needs and their passivity strivings, and the symptomatic expression of these needs as they oscillate and vary over time. They can relate to bits and pieces of themselves, symbolic objects of others within them.

All these patients have achieved a capacity to relate to others, often in a seductive and, on the surface, apparently "healthy" fashion. They can thus attract but they cannot hold. They can depend on; they can beguile; they can involve others in complicated, complex, oscillating and sadomasochistic maneuvers; they can entwine people in long-standing dependency, slave-master relations (Grunberger, 1960; Reich, 1949; Sarwer-Foner, 1972-1973; Stengel, 1945).

The majority of borderline patients lead restricted lives; do not achieve their full potentials; aspire to be many things but somehow fail in their achievement. They develop depressive, ruminative, oscillating, obsessional states with marked dependency and passivity strivings. They suffer from unbroken symbiotic relations, and from the incapacity to be a real person in real life, but are full of fantasies about achieving great things (Deutsch, 1942; Sarwer-Foner, 1972-1973; Tartakoff, et al., 1966)—the so-called as-if personality (Deutsch, 1942) of yesteryears. These patients have marked inhibitions to succeeding or completing a task; to being an adult individual, to being able to stand on their own; but they have little difficulty in being a childlike person. They limit their aggression in similar ways, they limit its expressions, or pour it out in totally inappropriate ways—inappropriate in terms of individuated achievement goals, but most appropriate in guaranteeing their inability to move forward and become independent people. All of the above operates on a large oscillating scale of to-and-from progression and regression (Masterson, 1975).

As a psychoanalyst, I am saying that these patients have achieved at least an anal level of integration (Grunberger, 1960; Sarwer-Foner, 1972-1973; Stengel, 1945), but they have not adequately worked out their adult separateness, their adult intactness, their sense of adult individualization in terms of Mahler's separation-individuation stages (Mahler, 1968, 1971; Mahler and Furer, 1963).

Their body image is complete in its organic schema, but incomplete in its intrapsychic totality. Such patients convert their awareness of their own inadequacy as a complete and separate being, and the resulting low self-esteem, into a feeling that what they are (i.e., their physical form and its mental and psychic representations [Fraiberg, 1969]) must be incomplete and inadequate. This feeling of incompleteness stems from very early roots in that whatever they felt they were able to integrate into their ego, superego, and concept of self at the completion of the Oedipus complex, somehow does not complete their individuation. They feel low, inadequate, or "wrong." Their bodies and what they are (later "the self" [Kohut, 1971]) are seen as inadequate, and as needing to have been different in order to be complete and whole. They feel that only then can they be an individual.

The perennial problem of splitting (Masterson, 1975) and projective mechanisms comes up here. These patients have to feel intrapsychically that they are totally good, or totally bad, at different times; that they are pleasing some internalized loved or feared, or externally existing object. They progress in life in terms of realistic goals to please this object, only to fall back when the real success of their moving forward and advancing toward an aim, toward a relation or an achievement, threatens them, and revives affective memories and deep-rooted patterns of fearing abandonment if they move away from a parent because this would really leave them alone as an adult — individuated and standing on their own, with a lost object relation as a result. Childhood memories of protection and being cared for, if they are submissive, are refreshed. Adulthood is here affectively perceived as a grave deprivation of their more pleasant childhood state. They thus rush back into the regressive symbiotic relation and do not complete their individuation as a reasonably intact adult.

Complicated, fused patterns of defense mechanisms are used. I say "patterns of defense mechanisms," because individualistically characteristic groupings of ego defenses are used in complex, repetitive patterns, producing oscillating (Scott, 1954) progressions and regressions, according to the patient's individual evolution of these defenses. Life crises or their absence play crucial, time-related roles in when, or even if, these patterns appear. It is difficult for the physician to even become aware of the complexities of each patient's patterns unless he follows them in psychoanalytic therapy over years (even then it is sometimes luck that gives you the pattern).

Negation and denial, dissociation and splitting (Masterson, 1975), fantasies of pseudo omnipotence (Deutsch, 1942; Tartakoff et al., 1966), can all be part of these patients' fundamental secondary narcissism (Kernberg, 1975; Kohut, 1971). Multiple or successive, rapid pseudo identifications with motherly, fatherly, or "strong" passing figures in their environment, along with identity diffusion, high temporary suggestibility, and "adhesive identification" occur only to oscillate regressively toward primary narcissism. Projective incorporation and projective identification can readily be seen in these patients. Hidden fantasies of creativeness, of greatness (Tartakoff et al., 1966), of achievement ("I know I can do it. I have a hidden power that only I know about, but I'm afraid to show it to the world") link them dynamically (but not in terms of the characterological defenses used) to some transvestite patients, at least at the level of some fixation points.

Reality testing about these areas is poor during periods of intense emotional turmoil when a life crisis (abandonment, rupture of some partial object relation, being faced with both the need to progress and their fear of progression, etc.) threatens these patients. Even in times of relative emotional quiescence, these patients show complex characterological resultants of defensive patterns, such as boredom, loneliness, and sexual promiscuity—the latter is often an attempt to combat loneliness and separateness. In order to feel wanted, they fuse with an object that at least temporarily completes the self. (I am using loneliness here not in the sense of being without company, but as the inner feeling of not being with the object one wishes or desires or longs for, even if one is surrounded by other people.)

One male patient gave a vague history of an episode which had occurred four years prior to his entering psychoanalysis—a "disturbance" which had resulted in four days of hospitalization, use of neuroleptic medication, and fearful distrust of the physician who had seen him then, followed by rapid recovery. Two short-lived, acute psychotic episodes (one of four days and one of two weeks) over the first four years of a seven-year analysis, the associations to these, and to one other threatening episode which was psychoanalytically aborted before it developed into a full psychosis in the fifth year of analysis, finally allowed the complex triggering patterns to be seen and known. The patient would become involved in an intense conflict over object choices in his life, which he settled by giving up one for another. Sometimes there were three such choices available with one to be chosen, e.g., a business, a wife, and a mistress, or a mistress, a wife, and the analyst. These were real crises in his life, but they were intrapsychically symbolized as the eternal father-mother dichotomy with resulting identity diffusion (man-woman choices). In addition, the patient would be in an exhausted physical state, usually produced by intense alertness, vigorous, even feverish social or professional activity, with lack of sleep and excessive alcohol consumption. There was also an upper respiratory tract infection with some fever, and in at least two of the three psychotic episodes (and perhaps all of them), an allergic crouplike mild laryngeal edema and hoarseness. This last element had to supervene after the first two existed, and only when an advanced state of exhaustion had already occurred. Without all of these, there was no psychosis.

Such patients only express the real patterns of their inhibitions to individuation in the transference, which is a symbolic reliving of the parental symbiosis (Mahler, 1968) that produced the inhibitions. Countertransference responses in the analyst, which can confirm the patient's inhibitions to growth, emerge in response to the transference emotions displayed by the patient. The meanings to the patient of the therapist's countertransference responses are subtle, intense, and crucial to success or failure of the treatment.

For these patients the psychoanalytic process involves reliving the patterns of oscillations described above in the transference and working them through, dealing with their genetic origins, and progressing to new experiences, as inhibitions are conquered and the patient develops new defenses and better adapted ways of dealing with life. Those patients who can adequately cathect and invest in the therapeutic relationship have a good fighting chance. It is also probable that some forms of intensive psychotherapy other than psychoanalysis, over time and with the right therapist, permit some patients to progress significantly.

At this point, I would like to return to my earlier question: Which patients belong under the rubric borderline? As already stated, the decision of whom to include depends partly on the type of patients one sees. If one is a psychoanalyst, seeing only selected, referred patients in office practice, the type of patients selected form a subgroup of a larger spectrum of cases. In general hospital units doing first- and second-line treatment and in many mental hospitals receiving acute patients, one sees another category of patient, presenting with an acute breakdown with degradation of ego defenses.

An example of this is the very acute schizo-affective psychosis of short duration and florid symptomatology, which the French call *une bouffée délirante*. The course of this acute episode (classified in North America as part of the schizo-affective schizophrenias, or in some cases as borderline disorders) is usually sharply delineated with proper therapy. Recovery is generally reasonably complete, and the patient usually returns close to his premorbid personality and functioning, often without overt signs of the confused, acute, and hallucinatory schizo-affective illness. Since those working with a therapeutic armamentarium limited to psychoanalytic psychotherapy and psychoanalysis of selected borderline patients in office practice do not see many of these patients, they would tend to exclude them from the borderline category. For those who take a phenomenological approach to classification, these patients' capacities to recover, their ability to function at large without psychotic symptoms but with neurotic character defenses, merit their inclusion in this category—once they are out of their psychosis.

And where do the psychopathic patients belong? Some sociopathic or psychopathic patients, including those who act out episodically, but have relatively stable object relations (particularly adolescents), can be included in the designation borderline (Schmideberg, 1959; M. Sim, personal communication, 1976). The remainder of psychopathic patients, although they belong phenomenologically on the borderline between neurosis and psychosis, and use ego-syntonic, impulse-ridden, pleasure-of-the-moment ego defenses (Sarwer-Foner, 1969) to protect their ego from further possible psychotic decompensation, are not readily treatable by currently available therapeutic techniques. (Exceptionally the odd patient does well in the hands of a particularly skilled therapist, who at the right time and place, selects and gets selected by a particular patient.) The usual psychopathic patient is therefore best left out of the classification borderline since he is best dealt with under the impulse-ridden character disorders, psychopathy or sociopathy (Sarwer-Foner, 1969).

My distinction here does not imply that many adolescents with acting-out behavior, great impulsivity, and poor control do not exhibit borderline disorders. However, those who use frankly antisocial, sociopathic behavior as their main symptomatic expression are best categorized and dealt with under a separate classification rather than as borderlines. A difference in the capacity to form an adequate transference relationship, differences in the techniques needed to treat them, the way impulsivity builds up with great speed and with little control before breaking into behavioral expression, all characterize and differentiate these patients from the more usual person included under the borderline syndrome. I recognize the arbitrary nature of such a classificatory decision, and that some eminent authorities disagree with it (Geleerd, 1958).

Classification of patients as borderline is sometimes made post hoc — after the initial diagnosis and only as one treats them. But depending on the clinical settings in which one sees them, the range of patients seen and the resulting diagnosis may vary. Does one first treat a patient in an acute receiving hospital with the threatening development of an acute psychosis, and then as he remits, does one become aware of his potential for better functioning? Or does one take a patient into psychoanalytic or intensive psychotherapeutic work in an office or outpatient setting and then find in his history, or as one treats him, the emergence of a borderline syndrome in the sudden threat of acute psychosis, or of an acute regression in his defenses in that direction? Or does the borderline syndrome emerge in the transference in the patterns of how the patient clings, in the way he moves back and forth to nowhere, in how he cannot advance to greater maturity, and in how he involves the physician in this oscillating pattern (Mahler, 1968; Masterson, 1972, 1975)? Does the patient abuse drugs to mask or hide this pattern? Does he use alcohol? Does the patient use acting-out behavior (as so many adolescents do) in an attempt to deal with these patterns? Does one see the patient in acute crisis intervention for a suicide attempt? Or is he a runaway, or a person with a tearful feeling of depersonalization?

Treatment Considerations

Therapeutic Alliance

An important aspect of the treatment of the borderline patient is the therapeutic alliance. What is the nature of the therapeutic alliance? What is the extent of the physician's interest, and the degree to which he is willing to involve himself in the therapeutic alliance with his patient? What are the therapeutic goals, and the limits of the setting in which the patient is seen? How long will the therapy last? Which therapeutic modalities does the physician know and use with expertise? In which of these is the patient willingly able to participate? Here we deal with both the setting and the limits of the physician's intentions and therapeutic armamentarium.

Is the physician doing a diagnostic consultation, or short-term therapy? Is he interested in only giving supportive therapy or in using psychopharmacology and some kind of supportive psychotherapy? Does he only feel comfortable with psychopharmacology? Does he use uncovering psychotherapy, or only psychoanalysis on selected patients? These factors, in combination with the setting and the type of patient, will determine the course, nature, and even the prognosis of the therapeutic process.

It is legitimate, of course, for doctors to have any and all of the above-mentioned limitations to their therapeutic abilities and styles, and thus to their therapeutic involvement. Such narrowness in turn limits the therapeutic alliance of the patient. It is equally legitimate for the selected physician to have the broadest training and abilities, and the deepest intention of committing himself in the therapeutic alliance for therapeutic work for as long as will be necessary for that patient's improvement.

Basic Therapeutic Attitude

What should be taught as the best attitude the physician can have for therapeutically approaching borderline patients? For me it is this: In all cases, regardless of the nature and length of therapy and the state of the patient's therapeutic alliance, one's therapeutic attitude should be to place directly on the patient (given the therapist's assistance) *his* responsibility for what he is, for what he wishes to become, and for where he is going. Everything one is, does, and feels should convey this.

Such an attitude, in common with the one I teach for general management of schizophrenic and other psychotic patients, places the innate responsibility of being the best person one can be directly on the patient, regardless of the level of his regressed state. Indeed, the more regressed the patient, the more important is the physician's attitude that the patient is not a helpless mobile, but is an interested and at least potentially able participant in the therapeutic process, *along with and helped by the physician*. The patient's motivation for progress should, with proper psychotherapeutic exploration, in the long run be at least as intense, and in principle more intense, than that of the physician, because it involves the patient's ability to solve or participate in solving his problems.

The physician has to use this therapeutic attitude, backed by the therapeutic alliance with the patient, to deal with the patient's resistances and defenses against becoming a more adequate, competent, less inhibition-ridden person. He does this in the reality of the moment and in the context of the transference manifestations. He must also meet the patient's fundamental tests of how reliable, steady, and really interested he, the therapist, is in the patient and his progress. Though the latter is important with every patient, it is a crucial cornerstone of the therapeutic alliance with the borderline patient since (just as with the schizophrenic patient) any unreliability, any limitations of commitment on the psychiatrist's part will be treated by the patient as a reliving of the ways in which the parents (particularly the mother) sent messages of relative or absolute rejection for any progression that threatened the parent-child fusion. It is therefore crucial over time (over a long time) to win the patient's trust by being really present in the reality of the therapy, through meeting the patient's testing maneuvers about one's reliability, steadiness, and real interest and commitment to the patient's therapeutic progress.

This form of treatment gets into the issue of character analysis (Kernberg, 1975; Kohut, 1971; Reich, 1949) and demonstrates, in the process, the physician's commitment to the therapeutic alliance. For it is a fundamental issue in the treatment of the borderline to stick to therapy long enough to solve the web of splitting, or projecting, to deal with the origins of patterns of refusing to complete individuation and separation.

WHAT KIND OF THERAPY?

These remarks are necessary for a discussion of which kind of therapy can be done, and of the techniques to be used. The teaching of management and handling of the borderline illnesses should be discussed, as well as where in the spectrum of such cases intervention should take place, and the nature of the best individual intervention, its intentions, aims, and goals.

There is a range of possible therapies: (1) crisis intervention: (2) supportive, reality-testing psychotherapy (short- or long-term ego-building and ego-integrative); (3) short-term, problem-oriented, uncovering psychotherapy; (4) longer-term, uncovering, psycho-analytically oriented psychotherapy (dealing with some character defenses, but not necessarily in a systematic and complete way); and (5) psychoanalysis aimed at character defenses and completing individuation as a complete adult. Psychopharmacology is used particularly at the level of crisis intervention. Sometimes it is used during a life crisis along with supportive, reality-testing psychotherapy. Occasionally psychopharmacology may help handle threatened acute psychotic eruptions in any of the other therapeutic situations.

In a particular case, should therapy be long-term, intermediate, or short-term? Are changes to be produced only in symptomatology —settling down an acute psychotic episode or preventing breakdown into psychosis with return of normative defenses; mitigating acute depression, acute anxiety, or suicidal problems; tempering aggression-impulsive or "spontaneous" outbursts; or dealing with dependency, passivity, or clinging behavior? Under what circumstances does one commit oneself (particularly with young and adolescent patients, but also with the selected adult) to therapy aimed at maturation, and the emergence of better characterological defenses? The latter involves psychoanalysis or psychoanalytically oriented psychotherapy of long duration.

Considerations of the therapeutic setting help us discuss how to tackle the various problems presented by these patients. In out-patient clinics or office practice, when a patient arrives in crisis one has to deal with the immediate problems (with panic, acute anxiety, threatened breakdown into schizophrenic or other psychotic dis-orders, severe depression, potential or actual suicide attempts, overt violence, or psychomotor agitation). Our intervention uses reality-testing psychotherapy and follows the percepts already outlined, i.e., placing on the patient, through one's attitude of respect for his individuality and personal integrity, whatever degrees of responsi-bility he is capable of accepting for himself. One does not shun, however, the realistic obligation of imposing on a patient, whose control or judgment is shattered, those limit-setting and external controls necessary to help protect him. Such restraints include hospitalization and certification as an involuntary patient, should it be needed. For example, a series of short-term, well-delivered ther-apeutic goals might be defined to help the patient remit from a threatened psychotic episode, i.e., to produce an upward progres-sion in his defenses and to carry out structured crisis intervention in the personal, family, work, or other situation that is producing the ego disruption. The patient's cooperation is elicited through the attitude described. It is then easier to form a solid therapeutic alliance with the patient around appropriate therapeutic modalities and goals. One must intervene therapeutically with "appropriate dosage and timing."

With adolescent patients, the issue of how many adolescents with acting-out behavior can be grouped together in open psychi-atric, general hospital units arises (Sarwer-Foner, 1969). Our policy is to "dilute them well," within a normative age spread of adult patients who then, almost automatically in a good therapeutic milieu (Sarwer-Foner, Ogle, and Dancey, 1960), act as behavior-limiting factors—grandfather, grandmother, uncle, and aunt model figures for these adolescent patients. This approach produces a diminution of the disruptive explosive potential created when too many disturbed, acting-out adolescents are in close contact with each other in a confined space. This is not to say that under some circumstances in state hospital or special units, well-organized adolescent wards or units do not have their place. In the acute general hospital, however, it is best to well dilute such patients among the predominant adult population (Sarwer-Foner, Ogle, and Dancey, 1960; Sarwer-Foner, 1967).

PHARMACOLOGY

Modern pharmacotherapy becomes important here and follows the rules established for other categories of patients (Klein, 1975; Sarwer-Foner, Ogle, and Dancey, 1960; Sarwer-Foner and Koranyi, 1960; Sarwer-Foner, 1960a, 1960b, 1975). We use pharmacotherapy in a specific way (Sarwer-Foner, 1975). It is not used to treat the entire disease process as "an antipsychotic," "antianxiety," or "antidepressant," for example. Rather, proper dosage of the appropriate agent is used to control the target symptoms we are aiming to reduce, such as hyperactivity, impulsivity with poor control, poorly controlled aggression, inability to sleep, psychomotor agitation, psychomotor retardation, etc. Our approach to pharmacotherapy is combined in a hospital setting with our therapeutic milieu (Sarwer-Foner, Ogle, and Dancey, 1960) and supportive psychotherapy. For suicidal patients with poor control and great impulsivity (Sarwer-Foner, 1969), electric shock can be instituted, and in such circumstances is often life saving.

The so-called antidepressive drugs are reserved largely for those patients with severe psychomotor retardation who have little capacity to invest energy in external relationships, in psychotherapeutic or social efforts. In these cases, *in adequate dosage,* antidepressives can give useful results. The disadvantages, of course, are that in the majority of patients, most drugs take one to three weeks to show significant, clear-cut clinical activity, although signs of their pharmacological action, as sleepiness or atropinelike side effects, appear within a few days. If one remembers that patients with depressive illness generally start to improve spontaneously in more than 30 days (Alexander, 1944) in a good therapeutic milieu (roughly 85 per cent of patients do this), one has to take this time factor into consideration in assessing the adequacy of so-called antidepressive medication. Nevertheless, in the so-called endogenous depressions, antidepressives probably have their most clear-cut indication. In patients who are neurotically depressed and can relate well, or in that minority of psychotically depressed patients who still have some capacity to relate (Sarwer-Foner, 1970) our psychotherapeutic programs are the keystone to which combined psychotherapy-psychopharmacology (Sarwer-Foner, 1960a) management can be added if necessary.

As the borderline patient recovers from his acute symptomatology, we are faced with the issue of whether to stop at the restricted goal of returning him to his premorbid level of functioning, or to engage in a new therapeutic endeavor which would, over time, improve his level of functioning beyond this. In other words, do we involve him in the struggle with his borderline core, and its multiple defenses? Here, the availability of trained therapeutic manpower and the motivation of the patient are determinant. I have already stressed the importance of meeting the testing maneuvers of the patient in establishing the therapeutic alliance, as a crucial phase of hospital treatment or of early contact in office work, since without this the patient can never permit himself to become involved with the longer-term therapeutic issues being raised.

In my own experience it is probably not terribly helpful to keep such patients on long-term pharmacotherapy, since they tend either not to use it at all or to use it improperly. Borderline patients often abuse drugs, developing dependency states and physiological addictions to certain categories such as the psychosedatives. They are also notorious for not taking medication on an organized basis, but rather only when it suits them — with the same oscillating patterns that we know so well. In the context, however, of a psychotherapeutic alliance with a competent physician, it can be useful to use appropriate medication, be it neuroleptic, "antidepressant," or psychosedative medication, for *emergency interventions* in situations where the patient feels helpless. The training in psychotherapeutic skills of the therapist will determine when and when not to resort to such therapy, since each time a drug is given it is an indication on at least one level that the therapist genuinely believes the patient cannot do better without it (Sarwer-Foner and Koranyi, 1960; Sarwer-Foner, 1960a, 1960b, 1975). When this is in fact the truth, the drug may be given with proper indication. When this is not so, i.e., when an appeal to the therapeutic alliance and proper levels of psychotherapeutic intervention by the treating physician suffice, giving a drug is relatively contraindicated (Sarwer-Foner and Koranyi, 1960).

Our data on the psychotropic drug therapy of borderline patients were not classified in terms of borderline disorders as such, but rather as to what pharmacological treatment does to the target symptoms being affected (Sarwer-Foner, 1960a, 1960b). I cannot thus give detailed statistical analysis in terms of its effect on the borderline disorders treated as a separate diagnostic entity (Klein, 1975). In this regard, however, our data do not seem to differ significantly from those shown by other authorities working within such a framework. Klein (1975) has classified his research data in terms of the borderline diagnosis and his data are interesting in this regard.

As a general statement, I do not feel that pharmacotherapy is in itself the answer or the ideal approach to the treatment of the borderline patient. It can usually only deal with the emergency or emergent aspect of certain disruptive symptoms or acute psychotic states, and this in itself is not always enough to help the borderline patient with the fundamental aspects of borderline disorder over time. Its use, however, in adequate doses is often essential in staving off decompensation in an emergency situation or in helping a patient achieve mastery over unacceptable impulses, mastery which helps the patient progress in his defenses to at least an acceptable level and to return to his usual state or to be able to decide whether he wants to have further, more intensive therapy. For the selected depressive patient, proper antidepressive medication can return the patient to a state of again cathecting external relationships, including psychotherapeutic and social contacts, when he was initially so psychomotorly retarded and withdrawn that he was unable to work with these modalities. Sometimes this is all the depressive patient wants (Sarwer-Foner, 1966), and as the psychopharmacological therapy returns him to his premorbid state, he leaves treatment.

I have said enough earlier about the use of pharmacotherapy in settings where one is dealing with cross-sections of illness (a cross-section of the longitudinal process involving a *present acute* decompensation of the patient's ego defenses). I see less utility for long-term or ongoing drug use in the hands of a psychotherapeutically skilled psychiatrist who has broader therapeutic goals with a particular patient. In the hands, however, of those who have short-term time-limited goals then, pharmacotherapy certainly becomes another therapeutic modality, useful and sometimes of critical importance when properly applied.

CONCLUSIONS

I realize that I am speaking of a specialized kind of psychotherapeutic interaction by a skilled psychiatrist, who has mastered both psychotherapy and pharmacotherapy. Nevertheless, I think this is the model that has to be advanced to those who are interested in the global treatment of the borderline patient. It is, of course, quite legitimate for physicians not so globally trained to use their own particular therapeutic modalities within the art of practicing medicine. We are then faced with the limits of the therapy, within the therapeutic alliance, and the question of the limited goals to be achieved. It must be remembered that patients can and do improve with all kinds of supportive therapy. The improvement is limited in these cases by the patient's innate capacity to grow and improve using these therapies. The nature of the regressive defenses seen in the borderline and the inability to complete individuation as an adult or an adolescent must be remembered. Such patients oscillate regressively to either real symbiotic relations with living family members or to narcissistic, intrapsychically unbroken, symbolic, symbiotic relations with mental representations involving heroic representations of their parents, and the heroes and ego ideals of their past and present, which are then used in oscillating progressions and regressions to ensure that the patient can never really achieve a separate status, can never individuate sufficiently to reasonably use his assets to achieve adult potentials. The limitations of those therapeutic techniques that do not voluntarily involve the patient in the struggle with this global process must be remembered.

REFERENCES

Alexander, G. H. (1944), Shock therapies: A method of more accurate estimation of their therapeutic efficacy. *J. Nerv. Ment. Dis.*, 99:922-924.

Brody, S. (1964), *Passivity.* New York: International Universities Press.

Deutsch, H. (1942), Some forms of emotional disturbance and their relationship to schizophrenia. *Psychoanal. Quart.,* 11:301-321.

Ekstein, R., & Wallerstein, J. (1954), Observations on the psychology of borderline and psychotic children. *The Psychoanalytic Study of the Child,* 9:344-369. New York: International Universities Press.

Federn, P. (1947), Principles of psychotherapy in latent schizophrenia. *Amer. J. Psychother.,* 1:129-144.

Fraiberg, S. (1969), Libidinal object constancy and mental representation. *The Psychoanalytic Study of the Child,* 24:9-47. New York: International Universities Press.

Geleerd, E. R. (1958), Borderline states in childhood and adolescence. *The Psychoanalytic Study of the Child,* 13:279-295. New York: International Universities Press.

Grinker, R. R., Sr., Werble, B., & Drye, R. C. (1968), *The Borderline Syndrome.* New York: Basic Books.

Grunberger, B. (1960), Etude sur la relation objectale anale. *Rev. Francaise Psychanal.,* 24:138-160, 166-168.

Hoch, P. H., & Polatin, P. (1949), Pseudoneurotic forms of schizophrenia. *Psychiat. Quart.,* 23:248-276.

Kernberg, O. F. (1967), Borderline personality organization. *J. Amer. Psychoanal. Assn.,* 15:641-685.

_____ (1968), The treatment of patients with borderline personality organization. *Internat. J. Psycho-Anal.,* 49:600-619.

_____ (1970), A psychoanalytic classification of character pathology. *J. Amer. Psychoanal. Assn.,* 18:800-822.

_____ (1975), *Borderline Conditions and Pathological Narcissism.* New York: Jason Aronson.

Klein, D. F. (1975), Psychopharmacology and the borderline patient. In: *Borderline States in Psychiatry,* ed. J. E. Mack. New York: Grune & Stratton, pp. 75-91.

Knight, R. P. (1953a), Borderline states. *Bull. Menninger Clinic,* 17:1-12.

_____ (1953b), Management and psychotherapy of the borderline schizophrenic patient. *Bull. Menninger Clinic,* 17:139-150.

Kohut, H. (1971), *The Analysis of the Self.* New York: International Universities Press.

Mack, J. E., ed. (1975), *Borderline States in Psychiatry.* New York: Grune & Stratton.

Mahler, M. S. (1968), *On Human Symbiosis and the Vicissitudes of Individuation.* Vol. I. *Infantile Psychosis.* New York: International Universities Press.

_____ (1971), A study of separation-individuation process: And its possible application to borderline phenomena in the psychoanalytic situation. *The Psychoanalytic Study of the Child,* 26:403-424. New York: Quadrangle.

_____ & Furer, M. (1963), Certain aspects of the separation-individuation phase. *Psychoanal. Quart.,* 32:1-14.

Masterson, J. F. (1971), Treatment of the adolescent with borderline syndrome: A problem in separation-individuation. *Bull. Menninger Clinic,* 35:5-18.

_____ (1972), *Treatment of the Borderline Adolescent: A Developmental Approach.* New York: Wiley.

_____ (1975), The splitting defense mechanism of the borderline adolescent: Developmental and clinical aspects. In: *Borderline States in Psychiatry,* ed. J. E. Mack. New York: Grune & Stratton, pp. 93-102.

Modell, A. H. (1963), Primitive object relationships and the predisposition to schizophrenia. *Internat. J. Psycho-Anal.,* 44:282-292.

_____ (1968), *Object Love and Reality.* New York: International Universities Press.

Panel (1956), The borderline case. L. L. Robbins, reporter. *J. Amer. Psychoanal. Assn.,* 4:550-562.

Parens, H., & Saul, L. J. (1971), *Dependence in Man.* New York: International Universities Press.

Reich, W. (1949), *Character Analysis.* New York: Orgone Press.

Sarwer-Foner, G. J. (1960a), Some therapeutic aspects of the use of neuroleptic drugs in schizophrenic, borderline states and in short-term psychotherapy of the neurosis. In: *The Dynamics of Psychiatric Drug Therapy,* ed. G. J. Sarwer-Foner. Springfield, Ill.: Thomas, pp. 517-529.

_____ (1960b), The role of neuroleptic medication in psychotherapeutic interaction. *Comprehen. Psychiat.,* 1:291-300.

_____ (1966), A psychoanalytic note on a specific delusion of time in psychotic depression. *Canad. Psychiat. Assn. J. Suppl.,* 11:S221-S228.

_____ (1967), Do adolescents need separate treatment facilities? In: *Panel Discussion in Adolescent Psychiatry,* ed. S. J. Shamsie. Montreal: Schering, pp. 67-84.

_____ (1969), Depression and suicide: On some particularly high risk suicidal patients. *Dis. Nerv. Sys. GWAN Suppl.,* 30:104-110.

_____ (1970), An object relationship evaluation of depressive illness. I. Patients who still relate to external objects. *Dis. Nerv. Sys. GWAN Suppl.,* 31:69-81.

_____ (1972-1973), Some aspects of anal object relationships. Seminars presented to students at Canadian Institute of Psychoanalysis.

_____ (1975), On psychiatric symptomatology: Its meaning and function in relation to the psychodynamic actions of drugs. In: *Psychopharmacological Treatment in Psychiatry,* ed. H. C. B. Denber. New York: Marcel Dekker.

_____ & Koranyi, E. K. (1960), The transference effects, the attitude of the treating physician and counter-transference in the use of neuroleptic drugs in psychiatry. In: *The Dynamics of Psychiatric Drug Therapy,* ed. G. J. Sarwer-Foner. Springfield, Ill.: Thomas, pp. 392-400.

_____ Ogle, W., & Dancey, T. E. (1960), A self-contained woman's ward as a therapeutic community. In: *Research Conference on the Therapeutic Community,* ed. H. C. B. Denber. Springfield, Ill.: Thomas, pp. 79-97.

Schmideberg, M. (1947), The treatment of psychopathic and borderline patients. *Amer. J. Psychother.,* 1:45-70.

_____ (1959), The borderline patient. In: *American Handbook of Psychiatry,* 1:398-416, ed. S. Arieti. New York: Basic Books.

Scott, W. C. M. (1954), A new hypothesis concerning the relationship of libidinal and aggressive instincts. *Internat. J. Psycho-Anal.,* 35:234-237.

Sifneos, P. E. (1972), *Short-term Psychotherapy and Emotional Crisis.* Cambridge, Mass.: Harvard University Press.

Stengel, E. (1945), A study of some clinical aspects of the relationship between obsessional neurosis and psychotic reaction types. *J. Ment. Sci.,* 91:166-187.

Stern, A. (1945), Psychoanalytic therapy in the borderline neuroses. *Psychoanal. Quart.,* 14:190-198.

Tartakoff, H. H., et al. (1966), The normal personality in our culture and the Nobel prize complex. In: *Psychoanalysis—A General Psychology,* ed. R. M. Loewenstein et al. New York: International Universities Press, pp. 222-252.

Zetzel, E. R. (1971), A developmental approach to the borderline patient. *Amer. J. Psychiat.,* 127:867-871.

Zilboorg, G. (1941), Ambulatory schizophrenias. *Psychiatry,* 4:149-155.

Psychopharmacological Treatment and Delineation of Borderline Disorders

DONALD F. KLEIN, M.D.

The label borderline is often used when a patient does not clearly fit a common diagnostic stereotype, but instead shows features suggestive of several diagnoses. In addition, while the patient may qualitatively belong to a diagnostic class usually considered to imply mild severity such as phobia, the diagnostician may be led by pervasive malfunction to prefer a label with more malignant implications. Terms such as latent schizophrenia and pseudoneurotic schizophrenia are often considered synonymous with borderline. The implication is usually that the patient is bordering on psychosis, although he does not manifest clear-cut Kraepelinian signs of schizophrenia (delusions, hallucinations), or psychotic degrees of depression. Indeed, some patients present such a welter of unique familial relationships, developmental idiosyncracies, social aberrations, affective states, cognitive disturbances, symptoms, defects, and maladaptations, that the significance of diagnostic signs is obscured.

GRINKER, WERBLE, AND DRYE'S STUDY

The most ambitious and methodical attempt to bring systematic descriptive inquiry to the concept of the "borderline syndrome" is that of Grinker, Werble, and Drye (1968). Their essential position is that among patients diagnosed as borderline, certain ego functions are rather severely impaired, though cognitive difficulties usually associated with schizophrenia are not found. They conceive that the

Director of Research, New York State Psychiatric Institute; Lecturer, Columbia University, College of Physicians and Surgeons, New York, New York.

Alfreda Howard was of editorial assistance in the preparation of this paper.

365

patient falls between neurosis and psychosis, thus calling for a borderline concept.

Grinker, Werble, and Drye believe that the growing attention paid to the borderline diagnosis by psychoanalysts is indicative of the increasing numbers of these patients seen in private practice. An alternative to this hypothesis is that analysts' progressive disillusionment with their ability to make permanent changes in nonpsychotic patients has been masked by terminological revision. The diagnosis of potential psychosis, i.e., borderline disorder, thus has honorific results. It preserves intact the belief that classical psychoanalysis is the uniformly effective treatment of choice for neurosis, since failures occur only with the borderline patient.

Grinker and his group propose that the hypothesized structural developmental ego defect of the borderline patient is due to a narcissistic trauma that produces a deficiency in identification processes. Identification is maintained at the infantile level of mimicry and does not reach the secondary level, characterized by confidence, independence, and development of regulatory structures. Affectionate relations are sought but feared; loneliness is sometimes defended against by participating with others on an "as-if" level (structured situations are more comfortable than the uncertainty of change); and the sense of identity is woefully weak. The borderline patients to whom Grinker and his associates refer cannot be defined by descriptive symptomatology, but only by the inferential ego defect. Nonetheless, the actual operational criteria for their study allows alternative inferences.

There were 51 young adult subjects in their study. The basic criteria for entering the study consisted of: (1) repeated short-term hospitalizations but good psychological functioning in the interim period; (2) florid, attention-provoking, histrionic episodes preceding hospitalization; (3) good accessibility during the diagnostic interview or easy possibility for this; (4) good intellectual contact and intact cognitive functions; (5) appropriate associations; (6) no systemized delusions or paranoid systems; and (7) an ego-alien quality to any transient psychoticlike behavior. Entering the study meant operationally that the patient required hospitalization but was not schizophrenic, organic, or toxic; the behavior prior to hospitalization, however, was in some sense florid.

One would guess that such criteria would encompass many patients with character or affective disorders. Nonetheless, all such patients were considered borderline for this study. My impression of these 51 patients is that they were characterized by marked affective disorder accompanied by disruptive behavior, the predominant affects being anxiety, anger, or depression (see Grinker, 1977).

REVIEW OF PHENOMENOLOGY AND POSSIBLE DRUG TREATMENT

Interestingly, three of the four groups Grinker, Werble, and Drye use to categorize their borderline patients are distinctly characterized as depressed. Furthermore, although Group III is not called depressed, their depression score is actually higher than that of Group I. Although the four groups are quite arbitrary in their composition, nonetheless it is interesting to review them from the standpoint of syndromal resemblance and possible psychopharmacological intervention.

Group I has angry, withdrawn, depressed, and hostile patients. The syndrome of hostile depression treatable with phenothiazines has been supported by Overall and his associates (1964). The case summary given, however, strongly resembles the hysteroid dysphoric patient described by Klein and Davis (1969), who support the use of monoamine oxidase inhibitors, as will be discussed below.

Group II distinctly resembles the extremely labile, vacillating, emotionally unstable character disorder also described by Klein and Davis, and shown to be improved by lithium in a controlled study by Rifkin et al. (1972), as will be discussed below.

It is interesting that Grinker, Werble, and Drye consider the labile Group II to be the core borderline state. A follow-up study of such labile patients by Rifkin et al. (1972a, 1972b) indicates that this group of patients, frequently considered schizophrenic by their hospital psychiatrists, in fact had a relatively benign course, as did the borderline patients in the Grinker study (Werble, 1970).

It is noteworthy that the second follow-up study of the borderline patients, made one to eight years after the original study, indicated that these patients had not deteriorated into schizophrenics, nor were they typically hospitalized or even in very long-term psychotherapy. They had stable, although not upwardly mobile, employment. Werble states that the patients showed defects in their interpersonal skills which he believes implied ego defect. The examples given, however, are quite uniformly expressions of depression, loneliness, and hopelessness. No attempt was made to relate longer-term follow-up to the four borderline groups nor is any evidence given that they changed in different ways.

Group III patients seem schizoid, obsessional, detached, and withdrawn, although they are adaptive and remain adaptive at follow-up. It is not clear what brought them into the hospital in the first place. The relevance of medication for this group is obscure. If they represent a phasic depression in a relatively well-integrated person, antidepressants may be useful.

Group IV patients appear similar to neurotic depressives, as Grinker, Werble, and Drye state, in that their behavior is clinging, anxious, and depressed. The case example presented, however, only appears passive and dependent. Anxiety is not manifest, although the group is described as clearly anxious. These patients appear to resemble the phobic anxious patients I have described (1964, 1973; Klein and Fink, 1962) who respond well to imipramine. Since the Grinker study ignores symptoms, it does not isolate specific phobias and phobic-dependent manipulations. It is therefore impossible to tell whether the resemblance I discern between group IV and phobic anxious patients is actually correct.

In sum, in reviewing various patient descriptions of the Grinker group, I am forcibly struck by the ubiquity of persistently labile, anxious, and depressive states associated with maladaptive interpersonal tactics. The assertion that the key is an ego defect seems unsupported by their data.

Studies on Pseudoneurotic Schizophrenia

The importance of affective derangement in borderline patients is emphasized by psychopharmacological studies. While I know of no drug studies with borderline patients, there are two dealing with patients treated as "pseudoneurotic" schizophrenics. Both studies involve comparisons of phenothiazine and antidepressant medication and allow the contrast of pseudoneurotics with other schizophrenic patients. Hedberg, Houck, and Glueck (1971) found that half of their pseudoneurotic patients responded best to tranylcypromine alone, as opposed to using it in combination with trifluoperazine or trifluoperazine alone. Non-pseudoneurotic schizophrenics did not respond as well to tranylcypromine.

In my study (Klein, 1967, 1968), a significant drug-placebo difference in favor of imipramine, but not for chlorpromazine, was shown with regard to global improvement of pseudoneurotic schizophrenics, associated with distinct mood elevation and decrease in clinging indecision. The success of the antidepressants with these patients should lead us to rethink the entire geographical relation of these syndromes. Perhaps the important border is with affective disorder rather than with neurosis, character disorder, or schizophrenia.

DEVELOPING TREATMENT PROGRAMS FOR BORDERLINE PATIENTS

Since borderline disorders do not have a neat set of psychopathological descriptors, development of a drug treatment program for these patients is a complex task. One way to develop a treatment course is to identify the syndromes frequently associated with these patients and to outline the treatments appropriate for each syndrome. It is important to note that some of our medication recommendations are based on clinical experience rather than controlled studies, of which there are a notable paucity.

We work from the assumption that the effects of most major psychotropic agents are related to their capacity to modify states of dysregulation of affect and activation (Klein and Davis, 1969), or vulnerability to such disruptions. It follows from this theory that psychotropic agents work through modification of activation-affective dysregulation, and that conditions not characterized by these defects should be refractory to these drugs.

It is therefore good strategy when confronted with a case that does not fit neatly into any diagnostic rubric to specifically and carefully explore for evidence that the patient's psychopathology can be attributed to an affective or activation disorder, or a stereotyped affective overresponse. Unfortunately such signs may not be immediately apparent or for that matter complained of by any patient, since patients frequently express their difficulty wholly in terms of interpersonal and intrapsychic conflicts. Even if during a mental-status examination the patient gives much evidence of affective disturbance, there can be a problem in figure-ground discrimination such that the examiner may, like the patient, see the affective disturbance as secondary and "understandable," with the result that these disturbances are quickly relegated to the background.

EMOTIONAL LABILITY

DESCRIPTION

One central psychopathological trait that is often overlooked or underemphasized in the borderline group is marked emotional lability. Labile, emotionally unstable patients, often female adolescents, are frequently treated with intensive exploratory psychotherapy because of their interesting personalities, high degree of interaction with the therapist, marked introspective capacities, manifest psychological distress, and dramatic life experiences. It is often noted that such patients overreact to the point that some would call them psychotic when they are frustrated by or lose an object upon which they have been exceedingly dependent. Although capable of forming intense, but brittle, attachments to their therapists and displaying much verbal insight, significant modification of their affective-behavior patterns is not regularly achieved. Some believe that by age 30 these patients become more mature, with or without treatment. It is often the case that the emotionally chaotic state of these patients makes it impossible for them to utilize new insights or to plan constructively and engage in a career-development program.

Antipsychotic agents are of some value in the treatment of this syndrome and can moderate both the high, giddy, excitable, impulsive, hedonistic phase and the sullen, hostile, depressive, withdrawn phase. Often feelings of confusion, perplexity, anxiety, and depression are replaced by a manner that is bland, placid, friendly, and ingratiating. Moreover a reduction in feelings of role diffusion and goallessness may occur, even in the absence of specific solutions. In their psychotherapy these patients move away from introspection toward a concern with day-to-day events and developing active and friendly peer relations. They do not, however, demonstrate any increased concern with long-range planning.

Interestingly, some psychotherapists may be distressed by the change in communications from apparent attempts at insight to minimization, denial, and lack of interest in introspection. The therapist will frequently attribute the change in lability to better environmental structuring and ignore the fact that previous structuring attempts resulted in negativistic impulsive actions. Sometimes therapists will conclude that medication is interfering with psychotherapy and discontinue it; their patients then promptly regress to emotional lability and episodic impulsiveness.

Such patients encourage medication discontinuation, since they usually do not like being on an even keel and frequently complain of feeling a lack of spontaneity and a certain deadness. External behavioral observation of these patients, who are often active and lively, does not, however, bear this out. Perhaps their complaints can be understood as expressions of regret that they no longer experience their high, giddy periods. In a sense such patients could be addicted to their elated stages, miss them, and derogate their comparatively normal states. Alternatively, it is possible that the neuroleptics actually do produce a feeling tone somewhat different from normal for these patients during their even periods, possibly related to parkinsonian akinesia. Since these patients accept lithium better than neuroleptics, this seems likely. Such complaints may lead patients to discontinue medication surreptitiously.

TREATMENT

1. *Neuroleptics.* Thioridazine, in doses of approximately 300 mg h.s., is effective and acceptable in this patient group. Larger doses are occasionally necessary. While it is our impression that nonaliphatic phenothiazines (e.g., trifluoperazine and fluphenazine) occasionally produce akathisia and irritability in these patients, they are, on the other hand, often effective and have a somewhat lower degree of lethargy and akinesia associated with their use.

2. *Lithium carbonate.* A double-blind placebo-controlled study has demonstrated that lithium carbonate is both very acceptable to such patients and of distinct value in dampening mood swings, supporting the belief that the patient's drug rejection is related to

extrapyramidal disorder (Rifkin et al., 1972). Lithium is also helpful in diminishing self-destructive (e.g., wrist-cutting) and assaultive behaviors. Lithium may be the drug of choice (dosage adjusted to achieve blood levels between .70 and 1.2 Mq/L), with occasional supplementation by small doses (50 mg at sleep) of thioridazine.

3. *Antidepressants.* Antidepressants have diverse effects in this group. Some patients respond very well with a marked increase in affective stability, whereas others become increasingly angry, irritable, and aggressive, although manic episodes are rare. These effects may occur in sequence, with initial benefit followed by exacerbation.

REJECTION-SENSITIVE DYSPHORIA (HYSTEROID DYSPHORIA)

DESCRIPTION

One subgroup of borderline patients, who may be labeled either a neurotic-depressive reaction or hysteroid character disorder, have a specific medication-response pattern. I believe it is this group that is often referred to in psychoanalytic discussions of the borderline.

The general psychopathological state of these patients is an extremely brittle, shallow mood ranging from giddy elation to desperate unhappiness, and markedly responsive to external sources of admiration and approval. Such a patient may appear hopelessly bereft when a love affair terminates, but upon meeting a new attentive man, feel perfectly fine and even slightly elated within a few days. Similarly, failure to win high praise for their work may devastate them, but the trauma is quickly forgotten if this gap is filled by commendation for another project.

This emotionality markedly affects their judgment. When euphoric, they minimize and deny shortcomings of a situation or personal relationships and idealize all achievements and love objects. On the other hand, when they are at the opposite emotional pole, feelings of desperation, disproportionate to actual circumstances, are expressed. While such patients refer to their dysphoric mood as "depression," the characteristic vegetative features of endogenous depressive states are not only absent, but seem to be reversed. These patients are prone to oversleep and overeat, and although they may express themselves despairingly, they are activity-oriented and often successfully strive to engage in new rewarding situations.

In general hysteroid patients are fickle, emotionally labile, irresponsible, shallow, love-intoxicated, giddy, and short-sighted. They tend to be egocentric, narcissistic, exhibitionistic, vain, and clothes-crazy. In addition, they are seductive, manipulative, exploitative, sexually provocative, and emotional and illogical in their thinking; they are easy prey to flattery and compliments. Their general manner is histrionic and flamboyant. In their sexual relations they are possessive, grasping, demanding, romantic, and foreplay-centered. When frustrated or disappointed they become reproachful, tearful, abusive, and vindictive, and often resort to alcohol.

The female hysteroid dysphoric patient is a caricature of femininity because her disorder drives her to attempt to repair her rejection-sensitive dysphoria by exaggerating the social, seductive, exhibitionistic tactics allowable to women in our society. It is the driven quality and repetitiveness of behavior that indicate the underlying affective vulnerability. Such patients often appear intact when they are able to latch onto someone, receiving affective reassurance and a more balanced perspective from the relationship, so that they are not swamped by their overreactions to life's vicissitudes, and the rejections that their intrusive possessiveness often elicits.

Although such patients, when deprived, speak fervently of the possibility of suicide, the act seems quite uncommon. Furthermore, although they speak frequently of loneliness, they are not dominated by separation anxiety, and rarely develop agoraphobic or travel-phobic trends. If they are in the company of a man who is dull and unadmiring, they will remove themselves as quickly as possible, whereas the patient dominated by separation anxiety will accept any type of companionship, even from a clod. The development of incapacitating depressive states can occur but is most unusual. These patients can be distinguished from those with an emotionally unstable character disorder by the clear-cut "reactive" nature of their dysphoria.

Finding a generally acceptable label for these patients would be most useful. They have been referred to as hysteroid characters because of their histrionic emotionality and sex-centered concerns. This term seems unfortunate in that it emphasizes their interpersonal tactics and fantasy goals. However, we view these character traits as secondary to the primary affective disturbance.

This shift in focus is not accidental but reflects our growing therapeutic armamentarium. Until very recently the psychotherapist's natural focus was upon those aspects of the patient that seemed modifiable by psychotherapy: object relations, intrapsychic conflicts, and interpersonal tactics. Affective lability and dependence on external sources of narcissistic supplies were considered secondary, reparative, anxiety-binding defenses not open to direct intervention. The ability of medication to directly change the affective reactivity of these patients now makes it appear that the maladaptive interpersonal tactics and object relations may be viewed as secondary reverberations and miscarried repairs related to the basic affective difficulty.

TREATMENT

1. *Psychotherapy.* Uncontrolled clinical experience with hysteroid dysphoric patients indicates that supportive and directive psychotherapy is of moderate value in getting them to organize their lives better, meet deadlines, and fulfill responsibilities. This may result from the patient's attempt to gain the therapist's approbation by accepting the therapist's values. In many instances, the affective disorder seems little changed by psychotherapy, but some skilled therapists may be able to help such patients to grow. The therapy often involves a careful alternation between some initial gratification of the patient's need for admiration and dependence with subsequent gradual frustration of these needs, to promote progressive autonomy and self-reliance. These patients can be educated to recognize the object-related nature of the dysphoria, but this may not help their overreactivity — a condition often referred to as intellectual insight.

2. *Antidepressants.* Imipramine often has negative effects with these patients who develop racing thoughts, somatic distress, feelings of depersonalization, or hypomanic states. An occasional patient, however, seems to respond to imipramine.

MAO inhibitors, although rarely used, can be of marked value here in reducing these patients' vulnerability to affective crash secondary to rejection. Their prophylactic effect should not be ignored. They seem to modify the patient's marked lability in both directions. While still tending to overvaluate approval and admiration, in a giddy fashion, the patient is able to make a more rational judgment of the situation.

A crucial consequence of putting these patients on MAO inhibitors is that they then do not become dysphoric upon loss of admiration. This affective modification makes it no longer necessary for them to fling themselves into self-destructive or unrewarding romantic involvements. Their frequent use of alcohol also becomes markedly diminished. Phenelzine, 45-90 mg daily, is an effective MAO inhibitor for this group. Higher doses may incur insomnia and an irritable hypomania. Prolonged treatment is necessary since drug termination regularly leads to a recurrence of emotional overreactivity. A rational goal is to maintain medication until the patient's life is organized well enough to ensure adequate external supplies of self-esteem. At this point weaning from medication may be attempted; this often fails, however. Dietary constraints must be carefully observed in patients taking MAO inhibitors.

Alcohol seems to work primarily upon anticipatory anxiety. Since these patients are in a chronic anxious state concerning the possibility of being rejected or failing, alcohol bolsters their courage.

3. *Neuroleptics.* Soporific neuroleptics are not well tolerated by these patients. Nonsedative neuroleptics may be of some value as an adjunctive medication to MAO inhibitors when used in small doses (e.g., 2 to 5 mg daily of trifluoperazine). In this dose range the patient appears more relaxed, less labile, and less hostile or irritable. Lithium may also be a useful adjunct.

CHRONIC ANXIETY-TENSION STATES

DESCRIPTION

The borderline patient also often presents with marked anxiety and tension, overshadowed by other more salient complaints. In particular, many patients have a syndrome that resembles mild agitated depression but are not diagnosed as such because of their numerous interpersonal difficulties.

TREATMENT

In primarily anxious-tense patients, without evidence of psychosis or panic attacks, the use of minor tranquilizers appears to have a role. While it is current practice to give such patients a benzodiazepine, hard evidence that these medications are particularly valuable in the complex borderline case with chronic anxiety is not available.

It is even conceivable that some patients react negatively to these agents, developing increased hostility or dysphoric complaints which are not recognized as attributable to their "tranquilizer." It is perhaps wise to minimize the use of such medications until other, possibly more definitive, interventions such as those provided by the tricyclic antidepressants, MAO inhibitors, phenothiazinelike drugs, and lithium have been exhausted. If the patient is suffering from a pervasive inability to enjoy himself that is quite unreactive to changes in his personal surroundings, associated with sleep disturbances, a loss of interest, and feeling overwhelmed, then the utility of antidepressants rather than minor tranquilizers becomes more evident.

PHOBIC NEUROSIS ASSOCIATED WITH SPONTANEOUS PANIC ATTACKS

DESCRIPTION

Certain patients present massive and diffuse anxiety with prominent autonomic and tension symptoms complicated by phobic avoidance and panic attacks — often termed pan-anxiety. The outstanding characteristic of this syndrome is that spontaneous panic attacks usually precede the secondary development of massive free-floating tension anxiety. The chronic anxiety represents the helpless anticipation of the irregularly recurrent, terrifying panic attacks. The panic attack is the proximal inciting cause of the chronic anxiety state, which then leads to a variety of phobic avoidances used by the patient in hopes of preventing a recurrence of these panics or at least guaranteeing easy, quick access to help and safety.

Phobic avoidance usually related to being alone, being blocked from aid, or traveling alone may misleadingly be referred to as agoraphobia. Recently, however, we have found that although phobic patients with spontaneous panic attacks may have many different situational avoidances, they have similar medication-response patterns.

TREATMENT

Spontaneous or situational predisposed panics can be blocked through the use of both tricyclic antidepressants and MAO inhibitors (Klein, 1964; Lipsedge et al., 1973; Tyrer, Candy, and Kelly, 1973; Zitrin et al., 1976). Although the panics respond within a few weeks, or even earlier, the chronic tensional, expectant anxiety requires a subsequent period of extinction, prior to the cessation of avoidance maneuvers. Panics, as in simple phobias, that are tied to specific stimuli (e.g., cats, heights, elevators) are not blocked by antidepressants.

Interestingly, benzodiazepines, the meprobamatelike drugs, alcohol, and barbiturates are all useful in decreasing the chronic anticipatory anxiety but are of no value in the panic attacks. Antidepressants stop spontaneous panic attacks but are of no value for chronic anxiety. This clearly indicates that these are two markedly different processes; the panic attacks are not simply the quantitative extension of chronic anxiety. Furthermore, panic anxiety, so defined, is refractory to antipsychotics and may be exacerbated by them. Because these patients are misleadingly referred to as borderlines, their condition is often worsened by antipsychotic treatment, leading to increased dosage and a vicious circle. Because alcohol and barbiturates decrease chronic anxiety, patients frequently become addicted as they continually raise the self-administered dosage in hope that their panics will also be relieved.

HISTRIONIC STATES

DESCRIPTION

A patient group causing grave problems in clinical management is comprised of tense histrionic patients who are characteristically labile, episodically agitated, erratic, unpredictable, and manipulative. Although they are usually rational, relevant, and coherent, they express occasional paranoid and hallucinatory verbalizations. It is their ability to change that is so startling; they can act frightened and panicky to the point of suicide and several minutes later be affably laughing with others. Thus, while these individuals maintain a high degree of social interaction and are at times friendly and supportive, they are at other times disturbing, hostile, argumentative and demanding, yet pleading for help and direction.

Such patients express great investment in their doctors and psychotherapy, endowing them with miraculous potentialities. Similarly, their therapists readily become emotionally involved and are frequently frustrated and perplexed by the inability to predict or modify these patients' behavior. In addition, these patients have a tendency to become mute under close questioning. This passive-aggressive maneuver is often inaccurately referred to as catatonic or micropsychotic. The diagnosis of histrionic reaction is difficult to defend in the fact of skepticism among colleagues as to one's diagnostic acumen. The apparent fluctuations in states of consciousness that occur with this illness should prompt a thorough neurological and electroencephalographic investigation.

One clinical feature of predictive value and theoretical import is the marked relation of these patients' symptoms to environmental impact. Unlike depressed patients, who may increase the vigor of their complaints in the presence of psychiatric staff in an attempt to obtain maximum caring from them, but who remain inactive or unproductively agitated when not under staff observation, this group of refractory patients may appear in good spirits when apparently unobserved by staff, engage in social games and gossip pleasantly with others, even shortly after an explosive affective display.

The key issue may be histrionic role-playing and symptom imitation. In other words, these patients' symptoms may not be the direct external manifestations of intolerable affective states, but rather may be environmentally oriented, learned, manipulative devices associated with loss of role distance. Agitation and depressive complaints in this group are not the same as similarly labeled phenomena in other patients.

It is frequently stated that classical grand hysteria is no longer seen. The diagnosis of schizophrenia, however, has become more and more prevalent, and atypical borderline or pseudoneurotic schizophrenias are widely reported. Since the knowledge of schizophrenic behavior is widespread in books, television, and movies, and it is common practice to house all patients with emotional disorders together, we speculate that hysteroschizophrenics learn and practice their behavior through observation and imitation in much the same fashion as the nineteenth-century hysteroepileptic.

The differential diagnosis of hysteroschizophrenia from true schizophrenia presents knotty problems. The major distinguishing feature would seem to be a variant upon the well-known hysterical phenomenon — "la belle indifference." Hysterics may have the most crippling disorders and yet not display appropriate concern or emotional reaction to their infirmities. If it is their motivation to attain the sick role, one can well understand this phenomenon as resulting from their natural satisfaction with attaining their goal.

An analogous phenomenon occurs in patients with hysteroschizophrenia. The attainment of the sick role is dependent upon their imitation of extreme emotional distress, including psychotic symptomatology. In the initial stages of disorders, therefore, rather than la belle indifference, there is a histrionic accentuation of numerous psychotic features in a confusing jumble. However, once the patient is adjudged psychiatrically ill, as by hospitalization, one is struck by the marked fluctuations in psychiatric status and by the patient's apparent indifference to the content of his expressed delusions. A schizophrenic, for instance, may express the belief that the food is poisoned and promptly give up eating. A hysteroschizophrenic may express the same belief and then eat with a good appetite 30 minutes later. Similarly, a schizophrenic who expresses suicidal ideation, because he is convinced that his persecutors are about to close in on him, is in an extremely dangerous state and must be kept under constant observation. His affective state remains constant — fear and agitation. A hysteroschizophrenic may express the same delusional content and then, when away from the immediate observation of professional staff, engage in conversation and banter with other patients. Marked fluctuation in symptomatic behavior, depending on its impact on the environment, is common with hysteroschizophrenics. Furthermore, these patients frequently resort to the use of sedatives, intoxicants, narcotics, or stimulants, thus obscuring their status.

TREATMENT

Hysteroschizophrenic patients are refractory or respond negatively to psychotropic medication and tend to abuse the use of stimulants and sedatives. Intolerance of distressing side effects due to medication is expressed dramatically. Because of these patients' lability, there is much uncertainty as to the effectiveness of medication, so that they may receive long treatment courses before medication is found ineffective. If the patient responds in a somatizing fashion, however, medication is terminated promptly.

Their disorganization is so severe that effective outpatient therapy can rarely be accomplished. On the other hand, inpatient therapy in permissive settings regularly offers these patients such regressive temptations that they are unable to progress toward accepting adult responsibilities. These patients present an unsolved problem. There is no firm evidence concerning the utility of either short-term or long-term hospitalization in the treatment of this heterogeneous collection of patients.

As indicated in the above discussion of hysteroschizophrenia, hospitalization is not an innocuous procedure and may serve to solidify demoralized, dependent, exploitative adaptations. Hospitalization in a high-level facility, however, does have a role in arriving at a clear-cut diagnostic formulation when this seems impossible. Hospitalization affords an opportunity to see the borderline patient in the round. One is continually amazed to see patients who present confusing pictures demonstrate glaring defects in affective regulation and cognitive ability that were simply undetectable from the patients' testimony and behavior in the office. Furthermore, hospitalization can afford a full overview of the patient's response to treatment that often cannot be gained in outpatient practice. For these reasons, judicious short-term participation in a well-structured day hospital program may afford a good diagnostic and therapeutic compromise.

Our personal experience does not support long-term intensive psychotherapy during full hospitalization as a prime means of effectively dealing with this heterogeneous group. Although it is possible that for some patients this may be the treatment of choice, before engaging in such a major, possibly regression-producing and dependency-affirming intervention, it would seem useful to be sure that all lesser interventions have failed.

Conclusions

The syndrome of borderline personality disorders comprises an extremely heterogeneous mixture, and I have enumerated only a few subgroups. Others, such as the eccentric-schizoid relatives of schizophrenics, probably exist.

A major difficulty in syndromal analysis is the low status of affective state as an independent variable in psychodynamic theory. Drive states and defenses are considered the basic reality. Affects are viewed primarily as mere expressions of drives either in action or blocked or as defenses against aggression.

This de-emphasis of affective state as an independent variable in analysis is quite understandable since dynamic theory has derived from the therapeutic endeavors of psychotherapists who had no method for directly affecting the patient's emotional state, except insofar as the emotional state was reactive to fantasies, transferences, interpretations, interpersonal relations, and so forth. Quite understandably then, the patient's emotional state was viewed as an epiphenomenon, since the therapist's focus was on the patient's character and intrapsychic conflicts. Peculiar repetitious behavior was therefore viewed in the framework of the patient's defective character, repetition compulsion, or ego defect. The possibility that the peculiar behavior might be an attempt to express or cope with recurrent intolerable affective states and reactions could not be handled in this dynamic framework.

It is only with the development of pharmacological agents, whose mode of action seems to be the direct amelioration of disordered affects and activation states or the reduction of specific affective vulnerabilities, that character and ego defect may be seen as more secondary than primary. For instance, the patient with an emotionally unstable character disorder who takes lithium still has functionally autonomous exploitative and impulsive adaptations; yet it seems far easier to understand these adaptations as being historically secondary to his constantly fluctuating emotional state than the other way around. Similarly, the phobic anxious dependent patient who responds to imipramine by cessation of panic still maintains a phobic, dependent, manipulative adaptation until he becomes convinced that the panic attacks will not recur — allowing a shift to more adaptive procedures. Again, it is the activation-affective disorder that results in the characterological "ego" peculiarities rather than vice versa. Another example occurs with character disorders complicated by retarded depressions who respond well to imipramine with a decrease in hostile, exploitative withdrawal once their depression is alleviated.

The phenomenological analysis of the borderline patient has been markedly impaired by the primary emphasis on ego structures and identificatory difficulties, i.e., "soft" thought disorder and characterological peculiarities. In contrast, focusing upon the patient's longitudinal affective status with special emphasis on reactivity or lack of reactivity of affective swings, as well as the specific nature of the stimuli-engendering reactive swings, appears a superior strategy. The so-called soft thought disorder seems an amalgam of emotional disorganization, histrionic self-dramatization, and loss of role distance.

Furthermore, response to medication plays a key role in the isolation of homogeneous subgroups. Such treatment responses were crucial to the discernment of the phobic anxious patient, the emotionally unstable character disorder, and the hysteroid dysphoric. Application of this systematic strategy of pharmacological behavioral dissection is extremely promising. The two approaches of concentrating on patient affectivity and their responses to medication dovetail neatly. A major problem is the development of adequate institutional facilities for pursuit of these objectives in the nonpsychotic patient.

Grinker, Werble, and Drye's studies have indicated the direction. Although I disagree with their conclusions, their respect for systematic fact gathering and data analysis deserves widespread emulation. Our field must go beyond the point of complex, and at times incomprehensible, theoretical formulations supported by snippets of ambiguous case material. To do this requires the establishment of clinical research institutes (Klein, 1970). One roadblock is the conviction that the uncontrolled psychoanalytic investigation is adequate to test hypotheses, rather than the recognition that at best it can only formulate hypotheses.

REFERENCES

Grinker, R. R., Sr. (1977), The borderline syndrome. A phenomenological view. *This Volume,* pp. 159-172.
_____ Werble, B., & Drye, R. C. (1968), *The Borderline Syndrome.* New York: Basic Books.
Hedberg, D. L., Houck, J. H., & Glueck, B. C. (1971), Tranylcypromine-trifluoperazine combination in the treatment of schizophrenia. *Amer. J. Psychiat.,* 127:1141-1146.
Klein, D. F. (1964), Delineation of two drug-responsive anxiety syndromes. *Psychopharmacologia,* 5:397-408.
_____ (1967), Importance of psychiatric diagnosis in prediction of clinical drug effects. *Arch. Gen. Psychiat.,* 16:118-126.
_____ (1968), Psychiatric diagnosis and a typology of clinical drug effects. *Psychopharmacologia,* 13:359-386.
_____ (1970), Non-scientific constraints on psychiatric treatment research produced by the organization of clinical services. In: *Non-Scientific Constraints on Medical Research,* ed. S. Merlis. New York: Raven Press.
_____ (1973), Drug therapy as a means of syndromal identification and nosological revision. In: *Psychopathology and Pharmacology,* ed. J. O. Cole & A. J. Friedhoff. Baltimore: Johns Hopkins Press.
_____ & Davis, J. M. (1969), *Diagnosis and Drug Treatment of Psychiatric Disorders.* Baltimore: Williams & Wilkins.
_____ & Fink, M. (1962), Psychiatric reaction patterns to imipramine. *Amer. J. Psychiat.,* 119:432-438.
Lipsedge, M. S., et al. (1973), The management of severe agoraphobia: A comparison of iproniazid and systematic desensitization. *Psychopharmacologia,* 32:67-80.
Overall, J. E., Hollister, L. E., Meyer, F., Kimbell, I., Jr., & Shelton, J. (1964), Imipramine and thioridazine in depressed and schizophrenic patients. Are there specific antidepressant drugs? *JAMA,* 189:605-608.
Rifkin, A., Levitan, S. J., Galewski, J., & Klein, D. F. (1972a), Emotionally unstable character disorder: A follow-up study: I. Description of patients and outcome. *Biol. Psychiat.,* 4:65-79.
_____ _____ _____ (1972b), Emotionally unstable character disorder. A follow-up study: II. Prediction of outcome. *Biol. Psychiat.,* 4:81-88.
_____ Quitkin, F., Carillo, C., & Klein, D. F. (1972), Lithium treatment in emotionally unstable character disorders. *Arch. Gen. Psychiat.,* 27:519-523.
Tyrer, P., Candy, J., & Kelly, D. (1973), A study of the clinical effects of phenelzine and placebo in the treatment of phobic anxiety. *Psychopharmacologia,* 32:237-254.
Werble, B. (1970), Second follow-up study of borderline patients. *Arch. Gen. Psychiat.,* 23:3-7.
Zitrin, C. M., et al. (1976), Comparison of short-term treatment regimens in phobic patients. In: *Evaluation of Psychological Therapies,* ed. R. L. Spitzer & D. F. Klein. Baltimore: Johns Hopkins Press.

Day Hospital Treatment
for Borderline Patients:
The Institution as Transitional Object

CLARENCE CRAFOORD, M.D.

AN EXPERIMENT IN SWEDEN

This report dates back to a four-year period, from 1968 to 1972, during which I functioned as senior psychiatrist at the Fruängen Day Hospital in Stockholm. My purpose in presenting this report is to describe a day hospital program for young borderline patients in Sweden, or, rather, how some borderline patients perceived a day hospital program set up to treat all kinds of seriously disturbed psychiatric patients and managed to change it according to their needs into a special treatment program for borderline patients.

The Fruängen Day Hospital, founded in 1966, was an innovation in Sweden at the time. Its founder, Dr. Bengt Berggren (Berggren, Rooth, and Szecsody, 1962, 1964), conceived of it as an alternative to psychiatric hospitalization. He wanted to show that many severely disturbed patients could be treated as well, or better, in a day hospital facility, where the cost would be lower than if they were treated in a full-time mental hospital. To this end, it was agreed that every third patient who presented himself to the public mental health system of the district and was judged to need hospitalization would be sent to the Fruängen Day Hospital to be treated there. Exempted were cases involving a fulminant psychotic episode, great suicidal risk, or heavy drug addiction (Berggren, 1966).

THE SETTING

The Fruängen Day Hospital is located in two stories of an ordinary office building in the shopping center of the suburb of

---

Psychiatrist-in-Chief, Luleå, Sweden.

Fruängen, ten miles southwest of central Stockholm. It belongs formally to Department Four of Langbro State Hospital, in the same part of Stockholm. The facility is open from 8 A.M. until 4 P.M., five days a week. Breakfast and lunch are served on the premises. All costs are covered by National Health Insurance, but a small daily fee equivalent to two dollars is expected from each patient. An average of 40 patients are treated every year, but the number of registered entries far exceeds this, as all patients are absent or discharged and then return and are reregistered many times during their career in the day hospital.

There are ten full-time staff members—two psychiatrists, one psychologist, one social worker, one psychiatric nurse, four psychiatric aides, and one occupational therapist.

During the four-year period covered by this report, the Fruängen Day Hospital had a daily patient census of 25. The male/female ratio was nine to six; the prevalent age 15 to 25. During the same period, three of our patients committed suicide, and five had to be transferred to closed wards in the nearby state hospital.

A TREATMENT PROGRAM IN EVOLUTION

When I took over the program in 1968, it included, briefly, social training in groups, occupational therapy, and group psychotherapy, one hour a week. The goal of treatment was mainly to improve social adaptation. While accepting this as basically sound, I decided to make treatment as psychodynamic as possible. Interpretation of behavior and clarification of the symbolic meaning of acts performed by patients or staff were to be the main instruments of treatment.

This of course caused many conflicts and much anxiety in the milieu, which became more of a challenge to both patients and staff. Many older staff members resisted the changes that I and my newer colleagues introduced. While the aim is to build an atmosphere which would encourage creativity in patients, as well as personnel, these changes created, in effect, unrest and anxiety. Many of the older staff members had a hard time seeing what was therapeutic about the new milieu. One nurse and one psychiatric aide resigned. Several others complained that the "analytic stuff" put too heavy a burden on them. Some patients left the hospital never to return. We began experiencing a shortage of patients and the policy of admitting only every third patient had to be abandoned.

We sent information about our program to the authorities of the nearby mental hospital and they decided that a number of their younger patients could be transferred to our day hospital for more intensive treatment. Some heavily drugged young schizophrenic patients quickly went mad and had to be returned to the hospital; some others began drinking heavily and stayed away from the facility for days in a row; some were frightened by the "toughness" of the new milieu.

At the same time that a more psychotherapeutic approach was introduced, the program was trying to adapt to the democratic trends of the modern therapeutic community. Patients were expected to participate in decisions affecting the milieu and their treatment. Some younger patients protested against the occupational therapy programs, which they found useless and meaningless. We took their criticisms seriously and began a thorough discussion with this rebellious group of young patients about occupational therapy in particular, and our day hospital treatment in general. New issues ensued. The rebellious group became, temporarily, a psychotherapeutic group. Discussion in this group became more meaningful to these patients than occupational therapy.

Partly as a result of our discussions with these young rebellious patients and partly because of broader considerations among our staff, the program at the day hospital changed in the direction of increased psychotherapy in small and big groups and away from occupational therapy, which was now less emphasized as such and more for its expressive potential in activities like art therapy, theater groups, or work for a patient newspaper. Inspired by the Norwegian milieu-therapy approach, we eventually established a big group every day, small groups three times a week, in addition to art-therapy or dramatic groups. The psychotherapeutic effect on the patients and its impact on the total milieu, including our staff, soon became noticeable.

These changes were brought about in a period of approximately a year and a half. During this time the often provocative arguments and acting-out behavior of the younger patients frightened and

angered the more depressed, neurotic older patients, who felt somewhat lost as the staff had to concentrate their attention on the more
outgoing younger patients. At the same time, some of us on the staff
felt we had more to offer these disturbed and disturbing younger
patients. They had been represented in the day hospital earlier, but
then usually only for short periods of time and often heavily under
drugs. Now, as the "easier" patients left, the population of our day
hospital facility changed decidedly in the direction of these younger,
more difficult patients.

Not all staff members favored this change. The new patients
were more demanding and challenging, craving more attention
and time. The nurses who, under our supervision, served as leaders
of the therapeutic community experienced a role confusion, as they
were expected to act as both therapists (in the discussion groups)
and comrades (in the workshops). Our solution to this was that the
more experienced staff members took over as group leaders in the
four psychotherapy groups, while the nurses stayed on as co-thera-
pists and leaders of the workshops. This change did not quite solve
the problem, as the nurses felt demoted, being deprived of their
status as group leaders. The psychiatrist and the psychologist thus
moved into the milieu. This movement also provoked suspicion
among the patients, and the groups eventually became more
frustrating and more demanding.

The problem of absenteeism from the day hospital indicated the
level of frustration among the patients. Some stayed away many
days at a time; some attended only on Fridays. It proved very difficult to regulate the patients' participation in the program and to
establish effective staff roles and leadership. Was this absenteeism
an indication that our program was wrong? We wondered. There
were sometimes as many staff members as patients around. The
atmosphere was one of mutual distrust and great anxiety, not only
for patients but for staff as well. We experienced the situation as a
vicious circle, as a test of our faith in the dynamic approach to treatment. Could we really believe in a treatment program that patients
chose not to attend? Finally, it occurred to us that in order to
achieve some stability in our program we had to offer individual as
well as group treatment. Until then we had operated on the belief
that group and milieu treatment alone should be sufficient and that

giving in to the constant demands of patients for individual attention would deprive the milieu of its importance.

The real breakthrough in our dilemma came when we discovered that, while patients constantly broke their contract with the institution, violating their time schedule, being frequently late or absent, or losing contact entirely with the program, they made themselves available in a more consistent fashion if they became attached to someone on the staff. That gave us the idea of promoting two contracts, one with the institution and one with a particular staff member — a therapist-patient contract — and we implicitly agreed to honor them independently of each other. Violation of the rules of the institution thus did not affect the bond between the patient and his individual psychotherapist. This arrangement proved very effective. The patient's maneuvers in the milieu could be examined in the individual setting and, even if he had to separate temporarily from the institution, he still remained in contact with his personal therapist. Whether the patient complied with or broke the rules of the larger program became an integral part of the treatment process, rather than an end in itself, as it tended to be in so many cases before. Dropping out thus came to be regarded as a sometimes necessary intermission, a pause that enabled the patient to return to the day hospital on new premises, perhaps many times over.

Many similar arrangements, maneuvers, or processes took place in different parts of the schedules and routines of the day hospital program, becoming the subject of seemingly never-ending discussions, not only between patient and therapist but also in the staff group and in the big group meetings. We came to realize that this fluidity, the option to evolve as we saw fit, was the life core of our day hospital milieu and that the whole treatment program would cease to exist the moment we looked upon it as ready.

A QUESTION OF DIAGNOSIS

During all this time, some two years since we started putting the emphasis on a psychotherapeutic, psychoanalytically oriented milieu, it had not occurred to us that the patients we had been dealing with were largely borderline. Even today, the diagnosis of borderline is not common in Scandinavia, and the concept itself does not exist in the Swedish psychiatric vocabulary. To some of us, it was known as a description of some exotic category of people with whom we were not acquainted in our practice.

In our day hospital setting we preferred to make light of diagnostic classifications, referring to our patients in vague terms as "depressed," "anxiety-ridden," "acting out," "drug abusers," and the like. Many of the patients who came to us from the state hospital were diagnosed as schizophrenic, and they would have remained there or returned home on heavy doses of psychotropic drugs as chronic patients, had they not been young and judged worthy of a chance at our day hospital. Among these patients, some 25 were with us over long periods of time. Even though they left us in anger and came back many times, they kept considering themselves our patients.

The first small group of four or five youths of 17 to 23 years of age came to constitute the nucleus of the hospital's program and community. Although we did not identify these patients as borderline, we all became heavily involved in their acting-out behavior, their stormy, unpredictable depressions, their episodic alcohol and drug abuse, and were astonished at the fact that they stayed on in spite of all the emotional turmoil, the constant clashes with the staff, and the frequent "relapses" all the way from delinquent behavior to schizophreniclike apathy. They did not really form a group; but they played cards together, ganging up against the assignments at the workshops. For a period, this nucleus of rebellious youths remained beyond their scheduled time of work and, enticing the rest of the patient group to join them, sat on the floor silently for a while, forming a human ring around a lit candle, in some kind of meaningless (to us) ritualistic act. They told us that the work our staff assigned to them was meaningless or at any rate not sufficient and insisted on having more group discussions or more meaningful assignments in the workshops and less "production of silly things."

Under the constant pressure of such acting-out behavior on the part of our patients, we were able slowly to develop a day hospital program such as we had hardly anticipated when we began the effort. The culture of the place and the information we conveyed to the outpatient clinics and mental health centers that supplied us with patients changed accordingly. Severely disturbed young people now came to our day hospital from all over Stockholm. Without actually knowing it, we had created a model therapeutic milieu for borderline patients. It was a self-selected group: the psychotic ones went mad in our milieu and had to be committed to a state hospital; the depressives and the older, more neurotic patients dropped out frightened, never to return; but the borderlines, mainly adolescents and young adults, stayed on.

Two Clinical Examples

Case 1

Harold came from a disturbed home, a split family beset with alcohol addiction and social problems. Early maladjustment had brought him to several correctional institutions for children and early adolescents. While in his teens, he began to abuse drugs and alcohol to a self-destructive degree and was committed to a mental hospital for juveniles. During periods of better adjustment he lived alone, working as a night guard or in similar lonely jobs. He looked upon himself as "a hopeless case." He began attending our program while living in the nearby state hospital; later he moved to his own flat. In the day hospital he was very negativistic, critical of everything and everybody, provocative and annoying to all of us. He would often come to the ward intoxicated, sometimes boastful, sometimes mute and sullen. He often talked of suicide.

Behind his aggressive behavior, Harold was really shy and scared. He soon attached himself to the art therapist, who encouraged his painting. For a period he attended only the art-therapy hours. He declared that the day hospital was the most "people-hating" and "cruel" institution there was. He said he hated it. Yet he came more and more regularly. When encouraged to stay longer, he would show up drunk and then be absent for a while. For a period he came only a few minutes before closing time and declared he would sleep in the facility. We had to fight to get him out, and some mornings we would find him lying asleep, often drunk, on the doorstep. For a while he came to the day hospital only to get a meal. We constantly pointed out to him that these were his own arrangements, not ours. Then one of the staff members suggested that he come at regular hours, regardless of whether he took part in the program or not. Soon afterward Harold came for the specified hours and periodically attended the hospital program, even though he still declared that it was all "shit." Then he told us he was going to school again, even though he felt the teachers and the whole school were crazy or foolish.

After a year of treatment, Harold's attachment to the day hospital began to loosen. He claimed that he came to us only to eat and drink, and denied that he made any progress. For one year after he stopped coming to the day hospital, he kept in continuous contact with his therapist and attended his technical studies. He still had anxiety spells when alone at night, and always carried some anxiolytic drugs in his pocket, using them as fetishes rather than taking them. Four years later and still in contact with the therapist, he reports living a normal life, working, and making plans to get married.

Case 2

Peter was eighteen when he came to the day hospital. His father had committed suicide when Peter was eight. His mother became psychotic and the family split for a while, Peter and his two siblings being placed in different foster homes. After some months the mother brought the elder siblings home, but Peter was brought back only a year later. He was told that he was a burden to his mother, as were the other children. "As soon as you are fifteen, you have to leave home," mother said. "My responsibility ends at fifteen."

Before he was fifteen, Peter sniffed rubber solvent and smoked marijuana. Once again child welfare placed him in a foster home. Peter became depressed and made a suicidal attempt, allegedly because the people in the foster home were too kind to him and he "could not stand it." He remained in this foster home for two years, attending school irregularly. Then he came to Stockholm, where he was to take a job and live with his mother again. But instead he went to a doctor, complaining of "liver trouble." He thought he had heard some peculiar noise coming from the right side of his body, which persuaded him that his liver was slowly breaking down. This he attributed to his earlier abuse of rubber solvent. He felt his liver was shrinking; and the thought of it so obsessed and terrified him that he could do nothing else but listen to his own liver and its shrinking noise. He felt his liver was moving in his stomach, contaminating other organs as well. He was admitted to the state hospital.

When Peter came to our day hospital he was very suspicious. He was critical of the program and soon joined those who protested against the occupational-therapy part. "Useless!" he exclaimed, and often left the groups in the middle of our discussions to take care of his liver in the toilet. He took part in a typewriting course and was awarded a diploma. This made him deeply anxious and he disappeared for a week, to come back drunk, deeply depressed, expressing feelings of total emptiness and despair. "I'll become a tramp," he declared. He was persuaded to join an art class, where he painted pictures of deserts with a lonely man lost in the middle. His engagement was now only in the art group and in the occupational-therapy discussion group, which eventually was dissolved.

Slowly Peter appeared less depressed and became more active in the day hospital. He became competitive, had a fight with another patient, and was a leader in the nuclear, rebellious group for some months. Eventually he became involved in the entire treatment program and was a superb guide to our weekly visitors. He began taking driving lessons and was considered very skillful. The staff became optimistic and encouraged him to get his driving license. When he succeeded, they congratulated him warmly, at which point he broke down completely and stopped coming to the day hospital.

Some days later he was admitted to the state hospital, confused and depressed. He thought of becoming "an old chronic schizophrenic." At the same time he wanted to discuss society's prejudice against people like himself. He was invited back to the day hospital, where this time he was provided with an individual psychotherapist. He remained in the program for two months, moved away from his mother's place, tried to go to school and to get a job, failing repeatedly. He had several depressive periods, but kept a once-afortnight contact with his therapist at the day hospital. Then he disappeared. Two years later we learned that he had presented himself to another mental hospital, complained about a liver problem again, and insisted on a liver puncture. At last he got one and was persuaded that his liver was normal. He began sending letters, poems, and paintings to his therapist at the day hospital but refused personal contact.

During the last five years Peter has kept up a sporadic correspondence with the day hospital; he describes a very quiet life. He is still painting the same lonely deserts and brooding about "the riddle of schizophrenia." He no longer complains about his liver, only because he considers it hopeless and all doctors incompetent. He occupies a flat of his own, and draws a pension, which affords him the use of an old car. He calls this his "accomplishment."

Peter's and Harold's cases depict some aspects of the Fruängen Day Hospital as a facility located in the metropolitan area of Stockholm, as well as the design and role of its program in the dynamics of the borderline youths around which it developed. These cases also illustrate the defense strategies against abandonment depressions, as Masterson (1972) has described them, which are always present in borderline patients. The extreme separation-individuation problem in achieving something real in the world is well portrayed by Peter's reaction to getting a typewriting diploma or a driver's license. Narcissistic traits are present in the diverse symptoms and behavior of both men.

The needs of the borderline patient were revealed by the patients themselves through their performance on the premises of the day hospital. They badly needed the security of the place, but they also needed to be able to abandon it, to despise it, to spit on it, or to love it. The institution was there, available, but not as the ever-present, obligatory reality of the mental hospital.

COMMENTS

At first we found the patients' erratic behavior, their constant coming and going very frustrating for our staff, but we also felt that our patients, as well as our staff, were subjected to repeated abandonments and interruptions of treatment by the institution itself. We eventually learned to look upon these repeated comings and goings as a process inherent in the patient's struggle for individuation. This change of attitude on our part meant a shift in the dynamics between the patients and the day hospital program. The two parallel contracts of individual therapy and commitment to the institution showed clearly how these patients used the facility, even its geography, as a testing ground for individuation. We learned that after a patient had been absent for some time, he would return under somewhat altered conditions. His commitment to the institution and the institution's commitment to him would be a little different. The day hospital's mode of operation — having patients leave and come back five times a week — is in itself an ever-repeating device of separation and fusion.

I would like to borrow Winnicott's (1953) concept of transitional object to illustrate the relation between the patient and the day hospital. The staff members of the day hospital or even the physical structure itself become a transitional object for the patient — a mother image without the threatening characteristics of a real mother, an object the patient may love, introject, toss around, spit out, and take in again. It offers the possibility of re-enacting the experience of separation over and over, enabling self- and object images to become integrated and ego boundaries to acquire stability. We coined the slogan "basic trust and confrontation" to characterize what the day hospital could offer as a transitional object for our patients (Crafoord, 1973).

We learned, on the other hand, that patients who adjusted themselves smoothly to the program, becoming instantly active in group discussions and work assignments, never being absent, ideal as they seemed to be for a day hospital system, were in fact resisting treatment. We came to recognize in the behavior of such patients, who might be diagnosed as borderline of the "as-if" type, a wish to find hospitalization in a day hospital, to turn the facility into a mental hospital. An example of such a patient was a very compliant youth who, during group discussions planning work activities, was very concerned with the concept of hospitalization and wondered whether the patients were not too "hospitalized." We interpreted his preoccupation with the idea of hospitalization as his own wish to be hospitalized, whereupon he began reconsidering his attachment to the place and his conformist behavior—until one day he did not show up and remained absent for some time.

In my view, the role of the day hospital as transitional object is fundamental during the phase of treatment that Masterson (1972) calls the "testing phase," which precedes the working through of depression that takes place mostly in the individual treatment parallel to the day hospital program, or, as in many of our cases, in the continual individual contact with a staff member after separation from the day hospital.

The great problem for the borderline patient in his struggle for identity, as I have observed it in our institution, is developing an attachment to somebody trustworthy enough (a "good-enough" mother substitute) so as to permit genuine separation depression to be contained by the patient. This paves the way for genuine self-development. The process of finding such a trustworthy person—not necessarily the psychotherapist—takes place in the turmoil of the "testing phase."

This is where I think that the Fruängen Day Hospital program, as we developed it with the help of our patients, possesses unique qualities. The dynamic structure of the program during weekdays, with its short interruptions for nights and longer ones for weekends, creates a basic rhythm, challenging and at the same time security-providing. The institution is always there; its conditions and schedules become familiar. But it forces you to come and go, to fuse and separate, to participate and integrate. Its framework is stable but not rigid, leaving room for individual variations in approach over longer or shorter periods of time. The people who comprise its staff are not away on irregular schedules, with days off, night duties, and so on, as in mental hospitals. They are available when the day hospital is open. Thus the day hospital has qualities which, as Chase and Hire (1966) have pointed out, are essential to the therapist of borderline patients: accepting, continuously the same, flexible, but providing well-defined boundaries.

REFERENCES

Berggren, B. (1966), [Memorandum from the Fruängen Day Hospital.] (Unpublished.)

———— Rooth, C. H., & Szecsody, I. (1962), [Day hospital care for psychiatric patients.] *J. Swedish Med. Assn.*, 59:2035.

———— ———— ———— (1964), [Day hospital care for psychiatric patients.] *J. Swedish Med. Assn.*, 61:2522.

Chase, L. S., & Hire, A. W. (1966), Countertransference in the analysis of borderlines. Presented to the Boston Psychoanalytic Society, Boston, Mass., March 23.

Crafoord, C. (1973), [Basic trust and confrontation. Experience from Fruängen Day Hospital 1968-1972.] *J. Swedish Med. Assn.*, 70:1640.

Masterson, J. F. (1972), *Treatment of the Borderline Adolescent. A Developmental Approach*. New York: Wiley.

Winnicott, D. W. (1953), Transitional objects and transitional phenomena: A study of the first not-me possession. *Internat. J. Psycho-Anal.*, 34:1-9.

Group Psychotherapy
of the Borderline Patient

LEONARD HORWITZ, PH.D.

Over the past decade the borderline patient has become a focus
of interest for mental health professionals. The reasons are not
entirely clear. Perhaps this phenomenon is related to the special
problems and challenges of diagnosis and treatment these patients
pose; perhaps it is related to the empirical and theoretical advances
in this field which occurred in the sixties under the leadership of
Grinker, Kernberg, Mahler, and others. Whatever the reasons, we
have not seen a parallel surge of interest within the group psychotherapy field. Although a moderate amount of literature deals with
this topic and a few papers are devoted primarily to this area, most
were written in the fifties (Feldberg, 1958; Freedman and Sweet,
1954; Shaskan, 1957; Spotnitz, 1957). This state of affairs is particularly surprising inasmuch as group therapists have long recognized the special contributions groups make to patients with significant ego weakness. I hope to alleviate the current drought
by a review of the pertinent literature and by a presentation of my
own perspective on this problem.

As a starting point, let me clarify my own orientation to the
main characteristics of the borderline patient. I see it as a diagnosis
of ego capacity and weakness and *not* one of characterological
problems. Borderline patients, like the rest of us, come in many
psychological sizes and shapes and manifest multiple varieties of
characterological features, personality attitudes, and behavioral
dispositions. They may be histrionic or inhibited, passively with-

Director of Group Psychotherapy, The Menninger Foundation; Faculty
Member, Topeka Institute for Psychoanalysis, Topeka, Kansas.

drawn or aggressive, grandiose or humble, paranoid or masochistic. In fact, more than most other types they often present erratically fluctuating behavioral pictures, to the dismay of their therapists.

The term borderline refers to a range of ego functions and object-relations developments which are more defective than in neurosis but more intact than in psychosis. Grinker, Werble, and Drye (1968) have demonstrated that the borderline syndrome embraces a wide range of pathology, with some patients falling closer to the neurotic end of the boundary, while others function closer to psychosis. With regard to their ego functions, these patients manifest a chronic instability with vulnerable reality testing and a low tolerance for disturbing affects. From the object-relations standpoint, they are given to splitting in all aspects of self- and object integration with resulting identity diffusion and unstable relatedness (Kernberg, 1967; Masterson and Rinsley, 1975).

Since the appearance of group psychotherapy as a significant treatment method over 30 years ago, borderline patients have been treated in many different settings and in groups of varying composition: outpatients and inpatients, homogeneous and mixed, combined with individual treatment and alone. A common denominator in many of the reports in the literature is that *certain* borderline patients may fail to progress in individual psychotherapy but respond well to group treatment, sometimes alone and sometimes in conjunction with individual treatment. No one is able to say with precision which kind of patient, combined with which kind of group, offers a favorable prognosis. On the other hand, the literature is fairly clear that there are special features of group treatment which make it especially unsuitable for certain patients. Wolman (1960) aptly observes that the group setting is particularly suitable for borderline patients when they can stand the group and the group can stand them.

The Appropriate Group and Parameters

Homogeneous versus Mixed Groups

A few workers have described successful experiences with groups composed entirely of borderline patients (Forer, 1961; Scheidlinger and Pyrke, 1961; Shaskan, 1971).[1] All were outpatient groups where the patients were also seen individually, at least in the initial phases of treatment. Each of the therapists stresses the importance of supportive measures, such as increased therapist transparency and activity, encouragement of socialization among members, symbolic as well as actual feeding of patients. The only suggestion of difficulties in conducting an all-borderline group is Wolman's (1960) observation that an all-psychotic group is not desirable because such patients tend to be too quiet, withdrawn, and demanding of nurturance.

A prominent feature of the literature, on the other hand, is the consistent recommendation that borderline patients are best treated in groups of neurotics and character disorders, provided they are carefully selected and do not exceed "more than one or two" in number (Day and Semrad, 1971; Hulse, 1958; Slavson, 1964). These cautions are introduced both because of the potential stress on the patient, as well as the strain such patients place upon the group. Since their pathology is of a more profound nature and they are clearly more handicapped than others in the group, they run the risk of being scapegoated or alienated from the more competent members. By the same token, neurotic patients often find it difficult to tolerate a fellow patient whose behavior is widely deviant from theirs. The therapist runs the risk of losing his better-integrated patients if the borderline patient is not admitted carefully and sparingly.

Concomitant Individual Treatment

Individual treatment at some point, either prior to or during the group experience, is recommended by practically every writer in this area (Day and Semrad, 1971; Greenbaum, 1957; Hulse, 1958; Scheidlinger and Holden, 1966; Slavson, 1964; Spotnitz, 1957).

---

[1] Since there is considerable variation in terminology used to designate the borderline patient, not all of the groups referred to here were specifically designated as such. Some of the patients were characterized as latent or ambulatory schizophrenics, schizophrenic syndromes, and primitive orally fixated personalities. Undoubtedly, not all of these patients fall precisely within the boundaries commonly designated as borderline, but most of them appear to do so.

Some authors recommend concomitant group and individual therapy for the majority of borderline patients taken into a group; usually the same therapist does both treatments (Greenbaum, 1957; Slavson, 1964; Spotnitz, 1957). Others, like Hulse (1958) or Day and Semrad (1971), suggest that individual therapy sessions should be available for the borderline patient on an intermittent basis to assist him at special times of stress. Slavson (1964) believes in a considerable period of prior individual therapy or an explicitly supportive group experience before entering a more demanding analytic group treatment. Greenbaum (1957) suggests that the individual therapist's introduction of group treatment should ideally be determined by some assessment of the patient's relative comfort with peers as compared with authority figures. Where the patient is more comfortable with peers, combined treatment should be started immediately. On the other hand, when the patient is more comfortable with parental figures, entry into a group should be postponed for some period of time. Thus, although there are differences of opinion with regard to using concomitant treatment as a standard procedure, all writers believe that some form of individual treatment must be made available to the borderline patient, even if only intermittently.

SPECIAL PARAMETERS OF TECHNIQUE

Another point of general agreement in the field is the necessity for special measures with these patients, whether they are treated in homogeneous or mixed groups. There appears to be a consensus that a therapeutic attitude which may best be described as active friendliness should be maintained in order to afford the patient the kind of emotional nourishment he needs to maintain his membership and participation. Wolman (1960) recommends that the therapist assume a warm, friendly, noncritical, and nondemanding attitude toward his patient. Shaskan (1957) stresses that the main therapeutic task is the support and improvement in the patient's ego functions. Likewise, Scheidlinger and Pyrke (1961) describe their group treatment of such patients as primarily a "supportive group approach." Of course, as Spotnitz (1957) makes clear, the support emanates not only from the therapist but also from the peer group, who are in a better position than the therapist to express openly their respect, admiration, and appreciation toward their fellow members. The particular emphasis on these supportive factors for borderline patients, certainly not emphasized to the same extent in writings about neurotic groups, points to a clear agreement that whatever other therapeutic techniques may be employed — clarifications, confrontations, or interpretations — these patients are in greater need than neurotics of active support from the therapist and the group.

With regard to the special problems of the borderline patient in a predominantly neurotic group, Hulse (1958) emphasizes that such patients need protection by the therapist against premature confrontations and against becoming the target of scapegoating. As the most fragile and vulnerable member of a group, the borderline requires special care and attention by the therapist.

The Appropriate Patient

Assuming the proper kind of group, either homogeneous or mixed, and the application of the necessary parameters in terms of the availability of concomitant individual treatment as well as supportive factors within the group treatment, what are the special indications and contraindications for the patient falling under the broad rubric of borderline disorder? We still lack precise criteria for inclusion or exclusion from a group, although certain general considerations have been noted by several writers. When Wolman (1960) points out that the patient must be able to "stand the group," he is referring to the patient's capacity to stick with the treatment despite the special strains and anxieties, along with the supports, a group experience generates. The borderline patient is characteristically plagued with those defects of ego and object relatedness that tend to make him a high-risk patient, at least in terms of his potential for dropping out — hence the universal caution in the literature for special care in selection and preparation (Slavson, 1964).

More often than not such patients are characterized by qualities that tend to merit exclusion. They often show poor tolerance for unpleasant affects; they have difficulty in permitting themselves to become attached to others; they have problems controlling hostility and are susceptible to paranoid anxieties and reactions. Slavson (1964) summarizes these considerations by stating that such patients should be excluded from a group when they manifest excessive narcissism, poorly controlled hostility, and excessive levels of anxiety. Although precision is lacking in assessing these variables, particularly in terms of their total configuration in the personality, there appears to be substantial agreement about the relevant factors.

Given such ego weaknesses which militate against optimal functioning in the group, why introduce a group modality at all? Paradoxically, the very qualities and defects that make the borderline patient a problematic group member are the same defects that are often best treated in a group setting. Groups are a medium par excellence for highlighting difficulties in relationships; they are frequently the ideal medium in which to resolve or attenuate these handicaps. When the patient's ego defects are sufficiently modulated both by his own capacities and by the application of special treatment parameters, there are special features in group psychotherapy which hold particular promise for this type of patient.

Special Features of Group Psychotherapy for Borderline Patients

Dilution of Transference

All of the writers on group treatment of borderline patients agree that the dilution of the transference, and of affects generally, is an important asset for the treatment of the borderline patient. It is this feature in particular that underlies the successful use of groups with patients who experience a dyadic relation as too stressful. Writers on the special indications for groups have emphasized that patients with chaotic, amorphous, fragile egos do especially well in group treatment because the transference dilution helps to prevent unwanted regressive reactions (Freedman and Sweet, 1954; Stein, 1963).

A complete discussion of the complicated phenomenon of dilution is beyond the scope of this paper, but a few of its components will be mentioned. The therapist as an authority figure "looms less large" in the group as opposed to a one-to-one relation (Scheidlinger and Pyrke, 1961). In addition, the intensity of emotional experiences, particularly negative transferences, tends to be attenuated (Spotnitz, 1957). These observations may be accounted for by the following factors:

1. There are opportunities for diffusing transference reactions upon the multiple targets present in the group so that negative feelings toward parental introjects, for example, may be directed toward one or more peers in addition to, or instead of, the therapist.

2. Group treatment, as opposed to individual treatment, affords the patient more opportunities for social and emotional distance, which may be necessary to the patient at a given time. He is less pressured to participate and this gives the opportunity to regulate, when necessary, the intensity of his emotional involvement. One patient, for example, fell asleep when the highly conflictual issue of the wish to return to one's parental home for nurturance was being discussed.

3. There is greater reality orientation in group as opposed to individual treatment. A group more closely simulates a social interaction and hence produces a greater pull toward appropriate social responses. Hulse (1958) offers an example of a marginally functioning psychotic patient who was able to maintain a much higher level of functioning in a group, in contrast to her regressive behavior in individual therapy.

While these factors are indeed valid, they represent only one side of a coin which includes pressures toward emotional intensification. We must not forget the contagion and resonance phenomena which tend to enhance emotional responsiveness in group members. Nor must we forget the dynamics of competition and sibling rivalry which heighten emotional life in a group. These factors are especially pronounced in groups employing a group-centered orientation (Horwitz, in press) which works in the direction of therapeutic regression. The point I wish to emphasize is that the group therapist must recognize tendencies toward dilution and intensification and, as in individual therapy, he may choose to exploit one set of factors over another when the clinical situation warrants it.

ACTIVATION

Group interaction stimulates or activates patients who would otherwise tend to be passive and withdrawn. One type of borderline patient is characterized by schizoid withdrawal, although obviously all schizoid patients are not borderline. These patients tend to be passive and weak in verbal participation; they maintain distance from others and rarely initiate contact spontaneously. They usually assume the role of observer in a group and, as such, may be quite perceptive and insightful. They are inclined to participate around the problems presented by others rather than disclose intimate facets of their own lives.

Such patients often experience difficulty in communicating in individual treatment because of their difficulties in tolerating personal closeness. The paucity of real relationships in their lives is a further deterrent to therapeutic work. A group provides the activation and stimulation such people may find useful. This point has been made most explicitly by Slavson (1964), who believes that the supportive setting of a group permits the patient to participate at his own pace and thus may contribute to drawing such people out of their protective shells. For such patients a group experience may indeed be their first opportunity to participate with others on an emotional level.

EMOTIONAL GRATIFICATION

Although groups have built-in frustrations, they also provide a wide variety of gratifications which make the group attractive and pleasurable despite the anxieties of participation. More often than not these gratifications may be ego building in themselves and may contribute silently and unobtrusively to significant personality change, especially in a borderline patient. A cohesive group whose members experience feelings of acceptance helps to bolster self-esteem and gratify dependency needs. In describing a successful group treatment of women with severe dependency problems who functioned mainly at a borderline level, Scheidlinger and Pyrke (1961) emphasize that the group as an entity affords symbolic and real ego support insofar as the collective unity of the group symbolically represents a maternal figure.[2] These authors stress not only the symbolic importance of the group, but also the significance of the real social experience for lonely, isolated people.

Another important form of gratification especially characteristic of groups is the positive reinforcement which flows from member to member. Feelings of acceptance and affection constitute a warm matrix within which patients may make significant gains in self-esteem and self-acceptance (Spotnitz, 1957).

EXPRESSION OF HOSTILITY

The dilution of transference is especially helpful in regard to borderline patients' acute difficulties in dealing with hostility and aggression. There is a general consensus that a central problem for these patients is their difficulty in dealing with vast amounts of latent destructive energy, presumably based upon excessive degrees of oral frustration and inability to integrate good and bad internalized objects (Kernberg, 1967). The clinical picture presented by these patients consists either of markedly poor impulse control or immobilized passivity, or, more usually, a picture fluctuating between these two extremes.

For the passive inhibited patient, the group provides an "unfreezing" experience, especially in the early stages, by permitting him to identify himself vicariously with both aggressor and victim in hostile exchanges transpiring in the group. Angry confrontations, attacks and counterattacks occur without permanent damage to either party or to the relationship. Later, with the support of the group, the patient may permit himself to express his anger toward other patients or toward the therapist. The presence of multiple transference targets contributes somewhat to the dilution of the experience.

With regard to the patient's gaining a better appreciation of his distorted attitudes, confrontation by peers or the group's consensual validation is often more effective than a similar observation by the therapist alone who tends to be seen as either a malevolent or over-idealized figure. The literature provides several examples of border-

[2] Scheidlinger (1974) has expanded and generalized this point.

line patients in a dyadic relationship who were unable to make satisfactory progress because they were immobilized by fear of their hostility (Greenbaum, 1957). When placed in a group, this fear was gradually attenuated, particularly by witnessing others express hostility toward the therapist without destructive results.

MULTIPLE IDENTIFICATIONS

A commonly recognized mechanism of change in individual psychotherapy is identification with and internalization of the therapist's attitudes and values, or of the therapeutic alliance itself (Horwitz, 1974). This process has often been referred to in the literature as borrowing the therapist's ego strength and is related to a corrective emotional experience. The identification process has tended to be depreciated by some analytic therapists as merely an educational process, rather than one involving conflict resolution and structural change. But for patients with significant ego weakness, the ego strengthening of identification with healthier ego attitudes and behaviors is commonly regarded as a desirable goal.

Group psychotherapy not only affords a patient the opportunity to identify himself with the therapist, but also with a variety of patients in the group. Slavson (1964) cautions that the borderline patient's tendency to make transient and intense identifications with others may produce undesirable effects in a group for certain patients. Perhaps he is referring here to the as-if personalities, but at any rate he stresses the importance of prolonged individual work with one therapist as a necessary preliminary to placing such persons in groups.

Other group therapists, however, stress the opportunities for finding identification models in a group. Shaskan (1957) refers to a patient "borrowing courage" from others who either support progressive moves or present examples in their own lives of adaptive responses to conflict and anxiety (Spotnitz, 1957). Thus, a patient who clung masochistically to a destructive, unfulfilling marriage because of her fears of loneliness was supported by another patient with similar fears who was nonetheless able to make the step successfully.

MODIFICATION OF CHARACTER ARMOR

The group is an especially good medium for the exploration and alteration of maladaptive character defenses. The group setting provides a multiplicity of stimuli and consequently elicits a wide range of reactions. Not only does it elicit attitudes toward authority figures, but also feelings of sibling rivalry, feelings about sharing a parent figure with others, reactions to hostile exchanges and demands by others for participation, reactions to displays of positive feelings, etc. In other words, many behaviors, which in individual therapy tend to get described by the patient rather than enacted, are seen in a group *in vivo* — hence the emphasis in the group therapy literature on the numerous here-and-now opportunities.

The more severe the character disorder, or the more prominent the ego weakness within which the character defenses are embedded, the more likely the patient will regard his character traits as ego syntonic. Glatzer (1972) has indicated that severe character disorders are able to accept confrontations from other group members more easily than from a therapist alone because the therapist tends to be viewed as a distorted figure, overvalued or devalued. In addition, she emphasizes the importance of the "mirror reaction" in a group in helping a patient to loosen his hold upon repressed, ego-syntonic traits. Whether they show excessive narcissism, tenacious masochism, clinging dependency, or infantile rage, their blindness to these characteristics in themselves tends to soften in seeing these characteristics in others. They may at first be repulsed and alienated by what they see, but this is then the beginning step in helping them to recognize these selfsame maladaptive defenses in themselves.

Character problems associated with orality are particularly well suited for treatment in groups. Because of the borderline patient's fixation at the level of oral deprivation and aggression, one would expect many such patients to be characterized by difficulties in tolerating the frustration of oral needs, the necessity to share the time and attention of the group with other people, and feelings of envy and disappointment in witnessing the successes of others. These oral problems and the variety of responses to them tend to be markedly highlighted in a therapeutic group. Provided such patients have the necessary minimum tolerance for frustration, or provided adequate adjuncts to group treatment are provided, such as concomitant individual therapy, these infantile and narcissistic strivings emerge readily and may be dealt with quite efficiently in a therapeutic group. The patient is not only confronted with his oral greed by the group, but he must cope with the task of dealing with these needs in a more adaptive way directly within the group. For this reason, Spotnitz (1957) has referred to the group experience as "first-rate training" for the borderline patient.

COUNTERTRANSFERENCE DILUTION

Borderline patients present a special challenge to all psychotherapists by virtue of the strong affective responses they evoke in the therapist. They have the capacity to create anger, disappointment, frustration, and feelings of inadequacy in others. Therapists must constantly cope with these feelings within themselves in order to be optimally therapeutic. The greater the patient's pathology and regression, the more intense the countertransference problems. Kleinian therapists have elaborated on the primitive defense of projective identification in which unwanted affects and unwanted part objects are projected onto others and the patient then strives to manipulate and control the malevolent impulses he perceives in the other person. A similar phenomenon is described by Racker (1968) as a complementary reaction in the countertransference, in which the patient's distorted perceptions of the therapist tend to elicit feelings within the therapist which complement what the patient is experiencing.

The earlier observations about dilution and intensification of transference apply equally well to the phenomenon of countertransference. Group psychotherapists have consistently observed that the intensity of their reactions to patients in a group tends to be somewhat muted when compared with their reactions to the same patient in a dyadic situation. In part, this observation may be based on the dilution of the patient's transference in a group, as well as on the parameters often introduced to deal with more difficult patients, such as concomitant individual therapy. Just as group psychotherapy promotes multiple targets of transference, so do the therapist and his group of therapist-surrogates help to diffuse countertransference reactions. On the other hand, there is frequently an intensification of countertransference toward the entire group when the cumulative affects of individual members resonate together to produce a powerful impact upon the therapist. Whether it is anger, sadness, or demands for dependency gratification, the therapist is pulled strongly into the group's affective life, often more intensely than occurs in individual therapy.

In enumerating the special features of group psychotherapy for the borderline patient, we must not overlook the equally important special risks mentioned earlier. A borderline patient in a neurotic group may not only be an easy target for scapegoating; by virtue of his greater difficulties in living he runs the risk of experiencing more alienation and greater feelings of inadequacy. He is a candidate for decompensation and increased regression when the group is undergoing tension or trauma in reaction to the vicissitudes of group life, such as the entry or departure of members, their successes and failures, or the inevitable interruptions of scheduled meetings. As has been mentioned, a borderline patient may alienate the better-integrated members of a group by his difficulties with commitment to relationships and by his occasional peculiar primitive behavior. Some writers (Yalom, 1975) have described how the poor choice of patients in an ongoing group can produce a virtual dissolution of a therapy group. Less emphasized, however, are the special contributions that borderline patients make to the functioning of a predominantly neurotic group. Hulse (1958) stresses the value such patients have by virtue of their easy access to unconscious thoughts and feelings. Because of their relatively weak capacity for repression of unconscious material, they tend to be in greater touch with primitive impulses and fears and hence are able to facilitate a group's coming to grips with such unconscious material. Hulse offers the example of a borderline patient who was able to facilitate group discussion regarding sexual frigidity. She spoke vividly about her conscious fear of orgasm lest she lose her identity and thus helped the others begin to uncover similar feelings within themselves, which were less available to consciousness. Feldberg (1958) claims that the borderline patient is able to see through neurotic

defenses with great clarity and is capable of unmasking rationalization and reaction formation.

SUPPORTIVE MEASURES

The borderline patient typically suffers from a deep-seated sense
of unacceptability, basic mistrust of others, and from an inability to
sustain satisfactory relationships. All writers consider it essential
that the group therapist take active measures to counteract the
patient's tendency to feel unaccepted, unloved, and even attacked.
Warmth, friendliness, empathy, and active demonstrations of the
desire to help are common prescriptions. This approach is easier in
an all-borderline group than it is in a predominantly neurotic
group. Even though it is possible for the therapist to offer differing
treatment to his patients depending on their individual needs, these
differential attitudes must be offered with sensitivity and discrimination.

Other kinds of supportive measures include the necessity to
protect the patient against being scapegoated, particularly when he
attempts to provoke other members into hostile reactions. Also
emphasized is the therapist's need to acknowledge the patient's
achievements or efforts without at the same time attempting to
seduce the patient into certain desired behaviors to which he is not
yet committed (Feldberg, 1958). Other writers discuss the importance of ego strengthening in the early phase of therapy (raising
self-esteem, overcoming mistrust, decreasing feelings of isolation)
before the more definitive tasks of ego repair and integration can
occur (Scheidlinger and Holden, 1966).

A more specific kind of support is emphasized by Feldberg
(1958) in his technique of stressing similarities among patients.
Whenever possible he attempts to comment on and underline the
similarities of concerns, preoccupations, and defenses manifested by
his patients. Such a technique helps to foster greater cohesiveness in
the group, a greater sense of belonging, and helps to neutralize
feelings of being different and an outsider. Furthermore, Feldberg
makes the interesting point that peer transferences tend to be kept

more fluid with this technique. As a consequence of their splitting defense, borderline persons tend to view others in black-and-white terms, as good or bad, friend or foe. When patients begin to perceive similarities between themselves and those whom they particularly regard as unacceptable or unfriendly, their hostile attitudes become less pronounced.

CONFRONTATION

All authors agree that one must go beyond mere friendliness and encouragement in order to be therapeutic. Several therapists recommend that the patient be confronted with his maladaptive character traits and some even recommend exploration of the roots of such behavior (Forer, 1961). Day and Semrad (1971) portray the borderline patient as tending to react to the therapist in an excessively passive way, surrendering and putting his trust for therapeutic change in the hands of the therapist — an attitude which must be challenged.

In a survey of a number of therapists as to their observations of borderline patients in a group, Colson (1974) reports considerable variability among therapists with regard to the reaction of borderline patients to confrontations regarding their behavior or defenses. Some observe a tendency for these patients to profit from confrontation, whether from their peers or therapist, while others report the opposite tendency of angry defensive, and even disorganized, reactions. But perhaps these views simply represent the chronic instability of the borderline patient. Certainly the technique of confrontation depends on the nature of the relation already established with the therapist and the group, as well as the extent of the patient's need for the particular behavior or defense in question. The oft-cited rule of thumb that borderline patients may be differentiated from schizophrenics by the fact that the former respond positively to confrontations while the latter tend to become more disorganized may only be a reflection of the relative degrees of vulnerability of the two groups.

Feldberg (1958) stresses the importance of observing a patient's reaction to comments or confrontations about his behavior and participation in the group. He considers it most important to avoid letting the patient retreat in silent anger or withdrawal after a confrontation has been made. The patient must be helped with his reaction, which often may be quite paranoid and distorted.

UNCOVERING AND INTERPRETATION

The trend within the group psychotherapy literature is best characterized by Slavson's (1964) advice to "confront but not explore." For the most part, group therapists believe that therapeutic change in borderline patients may best occur by means of strengthened identifications, increased awareness of their maladaptive behaviors, and help in correcting their reality-distorting tendencies. The uncovering of unconscious wishes and fears is usually not recommended for borderline patients for two reasons: the patient is already too much in contact with his unconscious wishes and hence needs help in repressing them; and an uncovering procedure runs the risk of excessive anxiety and strain on his defenses.

Once again there may be a difference between procedure in an all-borderline group and a mixed group. In writing about the latter, Hulse (1958) points out that borderline patients in a mixed group are able to tolerate greater exploration and interpretation in depth than they can in an individual-therapy setting. His explanation for this phenomenon is based on the "multiple identifications" or supportive effect of a group setting in which the interpretation usually pertains to more than one person. In another context I have referred to this phenomenon as the "protection of the group theme" (Horwitz, 1971).

AUTHOR'S PERSPECTIVE

The survey of the literature points to many characteristics of groups which make them particularly suited for treating borderline patients. I would like to underline my agreement with certain points and then introduce some issues with a more modern ring which group therapists have not yet confronted squarely.

First, I concur with other writers that most borderline patients in groups also need an individual-therapy relationship, preferably on a regular basis. The individual therapist will usually be a different person since it is antitherapeutic for the group therapist to see some patients individually while not seeing others privately as well. Further, the individual therapist ideally serves a supportive function. Many borderline individuals experience periodic flare-ups of extreme anxiety accompanied by some degree of disorganization and one can more effectively and flexibly deal with these reactions on a one-to-one basis. My own experience has been that failure to provide such patients with a regular supportive individual contact makes it difficult, if not impossible, for the patient to maintain his membership and participation in the therapy group.

Second, group treatment is an unqualified success with borderline patients in using confrontation to help them overcome egocentric and abrasive character traits, where they exist. While the diagnosis of borderline does not imply a particular character diagnosis, it is no surprise that many of these patients show severe narcissistic disturbances associated with their pregenital fixations and defenses. They are the group members who monopolize, alienate, and antagonize more frequently than the group's better-integrated patients. If they have other redeeming characteristics, they can achieve a satisfactory degree of acceptance as a member. And of course, only after the borderline patient has become integrated in the group and has developed a beginning therapeutic alliance, may the therapist or group member begin to confront him with his antisocial, self-defeating behavior.

Groups are especially suitable for these problems because the group setting portrays such behaviors in bold relief. Group patients necessarily compete with each other for time and attention. They must tolerate the frustration of not having their problems immediately and fully attended to. They are asked to listen to, explore, and try to understand the communications of their fellow patients. Small wonder, then, that problems of greed, vying for attention, and other oral-aggressive behaviors become highlighted, especially among patients who tend to be orally fixated. And confrontation about an undesirable characteristic or behavior is more effectively heard when a "jury" of one's peers passes judgment as opposed to the more ambivalently held therapist. An illustrative vignette follows.

A 23-year-old college student, diagnosed as a narcissistic and borderline personality, was hospitalized for drug addiction and manic episodes. In group psychotherapy he was a flamboyant raconteur, interesting and engaging, but tending to monopolize the group's time. He had some awareness of his greed in the group and rationalized that no one else was talking so he might as well use the time. An early characteristic, however, was his tendency to fall asleep when he was not in the center of the stage. His difficulty in listening to and in becoming interested in the problems other patients presented exactly paralleled his relationships outside the group, in particular with women, who only interested him insofar as they were an applauding and appreciative audience. Being confronted by the group with his egocentrism gave him a better appreciation of the impact of such behavior, made him see it as an ego-dystonic aspect of his character, and afforded him an opportunity to modify it first within the group, and later in his social relationships.

However useful character confrontation may be in helping borderline patients achieve more adaptive functioning, we must look more deeply into what a group may contribute to treating the patient's basic pathology. For the most part, group therapists have not incorporated the recent advances in understanding borderline pathology using object-relations concepts and developmental formulations. I am referring here particularly to the recently advanced view that borderline patients have been unable to integrate the primitive good and bad self-object representations and have resorted to the use of splitting to prevent the infiltration of aggression into the highly valued, overidealized introjected images of self and significant others (Kernberg, 1967). There is a fairly good consensus that this need to rely on the primitive defense of splitting is derived from the infant's experience of rage at his depriving mother and his need to protect the image of the good mother, or good breast, albeit at a considerable psychic cost.

Masterson and Rinsley (1975) have pushed this conceptualization further by describing borderline pathology as embedded in the matrix of the early mother-infant relationship—more particularly it is associated with the inability of the child to individuate or separate from an enveloping mother. They contend that the infant's beginning efforts to separate himself invariably resulted in the withdrawal of love by mother. The adult or adolescent patient with this developmental background and pathological pattern thus becomes overwhelmed with anxiety each time he embarks upon a successful, self-sufficient course.

Assuming that both conceptions described above are correct, what if anything can group treatment provide for these deep-seated pathological formations? Analytic group therapists are divided with regard to the usefulness of groups in dealing expressively with these problems. The prevalent view is probably that expressed by those who emphasize the dilution of transference in a group (Freedman and Sweet, 1954; Slavson, 1964; Stein, 1963). While they might subscribe to the notion that the borderline patient could benefit from the group's enhanced reality testing or from a corrective emotional experience, they would probably expect the group to attenuate transference reactions, especially negative transferences, and therefore a group would not contribute to the expressive treatment of the borderline person. He would presumably not be bringing his split positive and negative transferences clearly into the group because the group would diffuse or dilute these reactions.

This view of the limitations of group psychotherapy in the uncovering process is compatible with the findings of Spanjaard (1959), a psychoanalyst who treated five neurotic young men in an analytically oriented closed group over an extended period. While most of his patients achieved a successful result, he believed that the group, compared to individual psychoanalysis, failed to elicit a full transference neurosis and, in particular, did not uncover significant pregenital conflicts.

The opposite point of view is held by Bion (1961) and other group therapists with a group-centered orientation. They contend that a small unstructured group setting is capable of plumbing the depths of psychic conflict, of eliciting "psychotic anxieties" and primitive defenses via the group's basic assumption of life (Ganzaraín, 1960). Bion reports the frequent occurrence of projective identification in which unwanted impulses are projected onto others and are then reacted to as a real threat coming from the recipient. Insofar as a group may elicit such primitive reactions and genetically early levels of conflict, Bion has no trouble in seeing the potential usefulness of a group in treating borderline patients. In fact, he would probably say that the group, insofar as it facilitates the projection of good and bad introjects upon different parts of the group, is the ideal method of treating such pathology.

How may we reconcile these two highly discrepant ideas of group functioning? My view of the conflict is that both are right in the sense that a group has the potential for both dilution and intensification of the transference. Since Bion's experience was largely with professionals in a training or study group who could tolerate large doses of frustration and since he used a strictly group-centered approach, he was able to elicit strongly regressive responses. In other words, the better integrated the participants and the more frustrating the group experience, the more regressive the group's response. I believe that small groups are indeed capable of behaving closer to the intensification model than the dilution model when given the optimal conditions. My own work with analytic-expressive group psychotherapy has convinced me that groups are indeed capable of eliciting paranoid and depressive anxieties of a quite primitive kind. The problem is like the question of whether or not a dyadic relationship can result in a regressive transference neurosis. With the right patient and the right treatment structure, it can; without these conditions, it cannot.

We therefore seem to be on the threshold of answering affirmatively the question of whether the borderline patient's splitting defense can be treated effectively in a group. Borderlines are capable of finding the good-bad, overidealized-devalued dichotomy in a variety of figures in a group: sometimes the split is between patients and therapist, or between two different patients, or two different subgroups, or possibly between the entire group and another group. But there remains the crucial question of whether these splits can be healed in a group by intensifying the affects associated with them and then interpreting them as one would attempt to do with neurotics in a group.

Borderline patients are notoriously prone to narcissistic injury from comments that point out their infantile wishes, their strivings for special or exclusive attention, or their inordinate demands. In individual psychotherapy with borderlines, such interpretations tend to be received as a total assault upon the person's acceptability and a condemnation of his nonhuman qualities. Zetzel's (1971) recommendation that borderline patients in individual therapy be seen at a reduced frequency (once-a-week or less) is based on their difficulty in tolerating the arousal and interpretation of regressive transference wishes. In my own work on the Menninger Foundation Psychotherapy Research Project, I have observed (Horwitz, 1974) that a number of patients, many of whom were borderline, showed substantial improvement in treatment that was *not* mainly exploratory and uncovering. Rather, these patients were able to achieve significant and stable change through a variety of therapeutic methods emphasizing the consolidation of a therapeutic alliance, rather than the interpretation of the transference. Although several good neurotics profited considerably from psychoanalysis, a few borderline patients, who were mistakenly diagnosed as healthier than they actually were, did poorly in an uncovering procedure. We thus have an empirical question regarding the borderline's ability to use regressive-uncovering treatment in a group, which can only be answered by observational data; short of that, one can merely offer some reflections and impressions about the issue.

On the positive side is the fact that a group setting facilitates an uncovering process. I concur with those who have observed a greater readiness by borderline patients to accept both confrontations and interpretations in groups than in individual therapy. The group setting offers certain safeguards for these patients. First, they have the possibility for regulating the intensity of their reactions. Insofar as group-wide interpretations are offered to the entire group, individual members are considerably freer to accept or reject the therapist's comments as applicable to themselves. Second, insofar as other people are being addressed as well as themselves, particularly in a group-centered interpretation, the borderline individual is afforded the "protection of the group theme" (Horwitz, 1971). He finds it more difficult to react to the interpretation as a devastating criticism insofar as several others, if not the entire group, are simultaneously being told similar things about themselves.

Working with borderline patients in a predominantly neurotic group of course makes an expressive-uncovering approach difficult to implement, since the thrust of an analytic-expressive treatment effort is to interpret the transference and to impart insight into unconscious motivations and defenses. Wide variations among the group members in tolerating interpretations place a special burden on the group therapist and make it especially necessary for him to exercise tact and sound clinical judgment in gauging how "deep" his interpretations should be to the more vulnerable borderline person.

Despite the over-all facilitating effect of the group in making interpretations more acceptable, there are still some serious barriers to using an interpretive approach in a group. If the patient is simultaneously involved in an individual relationship, however supportive, he will be strongly tempted to maintain his distance in the group and thus avoid painful regressive reactions. My experience with several of these patients has suggested to me that their individual therapeutic relationships, whether with psychotherapists or hospital doctors or counselors, tend to become more significant than the group-therapy relationship and one therefore has minimal leverage in the group in eliciting transference reactions. Frequently negative attitudes may be acted out by the patient's distance-keeping behavior, but one is hard put to challenge the patient's commitment to the individual relationship since we generally believe he needs it.

Furthermore, we must consider that borderline patients tend to remain in treatment for considerable periods of time, sometimes indefinitely. They comprise a large number of the so-called lifers. In view of this tendency, there is a practical advantage to the patient's being connected to an individual therapist rather than a group, as tenure in a group rarely exceeds four or five years.

And finally, a theoretical consideration which requires further examination and study. Most writers agree that the borderline's fixation point of developmental arrest is one where the infant has begun, but has not achieved, separation and individuation from his mother. In order to successfully renegotiate this process, it makes theoretical sense that a dyad is the best crucible in which to re-experience these pregenital, two-person struggles and conflicts. Kosseff (1975) has recently proposed that a period of group psychotherapy with the same therapist could help the patient gain some distance, some breathing space, in the course of the struggle to separate from the individual therapist-mother. But he recommends that the eventual resolution of the paranoid anxieties should ideally be done within the individual setting which most closely approximates the conflictual life situation, i.e., the mother-infant dyad.

The group psychotherapy literature has not kept apace of the recent theoretical advances in the study of borderline patients. I hope we will begin accumulating observational and research data on the problems suggested by our new understandings. But until we do, I would suggest that a period of group psychotherapy primarily helps to attenuate abrasive, maladaptive behavior. Long-term individual psychotherapy, on the other hand, seems preferable in terms of resolving the underlying splits between good and bad, self- and object representations.

REFERENCES

Bion, W. R. (1961), *Experiences in Groups*. New York: Basic Books.

Colson, D. (1974), Behavior of borderline patients in groups. Interviews with therapists. (Unpublished.)

Day, M., & Semrad, E. (1971), Group therapy with neurotics and psychotics. In: *Comprehensive Group Psychotherapy*, ed. H. I. Kaplan & B. J. Sadock. Baltimore: Williams & Wilkins, pp. 566-580.

Feldberg, T. M. (1958), Treatment of "borderline" psychotics in groups of neurotic patients. *Internat. J. Group Psychother.*, 8:76-84.

Forer, B. R. (1961), Group psychotherapy with outpatient schizophrenics. *Internat. J. Group Psychother.*, 11:188-195.

Freedman, M. B., & Sweet, B. S. (1954), Some specific features of group psychotherapy and their implications for the selection of patients. *Internat. J. Group Psychother.*, 4:355-368.

Ganzaraín, R. (1960), "Psychotic" anxieties in group analytic psychotherapy. *Internat. Ment. Health Res. News.*, 2:15.

Glatzer, H. T. (1972), Treatment of oral character neurosis in group psychotherapy. In: *Progress in Group and Family Therapy*, ed. C. J. Sager & H. S. Kaplan. New York: Brunner/Mazel.

Greenbaum, H. (1957), Combined psychoanalytic therapy with negative therapeutic reactions. In: *Schizophrenia in Psychoanalytic Office Practice*, ed. A. H. Rifkin. New York: Grune & Stratton, pp. 56-65.

Grinker, R. R., Sr., Werble, B., & Drye, R. C. (1968), *The Borderline Syndrome*. New York: Basic Books.

Horwitz, L. (1971), Group-centered interventions in therapy groups. *Compar. Group Studies*, 2:311-331.

———— (1974), *Clinical Prediction in Psychotherapy*. New York: Jason Aronson.

———— (in press), A group-centered approach to group psychotherapy. *Internat. J. Group Psychother.*

Hulse, W. C. (1956), Private practice. In: *The Fields of Group Psychotherapy*, ed. S. R. Slavson. New York: International Universities Press, pp. 260-272.

_____ (1958), Psychotherapy with ambulatory schizophrenic patients in mixed analytic groups. *AMA Arch. Neurol. Psychiat.*, 79:681-687.

Kernberg, O. F. (1967), Borderline personality organization. *J. Amer. Psychoanal. Assn.*, 15:641-685.

Kosseff, J. (1975), The leader using object relations theory. In: *The Leader in the Group*, ed. Z. A. Liff. New York: Jason Aronson, pp. 212-242.

Masterson, J. F., & Rinsley, D. B. (1975), The borderline syndrome: The role of the mother in the genesis and structure of the borderline personality. *Internat. J. Psycho-Anal.*, 56:163-177.

Racker, H. (1968), *Transference and Countertransference*. New York: International Universities Press.

Scheidlinger, S. (1974), On the concept of the "mother-group." *Internat. J. Group Psychother.*, 24:417-428.

_____ & Holden, M. A. (1966), Group therapy of women with severe character disorders: The middle and final phases. *Internat. J. Group Psychother.*, 16:174-189.

_____ & Pyrke, M. (1961), Group therapy of women with severe dependency problems. *Amer. J. Orthopsychiat.*, 31:776-785.

Shaskan, D. A. (1957), Treatment of a borderline case with group analytically oriented psychotherapy. *J. Forens. Sci.*, 2:195-201.

_____ (1971), Management and group psychotherapy of borderline patients. Presented to Fifth World Congress of Psychiatry, Mexico City.

Slavson, S. R. (1964), *A Textbook in Analytic Group Psychotherapy*. New York: International Universities Press.

Spanjaard, J. (1959), Transference neurosis and psychoanalytic group psychotherapy. *Internat. J. Group Psychother.*, 9:31-42.

Spotnitz, H. (1957), The borderline schizophrenic in group psychotherapy: The importance of individualization. *Internat. J. Group Psychother.*, 7:155-174.

Stein, A. (1963), Indications for group psychotherapy and the selection of patients. *J. Hillside Hosp.*, 12:145-155.

Wolman, B. B. (1960), Group psychotherapy with latent schizophrenics. *Internat. J. Group Psychother.*, 10:301-312.

Yalom, I. D. (1975), *Theory and Practice of Group Psychotherapy*. New York: Basic Books.

Zetzel, E. R. (1971), A developmental approach to the borderline patient. *Amer. J. Psychiat.*, 127:867-871.

The Family Treatment of the Borderline Patient

ARTHUR MANDELBAUM, M.S.W.

> ... but how should they, who have already flung
> themselves together and no longer mark off and
> distinguish themselves from each other, who
> therefore no longer possess anything, be able
> to find a way out of themselves, out of the
> depth of their already shattered solitude ...
>
> —Rainer Maria Rilke

THE BORDERLINE PATIENT IN A BORDERLINE FAMILY STRUCTURE

It is my thesis that the borderline patient is likely to be immured in a family system which prevents his further development and makes the possibility of his change not only immensely difficult but hazardous. The family itself functions poorly as a unit, and a majority of its members are likely to pay a heavy psychological cost for their endeavors to keep the family afloat. The identified patient *may* (but not necessarily) present the most alarming symptoms, calling the most attention to himself, to the extent that all the other family members receive little or no attention, and their resources as well as difficulties are neglected in the treatment. When the family is included from the very beginning of the treatment process, and the therapeutic effort aimed at changing a dysfunctional system, borderline phenomena in the family itself may be altered, allowing the identified patient and others to free themselves sufficiently to risk change.

Director of Family Therapy, The Menninger Foundation, Topeka, Kansas.

For the borderline patient, his serious conflicts, with their potent mixture of fear of and allegiance to family ties, have a life of their own, independent of the current stresses which may bring them most blatantly to view. His fear of and allegiance to his family are ritualistic—sometimes the repetitive re-enactment of a history of reciprocal antagonisms, losses, hates, rivalries, loves, and connectedness which stretch back several or more generations. Glimpses of the enormous power of these ties allow a more comprehensive view of the complex mosaic formed by powerful forces merging with current stresses precisely at the point where breakdown occurs. These current stresses often arise at developmental phases where increased needs for support and nurturance occur and where there are more strivings for autonomy and separation.

THE POWER OF THE FAMILY

Since we are all members of a family molded and influenced by the history of past generations, most of which is seemingly forgotten and invisible, it is not surprising that we underestimate its incandescent dynamic power. We may prefer to see the situation as only an intrapsychic struggle, certain that skillful psychotherapy will alter the dynamics of the borderline personality, when in actuality a family system is at war with itself, drawing upon the fiery conflicts of years of dysfunctional forces. These forces catch the identified patient in a net of contradictory and painful confusions, paralyzing his resources, and even making him unaware that he has any available.

Resistances to the concept of the unconscious still linger, but ironically there may be more resistance to the concept of how powerfully the spirit of kinship exerts its pull on our attitudes. Not until recently has there been a systematic delineation of the distorting and malignant forces of separation and death on the development of children and spouses, as well as the other close relatives (Paul, 1967). We feel we should be free from the influence of parents, grandparents, and siblings, who may even live so far away that their images are difficult to recall spontaneously. This resistance to acknowledging the power of kinship implies that there is something shameful in it, as indeed there may be when we can recall such youthful indiscretions as secret acts of rebelliousness, sexual events, and longings for closeness with their concomitant wish for the elimination of rivals.

Family rituals and ceremonials, during holidays, weddings, and deaths, bring out regressions, recall and bring to life hidden conflicts, and dust off old roles long thought discarded but easily revived. We forget the original validity that made the family so central to our development, our survival, and safety and made it possible to hate and love, to belong and separate. The paradox posed by the dual nature of family kinship, sometimes excessive and overwhelming, yet also moderating, linking, and integrating, may make us apprehensive about approaching family affiliations to help free the patient, and other family members as well, from the primacy of such attachments, to modify its excesses, to disturb its disharmonious balance for the sake of breaking up the familial soil which has become hardened into a rigid clay, without nutrients and that porous quality which allows roots to spread and foliage to grow in new directions toward the sun.

The Logic of Family Treatment for the Identified Patient

During the past several decades the detailed study of the borderline personality organization has advanced considerably (Kernberg, 1975). The conceptual model focuses on the individual's life situation and links defects of faulty development to a causal chain of life events, usually in the early years, with stress on the mother-child relationship. The emphasis is on the study of intrapsychic structures, with the illness contained in the individual. The approach to treatment is also highly influenced by this conceptual model, with extensions into an understanding of onset, constitutional factors, particular current social-stress situations, losses of primary figures, and pernicious family influences. This conceptual model has produced invaluable theoretical knowledge and treatment approaches, almost all of which have as their focus helping the patient to alter and strengthen his inner resources, his self-esteem, his ability to cope with the world, to experience identity, and to view his therapist as a real person.

During the past two decades another approach to treatment has gradually developed which offers much promise for change. It is based on involving all family members in a joint and sustained effort to alter their social context, so that the identified patient can free himself from a web of family alliances which hold him immobile, fuse his energies, and merge his allegiances, which become paramount over his own individuality. In such a family-treatment effort, the psychiatric diagnosis of borderline personality organization is not sufficient for a thorough diagnostic understanding of family problems and family structure. Family diagnosis as currently practiced is not done via the medical model. Diagnosis is made and treatment approaches determined not by the identified patient alone, but from an appraisal of the structure and developmental level of the family system in which the patient lives, and the transactional behavior of family members with him and with each other.

The symptom picture or cluster of symptoms the patient presents, whether neurotic, borderline, or dominated by psychotic qualities, calls for an examination of those developmental factors in family life that have produced dysfunctional structures and roles. These structures and roles have skewed and immobilized the development of family members, as well as produced a chaotic family matrix. The symptoms of the identified patient are considered as one major indication that the process of individuation in the family has suffered a defeat. How many individuals are affected and at what level remains to be observed through a process which focuses on interactions between all family members, thereby seeking an assessment of over-all family functioning. The instrumentalities the family utilizes to solve the mundane problems of living, the negotiations they engage in, the roles they assign and are assigned, give a penetrating glimpse into whether self- and object representations are differentiated, whether reality testing is well defined by the family unit, whether mechanisms of defense such as projection and displacement are shared, interchanged, and occasionally seen through by the observing egos of various family members. At times, in the throes of anger, passion, guilt, or isolation, one or another family member may lose control, his sense of reality may temporarily diminish, but he can (at least momentarily) be brought to clear recognition and a sense of stability by other, more objective and cooler heads. This indicates that at times a higher level of ego development in the family is possible and the parents can be more effective in helping the children grow toward a higher level of self- and object differentiation.

STRUCTURE OF THE FAMILY

The noted composer, Elliot Carter (1975), in describing the structure of his Brass Quintet, 1974, stated that:

> ... another way of hearing the piece is to consider it as a meeting of five brass players who have come together to play slow, solemn music. As they start to do so, entering one after another, the weak member of the group interjects irrelevant, disruptive ideas that momentarily upset the plan. Given the atmosphere of discord that arises between the players, each begins to assert himself, joining partners in small groups, while the excluded ones try to bring back the slow music. The light, comic, flowing excitable or lyric duos and trios are heard between passages during which all five altercate and gradually stray from the project of playing slow music. Midway through, the horn deplores its alienation in a long, unaccompanied solo, which arouses the others to a menacing duo for trumpets and an angry trio for trombones and horn. All this leads to a violent altercation that is finally settled by an agreement to continue the slow music of the beginning. After quite a period of unanimity, the players again begin to disagree. The tenor trombone never having had a proper solo as have the others, stops them for his solo, which is accompanied by a muted trumpet. There is an abrupt and aggressive ending [p. 25].

There is no more apt description than the above of a disturbed family in interaction, where the weak member (perhaps the identified patient) expresses his irrelevant and disruptive ideas. In the seriously disturbed family, two aspects are notable. The family neither has a sense of itself as a whole, as a unit, nor does it have a sense that it consists of individuals, unique in their own right, who can be both together and separate. In this open-systems model, described by Minuchin and his colleagues (1976), the variety of feedback mechanisms consist of seemingly irrelevant yet hostile communications—reminiscent of the dialogue between the characters in a Pinter play, who menace each other with hidden, sinister meanings and threats, disguised longings, and wishes for closeness, but who also fear these aspects of their emotional needs. The enmeshment patterns of the pathological family system, also described by Minuchin and his colleagues (1976), consist not only of overresponsiveness and overinvolvement, but of distancing maneuvers as well. Family members live in constant fear of destruction and abandonment.

One or more of the parents in such highly disturbed families may have had parents, who in turn, were separated from their parents in the early formative years of life. As Bowen (1966) has written, it may take several generations of cumulative life insults to produce a family pattern which is volatile, inconsistent, enmeshed and distant, with poorly differentiated perception of self and others and with merging of personal space and absence of boundaries. The parents abandon their roles for immature, helpless, bewildered, childlike behaviors. The children in turn precociously assume "parental-executive" responsibilities. The parents characterize themselves as children. They left their families too early, either to go off to college, to work, or in a futile attempt at a lasting marriage. All of this results in abortive attempts to reunite with their families of origin, or to remain completely apart—although the latter is never really emotionally possible.

While the parents of the borderline child may seem to have a good grasp of reality issues outside of the family and fairly successful careers, their functioning as spouses and parents is a different matter. They are confused about the nature of their own family experiences, remembering one parent as good, the other as totally bad and recalling their parents' efforts to raise children as feeble and impotent. They sense their parents as unhappy, as incomplete and fragmented personalities, and they may carry memories and beliefs which in family treatment emerge as myths and rather serious distortions.

A mother, for instance, may see in her child all the demands for dependency and nurturing denied to her in early infancy, especially during the crucial developmental period of individuation and separation. These demands on the mother from her child are unacceptable, intolerable, and cause impatience, rage, and withdrawal. An eleven-year-old girl notes that when she approaches her mother, "She constantly cuts me off, and will find any excuse, any distraction to avoid my talking to her. Then I redouble my efforts and try harder, but this makes her even madder with me. Yet she calls me her baby, and everyone treats me like a baby, and tells me I talk like a baby. My sister dresses me, and tells me that if I dress myself, I would choose all of the wrong clothing."

After six sessions of family-therapy treatment, this girl reminded her sister quite firmly that she was the youngest member of the family, but not its baby. The therapist enthusiastically congratulated her, and urged her to continue to remind her family of that fact. She should also console her mother for no longer having babies in the family. The mother, picking up this cue, stated it was a relief to no longer have to baby her daughter. But now, who would meet her lonely needs? How could she give up her children, only to be left with a husband who was on his way toward serious invalidism? And what about her own mother who called her at least three times per day? The mother thus again communicated to her daughter that while dependency and nurturing needs were unacceptable demands, moves toward autonomy and growth were equally unacceptable. It is this contradiction that is one of the primary dilemmas characterizing borderline family structure: closeness and distance are unbalanced forces without a stable center and in chronic disequilibrium. Where there is no center, there is eccentricity, said the poet T. S. Eliot. Paradoxically, the lack of an integrated core at the center of family life produces a rigid, inflexible family system.

In such families one or more of the children may be selected to express the incompatibility of negative and positive vectors. These children are regarded as contaminatory and hazardous to the already tenuous balance of family life. The less-affected children look askance at the accused, hardly daring, except secretively, to form coalitions with him, for he now contains the projected, unacceptable parts of the parents. It is the father who complements the parental alliance in maintaining this homeostasis. In some instances, the father rigorously reinforces such a family triangle, for in his development as well dependency strivings met with an admixture of admonishment, rejection, and accusations of not fitting into the desired mold.

When a child is assigned this role by his parents, his siblings, or grandparents, it is hazardous for him to attempt to change it. His siblings may hold him to it, for it gives them some semblance of freedom from their parents' projections, although they are subject to much of its radiation. Their primary adult models do not mirror a stable integration of good and bad internalized objects. The interactions and transactions of daily family life are filled with brooding discontent and frustrations expressed in a projective, accusatory fashion. The second basic dilemma then which characterizes the borderline family structure is the spouses' need to complement each other in a projective pattern which enables them to keep at some distance any awareness of their own conflicts in developing autonomy from their families of origin, the hidden symbiotic ties between them which rigidify their relationship, their raging frustration at unmet oral needs, and their inability to modify and control aggressive outbursts.

TREATMENT CONSIDERATIONS

RESISTANCE TO TREATMENT

It is no wonder that change in the identified patient alone meets with silent, insidious, or overt resistance on the part of one or more of the parents, and then the entire family system. A survey of many hospitalized young adult patients shows that at the core of resistance to change is grave anxiety and panic that autonomy and independence will shatter the family unit and cause the parents to hurt one another, divorce, or abandon the patient forever, thus throwing him completely on his own fragile resources.

Freud (1916-1917), in describing his analytic attempts with an agoraphobic girl, understood that "she had made herself ill in order to keep her mother prisoner and to rob her of the freedom of movement that her [the mother's] relations with her lover required. The mother quickly made up her mind and brought the obnoxious treatment to an end. . . . the *liaison* between her mother and the well-to-do friend of the family was common knowledge in the city and ... it was probably connived at by the husband and father" (p. 460). "No one who has any experience of the rifts which so often divide a family will, if he is an analyst, be surprised to find that the patient's closest relatives betray less interest in his recovering than in his remaining as he is" (p. 459).

Haley (1973), who quotes this passage from Freud, points out that what was not available then was the knowledge that the patient was not the problem, it was the family. The child *had* to be ill to maintain the family's precarious structure. As Haley states: "Symptoms are contracts between people that serve many functions, including protective ones. Not only will parents resist improvement in a disturbed adolescent child, but the child will resist improvement if something is not done about his family.... Dealing with the relatives is essential to the treatment because they are the problem" (p. 232).

THE IDENTIFIED PATIENT

When a child feels he can do nothing to improve the quality of family life, improve his position in the family, or rescue his parents, he then experiences helplessness. He is likely to try to communicate his concern to his family by failure to learn, temper tantrums, soiling, enuresis, or a psychosomatic illness such as anorexia nervosa or asthma. To show his despair, in the family-therapy interview he may present random, restless behavior and disorganized thinking with the production of primary-process material. When the family therapist explores solutions, or when the family members together, in their appropriate roles, take responsibility for offering and testing solutions, the patient may then feel a sense of inner optimism and hope for his future. It is the parents who must ultimately give this hope and act upon it; this frees the child to risk more outside.

There is no question that the borderline personality is locked into his family of origin in ways which enslave him and cause him to be at the mercy of his inner and outer circumstances. What triggers off his inner chaos is often a chain of direct or subtle cues of a most confusing nature, but which are in essence threats of abandonment which reawaken dim memories of threats to survival in the early months of life. Such memories lead to rage reactions blaming one primary figure while idealizing another, confusions about identity, and regressions to earlier modes of behavior. The ways in which such a chain reaction is set in motion can best be observed with all family members present.

CASE EXAMPLE

Mary, a twelve-year-old diagnosed as a borderline personality with a symbiotic attachment to her mother, complained of confusion about herself, especially when away from the family. Her peers at school disliked her and resented her domineering, bossy ways and her accusations that they were unjust and discriminated against her. She was sometimes so angry she wanted to kill them, to blow them up, and she had further macabre fantasies about them when she felt persecuted.

Mary came to the first session with her young, slender, boyish-looking mother and her obese, sullen, depressed, withdrawn step-father. Also present were her half-brother Steve, age three, and her half-sister Sandy, age six months. Mary was bossy, argumentative, and teasing toward them. She kept sidling closer and closer to her mother. She felt that things at home were a mess, and that the noise and confusion produced severe headaches, for which all physical causes had been ruled out. She could hardly contain her aggression toward her siblings—kicking them, shoving them away, grasping them in a rough manner. There were few admonitions from the parents; her stepfather, in particular, sat in massive silence, his complexion getting redder and redder at the mounting rage inside him.

When Mary turned to her father with demands, he was confused, compliant, or unusually forceful in his refusals. When the parents disagreed about her demands, Mary's headaches became more severe. Her half-brother Steve, apparently oblivious to the family interchanges, would shout, "No! No!" at the most acute and sensitive moments, as if as early as at three years he were assuming the parental role of the father. Steve was impossible to get to bed—shouting, screaming his protests, and sometimes not falling asleep until 10 or 11 P.M.

When the therapist gently blocked Mary from dominating the session with her garrulous and forceful speech and pointed out that her parents needed to decide together how and when to put Steve to bed, how and when to accede to her requests and deny others, and that they, as her parents, had to work on these issues, she relapsed into sullen silence, but was far more relaxed and her random kicking motions diminished. When she returned to such behavior, the therapist again intervened, insisting that the stepfather, in particular, needed to be heard, since he was surrounded and overwhelmed by articulate women who found it so easy to talk. With laughter, the mother and daughter agreed; the husband smiled his agreement as well. At one point, when the parents were at an impasse about rules concerning the television set, Steve had a bowel movement, and his mother had to leave in order to change him. In this way, as the father was struggling to find his place in the family, Steve triangulated the mother away from the husband, as he undoubtedly did by his refusal to go to sleep. Several sessions later, it was apparent that Steve's sleep disturbances had diminished when the parents joined forces to structure his bedtime in a consistent no-nonsense fashion.

The history of both parents now emerged. The wife described her father as a "depressed, schizophrenic alcoholic" who "threw" all of the children out of the family when they reached adolescence. At nineteen she married a "manic-depressive, schizophrenic, alcoholic man." Mary intruded to give some early, frightening memories of her father. She recalled stealing down to the kitchen one night to take a bite out of a large chocolate bar. A huge, looming shadow suddenly appeared to threaten her life. The only warm memory Mary had of a caring person was of her 90-year-old maternal grandmother. She had only grim memories of her grandfather and her father. Slyly glancing at her stepfather, she began to attack him. The therapist intervened to ask the mother to resume the story of her history as she might desire to tell it.

The same intervention had to be made in order to allow the stepfather to tell, on his own, the story of his family, but this time, through glances, helplessness, and faulty memory, he invited his wife and stepdaughter to intervene. Ironically, he spoke of his interest in history, but could not remember the significant dates of his past. The therapist's intervention to reveal the systematic nature of these maneuvers and rigidly coded interactions succeeded in strengthening pathways toward individuation and self-esteem.

TREATMENT TECHNIQUES

The therapist's failure to intervene is an encouragement for boundaries to be violated: in the example given, the identified patient intruded into areas of her parents' lives, and was invited to intrude into their spouse functions. Not intervening sanctions the perpetuation of myths, of one hated parent pitted against a helpless idealized one. It allows for impulsive feelings or behavior to disrupt family interaction, thus increasing the sense of helplessness over establishing controls and self-discipline. Furthermore, a too-passive therapist does not help prevent irrational projection of the difficulties of living onto bad parents, uncontrollable children, or just happenstance. The children in these families are often *made* omnipotent, given power precociously, or sexually stimulated too early. Aggressions are not modulated or tempered so they come under good control. Kernberg (1975) suggests ". . . that in borderline patients, there is a development of pregenital and especially oral aggression, which tends to induce premature development of oedipal strivings, and as a consequence, there is a particular pathological condensation of pregenital and genital aims under the overriding influence of aggressive needs. It is this constellation of instinctual conflicts which determines the peculiar characteristics of the transference paradigm of the patients. . ." (p. 71).

Indeed, Kernberg's suggestions for the psychotherapy of such patients markedly resembles the techniques of treatment utilized in structural family therapy, with some modifications. The treatment is directed at the family matrix. The therapist establishes his "political" control early, setting the rules and boundaries for carrying out the treatment. He insists on which family members should be present, determines the length and frequency of the sessions, and selects priorities for the family to examine which lead to a systematic unfolding of those dysfunctional elements weakening and destroying the parental executive function. He suggests tasks to alter the structure of the environment and disequilibriate the chronically static, rigid structure which only leads to nonproductive, nongrowth gratifications. He calls attention to activities that violate boundaries, that triangulate the children, and that therefore produce ambiguous, bewildering communications and a lower order of ego functioning for all family members. Since the family has existed as a system for several decades or more, before meeting the therapist, its members are sensitively attuned to exploitation of each other. Eye glances, the motion of a hand or foot, facial grimaces suffice to invite intrusions into concerns and space which belong appropriately only to the parents, or to the children. Violations of territoriality are thus constant and may play havoc with treatment. Interventions into these game maneuvers are basic to change.

The therapist blocks projections of the problem onto one particular family member, which permit labeling and role fixation. He encourages constant negotiation between parents in regard to their setting rules and regulations, supports constructive powers, and offers new perspectives on drastic problems so that possibilities for new approaches can emerge. He praises the parents when they succeed in coming to a genuine agreement about how they wish to run the family. He praises the children when they unite as peers to support each other. Intrapsychic conflicts and the fantasies of each family member are translated into interpersonal and interactional terms at a level that permits discussion. Sexual conflicts between the parents are the business of the parents and theirs alone to solve. The children are blocked from solving adult difficulties, while the parents are freed from overinvolvement in those sexual developmental difficulties that children can work out on their own, with peers, or with the appropriate parent, at the appropriate time and place. The freedom to be autonomous, to begin the slow process of emancipation, is experientially demonstrated time and time again in the family process, with exploration of how the parents succeeded or did not succeed in emancipating themselves from their families of origin.

Mary was not permitted to boss and dominate her uncertain and indecisive stepfather. This freed her from being the transmitter of what was in reality the wife's criticism of her husband. When Mary took that role on cue from her mother, forced by an overinvolved identification with her mother, there was an admixture of confused aggressive feelings and oedipal longings. She tapped her stepfather coquettishly on the feet, soon kicking him vigorously, scornfully — frightened of his docility, his anger, his hidden invitation to continue her behavior with no limit setting by her mother.

The mother expressed fear that her daughter might become like her own father and her first husband. She was concerned that her second husband did not want their two youngest children. She had desired them so much that she had neglected to take her birth-control pills and did not tell her husband. He was furious with her, at his own two children, and depressed by his unhappiness with his career. The identified patient, Mary, having heard some of this intimate material over and over in family quarrels, was nevertheless dismissed from the session. She clapped her hands with delight. In her absence, the parents were encouraged to explore their conflict about having children. One night, Mary acted out this conflict when she was left alone with the children. She frightened a friend who was staying with her by placing a plastic bag over her infant sister's face.

When she returned to the session, Mary stated that her parents were always unhappy and angry. Her mother was often both strong and weak, domineering and dependent. Her father sulked and refused to help in the home. Mary turned to her father and said, "You can't make any decisions at all. When I want a Coke, you say, 'Ask your mother.' You don't know what's going on and I feel so mixed up all the time, that my head feels like blowing off."

The confusion of this child had an abnormal integrity. She acted in relation to her environment in erratic and inexplicable fashion, that is, until she was seen with her family and their gravitational pull on her and each other was understood. The question has been asked, "Do you know how they locate invisible planets? No? . . . Because the visible ones act in erratic and inexplicable fashion. Their orbits are . . . warped. So you apply gravitational theory and a little geometry of moving spheres and you say, Aha, if there is a planetary body right there of such and such a mass, and such and such an orbit, then all of the random movements of the other planets, become logical and even imperative" (MacDonald, 1974, p. 95).

Mary was a prisoner of a pattern, not only incapable of being otherwise, but lacking the resources on her own to be otherwise. She chose to be ill. When she had friends in for an overnight visit, she clung to them and bossed their activities, until they could no longer tolerate her. Like her daughter, the mother had no friends, except a close, angry relationship with her own mother, whom she called frequently.

In the family sessions, Mary was relieved when the therapist blocked her from her mother's voice, when he blocked her from assuming parental authority, when he refused to let her play a spouse role. Her mother attempted to describe her husband's background, but he was asked to speak for himself. His distancing himself from his wife, his stepdaughter, and his own children was softened when the therapist allowed no one to speak for him, when his sadness and withdrawal were noted but not criticized, and when he was permitted to speak without disruptions and coalitions being formed against him. At the same time, Mary was permitted to ask for and receive definite answers in regard to having friends over, study, and privileges appropriate to a young adolescent girl. The therapist emphasized that the family members should become clear and real to each other, consistent and dependable individuals who could be counted on to protect personal space, to give empathy, to express affect, to balance all good with some bad and all bad with some good.

Family treatment focuses on moving family structure from lower defensive structures to higher-level patterns. The family therapist moves rapidly to those substructures that must be strengthened in order to move the entire system upward. He may choose to appeal to those substructures already performing at higher levels and connect them to those lagging behind, thus moving the family to new effective heights. The more conflict-free areas he assists the family to add to its store of functioning resources, the more individuals in that family become experienced in observing egos, thus helping others to change their perspectives, to observe more precisely, to clarify their confusions, and to challenge misconceptions when they occur.

The borderline patient with such a family-treatment experience may indeed find himself confident enough and sufficiently independent of his parents to risk change. He is consistently and persistently advised that as he changes he will no longer be held accountable for the difficulties his parents have in their marital relationship, in their relationships with their families of origin, in their conflicts with their other children. This reassurance is experientially observed and tested, as in the treatment sessions he hears his parents deal with the unresolved dilemmas of their past and current life situations, but in new ways and in new directions. He cannot dare to alter until he views some alterations in the spouse and parental coalition. He cannot dare to alter until he views and feels the impact of change in the sibling subsystem, and changes himself in relation to his brothers and sisters. In family treatment powerful forces are set into new motion, altered and managed in new directions. These energy forces are harnessed to resolve failures to internalize and reconcile good and bad objects, to diminish aggressive tendencies, to endure and tolerate love feelings, without feeling a risk of merger and fusion, thus making autonomy and separation more possible.

REFERENCES

Bowen, M. (1966), The use of family theory in clinical practice. *Comprehen. Psychiat.,* 7:345-374.
Carter, E. (1975), Notes from the Aspen Music Festival Program.
Freud, S. (1916-1917), Introductory lectures on psycho-analysis. *Standard Edition,* 16. London: Hogarth Press, 1963.
Haley, J. (1973), *Uncommon Therapy.* New York: Ballantine Books.
Kernberg, O. F. (1975), *Borderline Conditions and Pathological Narcissism.* New York: Jason Aronson.
MacDonald, J. D. (1974), *The Dreadful Lemon Sky.* New York: Fawcett.
Minuchin, S., et al. (1976), A conceptual model of psychosomatic illness in children. *Arch. Gen. Psychiat.,* 32:1031-1038.
Paul, N. (1967), The role of mourning and empathy in conjoint marital therapy. In: *Family Therapy and Disturbed Families,* ed. G. H. Zuk & I. Boszormenyi-Nagy. Palo Alto, Calif.: Science & Behavior, pp. 186-205.

V

THE PATIENT

It's not the feeling of anything
I've ever done,
Which I might get away from,
Or of anything in me
I could get rid of —
But of emptiness, of failure
Toward someone, or something,
Outside of myself;
And I feel I must ... atone —
Is that the word?
Can you treat a patient
For such a state of mind?

—From *The Cocktail Party*, by T. S. Eliot

This concluding section deals with clinical matters. The contributors focus on conceptual and technical issues as they apply to clinical material. The emphasis is on the patient as a person.

Searles describes a particular dynamic that takes place between patient and therapist in treatment, specifically in the analytic situation, which may be characteristic of borderline patients, but which certainly transcends any particular pathology. It is indeed startling to recognize it in one's own, everyday pathology.

The chapter by Furer is based on Mahler's work. The case he presents comes out of their common "laboratory." Besides being an application of Mahler's theory to the treatment of a severely disturbed child, the case illustrates the development of an aspect of borderline personality organization, the so-called as-if personality.

439

Masterson's concise, succinct, task-oriented contribution addresses itself to a most puzzling clinical manifestation of what he considers a borderline personality disorder. He attempts to integrate his work on borderline adolescents with Hilde Bruch's ideas and experience with young persons suffering from anorexia nervosa. Masterson, like Rinsley, with whom he shares credit for the idea of the "split object-relations unit," has been heavily influenced by Mahler and Kernberg. His view in considering anorexia nervosa as a specific syndrome along a structural and developmental continuum may clarify what heretofore has been a very debatable and obscure issue.

My own paper on affects as they are ascribed to, described, and possibly experienced by borderline patients concludes this section of the book. How borderline patients feel or make others, in particular their therapists, feel is a relevant area of concern. What I have to say in this concluding piece is based, to a large extent, on what the other contributors taught me during this conference and reflects the previous chapters.

Dual- and Multiple-Identity Processes in Borderline Ego Functioning

HAROLD F. SEARLES, M.D.

Due in part to a too literal interpretation of some of Erikson's (1956) early writings concerning ego identity, I long thought the sense of identity in a healthy person to be essentially monolithic in nature, comprised in large part of well-digested part identifications with other persons. But in more recent years, especially in the course of exploring the psychodynamics of the borderline patient, in whom the sense of identity coexists simultaneously in two or more internal objects, I have come to see that the healthy individual's sense of identity is far from being monolithic in nature. Rather, it involves myriad internal objects functioning in lively and harmonious inter-relatedness, all contributing to a relatively coherent, consistent sense of identity which springs from and comprises all of them, but does not involve their being congealed into so unitary a mass as I once thought. I have come to believe that the more healthy a person is, the more consciously does he live in the knowledge that there are myriad "persons"—internal objects each bearing some sense-of-identity value—within him. He recognizes this state of his internal world to be what it is—not threatened insanity, but the strength resident in the human condition.

EXAMPLES OF THE PATIENT'S PHRASEOLOGY AS SUBTLY REVEALING OF MULTIPLE-IDENTITY FUNCTIONING

Often the content of a patient's remark seems ordinary enough, but the feeling tone conveyed gives the analyst a glimpse of the

Clinical Professor of Psychiatry, Georgetown University School of Medicine; Supervising and Training Analyst, Washington Psychoanalytic Institute, Washington, D.C.

patient's unconscious functioning in terms of a dual or multiple
identity. A married woman comments, "I suppose the most tolerable compromise with these hungers of mine is to go with another
couple, so I'd have a chance to share ideas with another man." Here
she reveals both her unconscious image of herself as a man, as well
as that of her being a couple. On another occasion, she describes,
"One time when I was smoking some grass, and *Bill were* [my italics]
having — and Bill and I were having an argument. . ." Her slip here
reveals her unconscious image of Bill as being two persons (a projection of her own internal state). A male patient makes a similarly
meaningful slip in speaking of one of his several cousins, "He's the
ones [my italics] — the one who's a lawyer." An attorney says of his
opponent in a forthcoming case, "He's filled with vindictiveness;
he's determined to *kill me off* [my italics] during the trial." Common usage tends to confine the phrase "kill off" to doing away with
multiple foes, rather than a single one.

A woman patient reproaches me with, "You *overran* [my italics]
me yesterday," unconsciously projecting on me her own multiple-
ego functioning in alluding to me as though I were a herd of stam-
peding horses, or a horde of insects. Another woman states, "My
mother has a large head, y'know." This seems mundane enough in
content, but it was said with an intonation that conveyed the
unconscious meaning, "My mother has a large head, *among other*
heads in her possession." This reminds me of a frankly psychotic
woman's delusion that either her head, or mine, was replaced by a
succession of other heads on innumerable occasions in the course of
our sessions.

Within another woman's ordinary-seeming statement that "I
feel terribly uneasy in my family, in my marriage, in my home" is a
feeling tone which reveals the existence, at an unconscious level, of
three separate identities in her — one having to do with her family; a
second, with her marriage; and a third, with her home. A much-
traveled woman says, "I feel more disturbed in England than I do in
other countries. . . . I feel more comfortable in Italy; I feel more
comfortable in France. I used to feel all right in Canada." Again,
this innocuous-seeming statement is said in a curious manner that
conveys the unintended meaning that, at an unconscious level, she is

living simultaneously as several different selves, in England and in other countries, including Italy and France.

Many patients who habitually and frequently add parenthetically, in the course of their reporting, "Y'know" imply the unconscious meaning that "You know, because you are having or have had the same experience; your experience is always a twin of mine."

Equally frequent is the patient who, in reporting some recently past incident, expresses puzzlement about some aspect of his own behavior, either implying or, much less often, explicitly stating that, "It wasn't like me to react as I did." Here is an allusion to the presence of another "me," this one unconscious, who governed his behavior in the past incident. This is a muted variation of the frankly paranoid person's delusion that occult forces were governing his mind and behavior. One paranoid patient was convinced for years that innumerable "doubles" of herself existed, and that supernatural forces unpredictably replaced her self with one or another of these doubles, which then carried out destructive behavior for which she herself was later held accountable. A borderline young woman revealed a subtle hint of paranoid reaction to one of her internal objects when, having found herself uncharacteristically late for her college classes, she said, "So I wonder if there's something cooking." Clearly she meant here, something at work in her own unconscious, but with the unintended, paranoid-flavored allusion to the possibility that external forces were influencing her. She added, in the same vein, "I wonder if there's something going on. It's not like me to be late for classes...."

The Patient Who Doesn't Know Where to Begin

It may not be deeply significant if a patient occasionally begins a session with the statement, "I don't know where to begin." It may be simply a realistic attempt to cope with, for example, the fact that much has been happening around him and within him of late. But I began to realize some two years ago that the patient who more often than not begins the session with this statement (or some variation upon it) is unconsciously saying, "It is not clear which one of my multiple I's will begin verbally reporting its thoughts, its feelings, its free associations, during this session." That is, it is not basically that there are too many competing subjects for this "I" to select among to begin the reporting, but rather that there are too many "I's" which are, at the moment, competing among "themselves" as to which one shall begin verbalizing. One such patient explained, after an initial silence in which his physical demeanor was expressive of "I don't know where to begin," that during that silence he had been feeling partly like Jimmy, a boyhood friend who was given to temper tantrums — and, evidently, partly like a much more adult, and quite different, person. A woman, who had become able, over the course of her analysis, to integrate into her conscious sense of identity many previously warded-off part identities, began a session by saying, in a manner which I felt expressive of much ego strength, in a kind of confident good humor, "Now let's see; which one of my several identities will materialize today?"

CERTAIN SIGNIFICANCES OF THE USE OF THE WORD "WE"

Some patients' reminiscences about childhood are expressed not in terms of "I," but rather in terms of "we." Such a patient almost invariably recalls that "we" used to do this or that. He scarcely ever says "I" in this connection, and the analyst is left largely in the dark as to whom "we" is meant to include. My impression is that the patient's sense of identity is essentially symbiotic in nature (as was true of each of the patients mentioned here), with the sense of identity being either dualistic or multiple, and with an ever-changing shifting of the symbiotic partners in that sense of identity.

Several years ago I encountered comparable data in a supervisory session, in which the female supervisee was describing her work with a hospitalized, frankly psychotic man who showed an extraordinarily severe problem in terms of multiple-identity functioning and, by the same token, of symbiotic interpersonal relatedness. Time after time, as the supervisee herself reported to me that "We decided to meet on the sun porch," or "We talked for a few minutes about that," it was impossible for me to know whether "We" referred to the supervisee and the patient, to the supervisee and one of the ward-staff members, or to the supervisee and the whole ward-staff collectively. I began to realize how impossible it was for the deeply confused patient to discern with whom he was dealing in the supervisee who was immersed in such an ambiguous and shifting "we"-identity.

A few weeks ago, in my third session with a male patient who was still occupied mainly with presenting details of his history, I suddenly realized that he was using "we" with the significance I am describing here. I had already become accustomed to his presenting himself more as a married couple than as an individual. He spoke of his wife nearly as much as he did of himself, so that it was as though the wife were ever-present in our sessions. In this third session I noticed that he would describe the events over a relatively long stretch of the marriage — detailing what "we" had done during that time, mentioning relatively briefly that his mother-in-law had intruded briefly but disruptively on the scene, then resuming his narrative that "we" had moved to another part of the country, detailing at length what "we" had done there, mentioning a brief affair he had had, then resuming his narrative of what "we" had done in subsequent years. I am oversimplifying here, but, in essence, I realized that at an unconscious level, "we" did not refer consistently to his symbiotic identity comprised of himself and his wife. Rather, at the time when the mother-in-law arrived on the scene, she had replaced his wife as his symbiotic partner. The "we" who had moved to another part of the country had been, in his unconscious experience, himself and his mother-in-law. Similarly, later on his mother-in-law had been replaced by his mistress; it was a symbiotic himself-and-his-mistress, not a symbiotic self-and-his-wife, who had participated in the things "we" had done in subsequent years. These were simply three among many symbiotic partners whom he evidently had had at an unconscious level.

Patients' use of "we" as having an unconscious symbiotic-*transference* significance is a phenomenon I find particularly valuable to note — privately, that is. I do not recommend an early interpretation of this phenomenon, lest premature interpretation interfere with the development of the nondefensive, healthy-identification aspects of this phenomenon (those aspects which relate to the patient's development of a constructive introject of the analyst).

A female patient, for example, comments at the beginning of the session, "Why did you move that plant over there?" After a very brief silence (my having made no reply), she goes on, "*We* [my italics] were invited out to a Chinese dinner with some people last evening, and went to the Kennedy Center afterward." "We" consciously refers to herself and her husband, as from long-established custom I was assumed to know. But unconsciously it refers, as I had come to realize from this and other transference data, to herself and me (a father-figure in the transference) as a symbiotic-marital partner.

A male patient details for several moments, at the beginning of a session, his feelings about what he experiences as the combative relatedness between us of late, making a number of references to our session of the preceding day. After a pause of only a couple of seconds, he goes on, "I was thinking about yesterday *we* [my italics] took the children to the zoo." Later in the session, referring to a girl friend he had had in California prior to his meeting his wife, he says, "When I think about her, and then I think about myself *here* [my italics], married and with three children. . . ." Data from many sessions substantiate my impression that the "we" who had taken the children to the zoo is, at an unconscious level, himself and me as his transference-mother.

Another male patient characteristically asked at the end of each session, "Time to go?", with such an intonation as to convey, "Time for us to go?" It had become clear to me that he carried an internal image of me within him between (as well as during) our sessions. He frequently began sessions by saying that "We" did thus-and-so with the children over the weekend, or that "We" had another nasty argument last night. It became more and more evident to me as the analysis went on that these communications, like his beginning a session with, "Night before last we had sex," contained unconscious references to me as his symbiotic-identity partner. In the transference, I represented mainly aspects of his symbiotically-related-to mother.

The psychodynamics described by Freud (1917), including the phenomenon of identification with the lost object, and the venting of hostility on the self as a representative of that ambivalently loved-and-hated lost object, when applied to the symbiotic transference phenomena described here, help to illuminate innumerable instances of patients' acting out. One female patient, for example, says, near the beginning of a session, "If I seem relatively unanxious to you this evening — I don't know whether I seem so to you or not; I feel relatively unanxious — it's probably because *we* [my italics; this ostensibly refers to her and her husband] didn't do any acting out [any tirading at their poorly disciplined children] last night."

In dozens of instances from my work over the years, it has been apparent that a patient's acting out (during my or his vacations, or in the usual interims between scheduled sessions) in the form of reckless driving, excessive drinking of alcohol, or self-detrimental behavior at work represents, to a significant degree, his rageful subjecting not of himself but of me, his symbiotic-transference identity-partner, to such punishment. Sometimes such a patient is conscious of his trying to emulate the analyst (or, in some instances, someone ostensibly outside the analytic situation), but then, time and again, he feels unable to carry through the identification successfully; he keeps falling on his face. He represses the fact that at an unconscious level, it is not that he is so much "unable" to maintain the identification, but rather that he keeps on, as it were, burning the other person in effigy within himself; he keeps throwing the internalized analyst upon the latter's face, within himself.

The Analyst's Feelings and Fantasies as Clues to Dual- or Multiple-Identity Functioning

In a discussion in 1973 of the role of jealousy in the fragmented ego, I wrote, concerning my work with a schizoid patient, that:

> For several years I found this man infuriatingly smug. But the time came when, to my astonishment, I realized that what I was feeling was jealousy; *he* so clearly favored his *self* over *me* that I felt deeply jealous, bitterly left out of this mutually cherishing and cozy relationship between the two "persons" who comprised him. . . . In retrospect, I saw that I previously had not developed sufficient personal significance to him . . . to sense these two now relatively well-differentiated "persons" in him and to feel myself capable of and desirous of participating in the "three"-way, intensely jealousy-laden competition. It is my impression that such schizoid patients usually prove so discouragingly inacces-

sible to psychoanalysis that the analyst and the patient give up ... before they have reached this lively but disturbing ... stratum in which the patient's ego fragmentation becomes revealed and the nature of the transference becomes one of a murderously jealous "three"-way competitiveness [pp. 256-257].

Since then I have collected many examples, largely from my work with borderline, schizoid, and narcissistic patients, concerning this phenomenon, which I have thought of as "intrapsychic" jealousy, or jealousy involving an internal object in one or the other of the two participants in the analytic interaction. Recently, for instance, when a woman suddenly interrupted her own reporting by telling herself with intense impatience and exasperation, in an appreciably different tone of voice, "Oh, *shut up*, you *idiot!*", I experienced that by-now-familiar feeling of jealousy of this idiot-"person." Her tone, despite all its furious impatience, was filled with possessive fondness. The "idiot" to whom she spoke was clearly mother's cherished little idiot.

I often sense that one or another patient is functioning unconsciously in a multiple-identity fashion when I feel not simply intimidated or overwhelmed by this overbearing patient but, curiously and more specifically, *outnumbered* by him. With one woman, relatively far along in her analysis, I had the thought, accompanied by a feeling of gratification and fulfillment, "She is moving." But along with this freely conscious thought and feeling, there emerged in me an entirely unbidden fantasy: in my mind's eye, I saw some fifty to a hundred people on foot in a caravan, moving in a straggling, undisciplined but clearly peaceable fashion across a landscape—all going essentially together in the same direction. They were clearly all related to one another, and it later occurred to me that the word "tribe" described that relationship. The fantasy was accompanied by a distinct sense of awe at the realization that, evidently for a long time, I had been perceiving, unconsciously, this woman as comprised of so many "persons."

During the long years of analysis before so coherent an internal object relatedness had developed within this patient, she unconsciously defended against the recognition of this internal state, partly through the projection of this or that internal object on the analyst at the slightest opportunity, as it were. As the analyst, I felt that I was somehow interrupting her train of thought, even when I was totally silent. It eventually became clear to her that if I "allowed" her to digress from her intended main path, I was thereby guilty of interrupting her. If I moved slightly in my chair, this tiny sound was reacted to as a gross interruption. She reacted fully as though a third person had come upon the scene, or as though this were the surreptitious sound of a copulating couple (another form of unconscious relatedness of her own internal objects), or, at times, as though a part of her own body-image had suddenly and dismember-ingly separated itself out from the rest of that body-image.

Such patients are, in my experience at least, by no means rare. The intensity of their projection of the internal objects which inter-fere, at an unconscious level, with their more conscious ego-identity functioning tends to have a severely constraining effect on the analyst's functioning at all overtly as an analyst during the sessions. One such patient implies that I am an enormous interference with his attempts to free associate. I often think of his silent and agonized demeanor as being that of a fly imprisoned in amber, and, further, I have noted privately that more often than not, when I venture some intendedly liberating brief interpretation, it is as if the fly in the amber now manages to appear, somehow, even *more* cramped than it was before.

As the patient becomes more aware that the interruptions come primarily from within, he speaks, for instance, of ". . . what I was going to tell you when I was interrupted by that remembrance of the fantasy I had on the way here," or he may explain that the reason he is silent so much of the time is "because I can't stand the sound of my own voice. . . . It is so grating; it sounds exactly like my mother's voice. . . ." Such patients make clear, on some of these occasions, that their "own" voice is experienced by them as thoroughly alien, fully equivalent to that of an antagonizing and entirely separate other person.

DEFENSIVE (TRANSFERENCE-RESISTANCE) VERSUS EGO-INTEGRATIVE ASPECTS OF THESE PHENOMENA

Any of these clinical phenomena, when it appears in the context of the transference, needs to be evaluated in terms of whether it is predominantly a defensive phenomenon—an instance of the patient's characteristic borderline, symbiotic mode of ego functioning in relation to other persons over the years—or whether it is a predominantly healthy development, signifying (among other things) the patient's having managed to develop a healthy internal object representation of the analyst in the latter's own right, beyond his transference significance to the patient. Presumably any one vignette represents to some degree a mixture of both kinds of elements.

As for the defensive functioning of these phenomena, much of the clinical material presented in my first published paper (Searles, 1951), concerning incorporation, is relevant. That material shows patients' unconscious utilization of incorporation as a mode of defense to maintain under repression, for example, feelings of hostility and rejection. On the other hand, most of the examples of dual- and multiple-identity processes described here are of essentially the same nature as those encountered in what I (Searles, 1961) have termed the phase of ambivalent symbiosis, a phase I have described as one traversed by the schizophrenic patient in the course of his improving ego integration. To my way of thinking, the ambivalently symbiotic, dual- and multiple-identity processes so characterologically typical of the borderline patient give way, over the course of psychoanalytic therapy, to better integrated functioning on the patient's part only if the therapist becomes able to function during the sessions in a fashion that allows the ambivalent symbiosis in the transference to become replaced, gradually, with a therapeutic symbiosis, the characteristics of which I have described elsewhere (Searles, 1965, 1973).

Space allows me to touch only briefly upon the defensive aspects of the processes under discussion. Time after time in my work with borderline patients, I find that the patient's not responding to my greeting upon his entering the office has come to infuriate me so much that I no longer greet him either. This is one of the ways in which we come to function as alike or as one. Such behavior on the analyst's part is clearly a fostering of symbiosis (or a succumbing to the patient's coercion toward symbiosis), but of a symbiosis which is defensive against antagonism.

A patient who says that "Yesterday when I walked in, you looked as if you were afraid I was gonna attack *me* [my italics]" is clearly fusing with me, unconsciously, at the moment of this slip, as a defense against his anxiety concerning his perception of me as being afraid of him. It is less threatening to him, unconsciously, to be the attacked than the attacking one.

A married man showed, relatively early in his analysis, a multiple-identity mode of ego functioning at an unconscious level. In reminiscing about his childhood, for example, he described the struggles that took place between his alcoholic uncle and his three older brothers, who had attempted to keep the uncle from drinking. "*I can remember fighting with him* [my italics]—not me personally but my three brothers. . . ." The italicized portion was said *fully* as if he personally had fought with the uncle; it was clear that "I" included his three brothers as well as himself. Incidentally, I was reminded, upon hearing him say this, of a chronically schizophrenic woman who had two sisters, two and four years younger than herself. She once said, in reminiscing about something in her childhood, "When I was six, four, and two," then corrected herself, "When we were six-four-and-two. . . ." The man whom I was just discussing soon established, in the treatment sessions, a defensively symbiotic mode of ego functioning which proved for years highly resistive to analysis. He essentially presented himself as a couple comprised of himself and his wife. This had, of course, various genetic roots; for one thing, he was identifying with a mother who had functioned in his upbringing as both mother and father. It gradually became clear that he was enormously threatened, at an unconscious level, lest I replace his wife as his symbiotic-marital partner, which would mean that I would become not merely, so to speak, his mate in a truly separate object relation, but that I would become the other half (so to speak) of the only ego identity he possessed.

A woman patient came, over the course of many months of analysis, to tell me during one of our sessions, "You are my self," in a way which I found very moving. She then added, with a kind of small-child shyness, the qualification, as though not to frighten me, "not *all* the time." The affective quality of this communication was such as to make me feel that it was not predominantly treatment-resistive in nature, but rather a manifestation of healthy growth in her, made possible partly by my no longer needing to shy away from a more therapeutically symbiotic mode of transference relatedness with her.

In my work with each of several patients, after a number of years the patient has finally asked me, with unusual simplicity and direct-ness, "What's the matter with me?", or "What's wrong with me?" In each instance this question seems consciously expressive of feelings of futility, helplessness, mystification, exasperation, discourage-ment, and so on, because of various tenacious treatment-resistant symptoms. But in each instance, the question proves to have been expressive, at an unconscious level, of oedipal longings. The patient in this regard is asking me why he or she still does not qualify, in my eyes, to become my romantic and sexual partner. But at a still deep-er level the question conveys the meaning, "Why have you still not accepted me fully as your symbiotic identity partner, and by the same token surrendered fully your individual identity and entered fully into a symbiotic identity with me?"

THE PATIENT'S MONOLOGUE AS BEING, UNCONSCIOUSLY, A DIALOGUE

In 1972 I devoted a paper to reporting a few of the developments in my psychoanalytic therapy with a deeply schizophrenic woman with whom I have been working for 23 years at this writing. For at least fifteen of those years I have been accustomed to her spending the bulk of many of her sessions in dialoguing vehemently with one or another part of herself, thus shutting me out to a high degree from talking at all directly with her.

In about 1962 I heard M. A. Woodbury describe, during a staff presentation at Chestnut Lodge, that the auditory-hallucinatory experiences of a chronically schizophrenic woman with whom he was working functioned, during the therapy sessions, to provide her with responses from another person, so to speak, at a time when he was not supplying any comments to her. A paper of mine (Searles, 1976) contains comparable data from another patient of mine, much less ill than the one mentioned above, but who has experi-enced auditory hallucinations for many years. One time this woman came into a session deeply worried about the persisting, and ap-parently undiagnosed, illness of a cousin. She asked, "What do you think Paul has, Dr. Searles?" I made no direct answer, but endeavored to evoke more of her thoughts in this regard. Within a few seconds, she reported, seriously, "I heard the voices say, 'It's a reaction.' " She quoted the voices as speaking in an explanatory tone, as if providing, authoritatively and decisively, the explanation she had sought in vain from me.

But many years of experiences such as those mentioned in the preceding paragraph did not lead me to recognize, until a very few years ago, how frequently the borderline patient's monologues during the session prove to be, on closer examination, unconscious dialogues—dialogues between two parts of the patient's self, one part being comprised of the introjected analyst, a symbiotic-identity partner, at an unconscious level, in the transference. I emphasize that the fact that he is involved in a dialogue is genuinely unconscious to the patient.

It is important that the analyst become aware of what is happening primarily because otherwise this symbiotic transference functions as a powerful resistance to further analysis. In addition, from the analyst's observing in detail the nature of the dialogue role he is unconsciously being assigned, he can see whether the patient tends to perceive him as being, say, an enthusiastically interested parent or a parent ridden with futility and having essentially nothing to offer him.

In one instance after another, subtle shifts in the patient's tone, as he vocalizes first one side of the dialogue and then the other, help one to detect that this unconscious dialogue is occurring. I shall present a few among a great many available examples, examples which emerge in relative profusion in any average working week for me.

A woman reports a dream in some detail. I say nothing, as usual. After a few seconds of silence, she comments in the tone, now, of an interested observer, "Rather interesting dream," and goes on with her seeming monologue.

Another woman complains, ". . . the *boredom* of the analysis is what gets me down . . . I wonder [tone of discovery] if that's why I've been getting into all these social activities lately?" Then, after a momentary pause, she says in a rather different tone of voice—one now of an interested rejoinder—"Hm! Could *be!*" I distinctly feel that in saying these last three words, she has been functioning unconsciously as though she were I, an interested symbiotic mother in the transference, responding with vocalized interest and acknowledgment of an interesting new idea on her part.

A man reports a detailed précis of a play he attended the previous evening, and which he found very interesting. After having completed this précis, he is silent for a few moments, during which I say nothing. He then gives an interested-sounding, emphatic grunt, and resumes his seeming monologue.

Another man speaks animatedly throughout the session, as usual, while I say little or nothing. Near the end of the session, he pauses briefly. then says in a tone which is now relatively unanimated, futile, and empty, "I don't really know what to say." I sense, here again, that in saying this he is speaking unconsciously as me in the transference — to the personification of his own schizoid-depressed, mother-identification qualities.

I can merely touch here on the matter of interpreting these symbiotic-transference phenomena to the patient. In general, I do not attempt to interpret them at all early. In line with my concepts about therapeutic symbiosis, it seems to me essential that the analyst come to recognize that these phenomena are representative not merely of unconscious defenses on the patient's part, but also of a need on his part for an appreciable degree of symbiotic relatedness with the analyst, relatedness having both reality as well as transference aspects. A too early attempt at interpretation tends to make the patient feel dismembered. In one instance I suggested to a patient, "When you say '_____,' are you speaking for me?" She replied, "For *you?* [her tone clearly indicating that she found this suggestion preposterous]. *No;* I have enough trouble speaking for *myself.* Why should I speak for *you,*" she added, not really asking a question, but making a bluntly decisive statement. But a few moments later she showed interest in my suggestion. "You mean that if you don't answer, I have to supply an answer?" I replied, ambiguously, "Mm." She did not go further with this matter directly, but within a few moments said, in reference to her brother, "Ed is *torn in two* [my italics] these days about whether to move to Massachusetts."

Conclusions

This paper is written with the assumption that unconscious dual- or multiple-identity processes are among the fundamental features of borderline ego functioning, and with the additional, implicit assumption that such processes can be found to some detectable degree in the analysis of any patient with an illness of whatever diagnosis. Most of the patients whose clinical material is included here were functioning, to a superficial view, as normal neurotic individuals; their dual- or multiple-identity functioning was at first subtle indeed.

Work with patients such as these has helped me to realize that the normal neurotic individual may be unconsciously reacted to by the other person as comprising, and may unconsciously experience himself as comprising, two or a group or a tribe or a multitude of persons. In the same process, I have also realized that individual psychoanalysis and sociology are, at base, essentially one field of study. This psychoanalytic work has given me a deeper appreciation of the multifarious creativity of the human being's unconscious than I possessed even a few years ago.

REFERENCES

Erikson, E. H. (1956), The problem of ego identity. *J. Amer. Psychoanal. Assn.*, 4:56-121.

Freud, S. (1917), Mourning and melancholia. *Standard Edition*, 14:243-258. London: Hogarth Press, 1957.

Searles, H. F. (1951), Data concerning certain manifestations of incorporation. In: *Collected Papers on Schizophrenia and Related Subjects*. New York: International Universities Press, 1965, pp. 39-69.

———— (1961), Phases of patient-therapist interaction in the psychotherapy of chronic schizophrenia. In: *Collected Papers on Schizophrenia and Related Subjects*. New York: International Universities Press, 1965, pp. 521-559.

———— (1965), *Collected Papers on Schizophrenia and Related Subjects*. New York: International Universities Press.

———— (1972), The function of the patient's realistic perceptions of the analyst in delusional transference. *Brit. J. Med. Psychol.*, 45:1-18.

———— (1973), Concerning therapeutic symbiosis. *The Annual of Psychoanalysis*, 1:247-262. New York: Quadrangle.

———— (1976), Transitional phenomena and therapeutic symbiosis. *Internat. J. Psychoanal. Psychother.*, 5:145-204.

Personality Organization during the Recovery of a Severely Disturbed Young Child

MANUEL FURER, M.D.

In this brief communication I hope to share with you what can be thought of either as a problem at the outcome or as an interesting development during the treatment of a psychotic girl, Cathy, from the ages of five through ten years. Essentially it was the appearance and consolidation of what we considered to be an as-if state of personality organization — an aspect of some borderline conditions — in the fourth and fifth year of treatment, although precursors of this state had been present earlier.

COMMUNICATION THROUGH SYMPTOMS:
THE FANTASY OF SYMBIOTIC UNION

Of particular interest was the form Cathy's psychosis took when she emerged, after only two months of treatment, from a state of secondary autism. She assumed a catatoniclike posturing in which she used her body to copy and represent various pictures she had seen in books. While this behavior was at its height, the child continued to ward off external human reality almost completely. At best we were able to infer her perceptions from the particular content or the changes in content of chanted bits of songs and stories which she had heard and repeated.

To begin with, the poses were not communications, but complex psychotic symptoms involving a regression to the stage of omnipotent symbiotic unity. What was most important for therapeutic

Supervising and Training Analyst, New York Psychoanalytic Institute, New York City, New York.

purposes, however, was that the poses contained memories which could be deciphered with the help of the mother, who in our tripartite treatment design, was not only present but participated in the therapeutic hours. The posing and withdrawal from contact with the therapist and the mother were in fact the child's response to the impingement of human objects, in particular their emotional expressions. Gradually, however, we were able to communicate our understanding of the memory, the wish, the missing affects, and the connections which began to appear between the past memory and present reality experience in the therapy room and at home.

One of Cathy's most frequent poses was a copy of a picture of Mary leaning over the baby Jesus. For the mother, Christmas was a focal point of the year, always awakening longings for closeness with her family, particularly her father. She cherished its rituals, most especially the setting up of the little figures of the Nativity Scene.

Cathy, I must explain, had been conceived unexpectedly in the first year of the parents' marriage, in a foreign country, where the father was on assignment for his company. Before relocating permanently in New York for the purpose of placing the child in treatment, mother and child had returned to the States only twice: at age two and a half when the maternal grandfather was dying of cancer, and again at age four and a half for the purpose of a full inpatient neurological and psychiatric evaluation. From the age of six months to two and a half years, Cathy's care had been turned over to a sixteen-year-old native girl, and it was in the language of this nursemaid that Cathy produced her first words and phrases. Development during this period was apparently normal or precocious. The visit to the States upon the grandfather's illness broke this connection, and Cathy never saw the nursemaid again.

Cathy, as we first knew her, presented echolalic speech, bizarre darting and grimacing, flailing of her arms, panic rages, autistic refusal of contact, sudden inexplicable fears and flight, and an attachment to little pieces of black plastic. The mother had ceased to regard the child's behavior as comprehensible or as a communication, and she directed her efforts to controlling displays of bizarre and hazardous behavior.

In the first months of treatment, as the mother was able to associate to Cathy's poses, the child's feeling of loss, her yearning and her rage related to the above events became a meaningful exchange between the mother and the child. The content was confirmed by another strange pose, the copying of the figure of a boy on skates pushing a girl on a sled — a scene taken from an illustration in a Mother Goose book. In this early period of the treatment, the crucial image was not in the pose, but in the picture, namely, the surrounding snow. It was at the age of two and a half, on the occasion of her grandfather's illness and death, that Cathy first saw snow, and it was also at that time that the mother became depressed and withdrawn. The pose of the happy child, by the child now age five, denied again the painful experience of this emotional separation from the mother, who so suddenly had become her sole caretaker.

By highlighting and selecting these particular phenomena and not detailing our procedures, one necessarily does violence to the case as a whole. I have to skip over the antecedent and concomitant re-establishment of a relationship between therapist, mother, and child, which required what we call the correct timing of both anticipatory and participatory empathy with Cathy's behavior, once we were able to read her cues. Summarizing very briefly, by this kind of bodily representation, the child was able to live out the fantasy of omnipotent symbiotic union to which she had regressed, and to ward off the painful affects associated with her perception of separateness, that is of self from object, which on a different psychic level was accentuated by her particular life history. The rage, and subsequently the sadness in response to our interventions, were first expressed in global fashion, then directed at the mother and the therapist, and eventually integrated, in a sense of being able to differentiate present reality from the past, present self from past self, and to an increasingly greater degree, self from object.

The warded-off affects tended to flood Cathy, and her defense now became an effort at omnipotent control by a fantasy of the mother's power, which was inferred from her behavior and way of life. When, for example, the mother was unable to make the sun go down or to restore images on the television screen, the child was thrown into a panic rage, and, in addition, viciously attacked her mother, whom she had come to see as cruelly withholding her power.

After two years of treatment, progress was substantial; poses appeared only in emergencies, having been replaced by renditions in play of the stories of ballets, particularly one taken from the fairy tale of Sleeping Beauty. The ballet-dancer pose (see Figure 1) had also been one of the frequent early rigid postures; the mother had wished to be a ballet dancer and the ultimate source of the interest was again the maternal grandfather. In addition, as an indication of a shifting from deanimated or inanimate objects to the original human object, the cherished possessions ceased to be the pieces of black plastic and became the figures of the Naciemento or Nativity Scene.

THE EMERGENCE OF SEXUAL CONFLICTS

As Cathy was approaching her seventh birthday, the material of the oedipal conflict burst upon the scene. She became aware or preoccupied with sexual differences with an intense anxiety closely related to her earlier fear of total bodily destruction (see Figure 2). Dogs, cats, and finally people were classified as to whether or not they possessed a penis or whether or not they menstruated. Her apparent sexual identification and her actual behavior took on a masochistic character. It was at this point that she developed a fetishlike symptom, a preoccupation with shoes, in particular shoes that could be glimpsed beneath the sill of a door. This preoccupation appeared in what now came to be an almost endless series of drawings of the ballet dancer and of the iceskater that we knew so well from her posing.

Cathy had a phobia of her mother's going into the bathroom, and as on later occasions during such periods of focused anxiety, the flooding by her own affects was less of an issue. The fear of the bathroom emerged as a fear of what was going on in the parents' bedroom and a concern that her mother was damaged in sexual intercourse. The shoes visible under the sill of the bathroom door represented the maternal phallus and reassured her that the mother was intact. Through the tripartite therapeutic process, the child's drawings and play behavior elicited from the mother the memory of an experience on the flight home from the grandfather's funeral;

FIGURE 1. This drawing illustrates Cathy's early need to pose stiffly in front of the mirror to counteract her fear of bodily disintegration. Being the ballet dancer also seemed to be Cathy's roundabout way of being close to her mother or getting her mother's attention and love, as the mother had always admired ballet and had wanted to be a ballerina herself.

FIGURE 2. This drawing shows Cathy's previous reaction to stress. She was going to the dentist to have a tooth extracted. We see here a clear illustration of her fear of complete bodily disintegration. Her psychosis here interfered severely with her reality testing and her body image.

she had hemorrhaged while in flight, having had a dilatation and curettage (for intermittent bleeding) a few days earlier. She had taken the child into the peculiar small bathroom on the airplane and it was clear that the child had seen the blood. The small bathroom was represented in Cathy's drawing, as were spots on her clothing. It appeared to me that there had been a deferred effect of that trauma, as in the case of the Wolf Man, which was now operative with the child's phallic genital development and involvement in the Oedipus complex. The reconstruction of the memory of the hemorrhage and of at least two periods of observation of the primal scene resulted in the disappearance of these fears and preoccupations.

The focus now became a conflict over Cathy's masochistic feminine wishes which overlaid an earlier bisexual identification with the baby Jesus. In essence, as enacted in the ballet fairy tale Sleeping Beauty, she participates in sexual activity, is damaged by pricking her finger on the spindle, and is punished by the mother, the wicked witch. On the other hand, she sleeps the quiet peaceful sleep of the asexual baby Jesus until the prince comes, a denial but at the same time a return of the repressed wishes, as well as a memory of the parents' activity, and of her own excitement (see Figures 3 and 4). In this child, however, the intensity of the play literally carried her out of reality into a dramatic although temporary delusional state — she was convinced that the mother was the persecutor. In the grip of her delusion, she would launch a sudden and violent physical attack on the mother, and later, when we were forced to have the mother wait on another floor, Cathy would seek her out there, raging. In the midst of one such Sleeping Beauty performance, when the mother was not in the room, the therapist grazed the child's cheek in passing. Cathy replied with full and fierce conviction, "Why did you slap me, mother?", but then returned to the play.

During this same period, the child's earlier hospitalization for psychiatric evaluation at age four and a half emerged in play, but with the concomitant quasi-delusional belief, she amalgamated the girl on what she called the operating table (for an EEG) with the penetration and pinning down of Jesus on the Cross. She played the mother as killer of Jesus and herself as the victim. Similarly, a gastrointestinal upset was proof that the mother, like the witch in the Snow White fairy tale, had poisoned her, and the contents of all food served to her had to be checked and verified first by the therapist.

FIGURE 3. This drawing and its companion (Figure 4) show Cathy's triangular conflict of wanting to marry her father and take her mother's place, but coping with it by playing out or making drawings of her fantasies. The two drawings show how marriage will come true in the future, when the prince will come, as in the fairy tale, take her to his castle, and marry her. Note the complexity of her composition, the expressions of the people, the decreased rigidity with which they are drawn—all signs of improved ego adaptation.

FIGURE 4. This drawing, like Figure 3, depicts the Sleeping Beauty fairy tale.

SUPEREGO DEVELOPMENT:
TRUTH, GOODNESS, AND ABSTRACT THINKING

At this point, Cathy began to show evidence of the development of a cruel and all-encompassing superego. Fear of injury from the persecutor varied erratically with fear of self-inflicted injury; masturbatory activity and sexual excitation were predominant; and her drawings featured elongated fingers, elaborately costumed princesses, and ballerinas disintegrating in consecutive drawings into arms, legs, and shoes. Cathy now concentrated on being the ballet dancer who was both good as a dancer and "good" as a child — holding her arms above her head, never touching herself. At the same time, Cathy displayed a capacity to think, in the analytic setting, on a very high level. She became preoccupied with what is truth and what is a lie — the lie consisted of her articulating the fear that mother would not return to her after a weekend off with father; the truth, she confessed, was her wish that only father would return.

As she began her first experiences with formal learning in school, exhibitionistic aspects of the ballet poses and an exaggerated narcissistic ego ideal, shared by mother and child, became evident. In entering school, Cathy had expected to be an instant success, and when this did not occur, she reverted, in the school room only, to the early catatoniclike posing, expressing the wish for omnipotence without the intrusion of reality. At the same time, material emerged revealing her idea that one had to be both good at what one does and "good" in moral terms, if one were to be like the mother — that is, to satisfy the mother's exhibitionistic longings — but also if one were to win the mother's love.

THE APPEARANCE OF AS-IF BEHAVIOR

As is evident from the above, Cathy, now into the third year of her treatment, was at this point able to retain the separate object image during therapy, despite temporary delusional episodes and transient regressions to earlier psychotic disguises. She could distinguish fantasy from reality in play and move in and out of fantasy and reality with impressive ease. At the end of the third year of treatment, an as-if type of behavior appeared. This was used as a defense and denial of feelings aroused by the impending separation from the therapist over the summer vacation. Her first reaction to this material was to say, "I do not like your voice, it is not my voice," and then to demand that the therapist change her dark eyes and hair to look exactly like Cathy. The response to the interpretation that being "the same" would undo the pain of "good-by" included the resurgence of regressive and more instinctualized mechanisms, such as the masochism described earlier, panic reactions to the loss of a shoe, and clear evidence of a return of the wish for fusion and of the fear of bodily disintegration. The last day of therapy that year permitted, for the first time since the above session, a discussion of the impending separation. Cathy asked, "Will I be the same Cathy Ruth J. when you are away?"

On her return the following fall, an enlarged school setting faced her with a conscious dilemma. She could no longer blot out the other children and their expression of emotions, which particularly frightened her. She knew her own emotions were overwhelming, and as often expressed in the past, she was never sure that any one feeling would ever stop. Her response was to imitate the voices, movements, and various other behaviors of her classmates, with the idea that the imitation would be real, but as her own creation manageable, and thus she could relate to the other children and control their responses as well as her own. Strikingly, instead of the stereotyped voice inflections and uncoordinated facial expressions and body movements other severely disturbed children adopt in response to potential affect, Cathy became apparently many different bodies, voices, and facial expressions. She practiced before the mirror, became dissatisfied, and then asked both therapist and mother to demonstrate the appropriate facial expressions for various emotions and situations, which she could then copy and use. At one point, she interrupted her practicing to paint her arms the color of the mother's favorite dress, and thus attired resumed work. The result was a façade of strangely mannered but fairly accurate renditions of a variety of affects. However, although she became adept at matching affect with gesture and "face," she recognized these creations as failures—or in her own words, "Why don't I have a real friend?" Nonetheless, this imitative as-if personality was impervious to interpretation, and comments or references to the behavior were so vigorously fought off that efforts to understand, empathize, and interpret were postponed.

To summarize another portion of the therapy of this period, in bringing the child into a relationship with mother and therapist certain aspects of the transference, in particular the idealization of the maternal figures and the exhibitionism, the beautiful, talented precocious child, were only sparsely analyzed. The idealized self became another portion of the as-if state and appeared in the transference during the fourth year of treatment.

THE STRUGGLE OVER MASTURBATION

At age nine Cathy began her fourth year of treatment, still driven by her sexual conflicts. She asked endless questions about anatomy, mating, and birth in an attempt to master her feelings. She remembered, as did the mother, several observations of parental sexual intercourse, and drew these scenes in great detail. She asked the therapist, "Do you take your nightgown off?" "Do you keep the covers on?", bringing the voyeuristic exhibitionistic focus in the forefront. "Do you do it every night?" she queried, indicating her nightly struggle with masturbation. Her drawings again showed people with grossly elongated middle fingers, and people mutilated, the punishment for masturbation.

At home, what would start as a wish to be either physically or emotionally close to her father could not be contained. She had fantasies of intercourse with him during which she was injured, and the wish was quite conscious. Again, in the treatment situation, these wishes took on hallucinatory reality, as in a session when her excitement culminated in the belief that she was having a nosebleed. As expected, this was dealt with by projection and the belief that the mother wanted her injured and killed. In the midst of these preoccupations, she once again demanded to learn the forms of social behavior from the therapist. She again became involved with the differences between truth and falsehood, real appearances as opposed to the "happy face" — the latter a demand from the distant past that the mother had made both of herself and the child. By now however, the imitation varied between the as-if defense and a yearning for identification with a separate and admired individual, the therapist, perceived as a beautiful golden-haired woman. In addition, the imitation of this period contained evidence of superego conflict — the copied happy face is false in the additional sense that the maternal figure in the transference is hated as well as admired.

Yearning for Identification with
the Therapist as a Good Mother Figure

In the final year of therapy, the child's anxiety was manifested in an effort to find out what she, Cathy, should be in order to elicit the therapist's admiration. She still presented a façade, the result of efforts at imitation and integration, which appeared peculiar, exaggerated, and hollow; to us, an as-if personality. It was felt, however, that Cathy had gained sufficient strength to deny her the borrowed personality and to interpret the defense. In response to a tentative introduction of this approach, she re-enacted those images that had previously brought her admiration: the imaginative child, the artist, the performer, the patient concerned with sexual problems, the polite and correct child. Her initial reaction to interpretation was terror and a return to catatonic posing, but this time of such grotesque form that it could only be understood as a depiction of an image of the destroyed and destructive self.

The as-if mechanism seemed to be Cathy's protection against impulses and emotions that, arising in ordinary situations, rapidly became extreme, fearfully unending, and finally, in fantasy, destructive. For instance, she finally expressed jealousy of the therapist: "You won't tell me about your private life. You won't tell me what your house and furniture look like. If you're Mrs. Blank, you must have a Mr. Blank. You don't understand because *you* always know where you are." Regression and primitive defenses followed rapidly, and the anger and betrayal were projected. In Cathy's fantasy, the therapist alone would have the only beautiful voice. She, Cathy, would then attack, take out all the therapist's blood and drink it, but the blood would then hurt her. Oh no, now she remembered, her tongue was cut out. Not only could she not have a beautiful voice, but she could not commit the destructive acts. Her face would show her emotions; her tongue cut out, she is the voiceless replication of the therapist and no one would be hurt.

This ambivalence in the transference was related to her struggle over masturbation. The therapist was the good nurse who fed her, and then the bad nurse who spanked her and kept her in bed at night. Cathy decided that both she and the therapist, the latter as both good and bad nurses, must sit imprisoned on a rock over water teaming with witches. If princes could vanquish the witches, the two of them would live. If the witches won out, they would die. The two of them together experiencing the same dangers seemed to us to represent a lessening in the extreme cruelty of her superego, plus a basis for empathy and genuine identification. The importance of this good maternal figure and the capacity for maintaining a relationship to a love object was such that Cathy was willing not only to control her impulses but to give them up in order to keep the good, kind therapist. One consequent solution was to give up men entirely, or as she explained, the therapist must be bored by her stories about Chris, a boy in school, so that they now could consider that there were only two people left to talk about — herself and the therapist. As Cathy, however, came to be fully aware of the actual relationship between the adult therapist trying to help her and the sick child driven by her wishes and fears, her relative helplessness became terrifying. The therapist was to play a devil; if the devil caught her, Cathy would die, but if Cathy let go of the devil, she would also die. Occasionally and fleetingly, Cathy experienced her conflicts as fully internal, which again frightened her. Hollowly and without affect, she said one time, "I'm sorry for you. You're such a good therapist and I don't try hard enough."

At this point, Cathy told a story, expressing in a creative way with a deliberate use of symbol and metaphor her understanding of what had been happening in her life, past and present. She said that she was "like Helen Keller, who was loved by her parents like a little dog. Then Anne Sullivan came, a woman who understood Helen since she herself was half blind and had had a terrible childhood. Anne decided that the child had had too much pity, that she was intelligent and could learn. Before the teacher came," Cathy explained, "Helen had been lonely. She had to feel the mouths of people talking. She thought, 'Why won't they play with me?' But then, and it's no wonder, she had tantrums and kicked and screamed. Still, if she could and she did make the same mouth movements, who would she be? The little dog? No one? Not herself and no one's friend." In association Cathy said, "Sometimes parents do cruel things to children without realizing it. Spankings aren't cruel. It is cruel when a child approaches a parent and the parent holds out her hand to stop you from touching her, and then she takes the child to its room."

TREATMENT INTERRUPTED:
CONSOLIDATION OF AN AS-IF PERSONALITY ORGANIZATION

The last half of this final year of therapy brought external stress into the treatment. The Masters' Center was to close in June after a prolonged effort by parents and staff to retain public funding — an effort of which Cathy was aware. Soon after the New Year, Cathy had to enter another new school. She was terrified by the complex social situations, by the sheer volume of children and their aggressive movements, and responded by standing in the stairway in rigid postures or by clinging tightly to adults. The failures all around her reactivated the wish and demand that the therapist be all-powerful and save her, like a princess in a tower, from the frightening prisons of home and school. Memories of her realities flooded her, however, and she saw the therapist as well as herself as weak and worthless. Perhaps if the therapist curled her hair and she, Cathy, looked prettier, school and home would be more appreciative. As these illusions were not sufficient, however, the demands became impossible and fantastic: the therapist should make her able to fly, to fly away.

A disguised return of the shoe fetish was expressed in the only wish she had in the world: a wish for a pair of high-buttoned antique shoes of very particular design. When these could not be found, she raged, but then settled on having the therapist sew her a pair of high-buttoned shoes out of flannel. During these sessions, Cathy would sit silently, reading one of her own books, occasionally glancing up to watch the therapist sew, and cutting off all comments with, "Don't talk." The shoes as omnipotent phallus were clearly a bridge between her and the maternal figure, the good maternal figure whom she feared would be lost in the destructive atmosphere. Only when the therapist tried a shoe on her foot for fit did Cathy relax briefly in the physical closeness. To recognize that any of her problems were internal, or that her difficulties with her parents, who were now both depressed and demanding, were real, made her feel too unhappy, too helpless, vulnerable, separate, disillusioned, and disappointed. She withdrew, spending her sessions reading, often not in the same room with the therapist, often not hearing the bell ring when the mother came to pick her up, and refusing to open the door herself.

The therapist broke into this new, and we felt disadvantageous, situation at termination, with a strong statement of the reality — namely, that Cathy was trying to say that they had no relationship and she, the therapist, could not continue to act as part of that belief. Cathy was living out a fantasy of despair and using her parents' scolding to support it. She was playing that she was being abandoned by her real mother, rather than acknowledge her hurt and disappointment. She was warding this off by becoming cold and dead, more cold and dead than she wished those on the outside to be. Cathy responded by confirming the interpretation, but then revealed that the therapist had not recognized that an old attempted solution was present — the as-if personality. She said, "I am not like other ten-year-olds. I am unordinary. I cannot feel. I can only copy. That is what I have been doing in my head. That is also part of it. My mother doesn't know what to do next."

The termination, it should be said, also meant for Cathy a change such as she had experienced many times in her life. Her family would be moving a very great distance away. She produced a fantasy of a girl named Glass Slipper who loses the maid she loves because her mother, conceited and strict, does not want her to play with grown-ups. Her mother dies and robbers come to kill Glass Slipper as they stupidly think she is guilty for her mother's death. In punishment, the robbers are taken to prison far away where they have clean air — a parental description of the future family home. Some of the latent content included the warding off of the pain of loss. Her own destructive feelings were projected onto the robbers who were taken away, but also taken home.

The libidinal attachment to the mother was now much stronger, as it was to the therapist. The analysis proceeded and a painful mourning reaction took place. Cathy was realistic about herself and her parents as she had not been before. She talked about yearning for a boy in her old school whom she would like to see again before leaving. However, she thought her mother would not want her to do that. As she described the closeness she wanted with this boy, the analyst was able to focus upon the feeling she had expressed before of the mother who holds out her hand to prevent contact, and then takes the child to its room. Cathy wept and said, "I have to work it out. I have felt pushed away, and many times I have been pushed away. Some of it is my fault, and I get so angry. But not being yourself doesn't help."

In the very last weeks of therapy, the fears of robbers and whirlwinds reappeared, behind which was the belief that the world was too dangerous, that the only safe place was with the therapist forever, whatever the therapist wished her to be she would be. In the main, however, Cathy and her therapist were able to think over the time they had spent together, sadly, and yet with the feeling that the therapist had a real and separate existence that would continue and that Cathy could thus remember her, as the therapist would remember Cathy.

Very briefly, as I understand this case, the as-if state was not a deficiency or defect in the ego of this child, but rather a defense against overwhelming stimuli. It was on a line of development from the posing in that it was a partial return to a lack of differentiation of the self from the object via incorporation — an attempt to blur the differences. In contrast to the earlier period of posing, however, the sense of reality in regard to the human object was never fully lost in this personality organization. Although the as-if mechanism was used as a defense, it was also an important part of a primitive mode of learning, evolving perhaps into higher-level functioning, but never fully integrated, as in the capacity to empathize with another human being.

Primary Anorexia Nervosa
in the Borderline Adolescent—
An Object-Relations View

JAMES F. MASTERSON, M.D.

This paper attempts to bridge Bruch's (1962, 1966, 1970, 1971, 1973) work on anorexia nervosa which stresses interpersonal theory and my own work on the borderline adolescent (Masterson, 1972, 1974, 1975) and adult (1976) which stresses object-relations theory. Bruch's (1973) thorough, painstaking work on eating disorders seems to have broken the theoretic and therapeutic log jam for the first time by getting beneath the anorexia nervosa syndrome to the underlying developmental arrest. Her reliance on interpersonal theory, however, omits the intrapsychic and therefore, in my judgment, leaves the clinical picture incomplete. This paper supplements her work by adding that intrapsychic dimension. It will demonstrate how the emphasis of object-relations theory (Fairbairn, 1954; Guntrip, 1969; Jacobson, 1964; Kernberg, 1971; Klein, 1946, 1948; Mahler, 1968; Masterson, 1976; Masterson and Rinsley, 1975) on intrapsychic structure specifies and clarifies the problem of anorexia nervosa and makes psychotherapy more specific and more effective.

A DEVELOPMENTAL, OBJECT-RELATIONS APPROACH TO
DIFFERENTIAL DIAGNOSIS OF ANOREXIA NERVOSA

The clinical syndrome of primary anorexia nervosa has been delineated by Bruch (1966) to consist of the following: (a) a relent-

---

Professor of Clinical Psychiatry, Cornell University; Attending Psychiatrist, New York Hospital, Payne-Whitney Clinic, New York City, New York.

less pursuit of thinness with body-image disturbance of delusional proportions; (b) a deficit in the accurate perception of bodily sensations manifested as lack of awareness of hunger and denial of fatigue; (c) an all-pervasive sense of ineffectiveness. This syndrome is not specific to any one diagnostic category, and the debate has raged for years as to whether a given anorexic patient is schizophrenic, borderline, or psychoneurotic.

A developmental, object-relations point of view, which goes beyond the symptomatic and descriptive to focus on the development of intrapsychic structure (the differentiation of self- and object representations and their related ego defense mechanisms), allows levels of development and types of intrapsychic structures to be distinguished from one another. It is therefore a useful tool to distinguish between the various underlying personality structures within which the anorexia nervosa syndrome can occur.

Intrapsychic structure develops (Jacobson, 1964; Kernberg, 1971; Mahler, 1968) through the slow, progressive differentiation of the self-representation from the object representation and the parallel and related maturation of ego defense mechanisms. Mahler (1968; Mahler, Pine, and Bergman, 1975) has reported this process as comprising four stages: autistic, symbiotic, separation-individuation, and on the way to object constancy. A developmental failure along this continuum results in an arrest in the differentiation of both the self- and object representations and in their related ego functions. The evidence for these arrested structures can then be observed in the patient. I shall outline three levels of developmental fixation that probably encompass the intrapsychic structure of most anorexia nervosa patients.

If the arrest occurs in the symbiotic phase, the self- and object representations are fused, and the patient's ego defenses are those of the psychotic — i.e., splitting, projection, very poor ego boundaries and reality testing, and often delusions and hallucinations. The clinical diagnosis is schizophrenia.

If the arrest occurs in the separation-individuation phase, the self- and object representations are separate but split into a good and bad object and self-representation. The ego defenses are still primitive but more mature than the psychotic — i.e., splitting, clinging, avoidance, denial, projection, acting out. Ego boundaries and reality testing are weaker than in the neurotic but stronger than in the psychotic. The clinical diagnosis is borderline personality organization (Kernberg, 1967; Masterson, 1972, 1976; Masterson and Rinsley, 1975).

If the arrest occurs late in the on-the-way-to-constancy phase or in the early phallic-oedipal phase, the self- and object representations are separate and whole rather than split—i.e., both good and bad combined rather than either good or bad. Ego defenses are more mature, with repression supplanting splitting and projection, denial and acting out giving way to reaction formation, sublimation, etc. The clinical diagnosis is psychoneurosis.

Most patients with anorexia nervosa probably have a developmental arrest at the symbiotic or separation-individuation phase. Their principal problems revolve around fears of loss of self (engulfment) or loss of the object (abandonment), feelings of emptiness, and struggles over autonomy. The principal problems of those patients with anorexia whose developmental arrest occurs in the fourth phase—on the way to object constancy—probably revolve around oral pregnancy wishes and fears, rather than fears of loss of self or loss of object.

An Object-Relations Theory of Anorexia Nervosa in the Borderline Adolescent

The cause of the developmental arrest in the borderline anorexic appears to be similar to the cause of the arrest in other borderline patients—i.e., the mother's withdrawal of her libidinal availability at the child's efforts to separate and individuate. This has been described in great detail elsewhere and will only be summarized here (Masterson, 1972, 1976; Masterson and Rinsley, 1975).

The borderline mother, herself suffering from a borderline syndrome, experiences significant gratification during her child's symbiotic phase. The crisis supervenes at the time of separation-individuation, specifically during the rapprochement subphase, when she finds herself unable to tolerate her toddler's ambivalence, curiosity, and assertiveness; the mutual cueing and communicative matching to these essential characteristics of individuation fail to develop. The mother is available if the child clings and behaves regressively, but withdraws if she attempts to separate and individuate. The child needs the mother's supplies in order to grow; if she grows, however, they are withdrawn from her. The child's excessive aggression becomes entrenched, in consequence of the mother's withdrawal, and is further aggravated by the child's inability to integrate positive and negative self- and object representations, since such integration would require further separation-individuation, which in turn would provoke further withdrawal of maternal libidinal supplies. A situation thus occurs in which aggression is repetitively provoked without any constructive means conducive to its neutralization.

The images of these two mothers are powerfully introjected by the child to form a split object-relations unit which consists of two separate part units, each of which comprises a part-self representation, a part-object representation, and an affective component linking the two together. These may be termed the withdrawing part unit and the rewarding part unit. The withdrawing part unit is cathected predominantly with aggressive energy, the rewarding part unit with libidinal energy, and both remain separated from each other, through the splitting defense mechanism (see Table 1).

SPLIT EGO

It is now necessary to inquire into the basis for the persistence of the split ego in these cases. As the child's self-representation begins to differentiate from the object representations of the mother—i.e., as the child begins to separate—she experiences abandonment depression in the wake of the threat of loss or withdrawal of supplies. At the same time, the mother continues to encourage and reward those aspects of her child's behavior—passivity and regressiveness—that enable her to continue to cling.

The mother thus encourages and rewards in the child the key defense mechanisms of denial of the reality of separation, which in turn allows the persistence of the wish for reunion (clinging), which later emerges as a defense against the abandonment depression. Part of the ego thus fails to undergo the necessary transformation from reliance upon the pleasure principle to reliance upon the reality principle, for to do so would mean acceptance of

TABLE 1
SUMMARY OF THE BORDERLINE SPLIT OBJECT-RELATIONS UNIT

Withdrawing of Aggressive Part Unit

Part-Object Representation	Affect	Part-Self Representation
A maternal part object which is attacking, critical, hostile, angry, withdrawing supplies and approval in the face of assertiveness or other efforts toward separation-individuation.	Chronic anger, frustration, and feeling thwarted, which cover profound underlying abandonment depression.	A part self which is inadequate, bad, helpless, guilty, ugly, empty, etc.

Rewarding or Libidinal Part Unit

Part-Object Representation	Affect	Part-Self Representation
A maternal part object which offers approval, support, and supplies for regressive and clinging behavior.	Feeling good, being fed, gratification of the wish for reunion.	A part self which is the good, passive, compliant child.

the reality of separation, which would bring on the abandonment depression. The ego structure is split into a pathological (pleasure) ego and a reality ego, the former pursuing relief from the feeling of abandonment, and the latter the reality principle. The pathological ego denies the reality of the separation, which permits the persistence of fantasies of reunion with the mother. These are then acted out through clinging and regressive behavior, thus defending against the abandonment depression and causing the patient to "feel good." Extensive fantasies of reunion are elaborated, projected onto the environment, and acted out, accompanied by increasing denial of reality. The two, operating in concert, create an ever-widening chasm between the patient's feelings and the reality of her functioning as she gradually emerges from the developmental years into adolescence.

THE RELATION BETWEEN THE SPLIT OBJECT-RELATIONS UNIT AND THE SPLIT EGO

The splitting defense keeps separate the rewarding and the withdrawing object-relations part units, including their associated affects. Both remain conscious but do not influence each other. Although both the rewarding and the withdrawing part units are pathological, the borderline experiences the rewarding part unit as increasingly ego syntonic, as it relieves the feelings of abandonment associated with the withdrawing part unit, with the result that the person "feels good." The affective state associated with the rewarding part unit is that of gratification at being fed, hence, "loved." The ensuing denial of reality—i.e., the lack of confidence in a self (Bruch's sense of personal ineffectiveness)—seems but a small price to pay for this affective state.

An alliance now develops between the child's rewarding maternal part unit and his pathological (pleasure) ego, the primary purpose of which is to promote the "good" feeling and to defend against the feeling of abandonment associated with the withdrawing part unit. This powerful alliance further promotes the denial of separateness and potentiates the child's acting out of reunion fantasies. The dramatic clinging behavior of the anorexic performs this function. The alliance has an important secondary function—the discharge of aggression, which is both associated with and directed toward the withdrawing part unit by means of symptoms (anorexia), inhibitions of perception of individuative stimuli—i.e., thoughts and feelings—and other kinds of self-destructive acts.

The withdrawing part unit (part-self representation, part-object representation, and feelings of abandonment) is activated by actual experiences of separation (or loss) or as a result of the patient's efforts toward separation-individuation within the therapeutic process, which symbolize earlier life experiences which provoked the mother's withdrawal of supplies.

The alliance between the rewarding part unit and the pathological (pleasure) ego is in turn activated by the resurgence of the withdrawing part unit. The purpose of this operation is defensive, i.e., to restore the wish for reunion, and thereby to relieve the feeling of abandonment. The rewarding part unit thus becomes the borderline's principal defense against the painful affective state associated with the withdrawing part unit. In terms of reality, however, both part units are pathological; it is as if the patient had but two alternatives—either to feel bad and abandoned (withdrawing part unit) or to feel good (rewarding part unit), at the cost of denial of reality and self-destructive behavior.

THE THERAPEUTIC ALLIANCE

The patient begins therapy feeling that the behavior motivated by the alliance between her rewarding part unit and her pathological (pleasure) ego is ego syntonic, i.e., it makes her feel good—anorexia, clinging, denial of individuation stimuli. She further denies the self-destructiveness of her behavior—the personal sense of ineffectiveness and other reality impairments.

The therapist's first objective is to render the functioning of this alliance ego alien by means of confrontative clarification of its destructiveness. Insofar as this therapeutic maneuver promotes control of the behavior, the withdrawing part unit becomes activated, which in turn reactivates the rewarding part unit, with the appearance of further resistance. A circular process results, sequentially including resistance, reality clarification, working through of feelings of abandonment (withdrawing part unit), further resistance (rewarding part unit), and further reality clarification, which leads in turn to further working through. This process of the alternate activation of the two part units and the defenses of the pathological ego in the transference demonstrates the patient's intrapsychic structure.

In those cases in which the circular working-through process proves successful, an alliance develops between the therapist's healthy ego and the patient's embattled reality ego. This therapeutic alliance, formed through the patient's having internalized the therapist as a positive external object who approves of separation-individuation, proceeds to function counter to the alliance between the patient's rewarding part unit and his pathological (pleasure) ego, battling with the latter, as it were, for ultimate control of the patient's motivations and actions. The structural realignments which can then ensue in the wake of this working-through process have been described elsewhere (Masterson, 1976; Masterson and Rinsley, 1975). In summary, the patient works through the pathological mourning (rage depression) associated with separation from the mother and, through the mechanisms of internalization and identification, forms a new intrapsychic structure based on whole-object relations.

CLINICAL ILLUSTRATION[1]

Connie, age fourteen, was admitted to the hospital after a suicidal attempt, with a five-year history of anorexia, vomiting, hyperactivity, depression, inability to express her feelings in words, and eventually rage reactions. The illness began at age nine during the summer of her first major trip away from home for a skating competition. She became depressed and escalated her already heavy skating practice schedule. The depression and overactivity continued episodically for the next two years until her eleventh summer, when Connie, at camp for the first time, became depressed and began to eat poorly with selective rejection of protein food. During her twelfth year she felt "pressured" in school and was angry with herself when she did not get "the top grades." That year she became terrified at a party when the other adolescents began to play a kissing game. She began to cling to her best friend and said she was "turned off" by boys. In her thirteenth year her brother began to withdraw from the family in preparation for his leaving for boarding school the next year and Connie took over many of his household tasks. During her thirteenth summer she again went away to camp and re-experienced the symptoms of the previous summer which cleared on her return.

In her fourteenth year Connie began to develop breast tissue and an interest in boys which was accompanied by a ten-pound

---

[1] I am indebted to Dr. Bruce Bienenstock, the patient's therapist, whom I supervised, for the material summarized here.

weight loss. Her mother then developed a severe depression in response to the death of the governess who had raised her, and her older brother left in September for boarding school. Connie became depressed and by November her selective eating pattern became more noticeable. She was "moody and irritable." By March she vomited regularly and by April she limited her diet exclusively to vegetables. The pediatrician's attempts to help were of no avail and in early September her parents found a suicide note saying she was sorry she was such a burden and describing suicidal attempts by scratching her lower abdomen and attempting to gag herself to death.

PAST HISTORY

Connie, the second of three children, had a normal birth and early development. She was breast-fed until three or four months of age, at which time her mother on stopping felt: "a separation, a loss of feeling of closeness like when she was in the womb. This seemed like a second separation."

Connie had a succession of nine maids who took care of her. At bedtime Connie often stood in her crib and screamed. Her brother comforted her. Her mother said, "There was no point in going in, that would prolong the agony. I was quite upset with guilt feelings." During Connie's first year, the mother remembers her as "helpful, never a complainer, never a discipline problem, a clown, mimic and independent, adventuresome, daring, obstinate."

Connie was increasingly unhappy during her second year of life. Her governess was dismissed and her mother gave birth to her sister, became depressed, and sent Connie for several months to live with her paternal grandparents. The parents recall little of Connie between two and five years. Connie was anxious on starting kindergarten, to the point that her mother went to school with her each morning for a month.

At age four, in nursery school, Connie was settling down after some minor reports of attention-getting behavior when the parents went away for a long weekend and returned to find Connie "dissolved, depressed" and again anxious about school. The mother had to return with her in the morning for a few weeks. After a tonsillectomy at seven, she became "hysterical" and would not let the nurses near her so that her mother took care of her. She did well at school both academically and socially until the last two years. On her mother's prompting the patient took up ice skating at age six and by age nine was deeply involved in practice and competitions.

PARENTS[2]

The parents each received individual psychotherapy once a week and group therapy once a week for sixteen months.

Connie's mother was an only child whose mother had died at her birth. She was raised by a governess with whom a strong mutual symbiotic relationship developed. The governess forced food on her charge and tried to influence her to become a champion ice skater. When Connie's mother was sixteen, her governess was dismissed by her father who had remarried and she reacted with a severe depression.

When Connie was born the mother consciously felt that her dream had come true, that her mother had returned in the person of her daughter. The symbiotic themes of reunion, dissolution, fusion, and death that sprang from the mother's relationship with the governess were repeated with Connie—including the problem with food and the ice-skating ambition.

These themes were evidenced in the family sessions when Connie said she no longer wanted to skate. Her mother later reported Connie's "freezing her out." She said, "I feel so hurt, it's like death, I withdraw." While working through her intense rage and depression at Connie's efforts to separate, the mother dreamed of Connie's death, of endless empty rooms. She gradually came to see Connie and herself as separate and to support Connie's individuation, while looking more realistically at her own life and desires.

Connie's father, a lawyer, was the eldest son of a wealthy, socially powerful family dominated by his mother. He was the "good" son fulfilling all the family expectations of him. He and his wife continued to live close to and be dominated by his mother up to

---

[2] I am indebted to Mrs. Grace Christ, the parents' therapist, for the material summarized here.

the time of admission. He had a sister, two years younger, who had died at age 23 of anorexia nervosa. There was evidence of unconscious collusion on the part of Connie's father and the rest of the family in this death. The father named Connie after his sister because, "I guess I wanted to resurrect her, to have another chance." It became clear that Connie and this dead sister were fused in the father's mind. In treatment the father began for the first time to mourn the loss of his sister and to explore the formerly repressed feelings of envy, rage, guilt, and sexual desire that he had toward her. He began to see the parallel between his interaction with Connie and her symptoms and his past interactions with his sister. He reported dreams of trying unsuccessfully to merge the two faces (daughter and sister) on one body. Gradually he was able to separate the two, which enabled him to become a father to his daughter.

INTRAPSYCHIC STRUCTURE

Connie's intrapsychic structure as derived from the history and from the recapitulation of the part units in the transference could be outlined as follows. The rewarding object-relations unit consisted of a part-object representation of an omnipotent mother who was perpetually caring and gave her special attention, a part-self representation of a good child who was loved for behaving as if she were sick and helpless and could not manage for herself, and an affect of feeling good, a cosmic feeling of safety and protection. The withdrawing object-relations part unit consisted of a part-object representation of a mother who varied from being indifferent to one who was "not there" and "hated her," a part-self representation as "a nobody, evil, fat pig, like I committed ten terrible sins, am ruining the whole family," and an affect of abandonment depression (Masterson, 1972).

The defense mechanisms of the pathological ego were: denial of separation, splitting, and acting out through clinging to the rewarding object-relations part unit, with a projection onto the mother and others of the wish for reunion. Behavior was helpless, childish, compliant, with avoidance and denial of individuative thoughts and feelings — to the point of "not thinking." The anger of the withdrawing object-relations part unit was expressed partly in the anorexia symptom and was partly reflected back on the self, as well as projected onto any and all who confronted her acting out of the rewarding object-relations part-unit fantasy.

TREATMENT

Connie was a short (58 inches), potentially attractive, but undernourished, gaunt-looking, depressed waif (64.9 pounds) who admitted depression but denied the anorexia, weight loss, and hyperactivity. Physical exam was negative and menarche had not occurred. Her behavior initially was hyperactive, overcompliant, clinging to staff. Her testing was limited to eating where she used various strategies to conceal from the staff that she was not eating and vomiting. She denied her cachexic state and hyperactivity and vomited because she was afraid of "getting fat." In interviews during this initial period she related historical data, expressed her sense of helplessness without her mother (Bruch's personal ineffectiveness) and her wish to return to her. Connie's acting out the rewarding object-relations part-unit fantasy to defend against the abandonment depression associated with the withdrawing object-relations part unit served the same defensive purpose as the acting out seen in the borderline patient who is overtly angry at the mother and whose behavior is destructive — i.e., taking drugs, truancy, etc. The difference between the two is that the latter patient is projecting and acting out the withdrawing object-relations part unit on the mother rather than the rewarding object-relations part unit — usually with these latter patients you can find a peer who becomes the recipient of the rewarding object-relations part-unit projection.

Limits were set to the patient's acting out by a minimum caloric intake per meal and the patient was restricted — i.e., sent to her room for failure to eat the minimum. The feelings associated with not eating became the subject for the next interview. At the same time, her denial and helplessness were confronted.

The confrontation and limit setting triggered the withdrawing object-relations part unit, with increased depression and anger. The withdrawing object-relations part unit was projected onto the therapist and for a long period of time Connie either made angry demands on her therapist, was silent, or attacked him for being stupid and upsetting her. Confrontation of this resistance finally led Connie to confront the withdrawing object-relations part unit and her feelings of abandonment. She said, "There were always so many things I wanted to tell them but couldn't, mostly it was how I felt. I guess I was afraid Mother would be angry or get upset. Whenever I told them when I was upset they would get upset too, as if I passed it on."

After five months of treatment her doctor's impending vacation triggered the withdrawing object-relations part unit which Connie acted out with a sign-out letter and loss of weight. When the destructiveness of the acting out was confronted, she turned to transference acting out: "I did trust you. I don't trust you any more. You turned against me just when I needed you." Then she moved to review the past: "I don't trust my brother any more either. When he came back from school he acted like he didn't even know me. We weren't even brother and sister any more [sobbing]. I had ruined it."

She then returned to transference acting out, acting helpless in the session, which was interpreted as a defense against the previously expressed feelings about being left. In the next session she no longer projected her feelings of being abandoned onto the therapist but continued her examination of the feelings surrounding her brother's departure for school. She again acted helpless to defend against the anger and depression, and again this was confronted. In the next session, after some transference acting out, she moved further into her dilemma. If she expressed anger at her mother, she felt she would be abandoned.

Connie explained, "I don't know why, I'm really mad at you. I feel like I could pull your hair out. I'm really mad. I'm scared to death of you more and more. I dread this. When I get mad you just leave. You make me feel like a pea or something. I've been building all of this inside me. I feel like I want to take it back, erase it. It's just like at home, everyone would just leave when I got angry. I'd do things for my parents so they'd forget I got mad at them." At this point, in keeping with her style of splitting the anger from the object and reflecting it back on herself, Connie acted out her helplessness and hopelessness by a suicide attempt, slashing her wrists to the point of requiring stitches.

She continued, however, to work through the abandonment depression: "When I was a little kid they understood and they showed it, like they loved me in a real way. But as I grew up they loved me in a fake way, like they didn't know how. If I grow up and move away, they won't be there any more. All my life I've been dreading moving away and when I think of it I get depressed."

Beneath the hopelessness and depression lay her intense anger:

All those things; hugging, kissing, I associated with caring and it was just the opposite. It's that they cared too much. Normal people care just by listening. I don't think they care unless they get down on their hands and knees and hug me. If they just listen it feels like they're mad. Caring was through actions and anger was through silence. That makes me mad to think about that now, that way of controlling me, and I used to be mad at everyone else for not caring because my parents exaggerated it so. Makes me mad, makes me furious to think about actions being everything. I was split inside. It was so difficult to decide when to appear better and when to appear worse. It was like they always wanted me to be happy and I always figured if I wasn't they'd do things to make me happy. When I was the worst [helpless] they'd do more things for me, like love me more. If I wanted to thank them, then I'd make myself perfect [clinging].

During this twelve-month period of working through there were a number of occasions when Connie regressed, stopped eating, and the eating restriction had to be resumed. These regressions were reactions either to the depression emerging in the interviews or, on two occasions, to her doctor's vacation. As she worked through her suicidal depression and homicidal rage, a slow, gradual, but drastic change occurred as her individuation began to flower. The clinging behavior stopped, eating restrictions were dropped permanently, depression lifted, she became assertive in interviews, and she began to gain weight and her appearance and dress became much more feminine and appropriate. She then had a series of twelve joint-family interviews with her parents which she managed well. She reported: "I feel good inside because I'm glad about the interviews with my family and feel different about myself. I feel different but in a weird way, it's something that I have that's mine. I don't feel as afraid of them, that I'm being controlled by them. After I saw them I knew no one told me how to be and I was glad."

She was discharged after sixteen months at a weight of 77 to attend a boarding school and continue in therapy three times a week with her therapist. She did well both at school and in therapy. Six months after discharge her therapist had to leave and she continued with the author three times a week for another ten months. She reacted to her therapist's departure with intense regression which seemed limited to her relationship with her mother and to the interviews. She did not become anorexic, continued to do well at school and with her friends. However, week in and week out she projected the withdrawing object-relations part unit onto me and acted out the transference to defend against her feelings of abandonment. Confrontation met only resistance. Perhaps she did not develop anorexia this time because she was discharging the rage in the interviews by transference acting out. Finally after eight months the transference acting out began to yield to confrontations and she began to work through her feelings of abandonment at her therapist's departure—she reported that she was so hurt and angry at his leaving her that she vowed to never allow a relationship like that to develop again. After 32 months of intensive psychotherapy she has come a long way, but still has a long way to go.

Discussion

The discussion will compare and contrast Bruch's interpersonal theory and object-relations theory on six critical issues.

Clinical Picture

PURSUIT OF THINNESS

Bruch postulates that the anorexia is due to a rigid effort to control the body to establish a "domain of selfhood" when faced with the adolescent growth task of independence and identity formation. Object-relations theory postulates that the anorexia has a number of adaptive and defensive purposes. In Connie's case its intrapsychic defensive purpose was to: (1) relieve her anxiety about loss of the object if she separated and individuated by avoiding growth of all kinds—physical, sexual, emotional; (2) to substitute obsessive control mechanisms for individuative feelings and thoughts as a source of motivations; and (3) to discharge the tension associated with her hostility to the object. Its adaptive purpose was to provoke the mother's attention at the same time that it expressed her hostility to the mother. The anorexic symptom was the keystone to a whole set of pathologic defenses whose purpose was to preserve the object at the cost of the self—the latter being denied. Confrontation of this denial in the therapeutic relationship led to a working through of the depression and rage at loss of the object and allowed separation-individuation to resume. The key difference between the two theories is that the object-relations theory links the symptoms with the self, the object, the affective state, and the defense mechanisms—i.e., the whole underlying problem in intrapsychic structure.

PERCEPTUAL DEFECTS

Bruch's evidence for a failure to learn body perceptions is very persuasive. There is much evidence, however, to suggest that the borderline patient suppresses and denies those individuative thoughts, feelings, and actions and maybe even perceptions that might interfere with the wish for supplies from the mother.

HELPLESSNESS

Bruch describes a sense of personal ineffectiveness related to always acting in response to others. Object-relations theory suggests that the helplessness (a common symptom in the borderline) is an inevitable consequence of the separation-individuation failure and the clinging. The predominant affect is invested in the object, not the self, and since efforts at coping and mastery are met by fear of loss of the object, the patient avoids efforts to cope and consequently feels helpless to cope on her own.

DEFECT IN INITIATIVE, AUTONOMY

Bruch describes the patient's not relying on her own thoughts, feelings, and body sensations. Object-relations theory suggests that this, like the helplessness, is again a necessary consequence of the separation-individuation problem—the patient denies and suppresses her own individuation to preserve the maternal supplies.

NEGATIVISM

Bruch describes "an unrelenting No" extending to every area of living, and aggressive negativism against all therapy. Object-relations theory suggests that the "No" represents an expression of the rage at the demand that the self be given up to obtain supplies; this rage is projected onto all expectations and expressed by opposition. The negativism to psychotherapy is more specific. Psychotherapy symbolizes separation-individuation and as such triggers the withdrawing object-relations part unit which is projected onto the psychotherapy, which is then resisted.

PARENTS

Bruch describes the parents as "appearing" normal, but superimposing their needs on the child and disregarding her signals — the child lacks appropriate confirming responses. We have not found the first point to be true and the second point, while true, requires substantial elaboration. None of our borderline parents, including the parents of patients with anorexia nervosa ever appeared normal. Both parents were clinically ill, the mother usually borderline and the father either borderline or one of the other severe character disorders. The mother clung to the patient to relieve her own anxiety. She responded to and confirmed the child's clinging behavior. She did not confirm individuative behavior. The father distanced himself from the patient, while at the same time reinforcing the mother's clinging. The patient's regressive behavior played a vital role in maintaining the mother's equilibrium and often was the linch pin of the whole family's system of emotional relationships. The complexities of the resultant depersonification have been described elsewhere (Masterson, 1972; Rinsley, 1971).

PAST HISTORY

Bruch describes the child's past history as being apparently normal with excellent performance and free of any difficulties. Object-relations theory asserts that this very performance based on the clinging mechanisms is most pathologic because it serves to avoid individuation. In addition, many of our patients had symptomatic episodes in their childhood.

PRECIPITATING EVENTS

Bruch suggests that adolescence itself or a new experience such as going to camp or entering a new school or college is the precipitating event. She discusses very little why these are precipitating events. Object-relations theory is of specific use here since it not only suggests what events are important, but also indicates why. Any environmental event that threatens the relationship with the person to whom the patient is clinging (i.e., death, divorce, depression, etc.) exposes her to separation anxiety and abandonment depression. Similarly, any event that poses a challenge that requires individuative coping (i.e., new school, camp, college) interrupts the patient's defense mechanisms and exposes her to separation anxiety. Many events combine both factors.

PSYCHODYNAMICS

Bruch suggests that the need for independence and identity that arises in adolescence precipitates the condition. Although these factors may play a role, object-relations theory makes clear that it is a precipitating factor only to the degree that it stirs up the earlier separation-individuation problem and brings on separation anxiety and abandonment depression.

Bruch states that the underlying structure of the disorder is not specific but resembles other disorders of adolescence. It is true that the symptom complex itself is not specific, but the underlying structure — be it borderline, schizophrenic, or psychoneurotic — is quite specific and should be so diagnosed for effective therapy.

PSYCHOTHERAPY

With the phrase "The Constructive Use of Ignorance," Bruch stresses the need to evoke awareness of impulse feelings and needs originating within the patient by the therapist's confirming or correcting responses to the patient's self-initiated expressions. I agree with this approach on the basis that its objective is to help the patient separate and individuate.

There is, however, one important exception in the initial phase of psychotherapy. The patient's denial of the destructiveness of the rewarding object-relations part unit – pathologic ego alliance to her own individuation is unconscious. She cannot initiate the processes necessary to overcome it herself. The therapist must aid her by questioning and confronting the denial. An independent self-motivated desire for therapy emerges as the patient becomes aware of her own individuative thoughts and feelings, on the one hand, and of how her behavior has been destructive to this essential image of her self, on the other. Transference distortions produced by this activity must be taken up later in psychotherapy as the patient becomes aware of the contrast between her own individuation and her clinging transference.

Conclusions

In my view, the advantages to supplementing Bruch's work with object-relations theory are:

1. It completes the puzzle of the clinical picture by providing the missing intrapsychic piece.

2. It ties the clinical manifestations to their developmental roots, and provides a more comprehensible and clearer picture of the disorder as a whole, which allows for the design of a more accurate psychotherapy.

3. It clearly emphasizes as well as explains why the objective of psychotherapy should be to go beyond weight gain to emotional growth — the patient's only guarantee against the future.

REFERENCES

Bruch, H. (1962), Perceptual and conceptual disturbances in anorexia nervosa. *Psychosom. Med.*, 24:187-194.

———— (1966), Anorexia nervosa and its differential diagnosis. *J. Nerv. Ment. Dis.*, 141:555-565.

———— (1970), Psychotherapy in primary anorexia nervosa. *J. Nerv. Ment. Dis.*, 150:51-67.

_____ (1971), Death in anorexia nervosa. *Psychosom. Med.*, 33:135-144.

_____ (1973), *Eating Disorders: Obesity, Anorexia Nervosa, and the Person Within.* New York: Basic Books.

Fairbairn, W. R. D. (1954), *An Object Relations Theory of the Personality.* New York: Basic Books.

Guntrip, H. (1969), *Schizoid Phenomena, Object Relations, and the Self.* New York: International Universities Press.

Jacobson, E. (1964), *The Self and the Object World.* New York: International Universities Press.

Kernberg, O. F. (1967), Borderline personality organization. *J. Amer. Psychoanal. Assn.*, 15:641-685.

_____ (1971), New developments in psychoanalytic object relations theory. Presented at 58th Annual Meeting of American Psychoanalytic Association, Washington, D.C. (Unpublished.)

Klein, M. (1946), Notes on some schizoid mechanisms. *Internat. J. Psycho-Anal.*, 27:99-110.

_____ (1948), Mourning and its relation to manic depressive states. In: *Love, Guilt, and Reparation: And Other Works.* New York: Delacorte, 1975, pp. 344-369.

Mahler, M. S. (1968), *On Human Symbiosis and the Vicissitudes of Individuation. Vol. I. Infantile Psychosis.* New York: International Universities Press.

_____ Pine, F., & Bergman, A. (1975), *The Psychological Birth of the Human Infant.* New York: Basic Books.

Masterson, J. F. (1972), *Treatment of the Borderline Adolescent: A Developmental Approach.* New York: Wiley.

_____ (1974), Intensive psychotherapy of the adolescent with a borderline syndrome. In: *American Handbook of Psychiatry,* Vol. II, ed. S. Arieti et al. New York: Basic Books, pp. 250-263.

_____ (1975), The splitting defense mechanism of the borderline adolescent: Developmental and clinical aspects. In: *Borderline States in Psychiatry,* ed. J. E. Mack. New York: Grune & Stratton, pp. 93-102.

_____ (1976), *Psychotherapy of the Borderline Adult: A Developmental Approach.* New York: Brunner/Mazel.

_____ & Rinsley, D. B. (1975), The borderline syndrome: The role of the mother in the genesis and psychic structure of the borderline personality. *Internat. J. Psycho-Anal.*, 56:163-177.

Rinsley, D. B. (1971), The adolescent inpatient: Patterns of depersonification. *Psychiat. Quart.*, 45:3-22.

Affects in Borderline Disorders

PETER HARTOCOLLIS, M.D., PH.D.

A Genetic Hypothesis

It was Kubie (1963) who first offered the hypothesis of a "central affective potential," suggesting that some early life situations or conflicts can imprint on the developing personality a proneness to certain affective experiences. Subsequently, Mahler (1966), in studying the separation-individuation period of early childhood development, described a characteristic affective responsiveness, a "basic mood" that presumably predisposes to certain emotional reactions in later life—depressive and anxiety spells, angry outbursts, boredom, or, on the other side of the affective continuum, elation, hypomanic excitement, and a sense of omnipotence. The basic mood reflects the child's emotional experience during the practicing and rapprochement subphases, specifically from the emergence of the self as a mental image around the ninth or tenth month of life, to the establishment of a firm mental image of the mother (object constancy) a year or two later.

The rapprochement subphase of the separation-individuation period corresponds to the anal phase of psychosexual development and forms the basis of a meaningful, secondary-process communication with the mother. If, for one reason or another, the mother-child relationship during this period is disturbed, the child's self-esteem becomes depleted, and a narcissistic vulnerability sets in. The ambivalence characterizing normal behavior during this phase intensifies, and as the child tries to ward off the fear of the love object—a fear which derives from the child's awareness of his aggressive fantasies against the frustrating mother—primitive de-

Director, C. F. Menninger Memorial Hospital; Training and Supervising Analyst, Topeka Institute for Psychoanalysis, Topeka, Kansas.

fenses such as splitting and projective identification prevail, resulting in a "basic depressive mood" and a strong predisposition to borderline personality disorder.

Some Basic Affects

On the basis of a comprehensive review of the literature, Gunderson and Singer (1975) conclude that anger is the most prevalent pathognomonic affect in borderline disorders. The borderline patient's anger is displayed dramatically in temper tantrums and hateful, seemingly irrational and unpredictable outbursts against love objects, people who try to help and bear no hostility to him. This anger has an omnipotent, destructive quality, which is most obvious when the patient turns against people who do not even know him—in fact, against the entire world.

Next to anger, the affect most frequently identified with borderline patients is depression. But it is usually qualified so as to sound more like loneliness, emptiness, or alienation rather than genuine, guilt-ridden depression. In fact, some have described it as "affectless" depression (Grinker, Werble, and Drye, 1968), and others as "anhedonia" (Hoch and Polatin, 1949).

The borderline patient's depressive affect contains a great deal of anger at what is experienced as rejection by a love object—a global parental image perceived alternatively as all "good" or all "bad"—as well as feelings of helplessness and hopelessness as the anger and the underlying aggression are turned inward. In other words, this angry depression is more masochistic than guilty in nature, involving very little concern for the missing love object, something that reflects the inadequate development of object constancy in such patients. Whatever feelings of grief or sadness accompany the sense of loss of the "good, need-satisfying, symbiotic mother" (Mahler, 1966) become readily overwhelmed by feelings of anger, helplessness, and hopelessness.

In contrast to anger and depression, boredom usually remains unnoticed or is mistaken for disgust, indifference, or depression— unless the patient actually complains about it. And borderline patients do complain about feeling bored, more than any other kind of patient. In fact, as is noted by Greenson (1953), boredom has little role in neurotic and psychotic conditions, which are usually characterized by anxiety, depression, guilt, obsessive fears and ruminations, or fatigue and apathy.

Boredom is experienced by healthy people, but as a transient affect or ego state. In the borderline person it becomes a prolonged, sometimes chronic affair. It is characterized by a sense of longing for something (or someone) that is not merely absent, but non-existent, or at best unidentifiable, something that leaves one feeling empty or hungry, passively expectant, hopeful in a helpless way. The sense of emptiness and helplessness that characterizes the borderline person's boredom represents, according to Greenson (1953), an unconscious ego state dominated by the image of "no mother," "no breasts," "mother will not come" — a negative hallucinatory image. Boredom stands for the denial of libidinal wishes that have come to represent a threat to the individual because of the destructive intensity of his fantasies toward the love object's frustrating image. To the extent that boredom is based on the mechanism of denial — the denial of threatening psychic reality in both its libidinal and aggressive content — boredom is related to elation and its concomitant sense of omnipotence, which is as characteristic, if not as common, an affect in borderline disorders.

Feelings of hatred and persecutory fear, along with depression, are stressed by authors of Kleinian persuasion. According to Grinberg (1977), the prevalence of hate and persecutory fear defines a more severely disturbed category of patients whom he labels "schizoid," while depression characterizes less severely disturbed patients whom he calls "melancholoid." These two groups of borderline patients seem to correspond closely to the two marginal types Grinker, Werble, and Drye (1968) describe. In addition to persecutory hatred and fear, Grinberg (1977) mentions "persecutory guilt," an affect he attributes to the interference of the primitive, sadistic superego that dominates the "psychotic part" of the borderline personality. The affects Grinberg describes are largely inferential, derived from his own experience in the analytic situation — his own countertransference presumably mirroring the patient's feelings transmitted to the analyst through the mechanism of projective identification. There is a controlling element in these feelings that makes the transference verge on psychosis ("psychotic transference"). An intense depressive affect is, on the other hand, experienced by "melancholoid" borderline patients when they are faced with the separation from, or loss of, an object on which they are extremely dependent. Such affects constitute what Grinberg refers to, in general, as "psychic suffering," which prompts the borderline person to mobilize primitive defense mechanisms that tend to blot out the awareness of these affects, or to distort them in such a manner as to render them hardly recognizable.

The affect of envy is also prevalent in borderline patients. It derives from the experience of frustration, usually oral, and a special pathognomonic intolerance for it. Borderline patients are frequently overwhelmed by a sense of futility, a variant of frustration and emptiness, which they try to counteract by resorting to fantasies that evoke the affect of elation or hypomanic euphoria.

A related affect borderline patients characteristically describe is disgust — feeling disgusted about something or someone and, above all, about themselves. Again, it may be argued that disgust, as borderline patients seem to experience it, is nothing more than anger, or a variant of anger. While there is no question that anger is involved, anger may not be the basic ingredient — that is, it is no more basic than it is to depression, of which it usually partakes. Essentially, disgust refers to prohibited sexual impulses of anal origin. A patient of mine, for example, complained that he felt dirty, while in his grandiose moments, he claimed he was the cleanest person in the world. He was also preoccupied with concerns of a homosexual nature and attributed one of his most disturbing symptoms, erythrophobia, to disgust at sexual thoughts he had about other men or other men allegedly had about him. The case of this patient, illustrating a gamut of affects characteristically experienced by borderline individuals, is presented below.

CASE REPORT

A 21-year-old, single man, a college drop-out, entered the Menninger Hospital because of extensive intake of drugs, suicidal threats, and homosexual preoccupation. He had been in psychotherapy with the referring physician, a psychoanalyst, for two and a half years.

In his first psychotherapy hour with me, the patient complained that he had "a problem with people." He wished to become a happier man by being able to "function," as he put it. He had difficulty finding a job and was afraid to go out and look for one. He recalled his previous therapist interpreting his problem as fear of "masculine competition." But he emphasized this point in order to negate it, claiming that he was never aware of such a fear, as he had never competed with any man. Almost immediately, and for a long time afterward, he tried to compete with me for the right of having the first and last word.

This young man talked incessantly, ignoring or evading whatever points I tried to make. He mentioned that he suffered from insomnia. That opened a prolonged, rambling presentation of symptoms such as blushing, headaches, and extensive daydreaming, which the patient interpreted as "defensive." He associated blushing with anger, and headaches with sexual fantasies, especially about men. In a monotonous, robotlike fashion, he verbalized feeling suspicious of everybody, suspecting that nobody liked him in spite of the fact that he tried very hard to make a good impression. He also stated that by talking about his illness, his odd wishes and practices, past and present, he meant to shock people. He added that the pathology of his life, present and past, made him feel exceptional, giving him a "claim to fame," as he put it.

In subsequent hours the patient elaborated on his many negative feelings about himself and others. He complained of feeling nervous, bored, angry, discouraged, and jealous. He declared that he had no identity and no one could help him. He expressed the wish to change, but observed he did not know how he wanted to change, or whether he wanted to change at all. He reiterated his wish to have attention, as much as he could get. He recalled that as a young adolescent he liked to play with dolls and had feminine interests. Later on, he revealed that he used to put on his mother's clothes and wander around the neighborhood in the dark.

On various occasions, he described his life in a depressed manner, and yet he did not seem concerned, indicating that his depression was ego syntonic. In fact, he did not see it as a symptom, but as a condition of his life, something he was willing to settle for. Repeatedly, he stated that he preferred to feel depressed rather than anxious, and that he was able to make himself feel depressed whenever he felt something or someone was going to make him anxious.

Not infrequently, he described feelings of happiness and then feelings of depression, restlessness, and nervousness — all in the same hour. At the same time that he enumerated all these feelings, he complained of boredom — as a matter of fact he did appear completely bored. When I pointed out the discrepancy, he explained that he was describing past feelings. He felt bored and did not know what to talk about to make the therapist feel interested, rather than bored as he himself felt.

As often, he talked about feelings of anger and feelings of disgust about himself and about everybody else. He wished to be excited, stimulated, but did not know how to get this stimulation. He felt doomed, like a "female whore"; he needed attention, he felt frustrated, all he could feel was frustration and hurt.

Sometimes he would say that he felt sad, not really depressed, just sad; or he was just acting sad, as he wanted others to pay attention to him. He did not really feel sad, he went on, because he could not feel anything; his feelings were very superficial. Actually he was feeling happy, although not very happy, he explained, because his feelings were superficial. He concluded by saying that he felt stupid. I said he looked sad. He replied, "Oh, I look sad, but I'm not really."

Another day, he observed that I seemed to be tired of listening to him; I was probably falling asleep. I admitted that I felt tired; he was talking in a very boring way, I had the feeling he himself was bored with what he was saying, and I noted perhaps that was why he thought I was bored with what he was saying (which indeed I was). I had expected him to get angry, but he remained calm, impassionate. He said he had no drives, no desires, except when he was here. I did not ask him what he meant. He started talking about his father, how he could not identify with his father and this made him feel very depressed. He had no identity; he had homosexual preferences; his life was empty, without interest, without hope. He hated himself, his best daydream was of trading places with someone else, no matter whom. He started talking again about being depressed. I commented that he looked relaxed. He said he relaxed as he talked about feeling depressed, talking this way relaxed him, being here was very relaxing, and that was why he did not want to feel depressed, because that relaxed him. He was afraid that if he felt relaxed he would start feeling excited and elated, and that would make him feel guilty. He repeated, "That's why I feel depressed or, at least, I try to convince myself and others that when I am depressed, I feel more relaxed that way."

Coming here was wasting his time, he asserted another day. He was talking about "trash"—whatever he said about his feelings was "trash"—it really did not represent what he felt, thought, or did. He claimed that whatever he did or said was in order to hide his real feelings; he spoke about feelings he did not really have, feelings like jealousy and the need for attention—"trash feelings."

I took exception to what he was saying, pointing out that he must be having all these feelings because he could describe them so vividly. Perhaps what he meant, I suggested, was that he liked to exaggerate when talking about his feelings. He agreed that indeed he had these feelings, except that he had them only to cover up for other feelings and thoughts which were more important. He refused to specify which feelings or thoughts were more important, declaring instead that he was really wasting his life; he was bored and wanted to change his life, to have a more stimulating life. He indicated that everything was going very smoothly in his life currently: he was working full-time, he had his own apartment, he was coming to therapy; but he felt bored and thought of creating a problem for himself—like insulting his boss—in order to make things more interesting. "But I like to be cold and look bored—like someone I know." He turned to me and smiled: "I did not mean you."

I said perhaps he was trying to make me feel cold and bored by saying things that were cold and boring. He replied that might be the case, he might be defending himself from coming too close to me. He did not like closeness, he would rather keep his distance. He explained that he tended to describe "trash feelings," what he called "trashing," in order to defend himself and to remain distant from others. He was afraid people might understand him. I commented that he often felt lonely, insecure, and discouraged. He did not respond. A little later he noted he was not only reluctant to talk here, but he felt sleepy and tired when he was here. He liked the kind of suspense he experienced with people when he was afraid that he might do something and lose them. I asked him whether he felt that he might lose me. He said he had no such fear; he more or less expected therapy to go on indefinitely. I would continue with him as long as he came and talked to me about his feelings, about being sick and lonely and in need of help—that is, unless his father stopped paying.

A PROBLEM OF IDENTITY

When a borderline individual, such as the patient just described, states that he feels one way or another, he does not necessarily experience what he says. He himself does not know how he feels. He is far more sure about the way you feel or the way he would like you to feel. He often feels bored and looks bored, as this is more of a neutral feeling, an affect that protects him from feeling anything dangerous or painful. Another way of describing such a feeling is to call it emptiness, feeling empty—which of course is not what one really is, empty of ideas or empty of a self-concept, but empty of personal feelings. The patient who complains that he feels empty, or who sounds empty, is empty only to the extent that he is unable to experience an affect that is outer-directed, that has an object or a goal attached to it. Feeling empty is equivalent to feeling lonely—a common complaint of borderline patients. Feeling empty corresponds to the awareness of one's inability to be self-sufficient and is accompanied by a sense of helplessness. Feeling lonely, on the other hand, is with reference to an object, when the feeling is about missing a "good" object rather than the narcissistic supplies that such an object can provide. This feeling is accompanied by a sense of hopelessness (Engel and Schmale, 1967). In borderline cases, the feeling of helplessness carries within it a sense of injustice, protest, and entitlement; the feeling of hopelessness is experienced as alienation and nihilism rather than as existential despair.

To the casual listener or observer, a borderline patient seems to report or experience a number of contradictory affects at the same time. But as Searles (1977) points out, this is not a case of multiple affects. It is not that the patient has too many contradictory or concomitant feelings, but that he is faced with a number of self-identities experiencing different feelings, which he finds difficult to identify with, as the "I" who is verbalizing them is one of the various "I's" who experience such affects—"I's" who compete among themselves as to which one will begin "verbalizing." And when a patient comes to identify with his therapist, the affects he describes as his own are likely to be affects shared with the therapist, at least in the patient's imagination, if not in reality—a case of projective identification. This reflects a sense of identity that could be thought of as symbiotic in nature, if it were not for the fact that the patient is able to deal with the therapist's identity as separate from his own conceptually, although not emotionally. The patient splits the therapist's identity into a conceptual and an emotional one and identifies momentarily with the emotional part. In fact, the patient manages to describe and to elicit in the therapist affects complementary to affects he really experiences or has good reason to experience. Thus, if he feels intensely excited about something, he claims that he feels bored, and manages to look bored, and moreover causes his listener to feel bored. It is also likely that the borderline patient who feels bored, empty, or depressed will express himself in anger and induce anger in the therapist in order to counteract an unbearable feeling of depression—a composite of emptiness, loneliness, abandonment, and loss of identity.

Experiences of separation and loss, even of a casual, ordinary, predictable nature, such as weekend interruptions of treatment or the mere termination of an analytic hour from one day to the next, can give rise to intense depressive reactions, felt as hopelessness, impotence, and inner emptiness of a catastrophic nature. Such reactions may be manifested defensively as anger, which is then experienced by both the patient and the therapist as such or, counterphobically, as disgust and boredom—if not as grandiose, omnipotent elation. Other defensive reactions to this depressive propensity are isolation, withdrawal, a display of self-sufficiency, exhibitionism, and also the experience of depersonalization, which signifies a deeper identity disturbance. Somatization, the equivalent of a conversion reaction, may also be used by a borderline person to handle unbearable feelings of loss and frustration resulting from the absence of a love object.

Affect and Object Relations

According to Deutsch (1942), borderline patients, at least those of the as-if variety, are completely lacking in affect. Stern (1938), who also describes borderline patients as "affectless," believes they are prone to anxiety—anxiety generated by narcissism rather than neurotic conflict. According to Kernberg (1975), patients with borderline personality organization suffer from chronic, diffuse, free-floating anxiety. But he, as well as others (Grinberg, 1977; Zetzel, 1971), point out that such patients find painful affect hard to tolerate, particularly anxiety. The implication is that any "affect-lessness" they may experience or exhibit is only apparent, probably defensive in nature. Indeed, most authors emphasize that border-line patients are easily hurt, very sensitive to criticism and interpretations that undercut the false image of themselves or their pathological narcissism. Significantly, all those who describe borderline patients as "affectless" refer to the superficiality characterizing the object relations of such patients rather than to any inability to experience affects. As Zilboorg (1941) points out, "Anxious or not, they are always angry. Their anger is diffuse, seldom directed against any person in particular. It is as 'pure' as their thoughts are 'pure'—seemingly unrelated to definite objects. Hence their thoughts give the impression of highly individualized abstractions without affect . . ." (p. 153).

Besides being envious of other people's qualities and privileges, the borderline patient tends to feel pathologically jealous, given to fantasies of hatred and sadistic violence against both his presumed rival and his love object. He may appear normally sociable and even charming, but he has no intimate friends and trusts no one. Incapable of experiencing tender feelings for other human beings, he engages in sexual promiscuity, at times of a "polymorphous-perverse" type (Kernberg, 1972), presumably to compensate for the absence of genuine love feelings.

Borderline individuals are prone to transitory, intense but superficial relationships, in which there is an urgent sense of hunger for something felt as missing, denied, or withheld from them. There is a clinging, helpless, and at the same time controlling dependence on the love object, with the latter becoming briefly idealized before being dropped, devaluated, or exploited—unless the love object happens to drop out of the relationship first, which is more often than not the case. Even though borderline persons, especially those of the narcissistic type, are able to fall in love, they cannot maintain themselves in love for any length of time, leaving the impression that theirs is no genuine love, but only a case of infatuation.

TIME AND AFFECTS

The readiness of the borderline person to shift from love to anger to hate, from anxiety to depression, from feeling omnipotently self-sufficient to feeling utterly helpless and lonely, is based on a compulsive need for the cognitive restructuring of a given situation or another person—a need that is defensively determined, reflecting a severe loss of self-esteem and, on a genetic level, the ambivalent, poorly integrated nature of his internal object world. The defense implied is, of course, splitting, a primitive defense that antedates the establishment of secondary-process thinking and the development of the concept of time. Splitting is a mental mechanism that defies reality testing in one of its most crucial determinants: the ability to time one's experience, to define it according to a temporal perspective. The use of splitting allows one to feel as if there were nothing but the here and now, in a way that completely ignores or negates past feelings or the prospect of feeling differently in the future.

All affects are bound in the present, felt in the here and now; but normally they are determined by some time perspective other than the present, they are future- or past-oriented (Hartocollis, 1972). Thus, anxiety and hope are felt in the present but are future-oriented. In order to feel anxious, one must be able to have a mental representation of oneself in a future situation, to assess one's adequacy or inadequacy in terms of a dangerous or challenging situation that is present only hypothetically as a future possibility, as a potential danger or challenge. In order to feel elated or depressed, one must be able to have a mental representation of oneself in a past situation, to assess one's adequacy in terms of a success or failure that cannot be changed, that is "located" in the past. The patient described earlier repeatedly explained that he felt depressed in order not to feel anxious, and insisted that he was able to make himself feel depressed whenever he felt threatened by anxiety, which he associated with some concern in the future. Then, instead of talking about the future, he would talk about the past, even when the past was characterized by failure and humiliation.

If the ability to perceive oneself as adequate or inadequate within a temporal perspective becomes, however, lost, as is the case with borderline patients, one is likely to feel suspended in a pleasant or unpleasant condition, which is akin to the infant's putative experience during the postsymbiotic phase of development, before the establishment of integrated self- and object images, when the self or the object is perceived as all "good" or all "bad" and felt as such. Elation, a feeling of omnipotent self-sufficiency, is the positive side of the experience; a feeling of helpless anger, boredom, emptiness, loneliness, or alienation, the negative side. The two sides alternate in rapid, seemingly unpredictable succession.

REFERENCES

Deutsch, H. (1942), Some forms of emotional disturbance and their relationship to schizophrenia. *Psychoanal. Quart.,* 11:301-321.

Engel, G. L., & Schmale, A. H., Jr. (1967), Psychoanalytic theory of somatic disorder: Conversion, specificity, and the disease onset situation. *J. Amer. Psychoanal. Assn.,* 15:344-365.

Greenson, R. R. (1953), On boredom. *J. Amer. Psychoanal. Assn.,* 1:7-21.

Grinberg, L. (1977), An approach to the understanding of borderline disorders. *This Volume,* pp. 123-141.

Grinker, R. R., Sr., Werble, B., & Drye, R. C. (1968), *The Borderline Syndrome.* New York: Basic Books.

Gunderson, J. G., & Singer, M. T. (1975), Defining borderline patients: An overview. *Amer. J. Psychiat.,* 132:1-10.

Hartocollis, P. (1972), Time as a dimension of affects. *J. Amer. Psychoanal. Assn.,* 20:92-108.

Hoch, P. H., & Polatin, P. (1949), Pseudoneurotic forms of schizophrenia. *Psychiat. Quart.,* 23:248-276.

Kernberg, O. F. (1972), Some preconditions and characteristics of mature love relations. (Unpublished.)

_____ (1975), *Borderline Conditions and Pathological Narcissism.* New York: Jason Aronson.

Kubie, L. S. (1963), The central affective potential and its trigger mechanisms. In: *Counterpoint: Libidinal Object and Subject,* ed. H. S. Gaskill. New York: International Universities Press, pp. 106-120.

Mahler, M. S. (1966), Notes on the development of basic moods: The depressive affect. In: *Psychoanalysis—A General Psychology*, ed. R. M. Loewenstein et al. New York: International Universities Press, pp. 152-168.

Searles, H. F. (1977), Dual- and multiple-identity processes in borderline ego functioning. *This Volume*, pp. 441-455.

Stern, A. (1938), Psychoanalytic investigation of and therapy in the borderline group of neuroses. *Psychoanal. Quart.*, 7:467-489.

Zetzel, E. R. (1971), A developmental approach to the borderline patient. *Amer. J. Psychiat.*, 127:867-871.

Zilboorg, G. (1941), Ambulatory schizophrenias. *Psychiatry*, 4:149-155.

ADDENDUM

On a Quotation from Freud

WILFRED R. BION, M.D.

I would like to start by reminding you of a quotation from Freud's *Inhibitions, Symptoms and Anxiety:* "There is much more continuity between intra-uterine life and earliest infancy than the impressive caesura of the act of birth would have us believe" (1926, p. 138). I hope that there will also turn out to be much more continuity between Doctor Mahler and myself with this intervening, impressive caesura of the conference.

"La réponse est le mahleur de la question." This quotation I owe to Doctor André Green, but I do not owe my pronunciation to him. That is my own original contribution.

Now I want to talk about the quotation from Freud. I don't know if I am misinterpreting it, but I think it is not inappropriate that he says this "impressive caesura . . . would have us believe," as if it were the caesura that governed us. This reminds me of the early Homeric description from which one gets the impression that the *phrenes* is really the origin of human thoughts and ideas. A very reasonable scientific conclusion, because it's obvious that when people express themselves, they go "uh-hu, uh-hu, uh-huh" — up and down with the diaphragm. What could be more sensible than that the *phrenes* would have us believe, whatever it is? I think it was Democritus of Abdera who decided that this extraordinary mass of stuff located in our heads has something to do with thinking — but in the meantime, the diaphragm is the important thing; the caesura is the important thing; that is the source of the thinking.

Editor's Note: When Doctor Bion arrived in Topeka for the Borderline Conference, he confided to me that he would rather not read his manuscript but use it, instead, as background for what he might feel like saying when his time came to address the audience. This is a nearly verbatim transcript of his presentation.

Picasso did something of this sort. He painted a picture on a piece of glass and you could see that there was a picture painted on one side of the glass, and if you looked on the other side, there was also a picture painted. Now I want to suggest that the same thing can be said of the caesura. It depends on which way you look at it, which way you are traveling: psychosomatic disorders or soma-psychotic—take your choice. The picture should be recognizably the same whether you look at it from the psychosomatic position, or whether you look at it from the soma-psychotic position.

Now, I want you to join me and try to achieve the same depths of ignorance I have managed to achieve, to get back to a frame of mind, which as nearly as possible is denuded of preconceptions, theories, and so forth. What I'm asking is really something of a mental acrobatic feat; I can well appreciate that. It is not easy for people well versed in anatomy, physiology, psychoanalysis, and psychiatry to get back to a state of primary ignorance, as it were.

I want to say something which sounds just like saying something for the sake of saying it; and perhaps it is, I don't know: "Bloody cunt. Bloody vagina." The first phrase is, I suspect, part of a universal language. It is not sexual; it is not physiological or anatomical, not medical. It is something quite different. "Bloody vagina," though, might be the sort of thing about which doctors talk, probably obstetricians or gynecologists. What about the other one? Now I am not going to try to produce the answer, not because I hope that the cure is ignorance, but temporarily, at any rate, I shall treat the answer as being a kind of disease of the question. I really want to talk about or draw attention to the sounds—"bloody cunt." As I say, "cunt" is not an anatomical or physiological phrase. What it is I don't know. Indeed, I throw it open to you, because if you investigate this question, you may find what this very primitive and archaic language is. "Bloody" does not have much to do with the white cells, red cells, or whatever. It is, in fact, an abbreviated way of talking about or using the term "by Our Lady." So it is really a part and parcel of what in more sophisticated terms we think of as being sacred.

This is very peculiar—"cunt" and this sacred term mixed up with it. I think that the sacred aspect of it would probably be much more meaningful to people familiar with the Roman Catholic religion. But I think one could find a similar sacred element without it necessarily having a Christian version. This is simply by way of introduction; this is simply to try to draw attention to the actual sounds of "bloody cunt" and whatever its counterparts are. I do not, for example, know to what extent this phrase could be translated or recognized, shall we say, in Chinese or in Russian. There seems to be a certain difference which the Chinese, at any rate, can detect by the peculiar difference in muscular movements of the face, which is not, in their observation, the same among Russians as it is among themselves. The advantage of a conference of this kind is that so many different kinds of experience can be brought to bear on these matters.

The queer thing about this language, if you call it that, is that it seems to have an archaic quality. Now this archaic quality nourishes the more intellectual and less lively aspects of one's characteristic thinking. Without its emerging to a point where one could verbalize it, it nevertheless nourishes it. A person, for example, who is very angry with somebody else might find that his intellectual and angry expression is nourished by these archaic factors which he can't express but which do make the angry expression much more alive if he calls the other person a "bloody cunt." It will almost certainly lead to a great deal of turmoil of one kind or another.

At this point I want to return to this idea of turmoil. Leonardo, in his notebooks, has a great many drawings of water and hair. Now this seems to me an artistic delineation of this same turmoil. When we disperse to the loneliness of our respective consulting rooms, offices, and so forth, I suggest that what is there is turmoil. It may appear in a form revealed in verbal expression. It may appear in a form that would seem more appropriately called latency phase. Palinurus is described — I think it is at the end of the fifth book of the *Aeniad* — as answering Somnus by saying that he must think he is very inexperienced if he is led off course while steering his fleet on the calm and beautiful surface of the Mediterranean. This, I think, is something we should not forget but I don't think we want to be misled by it, that is, by the superficial and beautiful calm which pervades our various consulting rooms and institutions.

A small child of my acquaintance, a little girl of about five or six, was lying on the floor studying a vast tome, the eleventh edition

of the *Encyclopaedia Britannica*. In comes one of those people we
call adults who says: "Well, Mary; how you have grown!" I am sure
we have all suffered from this kind of comment. Mary gets up,
points to the book, to an illustration of the ovum, and says: "I
should just think I have." There are many ways in which this can be
done. We have just heard one in Chiland and Lebovici's paper: the
child who dents the hat and puts it on the head. I don't think we
need sophisticated language to know what that means. Another
child, a baby who was apparently quite satisfactorily born, cried
and yelled at birth and could not be quieted. The more the mother
soothed the child, the more the child yelled. It became impossible
for the mother to sleep because of this apparently indefatigible yelling. What I want to suggest is that this was a very late event in the
story, only hidden because of the "impressive caesura of birth."

At this point I would like to indulge in some scientific fictions. I
don't mean by that that I am not taking the problem seriously, but I
know I shall never get anywhere nearer to a scientific statement. It
seems to me that from a very early stage the relation between
the germ-plasm and its environment operates. I don't see why it
shouldn't leave some kind of trace, even after the "impressive
caesura of birth." After all, if anatomists can say that they detect a
vestigial tail, if surgeons likewise can say they detect tumors which
really derive from the branchial cleft, well then, why should there
not be what we would call mental vestiges or archaic elements which
are operative in a way that is alarming and disturbing because it
breaks through the beautiful calm surface we ordinarily think of as
rational, sane behavior?

I don't suppose there will ever be any chance of knowing, so to
speak, what a fetus thinks; but to go on with my scientific fiction, I
suggest that there is no reason why it shouldn't feel. Indeed, I think
it would be quite useful to consider that some stages of fear, of
intense fear, are more easily visualized or imagined by us if one
thinks of them as thalamic fear, or as some sort of glandular manifestation, such as something to do with the adrenals or what later on
turn out to be the genital structures. Now you can look at this as you
like, say as memory traces, but these same memory traces can also
be considered a shadow which the future casts before. I could say
that this meeting itself can be regarded as an expression, as a

revision of such experience and knowledge as we have managed to pick up in the course of our lifetime. But it can also be regarded as showing the shadow of a future we don't know any more than we know the past, a shadow which it projects or casts before. The caesura that would have us believe, the future that would have us believe, or the past that would have us believe, depending on which direction you are traveling in and what you see. Now, it seems to me that there are certain premature and precocious developments that are too premature and too precocious to be tolerable. Therefore, the fetus, the id, if there is such a thing, does its best to sever that connection.

At a later stage, the patient can shut himself up. This happened with a man of thirty-odd years who drew the curtains of his room and as far as possible insulated himself from the universe in which he found himself. The patient objected to that universe and at the beginning objected to me sufficiently to bring his Smith and Wesson 450 revolver to the sessions, which he laid ostentatiously by his side so as to have available the means of putting a stop to the interpretation. Luckily, or unluckily, having been an instructor in small arms, I paid a great deal of attention to that Smith and Wesson. It did rather distract me from paying attention to what the patient was saying, and I think the patient was similarly saved from having to pay too much attention to what I was saying.

Another patient was extremely sensitive to sight, intolerably so; so sensitive, it was difficult for him to wear ordinary clothes because of the colors of the clothes. Another patient found it intolerable to listen to the Philharmonic Orchestra at a time when it was one of the really supreme orchestras, because, according to him, the clarinetist was sharp. I can't tell that kind of thing but I can believe he could; the problem then became how to shut this out. Now, I think that a patient of this kind is very often intelligent, sometimes I think wise. I remember one poor wretch who had committed a murder, but his sentence was limited because it was discovered that he was of very low intelligence. Unfortunately for him, by the time he saw me, his intelligence was not low enough to be less than that required by the British Western Command, which was anxious to punish him if he did not look after his rifle and bring it on parade. He said to me, "Sir, I am not fit to bear arms. I have been allowed out of jail because they said that I could be free if I would serve my country." Very difficult to do, very difficult, especially if the country insists on giving him a lethal weapon which he knows he is not capable of carrying.

Now, one can't very well say this about a fetus but, to continue with my science fiction, I can imagine a situation in which living in an environment of amniotic fluid, so to speak, one can be extremely sensitive to certain wavelengths, oscillations in the water. It would be useless to ask somebody about this, to ask, "When were you born?" The answer you would get would be an obstetrician's or gynecologist's dating, such and such a date. But what one really wants to know is: When was your character or personality born? Let me put it this way. When do your auditory or optic pits become functional? The variations in pressure of the fluid could have much the same effect as pressing on one's eyeball. One could see light, which might be intolerably bright. One could hear sounds, which might be intolerably loud. Anyhow, is a fetus at full-term a character and personality or not? When is that character or personality born? And when does that character or personality forget, get rid of, dispense with all the stuff it has picked up in the course of existence in a liquid medium? Now in this liquid medium, it seems to be possible, for certain animals at any rate, to achieve a kind of long-distance perception by being capable of smelling things. Dog-fish congregate around some piece of decaying matter, they can smell it out; mackerel, the same thing.

There appears to be quite an impressive change when this same animal, this fetus, changes to a gaseous medium. It is not a liquid medium, but it is fluid. Therefore you once again get these oscillations and wave senses and so forth, and you can contribute to them. I have to borrow this sort of language because I don't know what language to use when I am talking about the mind — believing that there is such a thing and that it isn't just an elaborate system of gap-filling theories to take up the space occupied by our ignorance. But I certainly do not see why there shouldn't be a carry-over of extremely primitive sensitiveness. Let's say that the fetus could be a quite healthy or sane object and yet have been subjected to pressures communicated long before we would think there was such a thing as a personality, and long after it.

When I was a student in the forecourt of the hospital in which I was studying, a small black cat used to appear at very regular hours, do its stuff, cover it up neatly, and walk off. It was known as Melanie Klein — Melanie, because it was black; Klein, because it was little; and Melanie Klein, because it had no inhibitions. I have a feeling that this is repeated, as it were, on a rather different level of the heliacal progress of the human mind, I am borrowing this idea from the molecular distribution of the DNA molecule. One comes back to these same things but on a somewhat different level. What we, I think, are trying to do is to get back onto the different levels, but without losing the vital contribution made by these archaisms.

REFERENCE

Freud, S. (1926), Inhibitions, symptoms and anxiety. *Standard Edition,* 20:87-156. London: Hogarth Press, 1962.

Name Index

519

Subject Index